PROTEST IN TOKYO

PROTEST IN TOKYO
THE SECURITY TREATY CRISIS
OF 1960

BY GEORGE R. PACKARD III

1966
PRINCETON UNIVERSITY PRESS
PRINCETON, NEW JERSEY

Publication of this book has been aided
by the Whitney Darrow Publication Reserve
Fund of Princeton University Press

Printed in the United States of America
By Quinn & Boden Company, Inc.,
Rahway, New Jersey

 PREFACE

GOOD REASONS have been advanced for not writing this book: it is too soon—we lack perspective; or it is too late—interest has subsided and the treaty crisis has been all but forgotten, even in Japan. Ignoring but respecting the truth in this advice, I have tried in these pages to answer two simple questions: what actually happened in Japan during May and June 1960, and why did it happen?

Future historians and social scientists will analyze and evaluate the events with more clarity and depth, but it is important to examine now the roots of Asia's first and most important democracy—and to understand how Western political concepts are transformed when they move to alien shores. In this study I have focused on the Japanese political process at a time when the nation was compelled to decide on a major national policy. I hope that it will shed light on the realities of that process and on the nature of the U.S.–Japanese alliance. Another reason for writing the book now can be expressed in the words of General Sir Ian Hamilton: "On the actual day of battle naked truths may be picked up for the asking: by the following morning they have already begun to get into their uniforms." I believe there may be some value in creating a record of the developments of May and June 1960 while memories are fresh and the principal actors available.

The treaty crisis was, for all involved, an emotional affair. Many Americans in Tokyo at the time saw it as a betrayal of trust—or worse—a confirmation of unpleasant suspicions. I have tried to see the issues in the cold morning light without the sense of bitterness and outrage that prevailed at the time. I should add here that I was not in Japan at the peak of the crisis, but resided there from 1956 to 1958 and again from 1960 to 1962 and 1963 to 1965, observing at first hand only a few of the events described herein. I carried out most of my research from the fall of 1960 to early 1962 while enrolled at Tokyo University, and did most of the writing in the U.S. during the following year. I returned to Japan in the summer of

1963, gathered some new material, shortened and rewrote several chapters, and benefited from comments on the manuscript by some of the principals in the treaty crisis.

I was first drawn to this subject by what seemed to me its paradoxes and ironies. Why were thousands of Japanese filling the streets of Tokyo day after day to block the new treaty when the only possible reward for their success would have been the continuance of the old treaty, which they insisted had been forced on them? Why was the old treaty, which had no time limit, considered better by the left wing than the new treaty, which offered the possibility of abrogation after eleven years? Why was Japan's worst postwar political crisis so intimately involved with the U.S. alliance? How did it happen that the President of the United States was prevented from visiting the country by a minority acting in the name of the "democratic process" and "human rights" that had been established under the U.S. occupation only fifteen years earlier? How could the Prime Minister of Japan be overthrown by street crowds without the slightest threat to the basic political and social order in Japan? Finally, was the crisis one of those periodic growth pains that plague all young democracies in rapidly modernizing nations, or was it a more ominous augury?

This book does not wholly answer these questions, and it raises some new ones. The focus has been upon the Japanese political process, and I have had to neglect many crucial aspects, including some of the underlying economic and social factors, as well as a deeper examination of the motivation of conservative interest groups, labor unions, intellectuals, and students. Nor have I fully covered the negotiations between the U.S. and Japan on revising the treaty, since the documents are not yet publicly available. This can be no more than a beginning; hopefully it will point the way to further study.

Readers who look here for a definitive new theory on Japanese politics will be disappointed. The primitive state of our knowledge of Japanese politics was well illustrated by the shock and surprise—even among those on the scene—caused by the events described herein. I did not start with any neat hypotheses nor have I consciously written from any "point of view." I have tried throughout to show that the crisis resulted from the convergence of international and domestic forces, and that no simple explanation of the causes is acceptable. I have, in short, tried to understand and not to judge.

I owe thanks to the Ford Foundation for enabling me to conduct research in Japan for 15 months (1960–1962) under a Foreign Area Research Fellowship and for an additional writing and research grant thereafter. Of course, all opinions expressed herein are my own and not necessarily those of the Foundation.

I am especially grateful to Director Matsumoto Shigeharu of the International House of Japan, as well as to other members of his staff: Messrs. Rōyama Michio, Tsurumi Yoshiyuki, and Miss Fukuda Naomi, Librarian, for facilitating my research in countless ways. I would like to thank Mrs. Maruyama Mitsuko of the Legislative Research Office in the National Diet Library for making available on special loan the Diet proceedings on the security treaty while the Library was moving to its new location in the summer of 1961, and Messrs. Tanabe Yutarō and Nakai Taijirō of that Library for their invaluable assistance in locating materials.

I would like to mention my gratitude to Professor Marius Jansen of Princeton University for his encouragement when I was first considering this project, to Professor Peter Berton of the University of Southern California, who loaned me his personal newspaper collection and provided many useful suggestions to solve the mysteries of research in Japan, to Professors Eguchi Bokurō and Etō Shinkichi of the General Education Department of Tokyo University, who were my faculty sponsors at the University, to Professor Ishida Takeshi for many hours of advice and constructive criticism, to Mr. Imai Masaya of Tokyo University for his help in tracking down materials, to Dr. Akashi Yōji of Georgetown University for his translation assistance, to Mr. Honda Shōjo of the Library of Congress for help in acquiring documents, to Professor James Morley of Columbia University for commenting on the manuscript, and to Miss Akiko Osawa and Miss Priscilla Rehn for typing aid.

I wish to thank those in the American Embassy in Tokyo who have read all or part of the manuscript and have given me the benefit of their wisdom and experience in Japan. These include: Ambassador Edwin O. Reischauer, Minister John K. Emmerson, the late Mr. John Goodyear, Mr. David L. Osborn, Mr. Ulrich Straus, and Mr. William L. Givens. Others from the Embassy who were kind enough to give me advice during the early stages of preparation were Mr. Robert A. Fearey, Mr. Coburn B. Kidd, and Mr. Albert L. Seligmann. It goes without saying that neither the individuals named here nor the United States Government should be associated with the facts, interpretations, or conclusions that I present in these pages; for these I alone am responsible.

I want to express my appreciation to the many Japanese individuals who were kind enough to contribute time and materials to my study. I was particularly gratified by the number of persons active in the anti-treaty movement who were willing to discuss the issues and events, and I am grateful to those leaders who read and commented on parts of the manuscript. Very few will agree with my interpretations but those who see this book will, I hope, find the facts in order and their own views fairly represented.

Finally I would like to thank Dr. Allan B. Cole, Professor of East Asian Studies at the Fletcher School of Law and Diplomacy, for his valuable suggestions during the preparation of the manuscript. His broad knowledge of Japanese political problems and his endless patience have improved the contents immeasurably. The mistakes that remain are my own.

To my wife and four kids, who put up with foolishness throughout, my thanks are deepest.

CONTENTS

Illustrations follow page 178

LIST OF ABBREVIATIONS
AND ORGANIZATIONS

JAPANESE NAMES appear in the text in the Japanese order: surnames first, except where the original document dictates otherwise. The macron over long vowels has been omitted in familiar names such as Tokyo, Kyoto, Osaka, Kyodo News, and the like. The short titles, "security treaty" and "administrative agreement" have been placed in lower case consistently by the author's preference. All citations of Japanese newspapers refer to the Tokyo morning editions unless otherwise specified.

Abbreviations

CC	Central Committee (Chūō Iinkai)
CEC	Central Executive Committee (Chūō Shikko Iinkai)
DSP	Democratic Socialist Party (Minshu Shakai Tō)
JCP	Japan Communist Party (Nihon Kyōsan Tō)
JSDF	Japan Self-defense Forces (Nihon Jieitai)
JSP	Japan Socialist Party (Nihon Shakai Tō)
LDP	Liberal Democratic Party (Jiyū Minshu Tō)
MITI	Ministry of International Trade and Industry (Tsūsanshō)
NCNA	New China News Agency
NPSC	National Public Safety Commission (Kōan Iinkai)
PSIA	Public Security Investigation Agency (Kōan Chōsa Chō)

Common Titles of Japanese Organizations

Ampo Hihan no Kai—Association for Criticizing the Security Treaty

Ampo Mondai Kenkyū Kai—Treaty Problems Research Association

Chūritsu Rōren—National Federation of Neutral Labor Unions

Gensuikyō—Council Against Atomic and Hydrogen Bombs

Kōan Chōsa Chō—Public Security Investigation Agency

Kokurō—National Railway Workers' Union

Kōrōkyō—Government Enterprise Workers' Union

Kyōsandō—Communist League

Mingakken—National Society of Scholars and Researchers for the Protection of Democracy

Nikkyōso—Japan Teachers' Union

Nitchū Kokkō—People's Council for Restoration of Japan-China Relations

Shinsanbetsu—National Federation of Industrial Organizations

Sōhyō—General Council of Trade Unions

Tanrō—Japan Federation of Coal Miners' Unions

Tokyo Chihyō—Tokyo Chapter of Sōhyō

Tōrōren—Federation of Tokyo Metropolitan Workers' Unions

Zengakuren—All Japan Federation of Student Self-government Associations

Zenjiren—All Japan Liaison Council of Self-government Associations

Zenkinzoku—All Japan Metal Industry Workers' Unions

Zenrō—Japan Trade Union Congress

PROTEST IN TOKYO

CHAPTER 1

Japan and the Original Security Treaty

THE IMAGE in the United States of Japan as a stable and trusted ally in the Pacific was shaken by the events of May and June 1960. The sudden cancellation of President Eisenhower's visit to Tokyo produced shock and incredulity around the world. The President who had been acclaimed as a hero by millions in Europe, Latin America, and India was rebuffed by the nation generally thought to be the strongest, friendliest democracy in Asia. What had happened?

We now know that the early, alarmist reports of a Japan on the eve of revolution were nonsense and that Japan's parliamentary government continues today perhaps stronger than befor the turmoil. But have we really grasped the meaning of May and June 1960? It is important to throw out the easy explanations, such as the one which blames international Communism for all the trouble. The Communists were involved, it is true, but the crisis was rooted deeply in Japanese domestic politics and in the dynamic, restless spirit of the Japanese people. There were, of course, a series of incidents—especially the U-2 affair and the summit conference breakup—followed by Prime Minister Kishi's unusual parliamentary tactics that created an extraordinary sense of crisis in Tokyo. It is possible to argue that if these events had not happened, or had happened differently, the whole affair might never have taken place in Japan. The fact remains, though, that it did take place and it laid bare the tensions that exist like coiled springs in Japanese society.

To really understand the Japan of 1960 or the Japan of today, it is necessary to go back to the origins of the United States–Japanese alliance and to reconsider the postwar history of the Japanese people. The United States and Japan became allies for the first time in history with the signing of a security treaty on September 8, 1951, in San Francisco. Only twenty years earlier, Japan had embarked on the conquest of Manchuria, a move that led to other aggressions and ultimately

3

drove her into a disastrous world war. Ten years earlier, Japan and America had locked in a bloody struggle across the Pacific. Then came Japan's crushing defeat and six years of occupation by American troops. The prologue to the new alliance, then, was a period of ambition, fear, hate, conquest, and foreign rule. No one could have imagined on December 7, 1941, the strange twist of history that, in less than ten years, would impel the two nations—with such different pasts and cultures—into the cold grip of military partnership. Those who asked in 1960 why the alliance was not working better might well have asked why it was working at all.

The security treaty was signed five hours after the conclusion of a peace treaty with Japan on September 8, 1951. The peace treaty, in which the United States and forty-eight other nations provided for the end of the occupation and restored defeated Japan to the community of independent nations, was based on the following considerations. By 1951 the goals of the occupation had been largely achieved: Japan's military machine had been wiped out, her war-torn economy revived, and a democratic form of government established. A longer occupation or a vindictive peace might have destroyed the gains or left a residue of bad feeling in Japan. At the same time, however, the United States faced a world in which the militant Communism of Stalin's last years was posing the greatest threat to its security in its entire history. A series of shattering events, from the fall of Czechoslovakia (1948) and the Berlin blockade (1948–1949) to the victory of Mao Tse-tung in China (1949), the Soviet possession of atomic weapons (1949), and the Communist offensive in Korea in 1950 forced Cold War considerations onto every U.S. foreign policy decision. In the Far East there was a new kind of shooting war in Korea against a nationalistic and bitterly hostile China allied with the Soviet Union. A dangerous power vacuum existed on the boundaries of Asia. Japan, with her enormous industrial potential, hung like a juicy plum outside the backyard of the two Communist giants. If the Communist surge were to be checked, the U.S. had to commit its own military strength along the vast arc stretching from the Aleutians in the North through Japan, Ko-

4

rea, Okinawa, and Taiwan to the Philippines in the South. A strong defensive anchor in Japan meant the stationing of American troops there, at least until an independent Japan, with an admitted stake in the free world, could bolster up its own defensive strength. In these circumstances, therefore, the security treaty became an essential part of the overall peace settlement.[1]

The security treaty was only one part of a complex set of agreements engineered by John Foster Dulles in what historians may some day regard as Dulles' most remarkable diplomatic feat.[2] In essence, it enabled the United States to achieve its two major objectives of giving Japan independence and providing for its own strategic security in the Far East. The occupation might end, but U.S. military power would remain in Japan under a new legal arrangement between sovereign nations.

The security treaty raised problems from the very outset, however. Opponents were quick to point out that Japan entered into it while still an occupied nation. In addition, the preamble noted that all nations have the right of individual and collective self-defense, and that the United States expected

[1] Deeply imbedded in the peace-making problem was the legitimate question whether a U.S.–Japan military alliance would, with its concomitant effects—the creation of a new Japanese Army, a revived munitions industry, and the formation of new military bureaucratic cliques—run counter to the democratic reforms of the occupation. The Cold War—particularly the outbreak of a shooting war in Korea—did not allow the U.S. the luxury of deliberation and choice: the military alliance became a necessary precaution for any peace settlement in 1950–1951.

[2] The peace treaty rested upon the following intricately meshed agreements: the U.S.–Japan security treaty (and the implementing administrative agreement), the Treaty of Mutual Defense between the United States, Australia, and New Zealand (ANZUS Pact) of 1951, and the Treaty of Mutual Defense between the United States and the Philippines (1951). The San Francisco peace treaty may be found in U.S. Department of State, *Treaty of Peace with Japan* (Vol. 3, *United States Treaties and Other International Agreements*, TIAS 2490), Washington: U.S. Government Printing Office, 1955, pp. 3169–3328. For excellent descriptions, respectively, of domestic and international aspects of the making of the peace treaty, see Bernard C. Cohen, *The Political Process and Foreign Policy: the Making of the Japanese Peace Settlement*, Princeton: Princeton University Press, 1957, and Frederick S. Dunn, *Peace-making and the Settlement with Japan*, Princeton: Princeton University Press, 1963.

Japan to ". . . increasingly assume responsibility for its own defense against direct and indirect aggression." This, of course, raised questions about Article IX, the controversial arms-renouncing clause of the Japanese Constitution. Article I of the treaty gave the United States the right to station troops in Japan and spelled out the purposes for which those troops could be used: to contribute to the maintenance of peace and security in the Far East and to the security of Japan. This gave the United States freedom to rush Japan-based troops or supplies to meet trouble anywhere in the Far East, but there was no specific commitment to defend Japan. In the negotiations leading to the revised treaty of 1960, Japan corrected this omission and sought U.S. assurances that Japan would be consulted before U.S. troops became involved in a crisis outside Japan. Article I also stated that American troops might, if expressly requested by the Japanese Government, help quell large-scale internal disturbances caused by an outside power. This provision was odious to the Communists against whom it was aimed, and it became increasingly unpalatable during the 1950's to patriotic Japanese who saw it as an infringement of sovereignty. This and Article II, which prohibited Japan from granting bases to any third power without U.S. consent, were both removed from the 1960 treaty. Article III left practical arrangements for the stationing of troops in Japan to a subsequent administrative agreement. The term of the treaty was indefinite; it would expire whenever both governments thought that the United Nations or alternative security arrangements assured international peace and security in the Far East (Article IV). Despite some misgivings and a small but vocal opposition in Japan, the treaty was ratified by a large majority in both Houses of the Japanese Diet in 1951 and entered into force with the peace treaty on April 28, 1952.

The administrative agreement, which laid down the detailed conditions for the presence of U.S. troops in Japan, was hammered out in Tokyo during the winter following the conclusion of the security treaty and was signed and made public on February 28, 1952. As an executive agreement between the two governments, it did not come before either the Diet or the

Senate, and it automatically went into effect with the security treaty, on April 28, 1952.[3] This long and technical contract, with its preamble and twenty-nine articles, provided for the practical operation of the security treaty, dealing with such matters as transportation, access to bases and communications, public utilities and services, procurement of labor, customs, taxes, claims for damages, foreign exchange control, and the legal status of U.S. troops and dependents. Special Ambassador Dean Rusk said at the time he negotiated the agreement that "we shall willingly try to find arrangements for the U.S. forces in Japan which will impose the least practicable burden upon the commercial, industrial, and agricultural processes by which the Japanese people must earn their livelihood." At the same time, Rusk pointed out, the U.S. force "must have the capability of carrying out its military mission." [4] In these two statements Rusk revealed the scope of an enormous problem: how could 100,000 U.S. troops, spread across Japan and held in combat readiness, avoid interfering with the economic and social life of Japan?

The agreement allowed for a good deal of flexibility and consultation between the two governments, but the United States was granted ". . . the rights, power, and authority within the facilities and areas which are necessary or appropriate for their establishment, use, operation, defense, or control," [5] as well as some other rights which gave her a strong hand in carrying out the terms of the treaty. The agreement set up a joint committee (Article XXVI) to handle the problems that might arise, and disagreements on the committee level were to be referred to higher levels in Washington and Tokyo for settlement.

But even the administrative agreement did not complete the

[3] For the complete text, see U.S. Department of State, *Administrative Agreement Under Article III of the Security Treaty Between the United States of America and Japan* (Vol. 3, *United States Treaties and Other International Agreements*, TIAS 2492), Washington: U.S. Government Printing Office, 1955, pp. 3341–3419.

[4] U.S. Department of State, "Statement by Dean Rusk, January 29, 1952," *Department of State Bulletin*, Vol. 26, No. 659, February 11, 1952, pp. 216–217.

[5] *Ibid.*, p. 145.

security arrangements, as the question of the number and location of U.S. bases was left to subsequent negotiations. It was not until July 26, 1952, that an agreement was reached (after five months of talks) by the joint committee. This agreement gave U.S. troops the use of "not more than" 1,400 installations and areas.[6] All the areas were to be provided to the United States free of charge, and Japan agreed to contribute an additional $155 million in yen annually. The Japanese Diet was told in March 1953 that the total area being used then by U.S. troops was 245,000 acres (two-thirds of which were for maneuver grounds).[7] The land under U.S. control thus amounted to about two-tenths of one percent of Japan's total area. These, then, were the arrangements which governed the U.S. military presence in Japan.

World Communist Reactions

The Soviet Union tried to break up the San Francisco Peace Conference, claiming that the peace treaty was drawn up unilaterally by the United States in violation of her pledges at Potsdam and of the declaration of the United Nations in 1942. She further objected that the treaty should not have been signed without the participation of Communist China, that it lacked guarantees against future Japanese aggression, that it should have awarded Taiwan to Communist China, and that it denied reparations to states damaged by Japan despite the "fact" that the United States had been taking reparations out of Ja-

[6] Of this number, 671 were private residences which had been requisitioned by the occupation and were scheduled to be returned to their owners by the spring of 1953. There were 603 land facilities and areas, which included 31 barracks, 32 land maneuver areas, 11 airfields, 18 airstrips, two naval bases (Yokosuka and Sasebo), and 18 collective residential quarters. Of this number about half would be returned to Japan by the spring of 1953, while about 300 would remain available to the United States indefinitely (*Nippon Times*, July 27, 1952).

[7] Testimony of the Japanese Foreign Office's International Cooperation Bureau Chief Iseki to the House of Representatives Foreign Affairs Committee, March 4, 1953, quoted in *Bōei Nenkan* (Defense Yearbook), Tokyo: Bōei Nenkan Hanko Kai, 1955, p. 77.

pan for the last six years.[8] The main thrust of Soviet propaganda was that the peace treaty was really an Anglo-American imperialistic pact aimed at the further exploitation of the peoples of Asia. Gromyko claimed in his speech to the San Francisco conference that he had received a petition representing five million Japanese who had objected to a unilateral peace treaty imposed on Japan.[9] He warned ominously that the treaty ". . . sowed the seeds of a new war in the Far East." [10]

As for the security treaty, Russia claimed that it revealed U.S. aggressive designs on the world, and that it aimed at reviving Japanese militarism.[11] The Soviets said that the United States, despite its disclaimers of territorial ambitions in World War II, was actually picking up real estate in the form of bases in Japan. They charged that Japan would be kept in a state of semicolonial subordination by the U.S., to be exploited by the monopoly capitalists of Wall Street.

Communist China echoed the Soviet attack on the peace settlement and added her own twists. The Chinese claimed that the war against Japan had been won mainly by China and the Soviet Union. The United States, according to this line, never waged an intensive war against Japan; she supplied Japan with war materials such as scrap iron in the 1930's and then after Pearl Harbor fought only half-heartedly. The United States dropped atomic bombs only after Russia had entered the war and scored great victories in Manchuria; [12] she then

[8] These charges and the U.S. replies are summarized in the *New York Times*, September 4, 1951.

[9] *New York Times*, September 9, 1951.

[10] *Ibid.* For a complete record of the proceedings at San Francisco, see U.S. Department of State Publication 4613, *Conference for Conclusion and Signature of Treaty of Peace with Japan*, San Francisco, 1951, Washington: U.S. Government Printing Office, 1952.

[11] In February 1950, Russia and Communist China had concluded a security pact of their own which named Japan and its allies as the potential aggressors; the text may be found in *Current Background*, No. 62, March 5, 1951.

[12] The first atomic bomb fell on Hiroshima on August 6, 1945; Russia entered the war on August 8 and fought for a week against the remnants of the once powerful Kwantung Army.

raced to grab bases in Japan after the war, and the security treaty was now her means of solidifying control of these bases, according to the Chinese line. A Radio Peking broadcast to Japan on September 25, 1951, claimed that there were eleven secret clauses in the treaty giving the United States complete control over Japan.[13]

The security treaty became a constant target for Russian and Chinese attacks during the 1950's. The Soviet Union used it as a pretext for blackballing Japan from the United Nations until 1956 and has continued up to now to use it to avoid signing a peace treaty on terms acceptable to Japan. Mixing threats and promises in their stormy romance with Japan during the 1950's, the Chinese reminded successive governments in Tokyo and hundreds of Japanese visitors to the mainland that relations could be patched up if, among other things, the security treaty were abolished; reversion to dangerous militarism under the treaty, they warned, would mean forfeiting all the advantages of trade and cultural exchange with the mainland and would lead Japan to new disasters. This anti-treaty propaganda was intended to appeal to the pacifist and neutralist sentiment in Japan, as well as to goad Japan's national pride. We shall see in the following chapters how the Communists stepped up their attacks on the treaty when the Japanese themselves began their serious movement for treaty revision in the late 1950's, and how these attacks found a sympathetic response.

Popular Japanese Reactions to the Treaties

It was against this Cold War background that Japanese reactions to the peace settlement can best be understood. In 1951 the Japanese people lacked a consensus on ideals and values. Loss of the war had swept away the old order: militarism, loyal obedience to the Emperor, a divine mission in Asia, and the

[13] This report caused enough stir in Japan to warrant a denial by Prime Minister Yoshida on September 27, 1951 (*Nippon Times*, September 26–27, 1951). See also the earlier Tass report which alleged that the United States planned to continue the occupation for thirty years and triple the size of the Japanese Self-defense Forces (*Mainichi Shimbun*, November 17, 1950).

10

new ideas from the West had scarcely had time to take root in this troubled land. In politics there had been a kind of suspension, in which authority had been yielded—almost with a sense of relief—to General MacArthur and the occupation. For most Japanese, this had been a period of shock, of tragedy, and of struggle for survival. The extremists, of course, rushed in to fill the void: the Communists noisily agitated for revolution while the older rightists lay quietly below the surface, waiting, for the moment, to emerge with their ancient formulae. But the vast majority of the Japanese people ignored the extremists as they ignored politics in general and set about to do the one thing on which all could agree, i.e., to mend the broken economy. It is true that by 1951 Japan had made a remarkable recovery, and a new kind of nationalism was beginning to emerge, this time from the left wing. But the inflow of new ideas and customs had left most of the people bewildered and pliable, and the Cold War descended on Japan at the moment when her ideological defenses were weakest.

As in the Meiji Period, when social and political reforms came largely from above rather than in response to popular movements from below, so under the occupation the people had accepted reforms with ingrained passivity and obedience. When the peace and security treaties were "handed down" to them by the winners of the Pacific War, they were not prepared to respond with great outbursts of emotion. The peace treaty was welcomed, to be sure, as a first step in liquidating the costly and humiliating defeat. The security treaty, clearly a condition of the peace treaty, was accepted with resignation and the belief that it could not be avoided. There was the feeling that Japan was in no position to insist on the removal of the very forces which were "giving" her the peace treaty. Foreign bases and troops were accepted simply as a further installment on the price that had to be paid for defeat in war—another phase of the occupation in fact, if not in name. No one was happy that U.S. soldiers would stay on in Japan; on the other hand, these were the same troops who had been here for six years, and they had not turned out (as Japanese militarists had warned before the surrender) to be "savage fiends." For

11

most Japanese, the idea of independence outweighed their repugnance for foreign troops and bases—which were seen in any case as temporary and destined for removal in the foreseeable future. Public opinion polls of that time suggest that a majority of Japanese supported the treaty itself, but that there was considerable doubt whether the treaty would enhance Japan's security.[14]

Absent from popular Japanese attitudes toward the treaty were the feelings that this would be a good way to contribute to the defense of the free world or to strengthen the cause of democracy. Sentimental Americans who looked to Japan as a kind of "Britain of the Pacific" sharing a common stake in the world order were in for a disappointment. One constant theme in Japan's recent diplomatic history has been the effort to avoid being dragged into purely Western quarrels, and even in the 1930's, when Japan was plunging down the road toward militarism and aggression, she resisted to the end an alliance with the Axis, keeping her hands free to negotiate with the Allies and succumbing only when Hitler's final victory seemed assured in September 1940. This same reluctance to become involved in the East-West confrontation after the War gave neutralism a powerful appeal. Neutralism seemed to many to be the best way for Japan to resume its rôle as an important power in Asia and in the world.

Japan's deep and longstanding fear of foreign domination

[14] In a *Mainichi Shimbun* poll of September 13–14, 1951, the question was asked, "Do you support the new Japan–U.S. security pact?" Of the respondents, 79.9% supported the pact; 6.8% were opposed; 10.4% did not know; 2.4% gave some other answer, and 0.5% did not know. A *Yomiuri Shimbun* poll of September 29–October 2, 1951 asked, "Do you think the Japan–U.S. Security Treaty will increase Japanese security?" 31.1% said "yes"; 16.4% said "no, it will bring danger"; and 52.5% said "don't know." Allan B. Cole and Naomichi Nakanishi, eds., *Japanese Public Opinion Polls with Socio-political Significance, 1947–1957*, 3 vols., Ann Arbor: University Microfilms, Inc., 1959, Vol. 3, pp. 664, 673. A *Yomiuri Shimbun* poll on attitudes toward bases published on August 15, 1951, showed that only 18.3% positively supported the idea of U.S. military bases in Japan; 33.6% felt that they couldn't be helped; 29.0% opposed bases; and 19.1% didn't know.

must also have lain behind her attitudes toward the new treaty. The treaty was bound to stir unpleasant emotions in a nation which, to a large degree, saw its modern history as a long struggle to resist foreign pressures in the form of unequal treaties, military threats, and economic sanctions. Many Japanese viewed their country's diplomacy of the past century as a continuous struggle to free Japan from dependence on or subordination to any outside power. Never had the goal of self-sufficiency been more remote than in 1951, yet it was a goal that retained its grip on the public mind. Japanese leaders in the Meiji Period had changed age-old legal and social institutions in a matter of some thirty years in order to rid themselves of unequal treaties by 1899; this was the land where no foreign troops had set foot since the Mongols were driven off in the twelfth century. One would hardly expect, therefore, that the security treaty, bringing inequalities and foreign troops, would become a popular alliance. The treaty could be tolerated at best for a brief period as a step toward national recovery, but by no stretch of the imagination could it be accepted as a permanent or even a long-term arrangement. If there is any doubt on this point, one need only look at the statements by the treaty's leading proponents in Japan; they all stressed the point that the treaty was an unavoidable measure—a provisional, unconventional, and irregular step for Japan.[15] The more extreme nationalist groups, which for the most part had adopted pro-American positions during the occupation and afterward, also insisted that the inequalities must be removed and that Japan must achieve true independence by revising the treaty.[16]

Paradoxically, the very fact that the treaty was seen as un-

[15] For example, Prime Minister Yoshida Shigeru stated, "That is why . . . we have concluded a security pact with the United States, under which American land, sea, and air forces, at our request, will be stationed within and about our territory. *Obviously such an arrangement cannot be continued indefinitely.* That is why we must undertake to build up a self defense power of our own . . ." (*Contemporary Japan*, Vol. 21, Nos. 1–3, 1952, p. 160, italics added). See also the statement by Dr. Koizumi Shinzō, *Nippon Times*, September 28, 1951.

[16] Ivan Morris, *Nationalism and the Right Wing in Japan*, London: Oxford University Press, 1960, p. 169.

avoidable made it less obnoxious to many Japanese. The old saying, "One must yield to the powerful" (*nagai mono niwa makare yō*), could be used to justify this arrangement. If the treaty were really unavoidable, according to this line of reasoning, then the people were not to be held responsible for any bad consequences that might result from it. If there was no choice, then there should be no anguish over the imperative or its results. This question of responsibility (or not) is a theme which recurs in the events of 1960.

One factor which tended to reduce opposition was the way in which the treaty was revealed in stages so that it could not be seen in full until well after all arrangements had become *faites accomplis*. The treaty's final text was kept secret until it was signed, and then it rode the wave of satisfaction that greeted the peace treaty and the coming of independence. Critics directed their fire against the "one-sided peace" rather than the security arrangements. When the security treaty came before the Diet in October 1951, it was no more than an agreement that Japan would allow American troops to stay on after the occupation; the unpleasant details were not made public until the conclusion of the administrative agreement on February 28, 1952. Even then, as we have seen, hard bargaining on the designation of bases and revision of domestic laws to conform to the treaty terms were put off until later. The result was that the treaty's opponents were unable to focus national attention on the whole pact at once, and this contrasted sharply with the situation in 1960 when the treaty and all its ramifications were well advertised in advance and when all eyes were turned on the Diet for a specific, limited, and tense period of national debate. It was not until 1960, in other words, that the opposition got a real chance to test its strength against the treaty.

The press took a generally resigned attitude toward the security treaty, though Prime Minister Yoshida was criticized for his "vague and arrogant" responses in the Diet. "There will be misgivings," said the *Tokyo Shimbun* on September 10, 1951, "both within and outside Japan about the stationing of troops on our territory, but it is also clear that there is simply no other way to protect Japan's security today." The *Yomiuri* felt that Japan's security had been guaranteed against the danger created by the power vacuum and added that "we hope that this treaty is not turned into a pretext for useless and hostile propaganda. But even if this should happen, there is no reason whatsoever for us to shrink back or be humble. A certain part of the world still acts with Machiavellian tactics, stopping at nothing to gain its ends."[17] *Nihon Keizai Shimbun* said on October 18, 1951, that it would be difficult to terminate the treaty, but that since any treaty assumes good will on both sides, it would trust to the good will of the United States on this matter. Japan's largest paper, the *Asahi*, agreed with the government that it was a treaty between two sovereign nations, but called for thorough Diet discussions and held that the United States should give its promise of aid in a more positive form. It asked that Japan not call for U.S. aid to settle internal disturbances, and that the treaty be kept purely defensive in nature.[18] Perhaps in part because the occupation was not yet over, the press was calm during the Diet debate in contrast with its excited attitude of May and June 1960.

Radio programs and magazines discussed the treaty widely in 1951, and prominent individuals from all walks of life issued statements for and against. The "man in the street" was asked for his views and, in some cases, formal public debates were organized. Popular objections to the treaty (as opposed to the more theoretical objections of the Socialists) tended to focus on the danger of Japan's being dragged into a new war. Doubts were raised, too, that Japan could be fully independent while allowing foreign garrisons on her soil. Some saw ominous signs in the fact that the treaty was prepared under a veil of secrecy and sprung on the people without warning, as in prewar days. Others regretted that it would make relations with Communist China more difficult. Questions were raised as to how much help the United States could be to Japan in the event of a nuclear war, and a few people said it was ridiculous for Japan,

[17] *Yomiuri Shimbun*, editorial, September 10, 1951.
[18] *Asahi Shimbun*, editorial, October 11, 1951.

15

while reaping nothing from the treaty herself, to become America's first line of defense. Despite all these anxieties, however, the polls showed surprising support for the treaty, as we noted above.

No Japanese could think of the treaty apart from a whole range of domestic and foreign problems. Rightly or wrongly, it was seen as the first great choice in the postwar era—perhaps not altogether voluntary—which would mold the social, economic, and political character of the nation for years to come. Whether or not they agreed with that choice, the Japanese thought of it in terms of related questions: was Japan a dangerous military vacuum, as the United States insisted? Were the Communists really an external threat? If U.S. troops were to fill the gap temporarily, what would happen when they left? [19] Could Japan rearm, and if so, how much without amending the Constitution? Could the left wing muster the one-third strength in either house to block an amendment? Would rearmament revive militarism and lead to a new police state? How much defense expenditure could the economy stand? If Japan were attacked by the Communists, would not the United States come to her aid even without the treaty? These and other imponderables lay before the Japanese Government and people in 1951, and continued to engage the nation's best minds in heated debate during the 1950's.

The Socialists

The three groups who fought hardest against the security treaty were the Socialists (JSP),[20] with powerful union support,

[19] In 1950 after the outbreak of war in Korea, a 75,000-man "National Police Reserve" was established despite protests that it would violate the Constitution; in 1952 it was reorganized as the National Security Force and it subsequently grew into Japan's current Ground Self-defense Forces. (See below, Chapter 1, pp. 19–21.)

[20] The Japan Socialist Party (*Nihon Shakai Tō*) is the name in direct translation from the Japanese. The party itself has translated its name since 1955 as the Social Democratic Party of Japan to suggest relations with the international socialist movement. For simplicity, we shall use the literal translation, Japan Socialist Party (JSP) or simply "the Socialists" to denote this major socialist party in Japan from 1945 to 1951 and from 1955 to this

the Communists (JCP), and a newly emerged group which became known as the "progressive intellectuals." The Socialists had taken their worst postwar beating in the last general elections before the signing of the peace and security treaties, winning only 48 of the 466 Lower House seats and 10.3 percent of the total vote in 1949. The party embraced an assortment of left wing elements ranging from Marxist theoreticians and militant labor leaders on the left to Fabians and Christians on the right. Japan's badly divided labor movement, as well as personal rivalries dating back to the 1920's, contributed to internal dissension, but a precarious sort of unity had been preserved during the occupation through the device of left and right wings.

Put simply, the left wing was strongly Marxist, with a "class approach" based on the support of Sōhyō (General Council of Trade Unions), the most powerful labor federation in Japan, with its more than three million members. Sōhyō had been anti-Communist (or at least anti-JCP) when it was founded in 1950, and it had even won the blessing of U.S. occupation authorities in its early days. But it had soon taken a turn to the left, and "the chicken grew up and became a duck instead of a docile hen," as its pro-Communist Chairman, Takano Minoru later boasted.[21] The left wing, with Sōhyō's militant backing, leaned toward cooperation with the Communists and favored the use of mass labor demonstrations to achieve political ends. In foreign affairs, its neutralism was very close to outright sympathy for the Communist Bloc. The right wing, on the other hand, believed in national or "mass" support rather than class support. It stressed parliamentarianism as the road to social democracy and shied away from mass action and violence. Its methods were gradual and it emphasized economic rather than political goals in the labor movement. In foreign policy, the

---

writing. The two wings into which the party divided from 1951 to 1955 are referred to as the Left and Right Wing Socialist Party, and the Nishio group which left the Socialist Party in 1959 to form the new Minshu Shakai Tō will be referred to as the Democratic Socialist Party (DSP).

[21] Quoted by Nakamura Kikuo in "Party Politics," *The New Leader*, Section Two, November 28, 1960, p. 21.

17

right wing leaned toward the free world and tried to avoid co-operation with the Communists at home. The left wing held the upper hand in the party's Central Executive Committee in 1951 but was outnumbered 17–33 in Lower House seats.

The Socialists faced a Lower House in which pro-treaty conservatives held about two-thirds of the seats at the end of the occupation. Prime Minister Yoshida's Liberal Party (conservative) had won 264 of the 466 seats in the 1949 general elections, and Yoshida's personal popularity was at its highest point since 1949. An *Asahi* poll taken right after the signing of the two treaties showed that 58 percent of Japan's eligible voters supported him, while only 17.7 percent were opposed.[22] Furthermore, the conservatives, though divided between the Liberal and Democratic Parties, maintained a solid front on the treaty question, and avoided the kind of internecine fighting that weakened them in 1960.[23] For these reasons, the Socialists had no chance of blocking the treaties in the Diet and were not even able to spark demands for general elections, even though two and a half years had elapsed since the previous elections. The best they could hope to do was use the Diet as a forum to publicize their objections to the treaties.

But even as the debate was taking place in the Diet in the fall of 1951, the Socialists were preparing for a showdown between the left and right wings over the peace treaty issue. The left wing and Sōhyō insisted on an overall peace settlement with Soviet and Communist Chinese participation; they demanded neutralism for Japan and opposed rearmament and all

[22] See results of the *Mainichi Shimbun* poll in the *Nippon Times*, July 11, 1951; and the results of the *Asahi Shimbun* poll in the *Nippon Times*, September 25, 1951.

[23] In August 1951 Yoshida agreed to the demands of the rival conservatives, the Democratic Party, for a three-day Diet session on the peace settlement in return for Democratic Party leader Tomabechi Gizō's presence and signature on the peace treaty at San Francisco. The Democrats, under Secretary-General Miki Takeo, expressed greater doubts about the security treaty than did the Liberals, and later attacked the administrative agreement, but they voted for the treaty in the Lower House. Miki Takeo was again on the side of the anti-government conservatives in 1960 and criticized the revised treaty for roughly the same domestic political reasons.

18

foreign bases. Thus they were adamantly opposed to both the peace and security treaties. The right wing, under Asanuma Inejirō, insisted that the Cold War in general and the Korean War in particular made an overall peace settlement impossible, and that Japan should therefore settle for the terms of the San Francisco Peace Treaty. The right wing argued that there was a limit to neutralism, and that there were compelling political and ideological reasons for accepting the "unilateral peace settlement." Like the left wing, however, they opposed the security treaty, and voted with the left wing on this issue.[24] The special convention called in October 1951 to resolve the peace treaty question ended in a spectacular brawl and a walkout in which separate Left and Right Wing Socialist Parties were formed.

It is worth noting that both wings opposed the security treaty and launched a sharp attack against it from the outset. Chairman Suzuki Mosaburō (left wing) summed up the party's position the day after the first text became public: "Just from looking at the text it is clear that, under the pretext of Japan's security, Japan has been bound hand and foot and will never again be able to loosen these bonds." [25] The Socialists portrayed the treaty as a blow to national pride; Suzuki declared that no real Japanese could approve even the best of security treaties (which this one was not), and he claimed that Prime Minister Yoshida had been forced into yielding to U.S. pressure against his will. "It cannot be helped," he said, "if countries like Egypt now say that we are subordinate to America." [26] Suzuki deplored the secrecy in which the negotiations had been carried out and noted that key points such as deployment and control of U.S. troops had been left to the administrative agreement.

In the Diet debate, the Socialists focused on the sensitive matter of rearmament and self-defense. This had become a major issue when General MacArthur formed a National Police

[24] The peace treaty was approved by the House of Representatives on October 26, 1951, by a vote of 307–47, while the security treaty passed by the lesser margin of 289–71.

[25] *Mainichi Shimbun*, September 10, 1951.

[26] *Ibid.*

Reserve of 75,000 men soon after the outbreak of the Korean War in 1950, a force which was to be the nucleus of Japan's present army. The Socialists held that Japan, by virtue of Article IX of her Constitution, had no right of self-defense and that the maintenance of any kind of armed force, whether for self-defense or otherwise, was unconstitutional.[27] The conservatives replied that no country can give up the inherent right of self-defense, and that Article IX did not rule out wars for self-defense, or the maintenance of self-defense forces, but only wars and war potential that might be used for settling international disputes.[28]

The security treaty poured gasoline on the flames of this controversy. It directly conflicted with the position of the Socialists by recognizing Japan's right of self-defense, and its preamble went on to say that the United States expected that ". . . Japan will itself increasingly assume responsibility for its own defense. . . ." The Socialists claimed that this clause obligated Japan to rearm even further, and that it would lead to the revival of militarism and aggression. They charged in the Diet debate that the maintenance of U.S. troops in Japan would constitute war potential banned by Article IX. In short, they held that the conservatives, in pushing the treaty through, were trampling on both the letter and the spirit of the Japanese Constitution.

The conservatives answered that keeping U.S. forces in Japan simply represented one of several Constitutional means open to them by which to provide Japan with a means of defense in case of trouble. In the sense that the treaty's aim was to preclude, not invite, war, they said, it in no way violated

[27] Article IX: "Aspiring sincerely to an international peace based on justice and order, the Japanese people forever renounce war as a sovereign right of the nation and the threat or use of force as a means of settling international disputes.

"In order to accomplish the aim of the preceding paragraph, land, sea, and air forces, as well as other war potential, will never be maintained. The right of belligerency of the state will not be recognized."

[28] This is known in Japan as the "Ashida–Kiyose interpretation." For a fuller treatment of the question, see Rōyama Masamichi, "Problems of Self-defense," *The Annals*, Vol. 308, November 1956, pp. 167–174.

either the letter or the spirit of the Constitution. On the matter of eventual rearmament, the conservatives had no single answer in 1951, but Prime Minister Yoshida held that the matter should be submitted to the will of the people at some later date when Japan's economy permitted its consideration. They observed that the preamble clause in which the United States expected Japan increasingly to share the burden of self-defense was nothing more than "an expectation" which had no binding force in international law.[29]

The Socialists raised other important problems in the Diet debate. They asserted that the security treaty would not contribute to the peace and security of the Far East and might even have the reverse effects. They wanted to know what the government would do if Japanese volunteers were dispatched to Korea or if U.S. forces in Japan arbitrarily launched an aggressive military action. They were concerned that the battle between the United States and Communist China might expand, and that U.S. bases in Japan might come under enemy bombing if the United States attacked Manchuria or otherwise threatened vital Chinese interests. They asked the government how it could prevent U.S. troops from pulling out of Japan at any moment. How would normal diplomatic relations be restored with the Soviet Union and Communist China? They objected strongly to the fact that there were no termination date and no precise obligation for the United States to defend Japan. They argued that the clause permitting U.S. troops to help put down internal disturbances (upon request by the government) was incompatible with Japan's status as a sovereign nation. Finally, they blasted the forthcoming administrative agreement: it would give the United States a *carte blanche* in Japan and would not even be subject to Diet approval.

The widely criticized administrative agreement was released on February 28, 1952, well after Diet ratification of the security

[29] The Liberal Party's official position on the security treaty was clarified in its statement of September 20, 1951, reported in the *Nippon Times,* September 21, 1951. The Foreign Office also published a pamphlet on September 26, 1951, in which it explained the terms of the treaty and said flatly that the treaty did not obligate Japan to rearm.

treaty, and it drew fire from some conservative sources as well as from the whole left wing. The Left Wing Socialists claimed that in effect it made Japan a military base for a foreign power and the Japanese people its soldiers. They charged that it gave away extensive extraterritorial rights and failed to ensure Japan's autonomy in the event of an emergency. Suzuki Mosaburō said repeatedly that Japan was being turned into a firing range. Right Wing Socialist Asanuma charged that the government had carried on "secret and humiliating diplomacy," and that the security treaty itself should have been signed after the peace treaty had gone into effect.[30] Conservative politician Miki Takeo of the Progressive (formerly Democratic) Party opposed the administrative agreement because of terms "disadvantageous for Japan in the light of accepted international customs and . . . also prejudicial to the mutual trust between the two nations." [31]

On these points, the Socialists found widespread support in the press, which was far more critical of the administrative agreement than it had been of the security treaty. Editorials demanded that the agreement be placed before the Diet, arguing that the United States should not be given such broad jurisdiction in criminal cases. There were complaints that major decisions by the new joint committee would reflect the predominant influence of the United States. Several editorials asked that the agreement be revised so that the Japanese people would not feel that the occupation was to continue. One writer described at length the harmful influence that the agreement would have on the Japanese economy.[32] The widely read critic, Ōya Sōichi, summed up much of the criticism when he wrote in the evening *Yomiuri* of February 28, 1952: "The Administrative Agreement gave me the impression that government leaders, from Prime Minister Yoshida down, deceived the people by being in collusion with foreigners. The result is that we are paying too dear a price for having them conclude a peace treaty for us. The

[30] *Nippon Times*, February 29, 1952.

[31] *Ibid.*

[32] Kimura Kihachirō, "Effects of the Administrative Agreement," *Contemporary Japan*, Vol. 21, Nos. 1–3, 1952, pp. 113–117; originally published in *New Age*, May 1952.

government should have frankly informed the people that its action was unavoidable, since the occupation in substance must continue, and thus seek their understanding." [33] Commentator Tokugawa Musei was more resigned: "It cannot be helped that we are pushed in this direction under the current of circumstances. The only thing we can do is make the best of it. It cannot be helped." [34]

The Socialists played essentially the same rôle in 1951 that they would again play in 1960: though they were unable to influence national policy and had no acceptable alternative for the Japanese voter, they were probably successful in stirring up antitreaty sentiment outside their own party, in the press and public. In this they were aided by the Communists.

The Communists

Though the Communists probably had less influence than the Socialists in turning public opinion against the new treaties, they had a distinctive position that is worth examining.

The Japan Communist Party (JCP) had taken a relatively calm line in the immediate postwar period, aiming at peaceful revolution and a "lovable image." But in January 1950, with the Korean War about to break out, Stalin ordered the JCP to adopt a strategy of terrorism and violence, sending guerrilla squads to the hills and causing Molotov cocktails to be hurled at police stations. It was in this second phase, when the party was most bitterly at odds with the U.S. occupation, that the treaty issue arose. The Japanese Communists echoed the Moscow-Peking line on the treaties and said that by allowing American imperialism to station troops in Japan, the Japanese Government was sacrificing its friendship with Russia and China, exposing the nation to atomic warfare and selling Japan's independence.

The Communists' underground tactics and use of violence backfired in 1950–1951, as they dropped from a postwar peak of thirty-five seats in the Lower House and three million votes

[33] Quoted in the *Nippon Times*, February 29, 1952.
[34] *Ibid.*

23

in 1949 to no seats and less than a million votes in 1952. Even though their moves to block the security treaty were of little consequence, it is nevertheless important to understand their theoretical approach to the treaty issues, for it was at the theoretical level that many important disputes would arise among leftists in the spring of 1960. The JCP's guide to action was essentially based on the Party Theses of 1927 and 1932, which held that Japan needed revolution in two stages: first, a national, bourgeois revolution and second, a socialist revolution led by the proletariat. (We shall see later how the two-stage (*Kōza-ha*) theorists and the one-stage (*Rōnō-ha*) theorists of the 1920's were to renew their battle in 1960.) The Communists, in accepting the old *Kōza-ha* or two-stage thesis, started from the assumption that the Meiji Era had not seen a full bourgeois revolution. But by 1951 they had also accepted the thesis that Japan was similar to pre-1949 China, i.e., a semicolonial area under the domination of the American imperialists. The task at hand, therefore, was to unite all the "democratic" elements among the Japanese people to throw out the imperialists. The social revolution would come later, at a second stage. The security treaty, legalizing the presence of U.S. troops in Japan, became the symbol of imperialist domination and the foremost target of attack. The Communists stressed appeals to nationalism more than did any other leftist group; they goaded Japanese pride by reiterating that the Japanese Government had "sold out" to the Americans. Oddly enough, these class-conscious Marxists found themselves working to unite all the classes against the common threat of imperialism. In this they differed significantly from the Left Wing Socialists, who emphasized the class struggle against Japan's own "monopoly capitalists" and saw Japan's economy at a more advanced stage in historical development—a stage which required an immediate Socialist revolution led by the proletariat. This theoretical difference was to affect their choice of tactics at the time of the 1960 crisis, and to weaken the effort by the left wing to unite in protest.

The Communists' attempt to unite all Japanese against the United States was more than party theory; it also meant a chance to embarrass the Americans in Japan and weaken their influence

—a course that was in line with the nationalistic objectives of Peking. Any moves that would result in the departure of U.S. troops from Japan or even lessen the effectiveness of U.S. bases in the Far East would have the highest support from the U.S.S.R. and Communist China. The JCP, therefore, looked for every possible opportunity to direct popular resentment against U.S. troops and bases, and to undermine the security treaty. As part of this strategy, the Communists succeeded in turning the May Day protest demonstrations of 1952 into anti-American riots.

The "Bloody May Day" of 1952 came just three days after Japan had regained independence. Next to the movement of May-June 1960 it was the largest disturbance since the war, and in some ways it was more violent. The immediate issue was Yoshida's attempt to pass the Anti-subversive Activities Law—a measure which the left saw as a threat to its survival.[35] Some 20,000 unionists, mostly under Communist leadership, tried to storm the out-of-bounds plaza in front of the Imperial Palace on May Day. There they clashed in a rock-throwing melee with 3,000 policemen. About 1,400 persons were injured—759 of them police—and 166 were arrested. During the fracas a few U.S. military vehicles were turned over and set on fire, and several Americans were hurt. These demonstrations had strong undertones of anti-Americanism and it was dangerous for a G.I. in uniform to be caught in the area of the riots. In 1960, on the other hand, the "mood" of the demonstrations was quite different; many Americans stood on the sidelines and watched the snake-dancing, and a few even participated in the demonstrations.

In their battle against the revised treaty in 1960, the Communists chose instead to sponsor a united front and, except in the special case of the Hagerty incident, when they had a unique chance to pursue their anti-American line, they found themselves in the new rôle of leading the calls for orderly and "respectable" demonstrating. They had come at least this far from the early days of the Molotov cocktails.

[35] It is ironic that the first application of this law came in 1964 against a *rightist* plot to overthrow the government (the "Sanmu Case").

The Progressive Intellectuals and the Treaty

The third major group to oppose the security treaty were the so-called progressive intellectuals (*kakushin interi*). They emerged from the war as a highly articulate, Marxist-oriented intelligentsia which captured the attention of Japan's vast reading public with a new brand of sweeping social criticism and commentary. With their panaceas for the social and economic hardships of the postwar period, they won prestige and influence extending well beyond the hard-core left wing into the more highly educated reading public that had been starved by the tightly controlled press under the militarists. Centering around the larger universities (especially Tokyo University), the intellectual journals (especially *Sekai*), and the newspapers, these progressive intellectuals proclaimed feelings of guilt for their prewar and wartime silence or collaboration; under the motto, "Never Again!" they attacked all conservative policies and governments, regarding themselves as jealous guardians of the new democracy. All of these intellectuals were committed to some form of socialism, but there were differences of viewpoint among them. Some became secret or overt members of the Communist Party, others joined the Socialists, while still others remained aloof from party politics altogether. As a group they exerted a strong influence on the postwar left wing movement in Japan.

By far the most famous and influential association of progressive intellectuals was the Peace Problems Symposium (Heiwa Mondai Danwa Kai). Led by Abe Yoshishige, President of Gakushūin (Peers College), Ōuchi Hyōe, professor of economics at Tokyo University, and Nishina Yoshinō, Director of the Science Research Institute, the group first assembled in November 1948 to discuss a UNESCO statement (issued on July 13, 1948) on the causes of war and the foundations of peace.[36] After a month of research and discussion, the participants in the symposium

---

[36] This statement and its background may be found in Hadley Cantril, ed., *Tensions that Cause Wars*, Urbana: University of Illinois Press, 1950, pp. 17–21.

issued a ten-point statement on the "problem of peace." [37] The group, approving the UNESCO ideas, further affirmed its own belief in the progress of man. It held that war was not inevitable but that peace was attainable only by abolishing the exploitation of man by man—through fundamental change in social organization and in modes of thinking. The achievement of the maximum degree of social justice ". . . through planning and adjusting the advance of productive forces and the utilization of resources, constitutes clearly a basic condition for prevention of war and establishment of peace. So long as these factors are monopolistically controlled by special groups within a country or by specific countries in the world, we cannot begin to hope to eradicate the root-cause of war." [38]

In essence, the statement held that peace and socialism went together; without socialism there could be no peace. It is fair to say that almost all these scholars accepted the Marxist principle that lay behind this statement: that the seeds of war may be found within the capitalist system itself. If one continued with this logic, it was an easy step to say that the socialist countries (Russia and Communist China) were peace-loving and the capitalist countries (led by the United States) were the true warmongers. This was precisely the position taken by most of the progressive intellectuals, and from these assumptions, all else followed. While many called themselves "nonparty" intellectuals, almost all inclined toward parties of the left, and their appeals for neutrality in foreign policy could not conceal their basic sympathy with the Soviet Bloc.[39]

After making the statement of December 1948, the members of the Peace Problems Symposium organized themselves more or less formally and met on a regular basis. The membership list

[37] Their statement appeared in *Sekai*, March 1949; an English translation may be found in Cantril, *op. cit.*, pp. 299–303.

[38] *Ibid.*, p. 301.

[39] There were a few exceptions in the group who questioned some Marxist tenets and advocated social democracy for different reasons; they subsequently dropped out of the category known as the "progressive intellectuals."

read like an all-star cast of Japan's academic world, and included such famous men as Tokyo University Professors Yanaihara Tadaō (later President of the University), Tsuji Kiyoaki (administrative law), Maruyama Masao (political science), Takagi Yasaka (U.S. affairs), and Ukai Nobushige (constitutional law). Some of the other well-known names were Tsuru Shigeto, Harvard graduate and internationally known economist, Shimizu Ikutarō, professor of sociology at Gakushūin, Rōyama Masamichi, political scientist and later President of Ochanomizu Women's College, Hani Gorō, historian, Suekawa Hiroshi, President of Ritsumeikan University, and Kuwabara Takeo, specialist in French literature.

When the issue of the peace treaty first arose, the Peace Problems Symposium issued its famous "Statement on the Peace Problem" of January 1950.[40] Being one of the first on the peace problem, it attracted considerable attention in Japan. Asserting the twin premises that any peace settlement must both contribute to world peace and preserve Japanese independence, it called for an overall peace settlement, opposition to military bases, and inviolable neutrality with membership for Japan in the United Nations.[41] A one-sided peace treaty would lead to the danger of a new war and hurt Japan's vital interest in achieving economic independence (i.e., avoiding dependence on the United States). The statement affirmed the possibility of peaceful coexistence and said that the spirit of Japan's peaceful Constitution ruled against siding with either of the Cold War adversaries. Leasing military bases to any foreign country as part of a one-sided peace settlement would not only violate the preamble and Article IX of the Constitution, but would also lead to the ruination of Japan and the world. Many of Japan's most famous scholars thus stood squarely against the idea of the security treaty over a year and a half before the treaty was signed.

The group issued still another statement, "Again on the Peace

[40] "Kōwa Mondai ni tsuite no Seimei," *Sekai*, detached appendix (*bessatsu furoku*), April 1950.

[41] It will be noted that these were basically the "three principles of peace" adopted by the Socialists in December 1949.

28

Problem," in the December 1950 issue of *Sekai*.[42] This statement was intended to present the group's thinking on the new problems arising since the start of the Korean War. Written mainly by Professors Maruyama Masao and Ukai Nobushige, it was to become the theoretical basis for many of the anti-treaty protests by intellectuals over the next few years.

The first two parts of this declaration repeated some of the points already mentioned above, and again called for absolute neutrality for Japan in the Cold War. The third, dealing with Japan's security and rearmament, said flatly that war as a means of self-defense for Japan was ruled out by the Constitution, and Japan's security must be assured by the United Nations. Japan must join the United Nations as Switzerland had joined the League: without obligation to join in collective security actions. Part Four took up the problem of peace and domestic reform, and concluded that Japan must set her own house in order before peace could be assured. Socialist reforms must be undertaken in Japan without reference to Soviet ideology or the Cold War. Resources at home must be utilized more effectively, and economic dependence on outside powers must be avoided as much as possible.

Running through these statements was a strong strain of nationalism—in the form of an attempt to escape the Cold War and turn inward on Japanese problems. The older ultranationalist goal of self-sufficiency for Japan was now taken up by the progressive intellectuals, and the old urge to escape from foreign pressures could be seen in the move toward neutrality and the desire to keep a free hand in world affairs. The security treaty, as an entangling alliance, ran counter to the spirit of the new nationalism. This brand of nationalism won quick support from the new generation of students and scholars who were tired of postwar defeatism and anxious to wed their newly discovered socialist concepts to the realities of the political scene. That their ideas were basically nationalistic was recognized by Professor Maruyama himself when he wrote in 1950: ". . . the position of the advocates of over-all peace and neutrality is

[42] "Mitabi Heiwa ni tsuite," *Sekai*, Vol. 60, December 1950, pp. 21–60.

29

broadly similar to that of Premier Nehru of India or the Socialists of West European nations. They are rightly or wrongly convinced that, if Japan were to conclude a separate peace with the United States and offer her military bases, thereby allying herself completely with one side of the divided world and isolating herself from the other, *the danger of losing political, economic, and psychological independence,* and of intensifying an armed conflict in the Far East, will be increased. They desire to belong to the third group of powers in a world divided between the two power blocks. *This trend represents one tendency of a new postwar nationalism."* [43] This element of nationalism became extremely significant among intellectuals in 1960, and we shall return to it in later chapters.

With some of Japan's most respected scholars and educators on record against the alliance with the United States many months before it was concluded and with their continued condemnation of the security treaty throughout the 1950's, the Japanese people could not be blamed for taking a careful second look at the treaty, and wondering about its value. How much influence did these intellectuals have over the nation as a whole? On one hand, many Japanese intellectuals (including some members of the group discussed above) tended toward ivory-tower elitism, and often seemed more interested in taking shots at each other than in converting the masses or even their own students. The eminently practical Japanese people have never placed national policy in the hands of their theorists. On the other hand, the progressive intellectuals had become a new sort of "elite" in Japan, and their opinions on every conceivable subject from nuclear testing to modern drama were eagerly sought after and disseminated through the country with the vast power of Japan's mass media. For years they directed their most scathing fire against the security treaty, and a decade of students sat at their feet. The judgment here is that they had considerable influence in stirring up the protest movement of 1960. They might have been even more effective in 1960 had they

[43] Maruyama Masao, "Nationalism in Post-war Japan," Japan Institute of Pacific Relations *Bulletin,* October 1950, p. 16 (italics added).

spoken with one voice, as they seemed to do in 1950. We shall see, however, how doctrinal and personal differences were to set them against each other and cause serious dissension.

Summary

Though there was heated opposition to the first security treaty from three distinct left wing groups—the Socialists, the Communists, and the progressive intellectuals—this criticism never seriously threatened the ratification process or the effectiveness of the treaty. These opponents were silenced to a degree by the way in which the treaty arrangements were gradually unfurled. The administrative agreement, signed after the treaty had been ratified, was the most unpopular aspect of the alliance. The discontent that did exist could never be focused upon the pact as a whole, and satisfaction with the peace treaty tended to overshadow doubts about the security treaty, which was accepted with a sense of resignation. High tension in the Cold War made some sort of defense arrangement seem acceptable to many Japanese.

Were there, in 1951–1952, any hints of future problems between the new allies? We have mentioned the abnormal period of twenty years leading up to the treaty and the special constitutional and emotional problems involved. With hindsight, we may pick out some additional factors that foreshadowed trouble. First, we have seen that the attacks on the treaty would, on grounds of self-interest or nationalism, inevitably appeal to many Japanese who were not leftists themselves. Second, no amount of good will on either side could hide the truth that no nation likes foreign troops on its soil, and the longer they stay the less they are liked. This was particularly true in the case of an Asian nation historically sensitive to Western encroachment. Third, the administrative agreement (as distinct from the security treaty) was badly received even by nonleftists from the moment it was made public. The Diet never had a chance to approve or disapprove it, and it remained a source of resentment.

A fourth point, and one that has often been overlooked, is that almost all Japanese, left, right, and center, shared certain assumptions about the pact. Everyone agreed it was a *temporary* expedient. While people disagreed over the alternatives—rearmament, neutrality, rapprochement with the Communists—everyone from Prime Minister Yoshida to the far left believed that the treaty had sometime to be revised or abolished, and most felt the sooner the better. All agreed that the U.S. bases and troops should be as few and as unobtrusive as possible, and that costs to Japan should be minimal. There was broad agreement that Japan should not get tied into a Pacific-wide pact that might lead to involvement in a war over someone else's interests or tie her fate to that of Chiang Kai-shek or the despised Syngman Rhee. The consensus on these points meant that the anti-treaty leftists would not be seen as a lunatic fringe, but as a mirror of the basic anxieties of the whole nation.

Finally, it is worth pointing out quite frankly that in 1951, most Japanese felt that, however burdensome or dangerous the alliance might prove to be, they were at least allying themselves to the stronger side in the Cold War struggle. They could, in other words, find comfort in the fact that they were "picking a winner." In 1960, the same people would entertain serious doubts as to which side was stronger, and this would lead to greater qualms about joining either side. The Japanese, like most of the other peoples of the world, are cool reckoners of the balance of power—a point that tends to be forgotten in the battle of ideologies. It was a point that the United States could ill afford to ignore.

This was the prelude to the 1960 crisis over the revised security treaty. While the seeds of protest may have been present from the outset, important changes took place during the 1950's, which were to create a troubled setting in 1960: dissension among the conservatives, a less popular prime minister, a rise of nationalism, a tense world situation, a new generation of Japanese students, and a new strategy by the left wing.

 CHAPTER 2

Treaty Diplomacy and Conservative Politics

THE CRISIS of May and June 1960 climaxed a three-year period in which Japan's revision of the security treaty became thoroughly embroiled in domestic politics. Radical discontent on the left and the conservative power struggle on the right came to focus increasingly on the treaty revision issues, and the political and intellectual life of the nation came to revolve about the forging of the new treaty. The period 1957–1960 (Kishi's term as Prime Minister) will probably be seen by future historians as the era of treaty revision, for even more than in Japan of the 1880's, the "unequal treaty" issue dominated the affairs of the nation. Kishi Nobusuke and the security treaty became in 1960 the objects of the greatest mass uprisings since the rice riots in 1918. To understand the national crisis, it is important to examine the changes that took place in Japan after the signing of the security treaty in 1951.

Pressures for Treaty Revision

Two factors created pressure for changes in the security treaty: the resurgence of Japanese nationalism and discontent with the presence of U.S. troops and bases in Japan.

We noted that the original security treaty was concluded in 1951 when Japan was still shocked and confused in the wake of the surrender and occupation. By 1957, however, the clouds of defeat and apathy were beginning to disappear, and a new sense of national pride was emerging hand in hand with the nation's growing strength and prestige. Though sharp ideological divisions still existed, there was an unspoken consensus that Japan must regain a leading role in world affairs. The trend was away from self-disparagement toward self-respect, from deep pessimism over the future to guarded optimism, from uncritical acceptance of foreign ideas and customs to a new search for the "Japanese essence" within the traditional culture.

There were good reasons for the new national pride. Economically, Japan's growth during the 1950's was phenomenal.

33

Between 1952 and 1958, the real gross national product grew at an average rate of 7 percent; between 1959 and 1961, the rate was nearly 13 percent, highest in the world. Between 1952 and 1960, Japan's exports tripled, and her imports more than doubled. Japanese manufacturers won universal respect for the motorcycles, cameras, and transistors that poured into world markets, and by 1956 Japan had surpassed Great Britain as the world's leading shipbuilder. The surge forward could be seen and felt and heard: modern buildings sprang up from the heaps of rubble. It was a standing joke to deplore the fact that some of the older and dirtier sections of the cities had been missed by the bombs! The vast energy of the people, long burdened by the war machine, was harnessed to new goals of individual and national prosperity, and consumption was higher than ever before in history. Not since the Emperor Jimmu (*Jimmu irai*) had things been so good, went the popular slogan of 1956–1957.[1]

On the international scene Japanese diplomats and politicians were beginning to speak with new authority and confidence. In 1956 Japan joined the United Nations, and by 1958 she had been elected to a seat on the Security Council. In 1956 she signed a declaration ending the state of war with the Soviet Union and reopened diplomatic relations with Moscow. In her relations toward Communist China, Japan showed increasing independence from the United States, and in 1957 she departed from the U.S.–backed Chincom trade controls to follow the British in liberalizing the list of exportable items to China. When the United States and Great Britain appeared to disagree over the Chincom issue, Japan even offered to mediate between them—an offer that would have amazed both sides several years earlier. On the issue of nuclear testing, the Japanese Government spoke out against the United States, Great Britain, and the U.S.S.R. with equal vehemence. Japan's presence on the world stage was coming to be felt again.

Yet the new prestige and national pride inevitably clashed with the realities of the world situation in which Japan found

[1] According to legend, the Emperor Jimmu founded the Yamato State in 660 B.C.

herself dependent upon the United States for military security and—to a degree—for trade and capital. The search for independence and self-sufficiency was frustrated by military and economic weakness, and the security treaty came to symbolize this frustration. The "unequal treaty," signed as it was when Japan was occupied and without world standing, was regarded as a legacy of defeat that had to be either abolished or overhauled in accordance with Japan's new prestige. Unhappy incidents, some of which will be discussed below, gave a sense of urgency to the desire for treaty revision, but even if there had been no friction at all, the new nationalism would have demanded a change in Japan's treaty-frozen status as an inferior. The treaty of 1951 was simply unsuited to the new Japan of 1957.

Thus by 1957 all the political parties were forced to grapple with the problem of treaty revision. The great struggle that attended the revision of the treaty was, from the start, a struggle over *how* and *how much* to change the treaty, for there was broad national agreement—as early as 1957—that some sort of changes were absolutely necessary.

Popular Attitudes Toward U.S. Troops and Bases

We observed in the last chapter that the Japanese people, like others, have traditionally been sensitive to the presence of foreigners in general and foreign troops in particular. The stationing on these crowded islands of 100,000 American servicemen of completely different cultural origin and economic status could not help but create tensions that no amount of good will could dispel. Had each U.S. soldier been a model of good behavior, there would still have been misunderstandings and friction. The conduct of the troops, however, was something less than ideal, and a number of unfortunate incidents stirred deep resentment among the Japanese people.

The most celebrated of these incidents was the "Girard Case" in which U.S. Army Specialist 3/c William S. Girard shot an empty shell case from his grenade launcher and killed an elderly Japanese woman brass-collector on a U.S.-leased firing range on January 30, 1957. The case became a national issue when

Girard's commander refused at first to transfer him to Japanese jurisdiction.[2] Girard was ultimately tried in a Japanese court and received a three-year (suspended) sentence in November 1957; he returned to the United States immediately thereafter. The dispute and the trial received sensational publicity for the better part of a year, however, and Japanese opinion was inflamed at the very moment when Kishi was trying to launch a "new era" in U.S.–Japanese relations in June 1957. For the Communists, it was powerful ammunition against the treaty: Girard was pictured as a typical cold-hearted American, contemptuous of "inferior yellow people." Socialist Party Secretary-General Asanuma Inejirō said on February 18, 1957 that the Girard Case had increased his party's determination to seek abolition of the security treaty, and he blamed the United States' "new style colonization policy" for the trouble.[3]

There were other incidents that irritated the people and helped the left wing to sow discontent with the treaty. There were cases of murder, theft, and rape as well as barroom brawls and black-marketeering.[4] None of these reached the proportions

[2] Under Article XVII of the administrative agreement, as revised in October 1953, crimes by U.S. troops against Japanese persons or property committed during off-duty hours were subject to the jurisdiction of Japanese courts. The point at issue in this case was whether Girard had been on or off duty. When the incident took place, Girard had been guarding a machine gun emplacement (as ordered) during a recess in firing practice. His commanding officer certified that the act had occurred while Girard was on duty; the Maebashi District Public Procurator's Office claimed that he had been off duty. After several months of argument, the United States agreed to turn Girard over to a Japanese court, a decision which was reviewed and approved by Secretary of State Dulles and Secretary of Defense Wilson. Girard's American lawyers then claimed that his constitutional rights would be violated if he were turned over to Japanese jurisdiction, and a U.S. District Court upheld their claim. The case went to the U.S. Supreme Court, which, on July 11, 1957, reversed the decision and ruled that Girard could constitutionally be turned over to Japanese jurisdiction. The Supreme Court held that the wisdom of the arrangement with Japan on jurisdiction was a matter for the exclusive determination of the executive and legislative branches.

[3] *Japan Times*, February 19, 1957.

[4] From October 29, 1953, when the Japanese jurisdiction clause under Article XVII of the administrative agreement went into effect, to Decem-

of the Girard Case, but their recurrence and publicity must certainly have had a cumulative effect in convincing the Japanese people that they would be better off without the U.S. forces in their midst.[5] Leftists' propaganda equated the American soldiers' attitudes with the high-handedness and brutality of their own discredited military leaders of the past.

Perhaps as important as the more sensational acts in creating hostility were the daily annoyances for the Japanese: the richer and taller GI's driving around in oversized cars with good-looking Japanese girls; the brash colonels who referred to all Japanese men as "boy-san"; the wives, living in fenced-off, centrally heated homes, with Japanese servants, who swore that they would never set foot on the Ginza because there were "too many Japanese down there"; the golf courses, the enclaves, the special privileges. As feelings of inferiority gave way to the new nationalism, these minor irritations caused growing indignation.

In stressing these sources of friction, it would be unfair to overlook the honest efforts of military commanders and personnel to create good will and understanding. As the "occupation mentality" wore off, public relations improved considerably. U.S. forces helped to rescue distressed Japanese fishermen, miners, and mountaineers, made generous contributions to local charities, joined international sporting and social events, and opened their bases and ships to inspection tours by the public on special occasions. The behavior of most of the troops was incomparably better than that of the Japanese troops in conquered areas before the surrender, and the people knew it. Some soldiers bothered to learn something of the language and made

ber 1, 1956, U.S. servicemen had been charged with 12,581 offenses which came under the primary jurisdiction of Japan. The vast majority of these were traffic violations. The Japanese waived jurisdiction at U.S. request or dropped the charges in all but 396 of these cases. Of the cases that went to Japanese courts, 87 resulted in jail sentences. *New York Times*, June 16, 1957.

[5] During the period when negotiations were under way for revising the treaty, two more unfavorable incidents occurred: in 1958 an airman shot and killed a Japanese student musician who was on his way to the U.S. base to take part in a concert (the "Longpre Case"); in 1959 a drunken GI burned a Japanese flag on a train in full view of the surrounding passengers.

37

real friendships; between 1945 and 1957, 25,000 servicemen married Japanese girls. Biracial orphans born out of wedlock were adopted by hundreds of U.S. military families. The tragedy in all this, of course, was that so much of the good will that did develop could be canceled by the thoughtless acts of the few individuals who should not have left their native shores.

Beyond these personal brushes between GI's and the Japanese people was the problem of U.S. bases disturbing the lives and economies of surrounding areas. Some of the grievances that developed were inspired or sharpened by leftist agitators, but the fact that some were legitimate is suggested by a discussion of base problems in the *Defense Yearbook* of 1955, which is not a leftist publication. It listed the following types of problems: fishermen caught less fish as a result of artillery fire on the beach at Uchinada; trees near the airport which had served farmers as windbreakers were cut down and harvests were thereby reduced in Fukuoka; pipes carrying drinking water to a U.S. base sucked in fish and reduced the catch at Lake Yamanaka; the submarine net at the mouth of Tokyo Bay reduced the catch by fishermen off Kanagawa. In addition, it continued, there was the "morals problem" created by the growth of red light districts in the vicinity of bases.[6] Still other kinds of difficulties arose: jet engine noises disturbed classroom activities, firing practice interrupted a geological survey, use of firing ranges kept farmers out of traditional grass-cutting areas, and locally employed labor had to be dismissed when troops were withdrawn, causing serious unemployment in some villages. There was the problem of strikes and rallies by base-laborers demanding higher dismissal allowances and other benefits. Finally, there were the inevitable mishaps—the stray shell, the plane crash, the traffic accidents—that brought death and tragedy to local families.[7]

[6] *Bōei Nenkan, 1955* (Defense Yearbook), Tokyo: Bōei Nenkan Hankō Kai, 1955, p. 78.

[7] A Kyodo report of February 9, 1957, stated that more than 150 persons had been killed or wounded by stray bullets or shells from some 100 U.S. firing ranges throughout Japan (*Japan Times*, February 10, 1957). Whether or not this figure was accurate, it at least indicates what the Japanese people were being led to believe in this matter.

Activists of the left wing, particularly the Communists, Zengakuren students, and some Sōhyō unionists, tried to turn the base problems into "base struggles." A national committee was set up to coordinate these struggles, and action squads were sent out to "educate" and organize the local farmers and fishermen. Intensive propaganda campaigns in areas affected by U.S. bases depicted the U.S. forces as the arm of U.S. imperialism ruthlessly exploiting the Japanese economy and cruelly depriving the farmer of his ancestral land and livelihood. Victims of accidents were portrayed as martyrs, and sympathy demonstrations were organized for the dead. Considering what must have been large expenditures of time and money in this work, however, the leftists were surprisingly ineffective. One reason for this was that the Japanese villagers tended to stick to their own problems and disregard those of the fellow on the other side of the mountain, so that it was hard to mobilize large protest campaigns in rural areas. Furthermore, peasants often resented the student and labor organizers who "came down" from Tokyo to tell them how to run their protest movements. People who were not directly affected by the bases and who were not leftists tended to view the agitators as professional trouble-makers, and showed little sympathy for their cause. Finally the U.S.–Japan Joint Committee set up under the administrative agreement dealt continuously with the difficulties and managed, through careful diplomacy and compensation for legitimate grievances, to negate some of the efforts of the hostile leftists. The one base problem that became an important national issue was the Sunakawa affair, which is discussed in Chapter 4.

That the anti-base struggles never became a major national movement, however, does not mean that the bases achieved any degree of popularity. An interesting study of public opinion on this matter was made by Douglas H. Mendel, Jr., who brought out the following points: (1) the presence of American troops never enjoyed majority support in Japan and became increasingly unpopular during the 1950's; (2) the Japanese people were not greatly worried about a Communist invasion and therefore did not appreciate the need for foreign troops on their soil; (3) more people saw the treaty as a source of potential danger than of security; and (4) the bases lacked the approval even of the conservative voters.[8] These points tend to support the conclusion (if support is needed) that the desire to revise the security treaty—with a view toward its abolition—was by the late 1950's shared by many nonleftists, and that the anti-treaty movement, though organized by the left wing, had at least some sympathy from a substantial part of the Japanese people. This sympathy contributed to the public tolerance of large-scale left wing agitation against the treaty in late 1959 and 1960. At local levels there were mixed feelings about the bases. On one day the gates of a U.S. base would be surrounded by red flags and demonstrators shouting "Go Home, Yankee!" and if the Yankees began packing up, an equally large demonstration of shop-keepers and base-workers would petition them to stay. In both cases, however, the publicity was generally unfavorable for the U.S. forces.

What did all this mean in terms of Japanese policies toward U.S. troops and bases? Should U.S. policy-makers have discerned a dangerous trend against the treaty well before the riots of 1960? This would be putting it too strongly. The real question was: *how* unpopular were the bases, and how far would the people go to express their disapproval? The mood of 1957 was less explosive than anxious and restless. Except for the extremists, there was grudging recognition that the security treaty in some form, distasteful as it might be, was still unavoidable. The new critical mood of 1957 sought ways to lessen the bad taste rather than remove it altogether. There was little support for mass action against the bases, and public opinion (as distinct from elements in press, student, and academic circles) had not yet crystallized around clear and meaningful ways to improve the treaty. The more extreme leftists, however, took the mood as a signal to launch new and harsher attacks on the treaty, and for them this was the beginning of a drive not just to improve the treaty but to abolish it altogether. The popular demand, on the other hand, was for removal of the inequalities, lessening the "danger of war," and paying due respect to Japan's new

[8] Douglas H. Mendel, Jr., *The Japanese People and Foreign Policy,* Berkeley and Los Angeles: University of California Press, 1961, Chapter 4.

national status and self-respect.[9] Prime Minister Kishi, though he was to become extremely unpopular in 1960, made a reasonable estimate of the prevailing mood when, from 1957, he tied his political fortunes to the great issue of negotiating a new treaty.

1957: Origins of the Treaty Revision Movement

From 1952 to 1957 there were all kinds of leftist attacks on the "San Francisco system," ranging from scholarly essays to street demonstrations and anti-base struggles. There was a sense of hollowness and futility in all this, however, for there seemed to be no immediate possibility of changing the system. The conservatives, who continued to win about two-thirds of the votes, ignored the treaty in their campaigns even as they made it the cornerstone of Japan's foreign policy. It was not until 1957 that the treaty issue took on a new urgency. Rising nationalism and the irritations over U.S. troops and bases created pressures against the treaty, and there were other developments that brought the issue into sharp focus in 1957 and gave rise to a reappraisal of Japan's entire foreign policy.

The nation's political and diplomatic fortunes seemed to

[9] The following polls support these conclusions. A poll by Yoron Kagaku Kyōkai of June 27, 1957 asked, "The U.S.A. is about to withdraw all its troops from Japan except its air and naval forces. What do you think about that?" The responses were: "Good": 66.3%; "Too soon": 15.9%; Others: 2.1%; "Indifferent": 4.9%; "Don't know": 10.4%; No answer: 0.4%.

The same poll asked, "The U.S.–Japan Security Treaty will be discussed by a U.S.–Japan Commission which will be established. What do you think about that?" The responses: "Good": 60.3%; "Unsatisfactory": 11.3%; "Don't know": 27.9%; No answer: 0.5%.

A Yomiuri Shimbun poll of August 23–25, 1957, asked, "The foreign policies of the Kishi Cabinet are closely related with U.S. foreign policies. What do you think about that?" The responses: "Good": 21%; "Not good": 8%; "Unavoidable": 43%; "Don't know": 28%. Allan B. Cole and Naomichi Nakanishi, eds., Japanese Public Opinion Polls with Sociopolitical Significance, 1947–1957, 3 vols., Ann Arbor: University Microfilms Inc., 1959, Vol. 3, pp. 757, 766. See also the results of the worldwide poll on U.S. bases published in the New York Herald Tribune, October 20, 1957, which showed Japan among the least anxious to have bases in her territory.

41

stand at a crossroads in early 1957. In the previous fall, three significant events had taken place: Japan's admission to the United Nations, the reopening of relations with the U.S.S.R., and the succession of Ishibashi to the office of Prime Minister. The combination of these events had produced, by New Year's Day 1957, a surge of popular interest and high expectation over the future course of Japanese diplomacy.

Prime Minister Hatoyama (1954–1956), backed by Shigemitsu Mamoru and Kōno Ichirō, had set the new style by seeming to play down relations with the United States in favor of a more independent course in world affairs. Hatoyama, no less than Yoshida, gave substantive recognition to the need for close ties with the United States, but he paid greater respect to the new desire for a flexible foreign policy. Instead of continually speaking in favor of close relations with the Anglo-American Bloc as Yoshida had done, Hatoyama leaned toward "third course" diplomacy in which Japan could move more freely between East and West, winning concessions from both sides and raising the price of her allegiance to the free world. The change was more of style than of substance, but it succeeded in winning for Hatoyama strong popular support. The Joint Declaration which he signed with the Soviet Union on October 19, 1956, unsatisfactory as it may have been from the Japanese standpoint, represented the first great departure from the "Yoshida line" in foreign affairs. When it was followed in December by Japan's admission to the United Nations, there was a surge of national self-confidence, as new diplomatic horizons seemed to be opening up. With the Russian problem "solved"—at least for the moment—and with United Nations membership as a badge of acceptance in the international community, all eyes turned to the next great foreign problem, Communist China, and to the man who succeeded Hatoyama as Prime Minister in December 1956, Ishibashi Tanzan.[10]

[10] Communist China was the "next great foreign problem" because this was the peak of the "China boom" of the mid-1950's. Since 1954, Communist China had waged an intensive drive for closer relations with Japan. The Chinese had released Japanese war criminals, given red-carpet tours of the mainland to hundreds of Japanese of all political views, and directed

The 72-year-old Ishibashi, former editor of the *Oriental Economist* and a "Keynesian liberal" by reputation, seemed in many ways a natural to tackle the China problem. More than any other conservative politician, Ishibashi suited the mood of 1957. The press gave play to his heroic resistance to occupation measures.[11] His knowledge of trade and economics and his vague professions of friendship for the Chinese people made him, in the popular image, the perfect man to defy the United States and restore relations with Communist China. Tentative support for Ishibashi came from some left wing elements, and even *Sekai* magazine, which was strongly anti-Government, felt that Ishibashi might pay more attention to the popular will and depart from a one-sided pro-American policy.[12] Throughout the nation the idea spread that Ishibashi might "deal with" the China problem as Hatoyama had dealt with Russia in 1956 and Yoshida had dealt with the United States in 1951: a progression toward greater independence for Japan.

No one will ever know what Ishibashi might have done about Communist China. In a crucial political turning point, he was forced by illness to resign just sixty-two days after taking office, and Kishi Nobusuke became Japan's seventh Prime Minister since the war. Kishi's background, experience, base of support, and "image" were quite different from those of Ishibashi, yet his rise to power did not end the speculation and excitement over Japan's foreign policy. Kishi had qualities that seemed to fit him for succession to the rôle of Hatoyama and Ishibashi. Young (sixty) and vigorous for a Japanese Prime Minister, he

---

into Japan a constant stream of propaganda aimed at weakening Japan's ties with Taiwan and the United States. The prevailing attitude in Japan at this time was to accept uncritically the achievements and claims of the mainland regime. The conservatives were impressed by the trade potential: by 1956, exports to the mainland exceeded in value exports to Taiwan. Ishibashi could have found considerable support within the LDP as well as across the nation for opening diplomatic relations with Communist China.

[11] See, for example, Hashimoto Tetsuma, "Tai-GHQ Tōsō Jidai" (Era of Struggle Against GHQ), *Bungei Shunjū*, February 1957, pp. 76–78.

[12] "Nihon no Ushio" (Japanese Tides), *Sekai*, February 1957, pp. 234–237.

had been a close political associate of Hatoyama, Shigemitsu, and Kōno since 1952; during his early days in office he encouraged the idea that he would "stand up to America" as well as increase trade with Communist China. In his first news conference as Prime Minister, he said that he favored increased trade with China and that, "from the point of view of national sentiment, the Japanese people desire that the present security treaty and administrative agreement between Japan and the United States should be abolished." [13] Kishi also stressed in his early speeches that Japan must seek closer relations with other Asian nations, another ideal of the new nationalism. To prove his point, Kishi traveled to Southeast Asia in May 1957— the first Japanese Prime Minister to do so since the war. All these gestures made the situation seem ripe for a shift in foreign policy away from close dependence on the United States, toward friendship with Communist China and a more assertive brand of diplomacy. This gave impetus to a new and critical scrutiny of the security treaty.

It is important to see that Kishi's original move to revise the security treaty was intimately tied in the public mind with the problem of Communist China.[14] As one newspaper saw it, both the conservatives and the Socialists were attempting, in 1957, to escape from the vice in which they were trapped between the two superpowers: the Socialists' solution was to negotiate directly with China, while Kishi approached the problem by way of America.[15] Leftists and some moderates, though they resented Kishi for other reasons, were willing to go along with his avowed aim of strengthening Japan's rôle in the U.S. alliance, so long as he seemed to be following the footsteps of Ha-

[13] New York Times, March 1, 1957.

[14] See, for example, the Asahi Shimbun editorial of April 28, 1957, "Ampo Jōyaku wa Kaitei Suru beki de aru" (The Security Treaty Should Be Revised), in which the Joint Japan–Soviet Declaration and the problem of "New China" are both linked to treaty revision.

[15] Yomiuri Shimbun, "Nichibei Ampo Jōyaku—Kaihai o Meguru Shomondai" (Japan–U.S. Security Treaty—Problems of Revision or Abolition), April 12, 1957.

toyama.[16] Kishi, with the unerring political instincts that had taken him to the Prime Ministership, sensed the size and strength of the public mood.

We shall have other occasions to refer to the "mood" in Japan, for though it defies precise analysis, it must be recognized as a vital element in the Japanese political scene. Other nations have moods, but it is doubtful whether any other civilized people act and react with so much unspoken consensus and emotional homogeneity as the Japanese do on some occasions. In recent years Japan has experienced a series of "booms" (known in Japanese as *būmu*) in which the nation, led by Tokyo, goes wild over a momentary fad, whether it be golf, leisure, travel, hair styles, or "winkie-dolls." The "mood" refers to the same sort of emotional response—an infectious type of attitude or popular feeling, such as sympathy for a particular sumo wrestler or receptivity to a certain political trend. An extremely long mood might last up to eighteen months, but most of them have been shorter. They are partly created and partly reflected by a far-reaching communications network in this highly literate, insular nation. When a mood gains momentum, the newspapers, TV, radio, and weekly and monthly magazines (some of which have enormous nationwide circulation) behave as if they were controlled by a single editor and uniformly devote their lead articles to the question at hand. The spread of television has added speed and momentum to the growth of booms and moods. The *Asahi Shimbun* in an editorial once deplored the importance of "mood" in politics: "We Japanese are usu-

[16] According to the interpretation of Professor Maruyama Masao, a leading leftist intellectual, Kishi did, in his early days as Prime Minister, follow the Hatoyama-Shigemitsu-Ishibashi line of conservative nationalism, but changes in both Japan and the United States during the next three years (the rapid growth of Japanese capitalism, the worsening of relations between Japan and China, and the remarkable growth of trade between Japan and Western Europe and the United States) led Kishi to adopt a new form of dependence on the free world. "Gikaisei Minshushugi no Yukue" (The Future of Parliamentary Democracy), *Ekonomisuto Bessatsu* ("Ampo ni Yureta Nihon no Kiroku"), Mainichi Shimbun Sha, September 10, 1960, p. 85.

ally swayed by our feelings in interpreting things and tend to believe everything we are told without grasping a clear picture. . . . This fad for the word 'mood' seems to pinpoint the weakness of the Japanese." [17] Moods and booms can come from reactions: Hatoyama's popularity as a reaction to Yoshida, Ikeda after Kishi, etc., or they can arise from a sudden or spectacular event: the winning of the Canada Cup in golf, the wedding of the Crown Prince, or an international crisis. The politician or legislator can ignore the direction and heat of a given mood only at his own peril.

In the spring of 1957, the low-keyed but widely shared mood was to take a critical and searching look at Japan's foreign affairs. It was a time when there was talk of Japan's serving as a "bridge" between East and West to relax world tension (a rôle which would also give her a stronger voice in world affairs).[18] Another popular idea favored a four-power nonaggression treaty between Japan, Communist China, Russia, and the United States. Politicians, commentators, scholars, and public figures joined in the public debate, and from February to May 1957 the press was filled with opinions on how and why to adapt the security treaty to the new circumstances. In the May 1957 issue of *Chuo Koron*, intellectuals ranging from moderate Professor Rōyama Masamichi to the "grand old man of the left," Yamakawa Hitoshi, called for changes in the treaty.[19]

[17] *Asahi Shimbun*, editorial, June 23, 1961.

[18] See, for example, Irie Keishirō, "Nihon wa Kokuren ni Nani o Kiyo Shi-uru ka?" (What Can Japan Contribute to the U.N.?), *Sekai*, February 1957, pp. 227–233.

[19] For a cross section of opinion on the treaty during this period, see the following articles: "Ampo Jōyaku wa Kaitei Subeki ka?" (Must the Security Treaty Be Revised?), a debate between Professors Kaino Michitaka and Ōhira Zengo, *Sankei Jiji Shimbun*, March 7, 1959; "Fubyōdō-sei no Genshō Hakaru" (Plan to Lessen Inequalities), *Nihon Keizai Shimbun*, March 18, 1957; "Nichibei Ampo Jōyaku—Kaihai o Meguru Shomondai" (Japan–U.S. Security Treaty: Problems of Revising or Abolishing), a series of 40 articles, *Yomiuri Shimbun*, March 13–May 1, 1957 (excepting March 16, 26–27, 31 and April 1, 5–6, 13, 18, and 23); "Ampo Jōyaku no Kaitei ka Kirikae ka?" (Revise or Change the Security Treaty?), editorial, *Tokyo Shimbun*, April 22, 1957; "Fubyōdō Jōyaku wa Nani ka?" (What Is the Unequal Treaty?), editorial, *Sankei Jiji Shimbun*, April 24, 1957; "Ampo

From all this argument and criticism, opinion hardened on the following major objections to the treaty: (1) it was one-sided and unequal in that it gave the United States the right to station troops in Japan but contained no specific obligation for the United States to defend Japan; (2) the treaty had no time limit; (3) the clause permitting U.S. troops to quell internal disturbances at the request of the Japanese Government was unsuited to a treaty between sovereign and equal nations; (4) the United States could use its Japan-based troops outside Japan without consulting Japan in advance: this could lead to retaliatory attacks against the bases by a future enemy of the U.S. and thus involve Japan in a war against her will; (5) nothing in the treaty prevented U.S. forces in Japan from being equipped with nuclear weapons; (6) there was no precise obligation for the U.S. to abide by the U.N. Charter in acting under the treaty. There were, of course, many variations and nuances of opinion, but there was considerable agreement on these six shortcomings. But if there was unity of opinion on the sickness, there was marked disagreement on the cure.

Against this background of heated public discussion Prime Minister Kishi assumed office and made plans for a visit to Washington in the spring of 1957. This was a period of high anticipation, and there was heavy pressure on Kishi.

The Second Rise of Kishi

Revision of the security treaty became so tightly entwined with the ambitions and political fortunes of Kishi Nobusuke that we should pause here to look briefly at the background of this extraordinary, controversial politician.[20]

Kishi was born in 1896 in a former *samurai* family in Yamaguchi Prefecture, earlier known as Choshu, which has produced

Jōyaku de Futatabi Seimei" (Another Statement on the Security Treaty), *Akahata*, April 27, 1957; and "Nichibei Kankei Saikentō no Toshi" (Year of Reexamining Japan–U.S. Relations), editorial, *Yomiuri Shimbun*, April 28, 1957. Many of the articles were occasioned by the fifth anniversaries of the signing of the administrative agreement (February 28, 1957) and the coming into effect of the security treaty (April 28, 1957).

[20] A biography of Kishi in Japanese was written in 1957 by Yoshimoto Shigeyoshi, *Kishi Nobusuke Den*, Tokyo: Tōyō Shokan, 1957.

47

more Prime Ministers (seven) than any other area in Japan.[21] Educated in the orthodox channels for the elite, he graduated with distinction from the Tokyo First Senior High School and the Law Faculty at Tokyo Imperial University. He attended college (1917–1920) during the period of social and political unrest that unsettled Japan after World War I. The atmosphere was one of excitement and confusion as new ideas from the West, such as Wilsonian liberalism and Bolshevik Marxism, collided with traditional Japanese concepts. Students and scholars formed associations to study and spread the new thoughts. Some students, such as Asanuma Inejirō at Waseda University, became attracted to the cause of socialism during these uneasy postwar years. Kishi, on the other hand, became a student of the nationalistic Professor Uesugi Shinkichi and fought against the more liberal views of such men as Professors Minobe Tatsukichi and Yoshino Sakuzō.[22] He was also deeply impressed, curiously, by the radical nationalist, Kita Ikki, whose home he visited occasionally.[23] For a time, Kishi was a member of the Gokoku Dōshikai (National Protection Comrades Group) which was set up to combat the radicals and their ideas on campus. As a student, Kishi read the works of Marx and Kautsky but rejected Marxism because, as he put it, "it goes against human nature." [24]

Kishi turned down an offer from Professor Uesugi to succeed to his chair and chose instead a traditional career in the government. He rose rapidly during the 1920's and 1930's in the Ministry of Commerce and Industry, where he came to be recognized as a brilliant leader and a promising bureaucrat. From 1936 to 1939 he served as second highest civilian official in the

[21] These are: Itō Hirobumi, Yamagata Aritomo, Katsura Tarō, Terauchi Seiki, Tanaka Giichi, Kishi, and Kishi's brother, Satō Eisaku. Two of Kishi's leading opponents in the treaty struggle also came from Yamaguchi: Miyamoto Kenji, Secretary-General of the Communist Party, and Kamiyama Shigeo, a leading JCP theoretician.

[22] Dan Kurzman, *Kishi and Japan*, New York: Ivan Obolensky, Inc., 1960, p. 95.

[23] "Kita was indeed one of the persons who profoundly influenced me during my university days" (Kurzman, *Kishi and Japan*, p. 92).

[24] Interview with Kishi Nobusuke, January 10, 1962.

Japanese puppet government of Manchukuo, responsible for planning the economic development of the vast Manchurian empire.[25] Returning to Tokyo in 1939, he became Vice-Minister of the Commerce Ministry, where he soon clashed with his superior, Commerce Minister Kobayashi Ichizō, over his (Kishi's) plan for tighter control of the economy. The upshot of this conflict was Kobayashi's resignation in April 1941; Kishi then became Minister of Commerce in the Tōjō Cabinet of October 1941. He was thus a cosigner of the declaration of war against the United States in December 1941. In 1943 Kishi became Vice-Minister for Military Procurement, a post directly under Tōjō, and Minister Without Portfolio, where he played a major rôle in holding together Japan's faltering economy during the war years. In 1944, soon after the Japanese loss of Saipan, Kishi resigned with the rest of the Tōjō Cabinet, reportedly helping to topple Tōjō from power. After the surrender, he was held (without trial) for three and a half years at Sugamo Prison as a Class A war criminal. Released in 1948, he took a job in the business of his close friend, Fujiyama Aiichirō, who was later to become his Foreign Minister. In 1952 he was depurged and began a new career in politics.

Kishi's comeback was as remarkable as the confused state of conservative politics after Japan's independence in 1952. Throughout much of the occupation and up to 1954, "One-man" Yoshida Shigeru had survived a series of crises and dominated the conservative camp. In December 1954, however, Yoshida was ousted by the aging (71) semi-invalid, Hatoyama Ichirō, and this set off a wild struggle among would-be successors, who expected the new administration to be short-lived (though it actually lasted until December 1956).[26] Kishi began

[25] Kishi was one of the famous "Ni-ki San-suke" group of five men who ran Manchuria. They were: Tōjō Hideki, Hoshino Naoki, Matsuoka Yōsuke (Kishi's uncle by marriage), Aikawa Yoshisuke, and Kishi Nobusuke. The "Ni-ki San-suke" refers to the two "ki's" and three "suke's" of the final character of their given names.

[26] For background on the Hatoyama purge and rivalry with Yoshida, see Hans H. Baerwald, *The Purge of Japanese Leaders under the Occupation*, Berkeley and Los Angeles: University of California Press, 1959, pp. 21–24, 85–86, 89–90.

his meteoric comeback by joining Yoshida's Liberal Party in 1953, but he soon combined with Miki Bukichi and Kōno Ichirō (and others) to support Hatoyama's rebellion against Yoshida and was expelled from the party in the same year. He thus played an important (some say decisive) part in forcing Yoshida into retirement in December 1954. In 1955, with the merger of the two conservative parties, Kishi became Secretary-General of the new Liberal-Democratic Party (LDP) and a leading candidate to succeed Hatoyama.

The ailing Hatoyama stepped down from office in December 1956, having fulfilled his pledge to normalize relations with the Soviet Union. In the factional scramble to replace him, the three leading candidates were Ishii Mitsujirō (former member of the Yoshida Cabinet), Ishibashi Tanzan, and Kishi. Kishi was still an "outsider" at this point, having no deep roots either in prewar party politics (like Hatoyama) or in the postwar "Yoshida school" of politics like Ishii. The latter, in Japanese political parlance, refers to the group of men drawn mostly from the ranks of the career bureaucrats, whom Yoshida brought into his successive cabinets. The "prize pupils" of this school included Ikeda Hayato, Satō Eisaku, Hori Shigeru, and Ishii Mitsujirō. One of the few constant factors in the shifting alignments within the LDP has been the enmity between the Yoshida and Hatoyama alliances.

Kishi was an outsider, but he had a foot in both camps: he was allied with Kōno Ichirō, a former Hatoyama man, and his younger brother, Satō Eisaku, was heir (along with Ikeda) to the Yoshida faction and loyal to Kishi.[27] He also

[27] Satō and Kishi are brothers but have different names for this reason: Kishi's father, Kishi Hidesuke, was originally adopted by the Satō family to marry Satō Moyo, Kishi's mother. The children of this marriage took the surname of Satō as is customary in such *"yoshi"* arrangements. When Kishi was in his teens he was adopted by his sonless uncle, Kishi Nobumasa, to marry one of the uncle's daughters, Yoshiko. At this point Kishi dropped the name Satō and assumed his present surname. In addition to his well-known younger brother (who at this writing is the Prime Minister of Japan), Kishi had an older brother Satō Ichirō, a former Rear Admiral who died in April 1958. Kishi had one other vague connection with Yoshida (which may or may not have been relevant): Yoshida's daughter was married to his cousin.

benefited from the sudden dearth of top conservative leaders in 1956 caused by the deaths of Ogata Taketora and Miki Bukichi and the retirement of Hatoyama. Thus, on the first ballot for LDP presidency on December 14, 1956, Kishi had a plurality, but he lost on a subsequent vote by the slight margin of seven votes when his rivals teamed up to back Ishibashi. The battle before and during this convention wracked the party and gave rise to charges of corruption and vote-buying.[28] In the new Ishibashi Cabinet of December 23, 1956, Kishi became Deputy Prime Minister and Minister of Foreign Affairs. After Ishibashi was forced by illness to retire in February 1957, Kishi moved into his place without a party contest and was voted President of the LDP as a formality on March 21, 1957.[29]

In five years Kishi had risen from the status of a depurged war criminal to Prime Minister of Japan. In thirteen years he had moved from Tōjō's Cabinet to leadership of the most important U.S. ally in the Pacific.

How was he viewed by the nation that had worked for twelve years to heal the physical and spiritual scars of the war he helped to start? Certainly Kishi would not have won a direct popular election to Japan's highest office in 1957 (although it is hard to say who would have won such an election). In his favor, with all but the hard-core left wing, was his apparent intention to follow the conservative nationalism of Hatoyama. Also in his favor were his relative youth and his reputation as a skilled administrator. Strongly against him, however, were his record of service with Tōjō, his designation as a Class A war criminal, and his "smoke-filled room" method of reaching the top. Among all of Japan's postwar Prime Ministers, Kishi had been most deeply involved in promoting the war effort. There

---

[28] Even the normally conservative *Japan Times* called it (editorial, January 3, 1957) "a disgraceful display of factional strife." Tsuji Masanobu, maverick LDP member of the House of Councillors, openly accused Kishi of vote-buying at this convention on December 10, 1958.

[29] The choice of Kishi for Prime Minister was apparently made at a closed meeting of LDP leaders including Kishi, Ikeda, Ishida Hirohide, Miki Takeo, Sunada Shigemasa, and others on the night of February 22, 1957. *Asahi Shimbun*, February 23, 1957.

was considerable doubt as to whether he had really been converted to democracy or whether, as his critics charged, he was simply riding the new tide. His early stand in favor of elevating the Emperor to Chief of State did nothing to dispel these doubts. Another source of concern was the fact that he was the first postwar Prime Minister to receive any measure of public support from the extreme nationalists.[30] There was not the slightest sign of a "Kishi boom" in 1957 and not until the LDP victory in the general elections of May 1958 did he have anything like a popular mandate. Even then there were those who argued that some other conservative Prime Minister would have turned out a better vote. It was this reservoir of mistrust by moderates that was Kishi's great liability; a misstep or assumption of a "high posture" could easily turn these suspicions into hostility.[31]

To the left wing, Kishi's rise to power was cause for alarm. Socialists, progressive intellectuals, and much of the younger generation saw Kishi as a symbol of everything they hated about prewar and wartime Japan. They were convinced he was an unreformed fascist plotting to turn back the hands of the clock. Kishi's subsequent moves to revise the police duties law, enforce the teachers' efficiency rating system, revise the constitution, restore Kigensetsu Day, increase pensions to former servicemen, pay reparations to South Vietnam, visit Chiang Kai-shek in Taiwan, rearm, and, finally, revise the security treaty with the United States seemed part of a single picture.

After Kishi's first speech to the Diet as Prime Minister, Socialist Party Secretary-General Asanuma declared: "There are some among the masses who are concerned about the fact that Prime Minister Kishi was one of those who signed the Imperial

---

[30] Ivan Morris, *Nationalism and the Right Wing in Japan,* London: Oxford University Press, 1960, p. 189, n.l.

[31] The term "high posture" (*kōshisei*) has become a popular term in Japanese politics to describe an inflexible or uncompromising approach to the opposition. Ordinarily a high posture by a conservative Prime Minister provokes more than usual hostility from the left and angers the press and political commentators. Too low a posture, however, leaves the conservative Prime Minister vulnerable to attack from his own right wing.

Rescript declaring war and was responsible for the wartime control of the economy; what does the Prime Minister think about these points?" Kishi replied, "I have fully searched my soul concerning my wartime responsibility, and today I am resolved to devote myself as a democratic statesman to the building of Japan with the people." [32] But Kishi's critics never gave him the benefit of the doubt, as they had given it to Ishibashi. In the troubled days of May-June 1960 the theme of war (guilt for the old one, fear of a new one) rumbled distantly behind the dust and the din of marching feet and angry voices. No matter how much of a "democratic statesman" Kishi had become, the pain and fear of the past could not be erased so soon.

Kishi's admirers saw his successful career and rapid rise after 1952 as evidence of the fact that he was a genius—that he had mastered the rules in the tough game of Japanese politics, made the right connections, and used to the utmost the opportunities that had presented themselves. They said that his experiences after the war converted him to a genuine believer in democracy although he remained a patriot with Japan's best interests at heart. His critics, who were far more vocal, credited his success to ruthless opportunism, money politics, and willingness to betray his superiors. They pointed to his turning against Kobayashi in 1941, Tōjō in 1944, and Yoshida in 1953, and even compared him to Akechi Mitsuhide (1528–1582), Japan's own Benedict Arnold, who turned on his master, Oda Nobunaga, and killed him in Honnoji Temple in 1582.[33]

Finally, there was a trait in Kishi's personality that alienated many Japanese who were not leftists. "He is too flawless," they

[32] *Japan Times*, quoted in an article by Murata Kiyoaki, March 2, 1957.

[33] For a variety of critical discussions of Kishi, see the following: Hidaka Rokurō, ed., *Gogatsu Jūkunichi* (May 19th), Tokyo: Iwanami Shinsho, 1960, pp. 57–64; Nakamura Kikuo, *Gikai Seiji to Taishū Kōdō* (Parliamentary Politics and Mass Movements), Tokyo: Bunka Shinsho, 1960, pp. 86–88; Tajima Taijirō, *"Jinbutsu Kishi Naikaku Ron"* (A View of the Characters in the Kishi Cabinet), *Chūō Kōron*, September 1957, pp. 106–114; and "Zadankai: Kishi Kaizō Naikaku o Shindan Suru" (Round-table Conference: Examining the Reorganized Kishi Cabinet), *Sekai*, September 1957, pp. 190–201.

said when they tried to articulate their hostility to Kishi. "He has no rough spots (*sotsu ga nai*)." He seemed to be the typical bureaucrat-turned-politician: cold, arrogant, legalistic, out of touch with the masses. Other critics added that he was a kind of parasite, first leaning on the Japanese militarists, and then on the United States, to stay in power. Some called him by the nickname "Ryō-Gishi" (a pun meaning "both banks of the river") to point up his straddling of issues.

Not everyone, but a substantial part of the Japanese people seemed to hold one or more of these uncomplimentary views of Kishi in the peak of the crisis in 1960. No one can say for certain which of the protests was stronger in 1960: against Kishi, against the security treaty, against "the system," or against the United States, but the judgment here is that the anti-Kishi sentiment was the prevailing one. We have jumped ahead of the main story, however; the tortuous road to treaty revision began in 1957.

Road to Negotiations: The "New Era"

It was a tradition by 1957 for Japanese Prime Ministers to strive for some major diplomatic feat during their administrations; Yoshida managed the San Francisco Peace Treaty, Hatoyama the reopening of relations with the U.S.S.R. As we noted above, the press played up the idea that Ishibashi's mandate was to solve the China problem. When Kishi took over, he gradually made it evident that his quest for fame would not be on the mainland of China but in Washington, D.C. He underlined the importance he attached to foreign affairs by keeping the job of Foreign Minister for the first five months of his administration, and then by conferring it on one of his closest friends, Fujiyama Aiichirō, in July 1957. Just three days after becoming Prime Minister, Kishi announced his plans to visit Washington at the close of the Diet session. During the spring of 1957, as the mood of criticism against the treaty grew stronger, he unfurled his intentions slowly, referring in vague terms to the need to place the security treaty on a footing of equality, but never committing himself to precise objectives. He gave the impression that he was acting to meet popular feelings but took care not to make bold promises. He was aware, no doubt, of the problems he would face in Washington and of the political dangers of coming home empty-handed when public expectations of a major *omiyage* (souvenir) were high.[34] Further pressure was placed on Kishi by a JSP mission to Peking in April 1957, where the Chinese lashed the security treaty as an infringement on Japanese sovereignty, and Mao Tse-tung offered to sign a nonaggression pact with Japan even before the abrogation of the security treaty. Kishi needed something to match this offer.

The state of U.S.–Japanese relations in 1957 (aside from the security treaty problem) was tolerably good. The differences that existed stemmed largely from the differing world outlooks of the two. The United States was relatively more concerned with military and security problems in the Far East; Japan was absorbed in rebuilding its economy. To many Japanese, the U.S. view of the world Communist threat seemed stubborn and emotional, particularly in the case of Communist China. They resented American interference in a problem that they had been handling for centuries.[35] Another strain on relations was the problem of nuclear testing. Japanese nervousness after Hiroshima had been aggravated by the "Lucky Dragon Incident" of 1954 in which a Japanese tuna boat was dusted by fall-out from a United States H-bomb near the Bikini testing grounds.[36] Still another potentially troublesome issue was commercial policy as trade grew by leaps and bounds during the 1950's.[37]

[34] Richard Storry observed at the time that trips abroad can make or break a prime minister, all else being equal, and pointed out that Prime Minister Yoshida visited the United States in October 1954, returned empty-handed, and was out of office by the end of the year. *Japan Times*, June 20, 1957.

[35] For an example of this sort of thinking, see Kano Hisaakira, "Views on U.S.–Japanese Relations," *Japan Quarterly*, Vol. 4, No. 2, April-June 1957, pp. 152–158.

[36] See Ralph Eugene Lapp, *The Voyage of the Lucky Dragon*, New York: Harper & Brothers, 1958, for an account of this episode.

[37] The remaining issues were: the question of how much and how fast Japan should rearm, Japan's desire for the immediate return of Okinawa and U.S. problems in administering it, the Government and Relief in Oc-

55

Kishi was prepared for the problems he would encounter in Washington over treaty revision, for he had traveled with then Foreign Minister Shigemitsu to the U.S. in August 1955 when Shigemitsu (according to press accounts) had suggested outright revision of the treaty and had been rebuffed by Secretary of State Dulles. Shigemitsu had apparently outlined to Dulles a six-year rearmament plan calling for an annual increase of 10,000 ground troops to bring the Ground Self-defense Forces' strength up to 180,000 by 1958 and the total Self-defense Force strength to 260,000 by 1960. Dulles, it is said, made the withdrawal of U.S. troops contingent upon the creation of still greater troop strength in Japan—possibly as large as 300,000 men, according to one report.[38] The Dulles-Shigemitsu Joint Communiqué did, in a sense, mark the first step in the process of treaty revision when it stated:

> It was agreed that efforts should be made, whenever practicable on a cooperative basis, to establish conditions such that Japan could, as rapidly as possible, assume primary responsibility for the defense of its homeland and be able to contribute to the preservation of international peace and security in the western Pacific. It was also agreed that when such conditions were brought about it would be appropriate to replace the present security treaty with one of greater mutuality.[39]

Behind this carefully guarded language it was clear that the sooner Japan rearmed, the sooner she could hope to revise the treaty. Thus Shigemitsu, the man who signed the surrender documents on the *Missouri* on September 2, 1945, returned to Tokyo to tell his government that the new Japanese army would

cupied Areas (GARIOA) account, and release of remaining war criminals. None of these issues threatened to shake the alliance, but it is worth noting that the security treaty was not the only matter that kept lights burning late at Kasumigaseki in the spring of 1957.

[38] *New York Times*, September 1, 1955; and *Japan Times*, article by Hirasawa Kazushige, August 17, 1957.

[39] U.S. Department of State, "Joint Statement of August 31, 1955," *Department of State Bulletin*, Vol. 33, No. 846, September 12, 1955, pp. 419–420.

have to be built up even faster if the treaty was soon to be revised.

Kishi met with greater success in Washington during his visit of June 1957. Arriving in the capital on the 19th, he was whisked out to Burning Tree for a round of golf with President Eisenhower, followed by two days of talks and a Joint Communiqué on June 21 proclaiming a "new era" in U.S.–Japanese relations.[40] The communiqué said that an intergovernmental committee would be established to study problems relating to the security treaty and to consult, when practicable, regarding the "disposition and employment in Japan by the United States of its forces." It would also consult to assure that any action taken under the treaty conformed to the principles of the United Nations Charter. Finally, the committee was to consider *"future adjustments in the relationships between the United States and Japan in these fields adequate to meet the needs and aspirations of the peoples of both countries."* The forming of the new committee took care of two problems: it appeared to give the Japanese side the desired consultation on disposition and employment of U.S. troops, plus assurance that the U.S. would act in accordance with the U.N. Charter to meet the criticism at home, and it hinted that future adjustments in the treaty could be considered.

The more tangible prize for Kishi in the communiqué was the announcement that the United States would withdraw, within the next year, all of its ground combat forces from Japan. Here was a major *omiyage* to take back to Tokyo: it would be seen, felt, and applauded all over the country. As for the Joint Committee, Kishi chose to consider it a "beach-head" or first stage in the revision process in which he would dispel U.S. misgivings and prove that Japan was a trusted ally. From the Joint Committee, he hinted that negotiations might proceed to a higher level.[41] When, soon after the Washington visit, Kishi was asked for comment on Dulles' remark that the treaty would not be revised, he replied that Dulles had meant, "Not for the

[40] See Appendix B.

[41] The committee was formally established on August 6, 1957 and met six times during the following year.

57

present." [42] When asked what Dulles meant by saying that the new Joint Committee was not designed to discuss the treaty, Kishi replied that this did not, nevertheless, prohibit discussion on the treaty.[43] Although Kishi had patently failed to win U.S. agreement to revise the treaty, he made the Washington visit and the "new era" communiqué appear to be little short of a diplomatic triumph.

The "new era" brought two new developments in the alliance. On one hand, the United States withdrew its ground troops, moved its installations to less obtrusive areas outside the big cities, and by gestures such as flying the Japanese flag next to the U.S. flag at its bases, paid greater deference to Japanese sensitivities. On the other hand, Japan continued its slow and steady program of rearming, with U.S. aid and encouragement. By 1959 the Self-defense Forces numbered 210,000 men, 1,300 aircraft, and over 400 ships.[44] It had the third largest navy in Asia. Japan's defense budget in fiscal 1959 (beginning April 1, 1959) accounted for 10.1 percent of the national budget and 1.2 percent of the gross national product.[45] Kishi could point out with some truth in October 1958 that Japan was no longer the dangerous military vacuum that it had been in 1952.

Foreign Policy Dilemmas for Japan

Since almost everybody in Japan had, at one time or another over the previous six years, called for changes in the security treaty, one might have expected that the U.S. agreement to negotiate a new treaty in September 1958 would be greeted with relief and satisfaction. Not for a moment. The entire treaty question was suddenly reopened, and the nation plunged into a controversy that almost tore it to pieces during the next two years.[46] The conservatives fell into utter disarray as faction lead-

[42] *Japan Times*, July 2, 1957.

[43] *Ibid.*

[44] Ardath W. Burks, *The Government of Japan*, New York: Thomas Y. Crowell Co., 1961, p. 236.

[45] Figures supplied by the U.S. Embassy, Tokyo.

[46] For a number of views on the new treaty situation, see the following: "Ampo Jōyaku Kaitei no Mondaiten" (Problems in Revising the Security

ers contradicted each other and fought to capitalize on the treaty issue. Underlying this confusion were two factors: the painful dilemmas of foreign policy that confronted Japan in this period and the complicated political infighting in the LDP.

In the months between Kishi's Washington visit of June 1957 and the formal opening of treaty negotiations in October 1958, one event—the Russian success with Sputnik—was to have an incalculable effect on the national debate over security. The sensational development of Sputnik—and by implication, the ICBM—shook the foundations of a long-accepted belief that the United States held an unchallengeable material and technical superiority over the Soviet Union and the rest of the world. It ended the popular notion that Russians were clumsy fellows capable of massive and energetic production but less than brilliant in scientific and technical matters.[47] The shock of Sputnik was magnified in December 1957 when the newsreels of America's first satellite attempt were shown in Japan; the Vanguard rocket exploded ignominiously on its pad in a billow of smoke. In the awkward laughter that filled the movie theaters there was, it seemed, the sort of embarrassment felt by the horse-racing fan who sees his mount stumble at the starting gate. We observed in the first chapter that, unpleasant as the treaty might have been, there was the conviction that it tied Japan to the stronger side in the Cold War. Now the question presented itself starkly: have we picked a winner or not?

Treaty), a round-table conference with Ōi Atsushi, Irie Keishirō, and Sugihara Arata, *Tokyo Shimbun*, October 5–9, 1958; "Ampo Kaitei o Megutte" (Concerning Treaty Revision), a round-table conference with Irie Keishirō, Nishimura Kumao, Sugihara Arata, Fukushima Shintarō, and Takano Yūichi, *Asahi Shimbun*, October 14–19 and 21, 1959; *Asahi Shimbun*, editorial, October 24, 1958; Ichimata Masao, "Dōdō to Shiseiken Motomeyo" (A Solemn Demand for Administrative Rights), *Yomiuri Shimbun*, October 26, 1958; "Seifu Yotō ni Shōgeki" (A Shock to the Government and LDP), *Nihon Keizai Shimbun*, October 30, 1958; and Nomura Kichisaburō, "Beigawa Sōan e no Iken" (An Opinion on the U.S. Draft), *Tokyo Shimbun* (evening), October 31, 1958.

[47] For an example, see Taketani Mitsuo, "*Saidai no Kyōkun*" (The Greatest Lesson), *Sekai*, December 1957, pp. 84–97.

The debate between pro-treaty conservatives and the left wing had always proceeded on two levels. On the surface were the labels: the peaceful constitution, U.S. imperialism, Communist aggression, Japanese independence, and so forth. Beneath these ideological terms was the basic dispute over the relative power of the two camps. The conservatives had deliberately chosen to argue on the grounds of the superior power of the United States, largely ignoring any ideological justification for the treaty. When Sputnik began to orbit the globe, the reaction of the Socialists and progressive intellectuals was to indulge in an orgy of self-congratulation, as if it somehow proved the truth of their *ideological* contentions. The conservatives now looked at each other in dismay, seemingly victimized by their own arguments on relative power. Government leaders argued defensively that the United States would soon catch up, and applauded each U.S. space success more loudly than was warranted. The Socialists shifted their attack on the Self-defense Forces from constitutional to pragmatic grounds: "The advent of missiles," said JSP Diet member Okada Sōji, "has completely changed the military situation. The Self-defense Forces have been rendered virtually valueless." [48]

The result of all this was that the security treaty came to be seen by many of its former supporters as a guarantee of *insecurity* in the event of war. The feeling was, in essence, that it would be like holding on to a lightning rod in the middle of a thunderstorm: wouldn't the U.S. bases simply attract a rain of Soviet missiles without in themselves being able to prevent the total destruction of these four islands? When Soviet bombers had been the only threat, the U.S. bases bristling with fighter planes had made sense. But now, might it not be better to get rid of these targets and take a chance with neutralism? In simple terms, there seemed to be two possible responses to the new power of the Communist Bloc: either strengthen the

[48] *Japan Times*, quoted in article by Kuroda Kazuo, November 8, 1957. It is interesting to note that the Sunakawa Case of 1959, which was supposed to have dealt with the specific question of whether or not the security treaty was constitutional, was argued to a great extent in terms of the relative power of the two sides in the Cold War.

alliance with the United States and get further under the U.S. protective shield or loosen the ties and work toward improving relations with the Communist Bloc. Neither choice seemed totally acceptable.

The second dilemma concerned rearmament, nuclear weapons, and the economy. We have already seen in the last chapter that the rearmament question was a hot constitutional and political issue in Japan, the world's only victim of atomic warfare. Nuclear weapons, as they became ready for tactical and defensive use in the late 1950's, posed a delicate problem: could the United States equip its Japan-based troops with nuclear arms and should the Japanese Self-defense Forces possess them? Public opinion was strongly opposed in both cases. But reports had circulated in Japan as early as February 1957 that the United States was contemplating the dispatch of atomic task force units to Japan, and these reports caused widespread consternation. The acceptance by some NATO countries of ballistic missiles at the Paris meeting of NATO in December 1957 added to the controversy. There were some conservatives in Japan, such as Nomura Kichisaburō and Hattori Takushirō, who publicly advocated equipping or at least training the Japanese Self-defense Forces with nuclear weapons; they argued that it would be a quick and perhaps cheaper way to build up Japan's defensive strength and thus to end the need for the security treaty. Kishi dropped a bombshell when he said on May 7, 1957, that he thought Japan could constitutionally possess atomic weapons so long as they were for defensive purposes. He quickly denied, however, any intention of permitting the U.S. forces or the Japanese to be equipped with such weapons.

The Socialists kept the issue on the front pages throughout the whole treaty negotiation period by suggesting that Kishi could not be sure that U.S. forces would not import atomic arms. They accused him of planning eventually to equip the Self-defense Forces with these weapons, and they were successful in stirring up deep anxieties. Even the Japanese acceptance of the nonnuclear "side-winder" air-to-air missile caused a storm of Socialist protest in the Diet. The result was that the conservatives were forced to seek an agreement with the United

States (during the treaty negotiations) that would put these worries to rest. The revised treaty, in the opinion of many, did not go far enough in this direction.

A related question was the amount of national outlay that could be devoted to defense. The rapid postwar recovery owed much to the fact that the U.S. had assumed almost total responsibility for Japan's defense. Japan in 1957 spent only 11.9 percent of her budget and 1.4 percent of her GNP for defense, low among the major powers of the world and far less than West Germany, which had similarly rearmed after defeat. Any lessening of the treaty ties with the U.S. would have meant, in the minds of most conservative leaders, a greater investment in arms at home, and the risk of a consequent slowdown in economic growth.

Another problem was the desire by the Japanese Government and leading financial interests to maintain Japan's international credit and image of trustworthiness at a high level, while at the same time committing Japan to the fewest international responsibilities beyond her direct and immediate interests. There was the nagging question whether trade and capital would continue to flow toward Japan at the same rate should Japan appear to suddenly reduce her commitment to the security of the free world. In the treaty's favor, of course, was the enormous inflow of dollars, averaging $570 million a year between 1953 and 1957, which resulted from the presence of U.S. troops and bases and which was crucial to Japan's balance of payments.

Thus there were delicate factors to weigh, and responsible conservatives, even if they agreed on the basic need for some sort of defense system, could honestly differ on ways and means of revising the treaty.

The third dilemma was the question of how to place a check on the military movements of the U.S. forces based in Japan. This issue was dormant during the relatively peaceful years between the end of the Korean War and 1958, but it became acute in 1958 when the Cold War took an ugly new turn. In that year, the Chinese Communists abruptly cut off all trade with Japan (May), British and American troops landed in Jordan and Lebanon (July), a new crisis loomed in the Taiwan

Straits (August), and Khrushchev opened his attack on the Western position in Berlin (November).

The unfortunate term, "brinkmanship," which had become current in 1957, was widely known and widely misunderstood in Japan. Even the conservatives were alarmed by it. What, they wondered, would the United States do with its forces in Japan if tension in the Far East should burst into a shooting war? A wave of "war nerves" swept the nation. Foreign Minister Fujiyama publicly disapproved of the dispatch of troops to Lebanon and Jordan.[49] In the Taiwan Straits crisis, the U.S. Seventh Fleet, partly supported by bases in Japan, was being used to convoy supplies to Quemoy—to the very brink of war. The idea that Japan should abdicate control over the question of war and peace and tie her fate to that of Chiang Kai-shek, whom she had fought for fifteen years in the recent past—to become involved in a war that involved no vital interest of Japan but threatened her with utter destruction—was the most unthinkable of disasters. A great many moderates and conservatives came to feel that any new security treaty *must* provide some voice for Japan in U.S. combat operations in the Far East, and the mounting tension in Southeast Asia reinforced this belief.

It was no coincidence that Foreign Minister Fujiyama appeared in Washington with a new demand for treaty revision at the very time that the shelling of Quemoy and Matsu was in full progress. Fujiyama in a statement to the Foreign Affairs Committee of the House of Representatives said, on August 30, 1958, what most Japanese were thinking: the battle in the Taiwan Straits was "an internal affair of China." [50] Here again Communist China emerged as a great force behind the drive to revise the treaty; the interesting point is that conservatives as

[49] *New York Times*, July 18, 1958.

[50] *New York Times*, article by Robert Trumbull, August 31, 1958. At a news conference on September 1, 1958, Fujiyama explained the Japanese desire for a voice in the deployment of U.S. forces to other parts of the Far East, and added dryly, "The United States policy towards Communist China has not always been successful in our eyes." *New York Times*, article by Robert Trumbull, September 2, 1958.

well as leftists actually feared the consequences of U.S. action in the absence of their restraining influence. The problem, of course, was U.S. reluctance to open up its entire Far Eastern defensive strategy to the risk of a Japanese veto in prior consultations at the moment of crisis.

These were the dilemmas facing the Japanese Government as the new treaty was being negotiated in the late 1950's. It is well to remember, in looking at the great struggle of 1960, that it was much more than a battle between left and right—between the free world and neutralism or Communism. The underlying question was: how to provide the greatest security for Japan— and on this question, the Japanese nation was deeply divided.

Kishi and the Conservative Factions

Communist China, U.S. "brinkmanship," rearmament, nuclear weapons, the economy, the balance of world power—all these provided the background and point of departure for the debate on the treaty negotiations. But having said this much, we should look at the domestic political side of the treaty negotiations, noting how personal ambitions and factional struggles became linked to the treaty issues. The results of the Liberal Democratic Party's undignified scramble would be strongly felt in the mass movement of May–June 1960.

Kishi announced, early in his regime, that he intended to eliminate factional strife and stay in office for a long period of time. It was clear that any success he might meet in his self-appointed mission of adjusting U.S.-Japanese relations would be used, not as Hatoyama did, to bow gracefully off the stage, but rather to tighten his grip on the reins of power. Both Kishi's implacable enemies of the left and his ambitious partners in the LDP were aware of these intentions—a fact which loaded the treaty revision question with political dynamite and complicated every phase of negotiations with the United States.

But Kishi's ambitions outran his political power in 1957. The LDP at that point was a party in name alone. In reality, it was more of "a working coalition of a number of political leaders, each with his following." [51] We noted earlier that Kishi rose to power as something of an outsider in that he was neither an alumnus of the "Yoshida school" nor a veteran of prewar party politics. This was a source of both strength and weakness: strength because it left him free to maneuver and bargain for support on all sides, weakness because he had no bedrock of support beyond his own faction and that of his brother, Satō Eisaku.[52] The key to Kishi's three-and-a-half year stay in office was his ability to divide his rivals against each other, seeing that none acquired too much "stature," and keeping them all guessing where he would throw his weight in the battle for succession. Kishi tried to strengthen his power base through popular support, making trips to Southeast Asia, Washington, Europe, and Latin America, but he never succeeded in launching a "Kishi boom" or even in developing a large popular following. Nor was he the type of politician who could play the "strong-man rôle" that Yoshida had made famous. Instead, he had to calculate every move in terms of its effect on the factional alignment of the LDP, and this is why negotiations on the treaty bogged down so badly in 1959.

Kishi's first Cabinet (February to July 1957), which he inherited intact from Ishibashi, was a balance between Kōno and Ōno, on one hand, and former Ishibashi supporters Ikeda, Miki, Matsumura, and Ishii on the other. Kōno and Ikeda were the principal antagonists, each trying to pull Kishi closer to his camp. This was a weak and provisional arrangement, and Kishi took steps to strengthen it after his Washington trip in June 1957. In a switch of top cabinet and party jobs, the former Ishibashi supporters were pushed out (except for Ishii, who be-

[51] Ike Nobutaka, *Japanese Politics*, New York: Alfred A. Knopf, 1957, p. 177. For an excellent discussion of LDP factions and party problems, see Robert A. Scalapino and Masumi Junnosuke, *Parties and Politics in Contemporary Japan*, Berkeley and Los Angeles: University of California Press, 1962, pp. 82–95.

[52] These two factions were relatively strong in themselves (see Scalapino and Masumi, *op. cit.*, p. 169) but they were not strong enough to outweigh a unified movement by rivals.

65

came Deputy Prime Minister) and the balance tipped in favor of Kōno, who now appeared to have the edge in the race to succeed Kishi. As Director of the Economic Planning Agency, Kōno spoke out on all subjects and became the "strong man" of the second Kishi Cabinet. He succeeded in annoying not only the Yoshida followers but also the Miki and Matsumura factions and Fujiyama, who was now beginning to take on political weight of his own.

Following the general elections in May 1958, Kishi again made key changes. The third Kishi Cabinet (June 1958–June 1959) included both Ikeda and Miki, and dropped Kōno. A new, tense balance was restored between Kōno and Ikeda. The mainstream of the party was still Kishi and Satō, backed by Ōno and Kōno. Ikeda was in the cabinet, but not very far in; he planned to oust Kishi in the LDP presidential elections of 1959. The Kōno forces plotted to keep Ikeda out of power and follow Kishi to the top.

The next major shift came after Kishi's defeat in the Police Bill affair in the fall of 1958.[53] The anti-Kishi group of Ikeda, Miki, Matsumura, Ishii, and others openly challenged Kishi's leadership and demanded sweeping cabinet and party changes. Kishi tried to compromise with the "rebels," but Ikeda, Miki, and Nadao Hirokichi (of the Ishii faction) resigned from the cabinet on December 27, 1958. Kishi was now in a dangerous spot, with his popularity at a new low, Ōno on the verge of deserting him to play mediator between the opposing factions, and Kōno reportedly disgusted with his willingness to compromise with the anti-mainstream. The truth was, however, that Kishi's opponents could not unite in time to beat him in the LDP election on January 24, 1959. They finally backed old Matsumura Kenzō, whom Kishi easily defeated, 320-166. As a result of party and cabinet changes in January 1959, a powerful group of politicians, including Kōno, Ikeda, Ishii, Miki, Matsumura, and Ishibashi, were left jobless.[54] With the im-

[53] Described in Chapter 3.

[54] This does not mean that they were all without influence, for members of their factions continued to hold important posts.

portant treaty issue looming, this sort of "weak" cabinet could not last for long.

Kishi's fortunes took a turn for the better in early 1959 as the nation's "mood" settled down from agitation over the Police Bill to enjoy Japan's greatest postwar spectacle up to the Olympics, the marriage of the Crown Prince, in April 1959. The economy was recovering well after a dip in 1957–1958, and the LDP won handily in the local and House of Councillor elections in the spring of 1959. During these months a showdown battle was looming between Ikeda and Kōno for the post of LDP Secretary-General in anticipation of the expected job changes in June 1959. Feeling mounted in the party that Kishi would have to strengthen party unity to pave the way for treaty revision, that this might be Kishi's last act, and that now was the time to get on the inside track.

At this point it is necessary to revert to a remarkable development behind the scenes in the LDP: the gradual return to power of former Prime Minister Yoshida Shigeru, who, after his resignation in December 1954, had almost disappeared from public view to his home in Oiso, 50 miles south of Tokyo on Sagami Bay.[55] Since the merger of the two conservative parties in 1955, Yoshida and his protégé, Satō Eisaku, had refused to join the new LDP, and Yoshida appeared to have retired from the affairs of state except for an occasional telephone call to

[55] We might observe here that this is the sort of development, like others in this chapter, that is hard to document or describe in the language of political science. This is not to subscribe to the "inscrutability" or "mysterious oriental" theories, but only to admit that it is a rare foreigner who can claim to have real insight into conservative politics in Japan. The spoken and unspoken nuance, the secret intermediary, the half-promise, the *machiai* bargain are enough to stump even the Japanese political scientist, who comes equipped not only with the language but also information on many other elements that go into the process of power-holding: the family relationships, business and financial connections, birthplace and electoral district roots, former and present factional associations and enmities, and the personalities, tastes, and philosophies of the human beings involved in the game. The description here, therefore, is based not on scientific research but on interviews with certain of the key figures involved, with reporters and scholars close to the scene, and, frankly, on the use of circumstantial evidence.

the Foreign Office or a meeting with former factional associates. In early 1957, however, the old man (at 80) had begun to stir. One press account reports that the Emperor, while passing through Oiso on the train, was reminded of old Yoshida and wrote a poem for him which so touched Yoshida that he became imbued with a spirit of service to the nation! [56] Whatever the reason, Yoshida and Satō rejoined the LDP on February 2, 1957, and became active again in party affairs.

Yoshida, whatever else may be said of him, was one of the few LDP leaders to hold and articulate consistent views on a number of issues.[57] Basically a conservative nationalist, he consistently backed closer relations between Japan and the Anglo-American Bloc in world affairs. By the late 1950's there seemed to be a curious revival of popular affection for the old man, even among some who had blasted him in 1954. His decisiveness and blunt language, once denounced as arrogant, were now viewed by some with nostalgia as the younger LDP leaders fell to bickering and wavering over the issues of the day. Yoshida was again an important LDP power when the treaty revision issue came to a head.

Since Kishi had helped overthrow Yoshida and was allied to the hated Kōno, the relationship between the two men had been strained. In the LDP elections of December 1956 Yoshida had supported first Ishii and then Ishibashi—both had seemed better than the Kishi-Kōno combination. In the party elections of January 1959 Yoshida again opposed Kishi in favor of Matsumura. But in the early months of 1959, with a new "treaty cabinet" about to be installed, there appeared an improvement in relations. This was happening even as the Satō faction moved away from Kōno and closer to Ikeda—in effect, a reunification of the old Yoshida forces.

The upshot was a dramatic shift in the conservative camp in June 1959. Kōno, annoyed by the failure of Ōno's compromise plan (which would have made him LDP Secretary-General), created a sensation on the night of June 12, 1959, by breaking

---

[56] *Japan Times*, article by Hirasawa Kazushige, January 11, 1957.

[57] See Yoshida Shigeru, *The Yoshida Memoirs*, Cambridge: Riverside Press, 1962, for an English language version of these views.

with Kishi and declaring that he would accept no cabinet or party post in the coming shuffle. The move put Kōno in the anti-mainstream, where he remained throughout the treaty struggle.

Faced with the desertion of Kōno—and with him, Ōno, from the mainstream—Kishi, in order to avoid isolation, did some of the fancy footwork for which he was justly famous. He now formed a working alliance with Ikeda, who had charged him with political corruption and incompetence only six months previously. The new Kishi Cabinet of June 1959 was jokingly called the "Sixth Yoshida Cabinet" because Ikeda and Satō now gained a major voice in the government, Ikeda taking over the Ministry of International Trade and Industry, and Satō remaining as Finance Minister.

The decisive change was that Kōno, along with Miki and Matsumura, were now left in the anti-mainstream of conservative politics, a fact that was to have an important effect on their positions with respect to the treaty negotiations and the revised treaty. Ikeda, as we shall see, took a cautious, middle-of-the-road position on the treaty and kept a reasonable distance from Kishi when the trouble began; it was clear, though, that he had moved into the lead in the race to succeed Kishi. It was also apparent that Yoshida, always close to the ear of Ikeda, now reigned as the new *genrō* in Oiso, in somewhat the manner of the illustrious Saionji Kimmochi before the war.

Now the conservative lineup for the treaty battle was set. We shall see that Kishi was not so near the end of the line as his rivals imagined. He had survived once again by pitting them against each other and cutting them down to size, and no one knew, least of all his leftist opponents, how long this could go on.

Conservative Factions and the Treaty Negotiations

The course of treaty negotiations and the LDP wrangling that accompanied it reveal some interesting aspects of policy-making in a country with a one-and-a-half-party system. We do not, of course, have the full story on the negotiations, as the documents are not yet publicly available. What we can do is observe briefly how the treaty revision process was affected by internal politics, and how it in turn affected the public as it dragged on for fifteen months. This transpired while the American press and public almost entirely ignored the issue—a cause of considerable annoyance to many Japanese.

Japan apparently put out feelers in the summer of 1958, over a year after Kishi's trip to Washington. According to Nishimura Kumao, former head of the Foreign Office Treaty Bureau, Foreign Minister Fujiyama on July 9, 1958, suggested to Ambassador MacArthur that negotiations toward revision of the security treaty be opened.[58] The United States then suggested three possibilities for a new treaty: (1) a simple base-lease agreement, (2) amendment of the present wording only, or (3) a new treaty of mutual defense. Kishi replied on August 25, 1958, that Japan wanted a new treaty of mutual defense.[59] According to one report, Kishi's decision overrode the advice of the Foreign Office, which favored amending the wording only and feared strong popular resistance against a mutual defense treaty.[60] Fujiyama flew to Washington and on September 12, 1958, issued a joint statement with Secretary of State Dulles which opened the way for treaty negotiations through regular diplomatic channels in Tokyo.[61] As preparations were being made for the opening of negotiations in Tokyo, loud rumblings were heard within the LDP.

"Once treaty revision became an actual problem, all sorts of opinions were advanced," said Nishimura in a vast understatement.[62] As we have noted, the LDP was split in the fall of 1958 into mainstream (Kishi-Satō-Ōno-Kōno) and anti-mainstream (Ikeda-Matsumura-Miki-Ishii-Ishibashi) groups. Fujiyama's sudden success in winning U.S. approval for negotiations seemed

[58] Nishimura Kumao, *Anzen Hoshō Jōyaku Ron* (A Discussion of the Security Treaty), Tokyo: Jiji Shinsho, 1960, pp. 121ff.

[59] "*Nichibei Sōgo Bōei Jōyaku—Seifu Mōshiire Ketsui*" (Government Decides on Proposal: Japan–U.S. Treaty of Mutual Defense), *Yomiuri Shimbun*, August 27, 1958.

[60] *Nihon Keizai Shimbun*, December 10, 1959.

[61] *New York Times*, September 12, 1958. See Appendix C.

[62] Nishimura, *Anzen Hoshō Jōyaku Ron*, p. 124.

to catch everybody by surprise. Alarm signals went up on all sides as it appeared that Kishi and Fujiyama were about to score a major diplomatic victory.[63] The party, having virtually committed itself to treaty revision for the past year and a half, now began to backtrack and fumble; obviously, Kishi and Fujiyama were not to be permitted to run away with the prize.

Only three official U.S.–Japanese meetings were held on the treaty in the fall of 1958 (October 4 and 22, and December 16).[64] The Police Bill disturbances, the feuding within the LDP, and questions over how to revise the treaty brought negotiations to a standstill in December, when a four-month recess was called. The major controversy involved the area to which the new mutual defense pact would apply. The United States reportedly urged that the joint defense area be "the western Pacific" but Japan, under its Constitution, could not agree to send troops to distant Guam or Taiwan in the event U.S. forces were attacked there.[65] Then the question boiled down to: could the constitutional right of self-defense be extended to the Ryūkyū Islands, where Japan held "residual sovereignty," but where the United States had kept administrative control?

LDP opinion on this matter was sharply divided. One group argued that Japan ought to help defend these islands on grounds that this might speed the recovery of Japan's administrative rights and silence Socialist demands for the return of Okinawa.

[63] On September 18, 1958, two foreign policy groups within the LDP met separately at the Akasaka Prince Hotel to coordinate reaction to the new development. The mainstream group was represented by the LDP's Gaikō Chōsa Kai (Foreign Affairs Research Council) chaired by Funada Naka, while the anti-mainstream was represented by the Gaikō Mondai Kenkyū Kai, chaired by ex-Prime Minister Ashida Hitoshi. In both groups, but especially the latter, doubts and objections were raised as to the advisability of treaty revision at that time. *Sankei Shimbun*, September 19, 1958.

[64] The word "official" is added because during the course of the negotiations there were a number of "unofficial" meetings between the two sides. In the late stages Foreign Minister Fujiyama had to resort to clandestine methods to avoid eager newsmen at his unofficial meetings with Ambassador MacArthur.

[65] Nishimura, *Anzen Hoshō Jōyaku Ron*, p. 123; and *New York Times*, article by Robert Trumbull, November 2, 1958.

71

Another group said that the dispatch of Japanese troops over-seas—even to Okinawa—could not be permitted under the Constitution; furthermore, if nuclear weapons were stationed in Okinawa, and if that island became part of the mutual defense area, then such weapons might also be stored in Japan, which would be unfortunate. A third group argued that Japan should offer to share in the defense of the islands provided she got immediate administrative control over them. Mixed into this debate were the questions whether Japan's forces were strong enough to help defend these islands, and whether Japan would be tying herself, if she agreed to defend them, into a sort of NEATO (Northeast Asia Treaty Organization) as the Socialists charged.[66] The problem, in short, was how to get the most administrative control over the islands with the least involvement in U.S. strategy. The U.S. position on the matter was firm and clear: Okinawa was not to be turned over to Japanese administration so long as the present tension lasted in the Far East.[67]

In December 1958 the factional positions within the party began to take shape on the treaty revision issue. Yoshida, leader of the so-called pro-American group, counseled against trying to place too many restrictions on the U.S. forces lest U.S.–Japanese relations be harmed in the process. In fact, Yoshida was opposed to the whole idea of treaty revision at this time and advised Fujiyama on December 8, 1958, to avoid rushing ahead with it.[68] He later told this writer that he had been opposed to treaty revision from start to finish—that the original treaty had been "his treaty" and that there was "no urgent need" to revise it at that time.[69] Ikeda echoed Yoshida's cautious attitude; at the time he was leading the revolt against the mainstream, a fact which also accounted for his opposition to Kishi's diplomacy. Other members of the anti-mainstream—Ishii, Ishibashi,

[66] U.S. forces in Okinawa were also covered by the U.S. treaties with the Republic of Korea, Nationalist China, and the Philippines.

[67] See the Eisenhower-Kishi Joint Communiqué of June 21, 1957, Appendix B.

[68] *Asahi Shimbun* (evening), "Ampo Kaitei wa Isogu na" (Don't Hurry Treaty Revision), December 8, 1958.

[69] Interview with Yoshida Shigeru, May 6, 1962.

Matsumura, and Miki—reiterated in various public statements that it was too early to revise the treaty. Nobody came out in direct opposition to treaty revision (this would have been politically suicidal) but their strategy was to delay Kishi and prevent him from winning a quick diplomatic success.[70] There was rising suspicion that Fujiyama might be using the treaty to hurdle over the others to the position of Kishi's heir-apparent; Fujiyama, a newcomer to politics, had won his first election to the Diet in May 1958 with the second largest number of votes in the country.

At this point even the mainstream began to waver. Not only did Kishi face a revolt within his own party, but the anti-Police Bill uprisings and the Russian and Chinese denunciations of the security treaty were ominous signs that the protest campaign against the revised treaty might be extremely serious—possibly even disastrous—for Kishi's regime. The confusion within the mainstream could be seen in the top level government-party conference of December 4, 1958, when the Ryūkyū and Bonin Island question was discussed. Fujiyama seemed to be in favor of excluding the islands from the treaty area. Kōno held that it would be improper to do so, but he reserved the right to change his position. Ōno and Satō seemed to agree with Kōno. Kishi said simply, "to include or exclude the Ryūkyūs and Bonins would each have its merits and demerits." [71]

Other questions on which the LDP could not agree were these: would it be dangerous or not to remove the clause allowing U.S. troops to be called to help put down internal disturbances? Former Admiral Nomura Kichisaburō thought it might be dangerous. Should the administrative agreement be overhauled completely or only partly revised? And should the treaty and administrative agreement be revised together or in two separate stages? With the anti-mainstream still opposed to any negotiations at all, and the mainstream quarreling on a number

[70] A top Foreign Office official was quoted as saying at this point that when treaty negotiations started, 80% of the problem was politics and 20% diplomacy; now, he added, the ratio was 95% to 5%. *Japan Times*, article by Shimizu Minoru, December 8, 1958.

[71] *Japan Times*, December 5, 1958.

of these questions, it was pointless for the government to continue the negotiations; for this reason the recess was called in December 1958.

During the next four months, Fujiyama Aiichirō worked to unify the factions behind his program of treaty revision and to win national support for his objectives. In spite of the strong opposition within his own party, he made frequent (and as it turned out, overly optimistic) predictions that the new treaty would soon be signed. This kept the treaty in the forefront of the news.

Kōno, who after January 1959 held neither government nor party posts, took the unusual step of approaching Ambassador MacArthur directly with a plan of his own for the Ryūkyūs and Bonins: place the islands in the treaty area, he suggested, but give Japan no responsibility for defending them until administrative control reverted to Japan. This proposal squarely contradicted Fujiyama's, which excluded the islands from the treaty area. When the problem of the administrative agreement came up in February 1959, Kōno again clashed with Fujiyama and asked for a major revision instead of merely deleting the defense contribution clause (in Article XXV). This revealed the growing antagonism between Fujiyama and Kōno—a rivalry that had much to do with the competition for the LDP presidency.

The anti-mainstream continued, early in 1959, to use delaying tactics. On March 7, 1959, they agreed on a common anti-revision policy: (1) to delay signing the new treaty until after the House of Councillors elections on June 2, and (2) to amend the security treaty and administrative agreement simultaneously, with substantial changes in the latter. It appeared that they were trying to set goals they knew the United States would not agree to, in order to embarrass Fujiyama and Kishi.

During these months Kishi seemed to be at the helm of a rudderless ship, as LDP leaders made conflicting statements and undercut each other at every turn. Having first agreed with Fujiyama that there should be no major revision of the administrative agreement, he came around to Ikeda's view that the agreement should be broadly revised. He tried to unify LDP opinion by setting up a ten-man "Cabinet Council on Foreign

Policy," consisting of five each from government and party, but since the new council merely reflected the existing divisions within the party, it made little progress.

Kishi's reluctance to forge ahead with a plan of his own was probably based on his realization that the left wing would stage a protest movement even larger than that against the Police Bill and that he would need maximum LDP unity to push the revised treaty through the Diet.[72] The result was that Kishi in early 1959 left the job of explaining and promoting treaty revision to Fujiyama while he sat through the endless rounds of meetings, compromises, and bargaining that characterize the decision-making process in Japanese politics. Had Kishi ridden roughshod over his LDP rivals, it is possible that he would not have lasted long enough in office to get the treaty ratified. But he had gone too far to turn back. By waiting for the House of Councillors election and a cabinet change in June, he hoped to gain a workable combination of forces that could push the treaty through to ratification.

The LDP finally adopted statements of policy and objectives on April 11, 1959, four months after negotiations had been broken off and two days before they were due to resume.[73] The statement on the treaty itself generally accorded with Fujiyama's known position, but the one on the administrative agreement simply incorporated the conflicting opinions without resolving them. On the same day, April 11, the LDP found it necessary to form another fourteen-member committee, the "Sub-committee for Adjusting Party Views on the Administrative Agreement," to be chaired by Funada Naka. Some observers saw the April 11 party statements simply as gimmicks to give the impression of unity in the coming House of Councillor elections,

[72] In February and March 1959 the left wing was forming the "People's Council" to oppose the revised treaty; this was formally inaugurated on March 28, 1959. Also the Date decision on the Sunakawa case (see below) of March 30, 1959, probably contributed to his hesitancy.

[73] The statements, prepared by the Party's Foreign Affairs Research Council and Executive Board, were entitled "Ampo Jōyaku Kaitei Yōkō" (A Synopsis on Revision of the Security Treaty), and "Gyōsei Kyōtei Chōsei Yōkō" (A Synopsis on Adjusting the Administrative Agreement). They may be found in the *Asahi Shimbun* (evening), April 8, 1959.

75

for they did not do away with party wrangling.[74] Kōno, still considered an adherent of the mainstream, stayed aloof from the Kishi-Fujiyama line and demanded concrete details on plans to change the administrative agreement. Ikeda, Miki, and Matsumura, the anti-mainstream leaders, took a "cautious attitude"; they wished to avoid giving the impression that they were using diplomacy as a domestic political weapon.[75]

The official LDP position on treaty negotiations was declared in a speech by Fujiyama on May 25, 1959. The party's main aims were as follows.[76]

1. To clarify the relationship of the treaty to the United Nations Charter.[77]

2. To clarify the cooperative relationship of the United States and Japan in the political and economic fields.

3. To clarify the American obligation to defend Japan, while restricting Japan's obligations to the limits of the constitution.

4. To establish the area of the treaty as Japanese territory. Japanese territory not then under Japanese administration would automatically become part of the treaty area when returned to Japanese control.

5. To allow U.S. forces to remain in Japan; to provide for prior consultations in cases where these troops were to be used in combat outside Japan and on major equipment changes.

6. To eliminate the "internal disturbance" clause; but, since the danger of indirect aggression still existed, if such aggression

[74] "Tōnai Chōsei Kusuburu" (Smouldering Adjustment within Party), *Asahi Shimbun*, April 12, 1959.

[75] *Asahi Shimbun*, April 12, 1959.

[76] The text may be found in Ampo Jōyaku Mondai Zenkoku Konwa Kai, *Ampo Jōyaku Mondai Tokyo Chiku Konwa Kai ni okeru Fujiyama Gaimu Daijin Enzetsu* (pamphlet), *Konwa Kai Shiryō*, No. 4, June 15, 1959, pp. 1–19. The summary here was made by Nishimura in *Anzen Hoshō Jōyaku Ron*, pp. 125–126. (Nishimura mistakenly gives the date of Fujiyama's speech as May 29 instead of May 25, 1959.)

[77] This relationship had been clarified in an exchange of notes at Tokyo on February 14, 1957 (United States Treaties and Other International Agreements, Vol. 8, Part 2, TIAS 3910, Washington: U.S. Government Printing Office, 1958, pp. 1571–1577) but the conservatives wished to embody it in the new treaty itself.

seemed about to take place, to provide in the new treaty a method of coping with it.

7. To eliminate the clause requiring U.S. prior consent for the forces of a third country to stay in or pass through Japan.

8. In order to ensure smooth functioning of the treaty, to insert a clause providing for consultations over the execution of the treaty.

9. To limit the duration to ten years, with one year's notice thereafter to abrogate.

These were the points on which Fujiyama tried to get LDP agreement between April and November 1959 as he simultaneously negotiated the new treaty with Ambassador MacArthur and sought to win the support of the nation.[78]

In spite of public and private wrangling within the LDP, negotiations between Fujiyama and MacArthur proceeded. Talks were reopened on April 13 and, after ten more official sessions, they halted for a summer recess on July 13. During this period, matters such as the area of the treaty, the internal disturbance clause, prior consultations, and the administrative agreement were discussed. There was hard bargaining on the details of the latter.

The next significant development in the LDP came with the party and cabinet shakeup of June 1959, when Ikeda returned to the government and Kōno moved into the anti-mainstream. The effect of this switch, not surprisingly, was that Ikeda withdrew his objections to the revision plan and stopped criticizing the Kishi-Fujiyama line publicly. There were rumors now that Kishi and Ikeda had made a deal through Masutani Shūji (with Yoshida's blessing) whereby Ikeda would stop obstructing treaty revision in return for Kishi's giving him a clear shot at the Prime Ministership after Kishi retired. According to these rumors, the deal was based on mutual need: without Ikeda, Kishi could not get the treaty approved; without Kishi's support, Ikeda could not beat the other contenders in the race to become Prime

[78] It should be noted that these points emerged after several negotiating sessions with the United States; they should not be taken as the government's optimum position but only the position that seemed reasonable after considering the U.S. position.

Minister. Ishii Mitsujirō, another former critic of the revision plan, now became chairman of the LDP executive board and gradually stopped resisting the government's line. Thus Kishi had cracked the phalanx of anti-mainstream opposition to win support for the revised treaty.

Kishi made some other important moves to strengthen his hand in the forthcoming treaty fight. On June 16, 1959, he brought a trusted follower, Kawashima Shōjirō, back to the job of party Secretary-General.[79] To the Chairmanship of the Policy Board, Kishi named Funada Naka, who had been an important backer of the treaty revision program from the beginning.[80] The key job of Chairman of the LDP's Foreign Affairs Research Council went on July 1st to Kaya Okinori, one of Kishi's oldest associates, a fellow member of the Tōjō Cabinet from 1941 to 1944, a convicted Class A war criminal, and alleged author of the plan for a "Greater East Asia Co-prosperity Sphere." [81] Whatever Kaya's political talents, Kishi could not have placed the treaty in the hands of a man more likely to disturb the neutralist and pacifist sentiment in Japan.

With the "treaty lineup" set, there were fresh rumors in June and July 1959 that the treaty would soon be signed. Once again, however, there were obstacles. Some details in the administrative agreement still had to be negotiated with the United States,

[79] Kawashima had been with him ever since the days of Kishi's Reconstruction League of 1952, and served as the only Kishi man in the second Hatoyama Cabinet. A man of recognized political talents, he had won in nine consecutive Diet elections and had been LDP Secretary-General during the second Kishi Cabinet.

[80] Though an Ōno faction member, Funada's long political career (first elected to the House of Representatives in 1930) and his tough views on defense made him a strong candidate for the job. As Director of the Defense Agency in the third Hatoyama Cabinet, Funada had created a furor by stating that the bombing of enemy bases did not constitute the dispatch of Japanese troops overseas.

[81] Kaya had made an astounding political comeback since his release from prison in 1955. He became an intimate adviser to Kishi on economic and diplomatic problems early in Kishi's regime. Joining the LDP in May 1957, he ran successfully for a Diet seat the following year. By 1959 he was a latent power within the LDP and one of Kishi's leading strategists in maneuvering the treaty through to completion.

and conflicts of opinion had to be ironed out in the LDP (notably on the question of the ten-year time limit). Both Kishi and Fujiyama had scheduled "prestige visits" around the world that summer and early autumn, and the LDP needed more time to run a publicity campaign in favor of the new treaty. Finally, the difficult problem of the Vietnam reparations agreement was to come before the Diet in the fall session. The earliest date the treaty could come up for ratification was therefore December 1959, at the regular Diet session.

The U.S.–Japanese negotiations began again on August 22, 1959, and went on through the fall: September 8, October 9 and 21, November 22 and 27, December 5, 9, 18, and 30. The main hurdles seemed to be the question of prior consultations and rights under the administrative agreement, with Japan seeking more control over the entry and exit of U.S. servicemen and their families, customs and postal inspection, contracting for goods and services, tax exemptions, labor procurement, and the airwaves. Finally, at the twenty-second official meeting on January 6, 1960, negotiations came to a close and the treaty and administrative agreement were ready for signing.[82]

From August 1959 on, Kōno became Kishi's most outspoken opponent on the treaty revision issue. In that month, Kōno publicly objected to the planned LDP publicity campaign for the treaty on the grounds that party opinion was not yet unified. He later protested the ten-year duration of the treaty many times, favoring a more flexible time limit. He wanted broad restrictions on the rights of U.S. forces in and around the bases and pressed for a Japanese veto in the prior consultations. At one point Kōno was said to have conditioned his support for the revised treaty on Kishi's taking over the negotiations from Fujiyama. He threw a scare into Kishi and Fujiyama by announcing plans for a trip—which he subsequently canceled—to Moscow in the fall of 1959. They feared he would try for a dramatic break-through on a peace treaty with Moscow, which would have undermined plans for treaty revision. Kōno was

---

[82] For the text of the treaty, see Appendix D. For a discussion of the nature of the agreements, see below.

living up to his reputation as the "time-bomb" in the LDP. Though one of Kishi's strongest supporters up to late 1958, he now proceeded to throw all his stubborn energy into knocking Kishi from the top. Apparently he reasoned that the way to the summit lay in disassociating himself from Kishi and the revised treaty; in this he may have shrewdly judged the temper of the nation, but he underestimated the Yoshida-Ikeda-Satō forces that were working to take over "from within." Former *Asahi Shimbun* reporter Kōno was characterized by another newspaperman, Hirasawa Kazushige, as follows: "The courage to meet an enemy head-on, the ability to make bold decisions, the energetic power to execute plans, the ruthless persuasive power, the shrewd sense to know when to grab opportunities, the enthusiasm to pursue ambitions and the ability to obtain abundant political funds—these are the qualities that combine to make Kōno the powerful man that he is." [83] We shall see in later chapters how this man of "dictatorial character and Machiavellian methods" [84] would try to capitalize on Kishi's troubles with the revised treaty.

The rest of the anti-mainstream tried to undermine Kishi by seeking diplomatic carrots in other fields. Miki went to Moscow, and Ishibashi and Matsumura both went to Peking in the autumn of 1959. None of them achieved anything spectacular and none was strong enough, even in combination with Kōno, to prevent Kishi from signing the treaty on January 19, 1960, in Washington, D.C., nor from placing it before the Diet for ratification. But the conservative party entered the final and decisive national debate on the revised treaty badly divided and bitterly quarreling. This dissension was to help the left wing in the end.

Summary

There were three important results from the protracted LDP struggle on treaty issues. First, it helped to spread through the country a sense of anxiety over the revised treaty. The very argu-

[83] *Japan Times*, January 30, 1959.
[84] *Ibid.*

ments used by the LDP leaders against each other (such as the ten-year time limit and the proposed Japanese veto) were used effectively by the opposition in the Diet debate of 1960. Second, the delays gave the anti-treaty professionals enough time to mount a new protest movement in 1960. Had the LDP been prepared to sign and present to the Diet a revised treaty in early or mid-1959, it is doubtful that the protest movement, coming hard on the heels of the anti-Police Bill movement, would have reached such proportions. Finally, the LDP struggle left Kishi on his way out—the treaty was clearly to be his "last act" as far as all the other LDP leaders were concerned. This changed the whole psychology of Kishi's position. No longer wielding the political leverage of a new premier, Kishi was forced to make last-resort bargains to get his treaty through. The press, which had never warmed up much to Kishi anyway, smelled blood by late 1959, and was beginning to snarl.

It has been observed by students of Japanese politics that the LDP leaders seemed far more interested in intraparty competition than in debate on national issues. The reason, of course, was that no opposition party had so far even slightly threatened their majority at the polls. The struggle within the LDP over the security treaty was admittedly caused in part by serious policy dilemmas. The conservatives were trapped between leftist-led nationalist demands for greater independence, on one hand, and what the United States would settle for, on the other. They also faced difficult problems in balancing national security and the requirements of the economy. But if there were ideological or philosophical convictions in the LDP as to the future course of Japan's diplomacy, one could scarcely detect them in the wild scramble for personal power. It appeared that the conservatives almost forgot the combustible nature of the issue until the mass explosions of 1960 jolted them back to their senses.

CHAPTER 3

The Left Wing and the People's Council, 1959

IN THE early spring of 1959, when the United States–Japan treaty negotiations were suspended and the conservatives were quarreling over ways to revise the treaty, the forces of the left wing were gathering to launch a massive drive against the security treaty and any revision of it that Kishi might propose. The left wing in postwar Japan had never been able to unify around generalized political objectives; a variety of coalitions had formed to battle the conservatives on particular issues, but these coalitions had quickly dissolved once the issue was settled. Security treaty revision provided a unique opportunity for harmony, since the entire left wing agreed that the alliance with the United States must be ended. In fact, the drive against the treaty threw together some strange bedfellows—tough union bosses, long-haired university professors, fiery eyed students and kimono-clad Marxist theoreticians—and though they agreed that the treaty must go, they were of many minds on the tactics and ideology of the "struggle." The leaders of the drive were the Socialists, Sōhyō, the Communists, and Zengakuren.

The Socialist Party

To understand how and why the Socialists acted as they did in the anti-treaty drive, it is necessary to examine the changes that had taken place in the party since 1952.[1] We saw in the

[1] For a more comprehensive view of the JSP, the reader may wish to consult the following English-language sources: "A Factional Analysis of the Socialist Party," *Japan Times*, January 20, 1957; Allan B. Cole, *Japanese Society and Politics*, Boston University Studies in Political Science, No. 1, 1956; Kenneth Colton, "Japan's Leaders, 1958," *Current History*, Vol. 34, No. 200, April 1958, pp. 228–236; William Dean Howells, "The Japanese Socialist Party and National Security, 1955–1960," Unpublished M.A. Thesis, East Asian Institute, Columbia University, 1960; Marius B. Jansen, "Education, Values and Politics in Japan," *Foreign Affairs*, Vol. 35, No. 4, July 1957, pp. 666–678; Hyman Kublin, "Japanese Politics and the Socialist Minority," *Yale Review*, Vol. 46, No. 4, June 1957, pp. 571–585; Nakamura Kikuo, "Party Politics," *New Leader*, Section Two, "Japan Today," November 28, 1960, pp. 20–26; Naoi Takeo, "Japanese Socialist

first chapter how the party split into Left and Right Wing Socialist Parties over the peace treaty question in 1951; the two wings merged in October 1955 in an uneasy compromise that collapsed again in the fall of 1959. In early 1959, when the People's Council was being formed, there were seven main factions in the party, grouped about an alliance of Suzuki (left-center) and Kawakami (right-center). The party was led by Chairman Suzuki Mosaburō and Secretary-General Asanuma Inejirō (Kawakami faction). To the left of Suzuki were the Wada, Matsumoto, Nomizo, and Kuroda factions, and to the right of Kawakami was the Nishio faction.[2] Party decisions were made by the Central Executive Committee, where the leftist factions held a 23-17 majority in 1958–1959. During the 1950's the left had increased its strength, and behind this trend lay the growing influence of Sōhyō in party affairs. The Socialists were supported

Mission to Peking," *New Leader*, Vol. 42, No. 15, April 13, 1959, pp. 9–10; and "Socialist Setback in Japan," *New Leader*, Vol. 42, No. 26, June 29, 1959, pp. 7–8; Herbert Passin, "The Sources of Protest in Japan," *American Political Science Review*, Vol. 56, No. 2, June 1962, pp. 391–403; Robert A. Scalapino, "Japanese Socialism in Crisis," *Foreign Affairs*, Vol. 38, No. 2, January 1960, pp. 318–328; Robert A. Scalapino and Masumi Junnosuke, *Parties and Politics in Contemporary Japan*, Berkeley and Los Angeles: University of California Press, 1962, especially Chapters 2 and 3; Davis C. S. Sissons, "Recent Developments in Japan's Socialist Movement," *Far Eastern Survey*, Vol. 29, March and June 1960, pp. 40–47, 89–92; George O. Totten, "Problems of Japanese Socialist Leadership," *Pacific Affairs*, Vol. 28, No. 2, June 1955, pp. 160–169; Cecil H. Uyehara, "The Social Democratic Movement," *Annals of the American Academy of Political and Social Science*, Vol. 308, November 1958, pp. 54–62; Wada Hiroo, "The Socialist Party," *New Politics*, Vol. 1, No. 2, Winter 1962, pp. 135–143; Chitoshi Yanaga, "Japanese Political Parties," *Parliamentary Affairs*, Vol. 10, No. 3, Summer 1957, pp. 265–276. The authoritative work on the JSP in the postwar period will be Allan B. Cole's *Japan's Postwar Social Democratic Parties*, New Haven: Yale University Press, 1966.

[2] The Diet strength of these factions in September 1959 was roughly as follows: in the House of Representatives (from right to left), Nishio 30, Kawakami 35, Suzuki 40, Wada 30, and the Nomizo-Matsumoto-Kuroda alliance 25; in the House of Councillors, Nishio 15, Kawakami 10, Suzuki 20, Wada 10, Nomizo-Matsumoto-Kuroda 15 (*Japan Times*, September 16, 1959). Some observers placed Wada, a left-leaning former bureaucrat, to the right of Suzuki.

in urban areas by important segments of the professional and technical people, younger women, intellectuals, white collar workers, junior bureaucrats, and some small merchants, but their real stronghold was organized labor; a growing number of Socialist Diet members owed their seats to union funds and votes.

At the polls, the Socialists had made impressive headway against the conservatives until the general elections of May 1958, when the party's rate of growth began to decline significantly.[3] In the House of Councillors elections of June 1959, the JSP percentage of the vote fell off while that of the LDP rose, causing the optimism of 1956–1957 to give way to gloom over the future. The Socialists were also badly defeated as usual in the gubernatorial and local assembly elections of April 1959. Fear that the party had reached an insurmountable "one-third barrier" led to critical self-examination and reopened the old left-right battle over the proper character of the party and the correct means of achieving the socialist revolution. The left wing factions, backed by Sōhyō, argued for a revolutionary class party (*kaikyū seitō*) using not only parliamentary methods but mass action to gain power; the right wing insisted on broadening the party's base of support to include nonlabor elements in a multiclass national party (*kokumin seitō*) with strict respect for the parliamentary process. This clash of viewpoints led to a new split in the party in October 1959.

A major problem for the party was its relationship with the Japan Communist Party. As election prospects grew dimmer in the late 1950's and reliance on extraparliamentary mass movements increased, the question of whether or not to permit joint action with the JCP took on new urgency. The JCP since 1955 had softened its line and tactics and in early 1959 it advocated a policy of neutrality for Japan that was virtually identical to that of the Socialists. The JSP now found less and less reason for *not* cooperating with the JCP on specific struggles, and left wing JSP factions argued convincingly for making use of the

[3] From a postwar low in 1949 when the JSP won only 48 seats in the Lower House with 13.5% of the vote, the party in May 1958 won 166 Lower House seats with 32.9% of the vote.

JCP's superior organizational resources in the mass movements. The dilemma was that by cooperating with the Communists, the Socialists lost the sympathy of many moderates as well as its own right wing and Zenrō and risked having its themes and objectives overshadowed by the JCP in the course of the struggle.[4] A major reason for this situation was the JSP's weakness in grass roots support. Despite drives to increase its membership to 100,000, the party had only about 80,000 members in 1959 and was making few inroads into conservative rural Japan.[5]

In foreign policy, the JSP continued to take a firm stand against the security treaty, urging that it be replaced by some form of nonaggression pact among Communist China, Russia, the United States, and Japan. Though there were important differences among the factions, the party continued to hold officially to the line that Japan had no right of self-defense, no constitutional basis for rearming. It called for the withdrawal of all U.S. bases, neutrality, restored relations with Communist China, and a peace treaty with Russia. The party's gradual shift to the left during the 1950's could be seen most strikingly in Secretary-General Asanuma's controversial statement of March 9, 1959, that "the United States is the common enemy of the Japanese and Chinese peoples." [6] His statement was to become a touchstone of militancy for subsequent Socialist leaders.[7]

[4] Zenrō (Zen Nihon Rōdō Kumiai Kaigi) or the Japan Trade Union Congress, was Japan's more conservative labor federation. Set up in April 1954, it was generally anti-Communist in outlook, supporting the right wing of the JSP (particularly Nishio), and upholding democratic socialism. Zenrō was far smaller than Sōhyō, with about 830,000 members (11.5% of organized labor) in June 1959 (*Japan Times*, December 20, 1959, figures from the Ministry of Labor). Zenrō's main strongholds were in private industry, notably the seamen's, and textile workers' unions. It concentrated on pure trade unionism more than Sōhyō, stressing economic over political goals.

[5] *Japan Times*, November 3, 1959.

[6] Asanuma later corrected this statement to read, "U.S. *imperialism* is the common enemy of the Japanese and Chinese peoples."

[7] JSP Chairman Suzuki Mosaburō reaffirmed the statement in Peking in January 1962, but later claimed he had been forced into it by his own left wing. JSP Chairman Sasaki Kōzō took an even more extreme stand in 1965, claiming that U.S. imperialism was the enemy of all the peoples of the world.

85

JSP relations with Prime Minister Kishi steadily deteriorated during Kishi's term in office. To the Socialists, it appeared increasingly evident that Kishi was trying to revert to prewar totalitarianism in fields where they had won vital rights since the war; in education, the Constitution, the police system, and finally the security treaty. Though the Socialists had long called for changes in the treaty system, it was plain by as early as 1957 that they would not agree to any revised treaty that Kishi might negotiate. The Socialists termed Kishi's trip to Washington in June 1957 "a conservative pilgrimage." [8] After the Eisenhower-Kishi Joint Communiqué of June 21, 1957, the JSP called Kishi's trip a "betrayal" which would increase Japan's involvement in American nuclear strategy.[9] The new joint committee was called "a step backward," and Kishi was said to be trying to perpetuate the present security setup rather than revise it fundamentally.[10] When Kishi finally won American agreement to revise the treaty, the Socialists had already gone beyond the point of compromise and their position of "absolute opposition" was inevitable even before they knew how the treaty would be revised. The party in 1959 took the position that Kishi was succumbing to pressure from Washington; the new treaty would strengthen the U.S. strategic system in the Far East and pave the way for the introduction of nuclear weapons into Japan. Kishi was using the treaty, according to this line, to shore up his tottering regime, rather than take a step toward "independence." [11]

By 1959 the last strands of confidence between Kishi and the Socialists had been worn away as a result of the Police Bill struggle of late 1958. Operation of the Diet was marked more and more by boycotts, physical violence, and trickery, nearing the point of complete collapse of the parliamentary system. The feeling was spreading among the minority Socialists that the

[8] *Ibid.*, April 5, 1957.
[9] *Ibid.*, June 23, 1957.
[10] *Ibid.*, September 14, 1957.
[11] Katsumata Seiichi (then chairman of the JSP Policy Deliberation Committee) explains why the United States took a "positive role" in revising the treaty in Ōhira Zengo, *Nihon no Anzen Hoshō to Kokusai Hō*, 5th ed., Tokyo: Yushindō, 1959, pp. 111–112.

only way to oppose Kishi successfully was to mobilize the masses outside the Diet. In this effort, they came to rely more and more on their strongest supporter, Sōhyō, the huge labor federation.

Sōhyō

Sōhyō (General Council of Japanese Trade Unions) was the largest federation of labor unions in Japan with about 3.7 million members or some 51 percent of all organized labor in June 1959.[12] More than any other single organization, Sōhyō gave the mass movement of 1960 its size and weight.[13]

Sōhyō had been politically rather than economically oriented throughout the 1950's, and its experiences with strikes, rallies, and demonstrations against the government had given it a hardened core of veteran leaders who could, at a moment's notice, mobilize thousands of workers in the Tokyo area. To Sōhyō, the government, rather than private industrialists, was the main class enemy; this was partly because of its Marxist ideology and partly because two-thirds of its members were government employees.

Until 1955, Sōhyō was led by Takano Minoru, whose position on most issues was very close to that of the Communist Party. The Takano faction, known as the "peace-force group" for its support of such "peace-loving" nations as Russia and Communist China, was ousted in 1955 by the slightly less radical "third-force group" under the leadership of Ōta Kaoru (Chairman since 1958) and Iwai Akira (Secretary-General since 1955). Ōta and Iwai, standing for left-leaning neutralism in foreign affairs, gave more emphasis to specific economic achievement rather than the "community-wide struggles" for general political

[12] *Japan Times*, December 20, 1959 (figures from the Ministry of Labor).

[13] I am indebted to (among others) the following sources of information on Sōhyō: Ayusawa Iwao, "Japanese Labor in 1959," *Oriental Economist*, Vol. 23, No. 591, January 1960, pp. 29–32; Sidney Hook, "Common Sense in Japan," *New Leader*, Vol. 42, October 5, 1959, pp. 10–12; and "Which Way Japan?" *New Leader*, Vol. 42, February 9, 1959, pp. 3–7; Solomon B. Levine, *Industrial Relations in Postwar Japan*, Urbana: University of Illinois Press, 1958; Benjamin Martin, "The Labor Scene," *Japan Times*, January 28, 1957 and July 14, 1957; James R. Soukup, "Labor and Politics in Japan: a study of interest-group attitudes and activities," *Journal of Politics*, Vol. 22, No. 2, May 1960, pp. 314–337.

ends that Takano had favored. They were less eager than Takano to bypass the Socialist Party and collaborate with the Communists in mass actions.

In spite of Takano's defeat in 1955, however, his influence remained strong in his own union, the All Japan Metal Industry Workers' Union (Zenkinzoku) as well as in the Japan Federation of Coal Miners' Union (Tanrō) and in certain national government workers' unions, such as the National Railroad Workers' Union (Kokurō). There was a running contest in many of Sōhyō's unions between the two major factions, as well as over the issue of whether to support the Communists or the Socialists. In addition to the pro-JCP sympathies of some Takano faction unions, Sōhyō embraced unions that were almost entirely Communist-controlled. This meant that, while the leadership of Sōhyō might officially oppose joint campaigns with the Communists, there could still be effective collaboration at local workshop levels on specific issues. The JCP, for its part, was cooperative with the Ōta-Iwai leadership at the national level, though it naturally favored the Takano faction.

Until 1959, Ōta and Iwai had stood firmly against allying Sōhyō with the Communist Party, either for limited or general political ends. An important shift in this policy took place on June 16, 1959, when the leaders announced to a union conference in Gifu Prefecture, that joint Socialist-Communist efforts were possible in "certain specific cases." [14] Sōhyō announced on June 20, 1959, that it would carry on joint struggles with the JCP if certain conditions were met, but that it could not give active support to the party as a whole.[15] Then on June 27, 1959, Ōta Kaoru stated in Osaka that Sōhyō would strengthen its ties with the JCP to fight revision of the security treaty in the coming autumn. For the first time in its history, Sōhyō's leaders pub-

[14] James R. Soukup, "Labor and Politics in Japan," *Journal of Politics*, Vol. 22, No. 2, May 1960, p. 323; and *Japan Times*, article by Benjamin Martin, July 13, 1959. The way had been opened for Sōhyō to cooperate with the JCP in the Sōhyō Convention of 1956 when the Takano forces succeeded in having the prohibition against joint action removed from Sōhyō policy statement.

[15] *Japan Times*, June 21, 1959.

licly endorsed a policy of limited joint action with the Communist Party—a turn to the left which was to have important results in the organized anti-treaty movement.[16]

Along with this new cordiality between Sōhyō and the Communists, there was new tension between Sōhyō and the right wing factions of the Socialist Party, especially after the JSP election defeats in the spring of 1959. Sōhyō leaders strongly supported the JSP left wing and the "Sakisaka Thesis" [17] and issued fresh demands for a class-based party centering on the power of organized labor. At its 12th National Convention, in August 1959, Sōhyō failed, for the first time in several years, to pass a resolution giving its exclusive support to the JSP. This pressure from Sōhyō hit the Socialists at a time when they badly needed Sōhyō's vast pool of organized manpower for the anti-treaty drive, and it finally succeeded in driving the right wing Nishio faction from the party in October 1959. The Socialists were caught in a vicious cycle: the more they relied on mass demonstrations, the more they needed Sōhyō; the greater Sōhyō's influence, the greater the emphasis on extraparliamentary action. Veteran Socialist leaders Suzuki and Asanuma were being carried along by a current that was not entirely congenial.

Sōhyō's foreign policy (or outlook on the world) was characterized aptly in 1959 by Professor Sidney Hook: "It (Sōhyō) is not officially Communist, but its position on foreign policy reads as if it were plagiarized from the official Communist analysis of the international scene, with its division of the world into the peace-loving nations headed by the Communist Bloc and the war-mongering nations led by the U.S." [18] Holding to its four principles of peace,[19] Sōhyō rarely criticized the Communist Bloc, saw the United States as imperialistic and warlike, and remained silent after the Hungarian uprisings of 1956.

[16] An analysis of the causes of Sōhyō's swing to the left can be found in David C. S. Sissons, "Recent Developments in Japan's Socialist Movement," *Far Eastern Survey*, Vol. 29, No. 1, March 1960, pp. 46–47.

[17] See below, Chapter 4.

[18] Sidney Hook, "Which Way Japan?" *New Leader*, Vol. 42, February 9, 1959, p. 3.

[19] Above, pp. 18–19.

Sōhyō's relationship with the Kishi Government was a story of growing bitterness. Kishi had cracked down hard on the railway strikes in 1957 and had enforced the teachers' efficiency rating system in 1958, which seemed to be direct blows against two of Sōhyō's most powerful unions, the Japan Teachers' Union, and the National Railway Workers' Union. When Kishi tried to revise the Police Duties Law in 1958, all organized labor took it as a grave threat to its basic rights of assembly and organization. Then, when the security treaty issue followed hard on the Police Bill affair, Sōhyō saw its implacable enemy, Kishi, using the new treaty to crush labor's resistance to his reactionary policies at home and abroad. The Sōhyō Action Program of 1959–1960 stated: "The Mutual Security System is the very source from which stem all forms of the capitalist offensives now being directed against us such as low wage standards, discharges, rationalization, oppressions, indoctrinations, and the fear of war." [20] In this way the treaty issue became the arena where Sōhyō chose to stage its most determined drive to unseat Kishi and to halt what it saw as dangerous gains by management over labor.[21]

Even though Sōhyō was ready and willing for a massive battle against Kishi in 1959–1960, it still had to face a number of serious problems, such as continuing political apathy in its rank and file, traditional enterprise-focused loyalties, the moderating influence of Zenrō and the right-leaning unions, the favorable trend of the economy in 1959, and finally the ever-present factionalism among its leaders.[22] The major problem

[20] *Japan Times*, quoted in Horii Etsurō, "The Labor Scene," September 9, 1959.

[21] Adding to the sense of climax in 1960 was the Miike Strike, near Fukuoka, which Sōhyō viewed as a kind of final showdown between management and labor, over the question of rationalizing Japan's weak coal-mining industry in the face of competition from oil (see below).

[22] Sōhyō factions reportedly corresponded to JSP factions as follows: Ōta Kaoru (originally of the Japan Federation of Synthetic Chemical Workers' Union) supported the Wada faction; Iwai Akira (originally of the National Railway Workers' Union) supported the Suzuki faction, and Takano Minoru supported the far-left Matsumoto faction. James Soukup, "Labor and Politics in Japan," *Journal of Politics*, Vol. 22, No. 2, May 1960, pp. 332–333.

was how to tie each local or industry-wide grievance into the unified mass movement against Kishi and the revised treaty. This effort required considerable organization and propaganda at the local levels, and the rôle of the Communist Party in fomenting the drive was an important one.

The Communist Party

The Communists enjoyed their "finest hour" in Japan during the treaty crisis of 1960. The tactics they used to involve themselves in the movement revealed new flexibility in pursuit of their long-standing goals.

We saw in Chapter 1 how the "Bloody May Day" of 1952 climaxed the JCP's campaign of revolutionary violence which had begun with Stalin's directive of January 1950. The Communists suffered at the polls for these unpopular tactics, losing about two million votes and all 35 of their Lower House seats in the elections of October 1952. During the next few years the party gradually softened its line and emerged from underground, returning to its "lovable image" of the early occupation period. At the JCP's Sixth National Convention in July 1955, the former violent tactics were disavowed as "extreme leftist adventurism." Then in July 1956, four silent months after the Twentieth Congress of the C.P.S.U., the party's Central Committee decided to revise the 1951 Program and affirmed (as Khrushchev had done in February) that the changeover to Socialism might be achieved through peaceful means. The party now called for a "united democratic front of national liberation" consisting of all progressive elements opposed to imperialism, including certain sections of the bourgeoisie.[23] Japan was called a dependent country (subordinate to the U.S.) and the first task was to overthrow U.S. imperialism, following which the socialist revolution might occur.

The Communists, because of their weakness, had no choice but to work through a united front in the late 1950's. The party leaders had been among the most faithful of Stalin's fol-

[23] Paul F. Langer, "Communism in Independent Japan," *Japan Between East and West*, eds. Hugh Borton *et al.*, New York: Harper and Brothers, 1957, p. 50.

lowers, and they had been badly weakened by "de-Stalinization" and the Hungarian Revolution of 1956. In addition, they had been hurt by scandals (Shida's expulsion in 1957), internal dissension and rising prosperity. In the elections of May 1958, the JCP won just over a million votes (2.6 percent of the total) and one seat in the Lower House.[24] This was better than in 1952, but it was clear that the Socialists had captured the bulk of Japan's protest vote, and that a united front was the JCP's only means of exercising real political influence.[25]

The Communists and Socialists began to cooperate informally in 1957 and with treaty negotiations on the horizon in the summer of 1958, the Communists increased their efforts for a united front. At the JCP's Seventh National Convention in July 1958, the party called for cooperation with the JSP and urged the formation of a multiclass coalition, led by labor, but also including farmers and fishermen, students and women, intellectuals and small businessmen, and even some rich villagers.[26] A party directive in December 1958 spelled out the concrete policies to be followed: under these policies the party would (1) break up the treaty revision plot by developing joint struggle organizations, (2) carry out a struggle to end treaty negotiations, and (3) build a people's democratic united front.[27]

The Communists moved one step closer to the Socialists in late 1958, at the time when all left wing forces were in ferment over the nature of the new coalition to be formed against the

[24] By 1959 membership was down to 45,000, according to PSIA figures published in the *Japan Times*, March 25, 1959.

[25] Langer, *op. cit.*, pp. 60–65, lists the factors favoring a united front.

[26] The Communists even envisaged joining hands with certain elements of the LDP, in a national coalition reminiscent of the Communist Chinese united front prior to 1949. See Kamiyama Shigeo's article in *Zenei*, June 1958, reprinted in Kamiyama Shigeo, *Ampo Tōsō to Tōitsu Sensen*, Tokyo: Shindokusho Sha, pp. 85–86.

[27] JCP Central Secretariat Directive, No. 32, *Ampo Jōyaku Kaitei Kōshō Uchikiri to Haki o Chūshin to Suru Tomen no Taishū Tōsō o Hatten Saseru Tame ni* (Cutting Off and Ending Negotiations for Revising the Security Treaty Are Central to Advancing the Present Mass Struggle), summarized in Kōan Chōsa Chō, *Ampo Tōsō no Gaiyō* (An Outline of the Security Treaty Struggle), Tokyo: 1960, pp. 20–21.

revised security treaty. On December 11, 1958, the JCP announced a new policy supporting neutralism for Japan.[28] This statement followed declarations by Communist China (November 19, 1958) and Russia (December 2, 1958) supporting the idea of a neutral Japan, and signaled an important shift in the international Communist line.[29] The JCP had now stepped squarely into the position occupied by Sōhyō and the Socialists; for the first time they paraded openly under the banner of "friendly relations with all countries." With this shift in JCP policy there seemed to be even less reason for the Socialists not to cooperate; in fact the JSP and JCP could speak with one voice on almost all foreign issues: nuclear arms, disarmament, Okinawa, peaceful coexistence, relations with China, and a peace treaty with Russia. In this way the Communists tailored their line to fit the needs of the intensive drive to form a united front against the security treaty.

The remaining differences between the Communists and the left wing Socialists stemmed from differing analyses of Japan's stage of economic development. In short, the left Socialists saw Japan as an independent, advanced capitalist nation with Kishi, representing monopoly capital, as the prime enemy. In the tactics of revolution, they gave slightly greater importance than the Communists to the struggle against the conservatives inside the Diet. The Communists, by 1959, saw Japan as a semi-dependent country (*hanjūzokukoku*) with U.S. imperialism the major enemy. The Communists, therefore, were less eager than the left Socialists to attack and overthrow Kishi; they took the somewhat surprising position that anti-Kishi attacks were divisive and distracting, and that national sentiment should be unified around the main drive to remove the U.S. presence in Japan. During the crisis of May-June 1960, these differences produced serious controversies over whether to demonstrate at the Diet (the JSP view), or the U.S. Embassy (the Communist view).

The JCP line on the security treaty itself collided with those

[28] The statement, entitled "Nihon Jinmin no Dokuritsu to Anzen e No Michi," is discussed in Kōan Chōsa Chō, *Ampo Tōsō*, p. 20.

[29] *Japan Times*, November 20, 1958, and December 14, 1958.

of other left wing elements, notably Zengakuren. To the Communists, the revised treaty was a humiliating defeat for the Japanese people; it was being forced down their throats by U.S. monopoly capital.[30] Kamiyama Shigeo, a JCP Central Committee member, wrote in *Sekai* in May 1958 that the purposes of revising the treaty were: (1) to secure U.S. military rights and make Japan an American nuclear rocket base; (2) to include Japan in the aggressive U.S. military bloc and make her part of the American strategic system in the Far East; (3) to set up Japan as the front line of aggression while the United States retired to the rear. The results of the new treaty, continued Kamiyama, would be as follows: Japan's obligation to build up her arms and increase her military commitments to the United States would be strengthened, Japanese troops would be sent overseas, Article IX of the Constitution would become meaningless, various reactionary laws would be forced through, all kinds of suppression would increase, and independence for the Japanese people would be further postponed. Finally, the recent Sino-Soviet proposals for a neutral Japan would be left by the wayside.[31] Thus did the Communists tie the security treaty into the whole range of domestic protest in Japan.

The Communist Party in 1959 carried on its united front policies at two levels: at the top, they wooed Socialist and Sōhyō leaders with their new soft line of peaceful revolution and neutralism, and at the bottom, they stepped up their efforts to carry on "joint struggles" with local, grass roots elements in the left wing, through organized infiltration. The measure of their success could be seen in their wide participation and influence in the new coalition of March 28, 1959.

Zengakuren

The fourth major component in the left wing coalition against the security treaty was Zengakuren (the All-Japan Fed-

[30] The fact that Kishi had initiated treaty revision was dismissed by the orthodox explanation that U.S. imperialism lay behind the plot and Kishi was an agent of that force.

[31] Kamiyama, *op. cit.*, p. 63 (reprinted from *Sekai*, May 1958).

eration of Student Self-government Associations).[32] Zengakuren was founded in September 1948 in the poverty and despair of war-torn Japan, but it rose to its highest peak, paradoxically, when the miserable conditions at the time of its birth had all but disappeared. It played a major part in preventing President Eisenhower's visit to Japan and in toppling Prime Minister Kishi from power in 1960. Furthermore, it split the ranks of the left wing and came back, like a Frankenstein, to haunt its former masters in the Communist Party. Though not a political party, Zengakuren had come to be a powerful political force in time of crisis.

Zengakuren fell under JCP control in its early days, and participated in various postwar leftist struggles against the "reverse course" and "militaristic" acts of the government and "U.S. imperialism." Imbued with an historic sense of mission, highly theoretical, and always prepared for violence, the student leaders of Zengakuren lent their own distinctive flavor to the more orthodox left wing forces in Japan.

University students in Japan occupied a special position. They were, in their own eyes, and in fact, an elite group who had survived the fiercely competitive examination system, and their leaders, representing all classes, felt it their distinct duty and privilege to enlighten the "masses" and cure society's ills. They scorned politics and election campaigns, preferring instead to wage "struggles" as a kind of vanguard of the oppressed. Exposed in college to the heady works of Marx and Lenin after

[32] Zengakuren is the abbreviated form of Zen Nihon Gakusei Jichikai Sōrengō. For background on the student movement in Japan, see the following sources in English: Lawrence H. Battistini, *The Postwar Student Struggle in Japan*, Tokyo: Charles E. Tuttle Co., 1956; I. I. Morris, *Nationalism and the Right Wing in Japan*, London: Oxford University Press, 1960, Chapter 7, and "Policeman and Student in Japanese Politics," *Pacific Affairs*, Vol. 32, No. 1, March 1959, pp. 5–17. In Japanese, see: Gakusei Undō Kenkyū Kai, *Gendai no Gakusei Undō—Sono Shisō to Kōdō*, Tokyo: Shinkō Shuppan Sha, 1961; Inaoka Susumu and Itoya Hisao, *Nihon no Gakusei Undō—Sono Rekishiteki Yakuwari ga Oshieru Mono*, Tokyo: Aoki Shoten, 1961; and Yamanaka Akira, *Sengo Gakusei Undō Shi —Nihon no Yoru to Kiri no naka de*, Tokyo: Aoki Shoten, 1961. In addition to these and the sources cited below, information in this section is based on talks with Zengakuren leaders and members during 1960–1962.

years of learning by rote, and cut off from normal social relationships, the student activists threw themselves into causes with raw energy and naive idealism, and were tolerated, if not openly admired, by much of the rest of society.

Zengakuren reached a high point in membership and activity in 1949 (along with the JCP), declined from 1950 to 1955, and began a "renaissance" in 1956. Between 1956 and 1958, the revitalized students clashed with the government at Sunakawa,[33] and demonstrated wildly against U.S. and U.K. nuclear testing, the teachers' efficiency rating system, moral education, and the Police Bill. With some 300,000 members scattered in about 140 colleges and universities throughout the country, Zengakuren leaders were spoiling for a new battle with the government as the anti-treaty movement was being organized in 1959.[34] Of the 300,000 members, only about 2,000 could be considered active, while another 10,000 to 20,000 might be counted on for an occasional demonstration. The rest were surprisingly apathetic about politics, leaving control of the organization in the hands of the highly motivated Marxist leadership.

Individual students did not opt for membership in Zengakuren; they were automatically enrolled when they entered a faculty or class whose student government association belonged.[35] The basic unit of membership in Zengakuren was the student self-government association (*jichikai*) elected by

[33] See below, Chapter 4.

[34] It is impossible to get precise figures on Zengakuren membership; neither its own officers nor the Education Ministry nor the public security officials claimed accuracy. One reason is that student self-government associations at the various universities voted themselves in and out of Zengakuren with confusing frequency. The government exercised no overall authority over student organizations, leaving it to each university to see that its students reported any ties to outside organizations—a formality that was almost never observed. (Interview with Nemoto Matsuhiko, Assistant Chief of the Student Section, Ministry of Education, December 18, 1961.)

[35] It was a common practice for universities to collect membership dues for the student self-government associations along with tuition fees, turning over these funds to the student officers of the associations later on. Thus individual students at these universities had little choice but to pay the dues, whether or not they supported Zengakuren's political positions.

students within a particular faculty or department of a university. This consisted of a self-government committee (*jichi iinkai*) which in turn elected a standing committee (*jōnin iin*) and a chairman (*iinchō*) to take care of day-to-day problems and decisions. Though in theory anyone could run for these positions, it usually happened that the elected leaders of these bodies were active Communists with close ties to the national headquarters of Zengakuren. This was due partly to student tolerance and sympathy for Communism, partly to student apathy, and partly to the efficiency with which the Communists organized and ran the various activities.

Each self-government association sent from one to fifteen representatives (depending on the size of its membership) to the Zengakuren National Convention (*zenkoku taikai*) of about 500 delegates, which met once a year or more often as events demanded.[36] As might be expected, the principle of democratic centralism operated in Zengakuren, and the real decision-making power rested in 1959 with the Central Executive Committee (CEC), or, more precisely, with the most powerful faction within the CEC. As a rule, the CEC members held political views far more extreme than the mass of students they purported to represent, and this was particularly true in 1959.[37]

[36] At an intermediate level between the self-government associations and the national convention were fifteen regional chapters (*chihō gakuren*) which coordinated activities in their own areas; most active in the antitreaty demonstrations was the Tokyo Regional Chapter (Togakuren) with its approximately 80,000 members. The National Convention elected the Central Committee (Chūō Iinkai) of some 150 members and the Central Executive Committee (Chūō Shikko Iinkai) of about 35 members. This Central Executive Committee (CEC) elected Zengakuren's national chairman, two vice-chairmen, and a secretary-general, and staffed a secretariat with its finance, information and propaganda, organization, and various other departments.

[37] However, each member association was required by Zengakuren rules to abide by policies laid down by the National Convention, which generally rubber-stamped the policies decided on by the CEC in advance; see Article XII, Zengakuren Charter; the complete Charter may be found in Zengakuren, Chūō Shoki Kyoku Jōsenbu, ed., *Tatakau Zengakuren: Daijūgokai Rinji Zenkoku Taikai Hōkoku narabi ni Kettei Shu*, April 5, 1960, pp. 187–194.

During the anti-treaty movement, the prevailing faction in the Zengakuren CEC was a radical group belonging to the Communist League (Kyōsanshugi Dōmei, also known by its short form Kyōsandō and its nickname *Bundo*, from the German). The Communist League was set up in December 1958 by a group of students who had rebelled against the JCP in the dramatic "June 1 Incident," and consisted of about 2,000 members.[38] Together with other student factions that opposed JCP control over the student movement, these students came to be known as the "mainstream" of Zengakuren during the anti-treaty movement. Those who remained loyal to and largely directed by the JCP were called the "anti-mainstream." In 1959–1960, the mainstream held about a 60–40 edge over the pro-JCP anti-mainstream, though there was a good deal of shifting back and forth by individuals and self-government associations as the two factions competed for student loyalties.[39]

[38] On June 1, 1958, 105 of the 130-odd students who were delegates to Zengakuren's 11th National Convention, and who were also JCP members (known as the "Daigiin Gurūpu") passed a resolution of nonconfidence in the JCP Central Committee in JCP headquarters at Yoyogi. The students were dissatisfied with what they considered the "insufficient de-Stalinization of the JCP" and resentful of JCP attempts to intervene in their affairs. The result was physical violence, recriminations on both sides, and the expulsion from the JCP of most of the dissident students. For the Zengakuren side of the dispute see (in Japanese) Koyama Kenichi, ed., *Nihon Kyōsantō no Kiki to Gakusei Undō—Zengakuren Ikensho* (A Zengakuren Statement: The Crisis in the JCP and the Student Movement), January 1, 1959. For JCP accounts, see *Akahata*, June 5, 10–12, 23, 1958; and *Zenei*, No. 143, unsigned article, "Tō no Konran o Nerau Torotsukisuto no Sakudō ni Tsuite" (On the Plot of the Trotskyites Who Aim to Stir up Trouble within the Party), pp. 15–30, August 1958. In English, see *Japan Times*, article by Murata Kiyoaki, December 24, 1958, and Koyama Kenichi, "The Zengakuren," *New Politics*, Vol. 1, No. 2, Winter 1962, pp. 124–134.

[39] The anti-mainstream (pro-JCP) students were organized into an anti-leadership faction by the JCP as early as 1957; after the June 1, 1958 Incident these students went their own way and ran separate activities. The decisive break came in March 1960 when the anti-mainstreamers refused to recognize the validity of the Zengakuren 15th Extraordinary Convention (run by the mainstream) and formed their own organization in Tokyo, *Tōjiren* (*Tokyo-to Jichikai Renraku Kaigi*) or Tokyo City Self-

The battle between the Communist Party and the leftist students had complex origins involving the traditional elitism of the students, their sense of a distinct, historical mission, their disillusionment with world Communism in general, and the growth of nationalism among the younger generation in Japan. For our purposes, it is enough to observe how the split affected the left wing during the anti-treaty movement, and to see in the welter of events in those hectic days of May-June 1960 the ideological commitments that drove the students on to desperate charges against the gates of the Diet.

The JCP branded the students of the mainstream "Trotskyites," accused them of being "anachronistic" and guilty of "petty bourgeois revisionism." The students countered with charges of "opportunism, Stalinism, and bureaucratism" against the party. The truth behind these epithets was that the mainstream students had no firm ideology and were united only by a shared mistrust of the JCP and a basic faith in Marxism. They were divided into many factions,[40] and though Trotsky

---

government Association Liaison Council, for the purpose of acting in the anti-treaty movement. In July 1960 this group became part of a national pro-JCP student movement called *Zenjiren* (*Zen Nihon Jichikai Renraku Kaigi*) or All-Japan Liaison Council of Self-government Associations. For background on Zengakuren factional problems see (in Japanese) Nikkan Rōdō Tsūshin Sha, ed., *Zengakuren no Jittai—Sono Habatsu o Chūshin to Shite* (The Actual State of Zengakuren: Focusing on Its Factions), Tokyo: Nikkan Rōdō Tsūshin Sha, 1959, and *Mainichi Shimbun*, July 11, 1961; in English, see *Asahi Evening News*, June 10 and July 8, 1960.

[40] Besides the Communist League, many other new factions sprang up within the Zengakuren mainstream, of which the following were most influential: (1) the Revolutionary Communist League (Kakumeiteki Kyōsanshugisha Dōmei or Kakkyōdō), a more radical, more theoretical, more anti-American group, smaller than the Communist League. It often participated in Communist League activities but it maintained its own distinct ideology. Set up in June 1958, it was strongly influenced by the writings of Trotsky, and its intellectual leader was a nearly blind, self-educated philosopher and writer named Kuroda Kanichi. In 1959 the Tokyo branch of this faction (Kakkyōdō Zenkoku Iinkai) became better known as the Marxist Student League (Marugakudō), which then began to function as a kind of action or mass organization, enlisting students who were not necessarily members of the Revolutionary Communist League. In April 1961, at the 27th Meeting of the Zengakuren CEC, it replaced the Revolutionary Communist

was widely read and admired, he was for the students simply one of a number of great men who had rejected Stalinist orthodoxy.

In the view of most mainstream students, Stalin's "Socialism in one country" had been a catastrophe for the Marxist revolution; they felt that an immediate, world-wide revolution of the proletariat was needed, and that Khrushchev's peaceful coexistence was no more than an extension of Stalin's error. The struggle at home must be centered on Japanese labor, with Japanese monopoly capital (not U.S. imperialism) the prime target. The students felt they must disassociate themselves from the "opportunistic" JCP, which was ignoring the revived threat of Japanese monopoly capital and which offered no hope of strong leadership to the proletariat. The JCP emphasis on a united front with the Socialists was considered weak-kneed and doomed to failure. The security treaty issue was seen as an opportunity to use carefully planned violence with "correct political timing" to deliver a "shock" to the nation. By the use of shock tactics, the political consciousness of the labor class might be heightened, causing it to break away from its encrusted leadership and surge toward a real revolution. It was within this framework that all Zengakuren demonstrations and activities were formulated. The leaders saw themselves engaged not in senseless violence (as it appeared to many) but in an intricate problem of revolutionary struggle in which the sparks flying from a well-placed incident might ignite the dry tinder in Japanese society.

If this scheme sounds grandiose for a small group of college

League as the dominant faction in Zengakuren. (2) The Kansai Branch of the Revolutionary Communist League (Kakkyōdō Kansai-ha) was an offshoot of No. 1 above, with its base in Kyoto and Osaka. (3) The Socialist Youth League (Shakaishugi Seinen Dōmei or Shaseidō) was composed of students who, though far to the left of the JSP, looked to the JSP left wing factions for leadership of the student movement and worked to "radicalize" JSP policies from within. This group was not officially organized by the JSP until after the treaty crisis, but during the demonstrations it earned a reputation for violence and was one of the most feared action groups around the Diet. *Asahi Shimbun*, July 11, 1961, partly explains the relationship of these groups, though with certain minor errors.

students to have entertained, let no one doubt that they were deadly serious in their work: "In this student movement lies the promise of the future and the revolutionary power needed to achieve it. Those who ignore or mock at this will be ignored by history itself," wrote a Zengakuren leader.[41] It was with mixed feelings that the older leftist union leaders, intellectuals, and politicians embraced Zengakuren in the coalition against the security treaty. The student leaders, bursting with the energy of Japan's postwar generation and resentful of the discredited leaders from another era, were to plague the anti-treaty movement with their independent actions. The discord between Zengakuren and the People's Council was symptomatic of the confusion of values and ideals in Japanese society as a whole and raised new questions about the future of the left wing movement in Japan.

The Police Bill Controversy

If the May-June disturbances of 1960 were unprecedented in size and gravity in postwar Japan, it is also true that since the war there had been a long series of left-right battles involving violence inside and outside the Diet which had set the patterns for the events of 1960. The Police Bill controversy of October-November 1958 climaxed all the other struggles up to that time, and in a very real sense, served as a "dress rehearsal" for the more serious treaty crisis of 1960.

The bare facts of the Police Bill controversy are as follows.[42] On October 8, 1958, four days after the opening of the Mac-Arthur-Fujiyama treaty talks, the government presented to the Diet a bill to revise the Police Duties Performance Law, a bill

---

[41] Koyama Kenichi, "The Zengakuren," *New Politics*, Vol. 1, No. 2, Winter 1962, p. 124.

[42] For details on the points at issue and the course of events see Chiba Yūjirō, "Revision of the Police Duties Law," *Contemporary Japan*, Vol. 25, No. 4, March 1959, pp. 621–634; "Basic Trends, Bureaucracy on the Move," *Japan Quarterly*, Vol. 6, No. 1, January-March 1959, pp. 1–5; Lawrence Olson, "The Police Bill Controversy," *American Universities Field Staff Letter*, LO-12-'58, November 28, 1959; David C. S. Sissons, "The Dispute over Japan's Police Law," *Pacific Affairs*, Vol. 32, No. 1, March 1959, pp. 34–45.

101

which would have enlarged the powers of the police in preventive action, including interrogation, search, and arrest.[43] The left wing strongly opposed the bill on the grounds that it would lead to abuses, violate basic human rights, and turn Japan back into a police state. The Socialists boycotted the Diet and barricaded committee rooms to prevent deliberations. A "People's Council to Oppose Mal-revision of the Police Duties Law" (Keishoku Hō Kaiaku Hantai Kokumin Kaigi) was formed by a number of leftist organizations, with some moderate elements joining in. On November 4, 1958, the Kishi Government extended the Diet session (due to end November 7) in a surprise maneuver, leading to strikes and workshop rallies by some four million workers and strong protests from the press, public figures, and "neutral elements" in Japan. After several weeks of uproar and political negotiations, Kishi and JSP Chairman Suzuki worked out a compromise on November 22 whereby the JSP recognized the extension of the Diet session while the LDP shelved the Police Bill for an indefinite period.

The left wing and a sizable number of moderates considered the Police Bill and security treaty revision part of a single plot to restore authoritarian government under tight bureaucratic control. Though the Police Bill was hotly debated on its own merits, there lurked a suspicion in many minds that Kishi was paving the road to personal diplomatic success by first buttressing his coercive power at home. The timing, whereby the Police Bill was placed before the Diet at the very moment that U.S.–Japanese treaty negotiations were starting seemed in itself evidence of Kishi's plotting. If Kishi could strengthen the police and curb the power of organized labor to launch mass protest movements, he would, it seemed, assure himself of smooth ratification of the revised security treaty, and a longer term in office. Then he might go on to try to revise the Constitution and press through other "reactionary legislation" which would effectively restore the police state and militarism of the 1930's. The Police Bill and the treaty were thus seen as successive steps

[43] For the background to this issue see S. Sugai, "The Japanese Police System," in Robert E. Ward, ed., *Five Studies in Japanese Politics*, Ann Arbor: University of Michigan Press, 1957.

102

in Kishi's master plan, and for this reason many people, some of whom admitted the wisdom of revising both the police law and the security treaty, were nevertheless sympathetic to or active in protest movements against both measures.

As a dress rehearsal for the anti-treaty movement, the Police Bill affair had the following features. The Socialists, in adamant opposition, used physical measures to block Diet deliberations, and tried to prevent extension of the Diet by surrounding the speaker's rostrum in the lower house. The government countered by having the Vice-Speaker pass the extension from the floor of the house (on May 19, 1960, a different tactic was used). The press and public, almost entirely ignoring the questionable Socialist Diet tactics, sided overwhelmingly against Kishi for this act. The LDP Diet tactics came to replace the substantive aspects of the bill at hand as the primary issue in the public mind. The conservatives, instead of rallying around Kishi, showed open dissension, and anti-mainstream leaders attacked Kishi in public to improve their own standing in the party. This in turn encouraged the left wing and moderates to step up the attack against Kishi.[44] The organized left wing founded a "people's council" to oppose the bill and mobilized labor and students to run "united actions" with demonstrations, rallies, and strikes. Labor launched its first purely political strike since 1952. Small bands of rightists engaged in scuffles with leftist demonstrators. Unorganized groups and individuals (many for the first time) involved themselves in the political movement with statements and protest demonstrations.[45] These features would recur in more intense and dramatic form in the treaty crisis of 1960; the fact that they had occurred once probably helped the anti-treaty movement gather steam.

[44] It is interesting to note that Kōno Ichirō, most outspoken LDP opponent of Kishi in the security treaty affair of 1960, was still in the mainstream in the fall of 1958 and, with Ōno Bamboku, urged Kishi to take an unyielding stand against the left and press the Police Bill through to completion. In 1960 he found fault with Kishi's forceful methods, which were very similar.

[45] One of the most notable of these was the protest by Mrs. Uemura Tamaki, Director of the Y.W.C.A.

The results of the Police Bill battle were highly important. First, the movement was successful and the bill was shelved. This tended to strengthen the radicals in all leftist groups who had long argued that the only way to beat Kishi was by mass popular action outside the Diet. The left wing, more than at any time since 1952, took heart from the government's apparent loss of confidence in the moment of crisis. If victory could be achieved in the streets over the Police Bill, why not over the revised security treaty and the rest of the conservative program? This argument seemed all the more logical after the Socialists were badly beaten in the elections of the spring of 1959. Secondly, Kishi was weakened permanently by the Police Bill affair, both within the LDP and in the eyes of the public. Though he recovered in 1959 to throw together a new "treaty cabinet," he was clearly on his way out with the passage of the treaty as far as the other LDP faction heads were concerned. Third, labor leaders gained a new view of the hitherto unsuspected energy potential in their own rank-and-file that might be turned against the government. Unionists in the Tokyo area, for their part, picked up confidence and valuable experience in the "art" of successfully demonstrating, so that in 1960 they could be rapidly mobilized and thrown into action under firm discipline. Finally, the moderates and conservatives who might have countenanced the forceful passage of the treaty in 1960 by some other Prime Minister, came to harbor deep mistrust for Kishi and were quickly alienated by his tactics in forcing through the treaty on May 19–20, 1960. In May 1960, they reacted almost instinctively with the thought that "Kishi has done it again!"

The important difference between the two protest movements was in the grouping of forces in the left wing coalition. The People's Council to Oppose Mal-revision of the Police Duties Law included the moderate Zenrō and Shinsanbetsu labor federations as well as a united Socialist Party. The emphasis was on "protecting democracy" (not "peace") and the coalition excluded the Communists from formal participation. The axis of the coalition was thus several steps to the right of the anti-treaty coalition, which excluded Zenrō, Shinsanbetsu, and the Nishio wing of the JSP and included the Communists. The more moderate, centrist character of the anti-Police Bill forces allowed ultimately for a negotiated settlement of the crisis and a seemingly popular victory for the Socialists; in 1960 the Communists were better able to give the movement their own special flavor and divert attention to their own goals.

Formation of the People's Council

We have looked briefly at the four main groups behind the drive against the security treaty that began in 1959: the Socialists, verging on a new split and moving leftward; Sōhyō, gradually overcoming its qualms against open cooperation with the Communists; the JCP, backing a broad united front against U.S. imperialism; and Zengakuren, at odds with the Communists and straining for an immediate revolution of the proletariat. In early 1959 the leaders of these groups and other left wing organizations sought to follow up their Police Bill campaign with a new and massive movement against the revised security treaty. The new coalition that finally developed was called the People's Council for Preventing Revision of the Security Treaty (Ampo Jōyaku Kaitei Soshi Kokumin Kaigi).[46] How this council was formed and how it functioned tells much of the story of the frustration that has marked all attempts to unify the left wing since the war.[47]

Inspiration for the new People's Council came from the body that was formed in October 1958 to combat the Police Bill, the People's Council to Oppose Mal-revision of the Police Duties Law. Fresh from their victory over Kishi in the late fall of 1958, various leftist groups sought to convert the old council into a new anti-treaty coalition. At a followup meeting of the old

[46] Hereinafter referred to simply as "the People's Council." The name of this organization has also been translated as "The National Council for Blocking Revision of the Security Treaty."

[47] I am indebted to the Director and members of the Secretariat of the People's Council for making available a number of publications and records in their offices, as well as for the hours of interviews granted. Other sources of information for this section are cited in the text below. Of all the accounts of the anti-treaty struggle, the officers of the People's Council endorsed Ide Busaburō's *Ampo Tōsō*, Tokyo: San'ichi Shobō, 1960, as the most accurate.

council on November 28, 1958, the Socialists proposed that it perpetuate itself under the new name, People's Council for Safeguarding Democracy and Peace (Minshushugi to Heiwa o Mamoru Kokumin Kaigi).[48] Sōhyō was an enthusiastic backer of this idea. The JCP also concurred quickly, based on decisions taken at its 13th Central Committee Meeting, November 23, 1958. But Zenrō and Shinsanbetsu hesitated; they had joined in the Police Bill effort, but during the course of the movement they had become increasingly concerned over the extent of informal Communist participation. They now made it clear that the price for their agreement would be the explicit exclusion of the Communists from the new council. The Socialists, basking in praise from the press for their wise choice of tactics in the Police Bill affair, argued among themselves whether to move ahead without Zenrō and Shinsanbetsu. The Sōhyō-backed left wing faction held that it was precisely because of Zenrō's (and Nishio's) willingness to negotiate with Kishi that the Police Bill movement had "collapsed" (in their view) at the crucial moment. Of course the right and center elements in the JSP favored a broad coalition against the treaty and insisted that Zenrō and Shinsanbetsu be included and the Communists kept out of the new council. While the Socialists debated this problem, other groups seized the initiative and moved ahead.

Sōhyō did the most to promote the new council. Its leaders foresaw a dangerous period in April 1959 when a new treaty might be signed and the LDP might use the political calm surrounding the Crown Prince's wedding to whisk the treaty through the Diet. The Takano faction, with support from the far-left factions in the JSP, was anxious to dump Zenrō from the start. Ōta and Iwai, somewhat more cautious, were eager to get the new council launched in time to tie in the anti-treaty activities with the spring labor offensive. They doubted that Zenrō and Shinsanbetsu would join, no matter how much time and bargaining went into the effort. Thus at a meeting

[48] The JSP had formulated this policy at its 15th National Convention, November 12, 1958.

of Sōhyō directors on March 4, 1959, the crucial decision was taken to go forward without Zenrō, and to allow the Communists to participate as "observers" in the new organization. From this point on events moved rapidly.

On March 6, 1959, Sōhyō called a meeting of representatives from the following organizations: the JSP, JCP, Japan Council Against Atomic and Hydrogen Bombs (Gensuikyō),[49] Japan Peace Committee (Nihon Heiwa Iinkai), and the People's Council for Restoration of Japan-China Relations (Nitchū Kokkō Kaifuku Kokumin Kaigi). At this meeting Sōhyō's Chairman Ōta Kaoru urged that the Communist Party be allowed to sit on the new People's Council; he blamed the "collapse" (as he saw it) of the anti-Police Bill drive on the insistence by Zenrō and Shinsanbetsu that the JCP be excluded. The Socialist representative at the meeting, Ioka Daiji, objected to Ōta's proposal, but all the other representatives concurred. The Socialists now found that they were rapidly being isolated from the new movement.[50]

In addition to Sōhyō's efforts, initiative in forming the new council also came from several pro-Communist "peace groups." This began as early as December 8, 1958, with an appeal from two organizations which favored relations with Communist China.[51] This appeal urged all "democratic organizations" to pursue their struggles with new vigor and join hands in the spring of 1959 in a new struggle against the security treaty.[52] The pro-Communist Japan Peace Committee also worked to unite labor and peace groups against the treaty, and on January 16, 1959, sponsored a "peace rally" which called for an end to the treaty and for peaceful coexistence. Then, on February 5, 1959, Sōhyō and four other groups issued a joint state-

---

[49] The Japan Council Against Atomic and Hydrogen Bombs is hereinafter referred to by its familiar Japanese abbreviation, Gensuikyō.

[50] Kōan Chōsa Chō, *Ampo Tōsō*, pp. 32–33.

[51] These were: The People's Rally to Solve Japan-China Relations and Prohibit Nuclear Weapons (Nitchū Kankei Dakai Kakubusō Kinshi Kokumin Shūkai) and the People's Council for Restoration of Japan-China Relations (Nitchū Kokkō Kaifuku Kokumin Kaigi).

[52] Kōan Chōsa Chō, *Ampo Tōsō*, p. 35.

ment calling on the whole nation for a united struggle against the security treaty and for restored relations with Communist China.[53] They declared that February 28, 1959 (seventh anniversary of signing the administrative agreement), would be a day of nationwide united action against the treaty and of breaking the deadlock in relations with Communist China. Representatives of the five organizations met with Kishi and demanded that negotiations with the United States on treaty revision be cut off and that talks be started on abolishing the treaty and administrative agreement. Through these front groups, the Communists played a large role in whipping up enthusiasm for the new People's Council.[54]

In the face of this rolling movement to form a new council *with* JCP participation, the Socialists backed down. On March 10, 1959, the party announced it would join Sōhyō and seven other organizations in forming a council on which the JCP would be represented.[55] This represented a decisive change from the policy set down in the JSP Convention of November 1958, when cooperation with the Communists had been ruled out. It clearly spelled victory for the left wing factions over Nishio, and foreshadowed the party split of the fall of 1959.

On the following day, Sōhyō held a meeting at which representatives from the following eight organizations were present: JSP, JCP, Gensuikyō, Japan Peace Committee, People's Council for Restoration of Japan-China Relations, National Federation for Safeguarding the Constitution, National Liaison Council Against Military Bases, and the Japan-China Friendship Association (Nitchū Yūkō Kyōkai). At this meeting it was decided that the new council would be officially inaugurated on March 28, 1959, that there would be thirteen sponsoring organizations, and the JCP would not be among the thirteen

[53] These were: Gensuikyō, the National Federation for Safeguarding the Constitution (Goken Rengō), People's Council for Restoration of Japan-China Relations (Nitchū Kokkō Kaifuku Kokumin Kaigi), and the National Liaison Council Against Military Bases (Zenkoku Kichiren).

[54] Kōan Chōsa Chō, *Ampo Tōsō*, pp. 34–35, and Ide Busaburō, *Ampo Tōsō*, p. 53.

[55] *Yomiuri Shimbun* (evening), March 10, 1959.

original sponsors.[56] Each of the thirteen bodies would have one representative on the Board of Directors but the JCP would join as an "observer" (*obuzābā*) only. The JCP would, however, be represented on the council's secretariat.[57] At this meeting JCP representatives Kamiyama Shigeo and Yanagida Haruo fought hard to get full representation on the Board of Directors. They were supported by representatives from the Japan Peace Committee and the Japan-China Friendship Association. But the Socialists held out for observer status only, and finally won at least this concession.[58]

Between March 12 and 28, preparations for the new council advanced swiftly. Invitations to participate were sent out to hundreds of "democratic organizations" and plans were made for the inaugural. But several serious controversies flared up in this interval which threatened the unity of the new council before it was even launched. As a name for the new body, the JCP and several of its supporters wanted "the People's Council for Smashing the Security System" (Ampo Taisei Daha Kokumin Kaigi). The JSP argued that, though the ultimate goal was to abolish the treaty system, the present aim must be merely to block treaty revision, and the name must appeal to a broad cross section of the nation.[59] The Socialists finally succeeded in naming it the People's Council to Prevent Revision of the Security Treaty.[60]

During this interval the JCP went on fighting for a position on the Board of Directors, continuing the quarrel down

[56] The thirteen included the above-mentioned nine, minus the JCP, plus these five: the All-Japan Farmers' Union (Zen Nichirō), the Joint Struggle Council of Youths and Students (Seinen Gakusei Kyōtō Kaigi), the Women's Council for Safeguarding Human Rights (Jinken o Mamoru Fujin Kyōgi Kai), the National Federation of Neutral Labor Unions (Chūritsu Rōren), and the Tokyo Joint Struggle Council for Safeguarding Peace and Democracy (Heiwa to Minshushugi o Mamoru Tokyo Kyōtō Kaigi).

[57] Kōan Chōsa Chō, *Ampo Tōsō*, pp. 36–37.

[58] *Ibid.*, p. 37.

[59] The JCP name was slightly more anti-American in focus, and the JSP name slightly more anti-Kishi.

[60] As a compromise, one of the three policy aims declared at the inaugural was the abolition of the security system.

to the day before the inaugural, but the JSP held out and prevented the change.[61] In addition, there was the problem of Zengakuren. The students naturally demanded a full seat on the council, but the older leaders were wary of the wild-eyed young Communists and decided to put them, with a number of other youth groups, in the Joint Struggle Council of Youths and Students. This was annoying to Zengakuren leaders, but as it later developed, they came to dominate the youth and student council and sent one of their own representatives to the directors' meetings anyway. Though all of these controversies were temporarily settled in March 1959, they continued to simmer beneath the surface and disturb the unity of the new coalition.

When Zenrō and Shinsanbetsu saw the trend of these events, they were quick to announce their opposition. Opposed to treaty revision, but equally opposed to cooperating with the Communists, Zenrō announced on March 24, 1959 (despite last minute talks with JSP leaders) that it would not join the new council; it warned the JSP that cooperation with the Communists would only lose them the support of the masses. Shinsanbetsu, in a similar statement on March 16, 1959, also announced that it would not participate.[62] This meant that the new anti-Government movement would lack the unified support of organized labor, a factor so important in the anti-Police Bill struggle. It also meant that, as the anti-treaty movement gathered momentum, mounting strain would be placed on relations between the left and right wings of the Socialist Party.

In the early spring of 1959, then, the political scene in Japan was outwardly calm, but there was ferment on both the left and right over the forthcoming treaty. The new People's Council in March 1959 committed the whole "Progressive camp" (excepting only Zenrō and right socialist elements) to a policy of

[61] As we shall see, the JCP came to sit on the key "Strategy Committee" in April 1960, so that its status as an observer did not keep it from influencing the action.

[62] Shinsanbetsu, organized in 1949 to combat Communist control over labor unions, had only 43,000 members in June 1959 (*Japan Times*, December 20, 1959), and stood somewhere between Sōhyō and Zenrō in outlook.

unyielding opposition to a revised security treaty. No matter what concession Kishi or Fujiyama might wring from U.S. diplomats, the political forces representing about one-third of the Japanese people had now committed themselves to absolute opposition. Since Kishi by this time was hopelessly committed to revising the treaty, the clash of 1960 was therefore written on the wall over a year before it occurred. No amount of diplomacy or verbiage in the Diet could obscure this fundamental political reality.

Organization and Activities of the People's Council

The new People's Council was officially inaugurated on March 28, 1959, at the National Railway Workers Hall. A total of 134 organizations (including the 13 original sponsors) sent 620 representatives to this first meeting.[63] Every conceivable type of "progressive organization" was represented: the Women's Socialist League, Japan Anarchists' League, Executive Committee of the Japan Group Singing Association, League for the Emancipation of Outcasts, Christian Peace Association, and so forth. The slogans adopted at the meeting reflected the nature of the new organization, covering the whole range of leftist grievances: opposition to nuclear weapons, foreign bases, "alliance" with South Korea and rearmament, and support for the "peace constitution," neutralism, and human rights. The Council's three stated policy aims were to prevent revision of the security treaty, achieve neutralism, and abolish the security system.

The thirteen original sponsors formed a thirteen-member Board of Directors (see organization chart, below). This was the overall coordinating body, where the principle of unanimity applied to all decision-making. A secretariat with a director, two vice-directors, two secretaries, and several part-time students was set up to handle the daily business of the Board of Directors. In each prefecture, a regional joint struggle council (Kenmin Kyōtō Kaigi) was formed, made up of the particular "mix"

[63] A list of the participating organizations can be found in Kōan Chōsa Chō, Ampo Tōsō, pp. 42–44.

111

PEOPLE'S COUNCIL FOR PREVENTING REVISION OF THE SECURITY TREATY

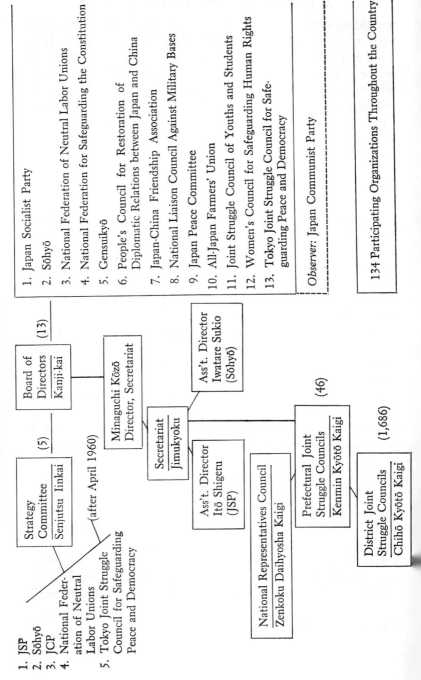

Strategy Committee / Senjutsu Iinkai (5)

1. JSP
2. Sōhyō
3. JCP
4. National Federation of Neutral Labor Unions
5. Tokyo Joint Struggle Council for Safeguarding Peace and Democracy

Board of Directors / Kanji-kai (13)

1. Japan Socialist Party
2. Sōhyō
3. National Federation of Neutral Labor Unions
4. National Federation for Safeguarding the Constitution
5. Gensuikyō
6. People's Council for Restoration of Diplomatic Relations between Japan and China
7. Japan-China Friendship Association
8. National Liaison Council Against Military Bases
9. Japan Peace Committee
10. All-Japan Farmers' Union
11. Joint Struggle Council of Youths and Students
12. Women's Council for Safeguarding Human Rights
13. Tokyo Joint Struggle Council for Safeguarding Peace and Democracy

Observer: Japan Communist Party

134 Participating Organizations Throughout the Country

Minaguchi Kōzō Director, Secretariat

(after April 1960)

Secretariat / Jimukyoku

Ass't. Director Iwatare Sukio (Sōhyō)

Ass't. Director Itō Shigeru (JSP)

National Representatives Council / Zenkoku Daihyosha Kaigi

Prefectural Joint Struggle Councils / Kenmin Kyōtō Kaigi (46)

District Joint Struggle Councils / Chihō Kyōtō Kaigi (1,686)

of left wing elements that prevailed in that area. Below the prefectural joint struggle councils were district joint struggle councils (*chihō kyōtō kaigi*), again formed of the local left wing groups in towns and villages throughout the nation. By August 1, 1959, all 46 prefectures and metropolitan areas (*todōfuken*) had regional councils, and by July 1960, 1,686 district councils had been formed.[64] These local councils were coordinated from the center by instructions and "requests" from the Board of Directors in Tokyo and by occasional meetings of a National Representatives Council (Zenkoku Daihyōsha Kaigi) to which the local councils sent delegates. The National Representatives Council had no power of decision- or policy-making, but served rather as a forum for transmitting information and enthusiasm from Tokyo to the outlying districts. A Strategy Committee (Senjutsu Iinkai) was formed in April 1960 to resolve arguments over tactics among the Directors. This committee consisted of representatives from the JSP, JCP, Sōhyō, the Tokyo Joint Struggle Council, and the National Federation of Neutral Labor Unions.

Headquarters for the council were set up in an office and conference room provided by the Socialist Party on the second floor of the House of Councillors Annex, within the Diet compound. "These rooms were not too inspiring in outward appearance," commented a leftist writer, "considering they were the home of the organization of Japan's united progressive camp."[65] In these two rooms, furnished with two telephones, several desks, and a long conference table, the People's Council went about its work. The main activities at headquarters were the writing of handbills and posters, publishing a small news bulletin, and serving as a liaison point for representatives

[64] *Ibid.*, pp. 49–50. Officers of the People's Council said that about 2,000 of these councils had been formed by July 1960; Ide Busaburō in *Ampo Tōsō*, p. 55, also said 2,000. *Sayoku Dantai Jiten*, Shakai Undō Chōsa Kai, ed., Tokyo: Musashi Shobō, 1961, p. 17, gives the number as 1,500.

[65] Ide Busaburō, *Ampo Tōsō*, p. 54. It is interesting, though, that the headquarters of the organization that planned the largest demonstration in history at the Japanese Diet should have been housed within the compound of the Diet!

of the other participating organizations, especially around the time of "united action" events.

The People's Council functioned without an official leader for six months; thought was given to a number of candidates, including Nambara Shigeru, former President of Tokyo University, Nakajima Kenzō, pro-Communist writer and scholar, and Uehara Senroku, well-known leftist professor from Hitotsubashi University, but the members could not agree among themselves on a chairman who was famous, but sufficiently neutral toward the competing leftist groups. In October 1959 the job was finally given to a virtually unknown figure, Minaguchi Kōzō, but instead of becoming chairman (*gichō*), he was given the lesser title of "Director of the Secretariat" (*jimukyoku-chō*).[66]

Minaguchi was in many ways typical of a new breed in Japan, the "leftist organization man." At 45—with long, slightly graying hair, horn-rimmed glasses, and wearing a brown business suit—his appearance was more like that of a college professor or a businessman. He had studied in the Faculty of Agriculture of Tokyo Imperial University, and in his student days had interested himself in leftist activities. After graduating in 1938 he went to work for the Ministry of Agriculture, where he enjoyed the "progressive atmosphere" in dealing with tenancy disputes (*kosaku sōgi*) of that period. Immediately after the war, he organized and became head of a union in the Ministry of Agriculture, and from 1946 to 1948 he was Chairman of the Government Workers Union (Kanchō Rōdō Kumiai). In 1952, having risen to a position of section-chief (*kachō*) in the Ministry of Agriculture, he left his job and for three years engaged in research in farm villages. In 1954 he became assistant to the head of the National Federation for Safeguarding the Constitution, under former Prime Minister Katayama Tetsu; today he runs that organization from spacious offices in the fifth floor of the new Diet Library.[67]

---

[66] Minaguchi had already been a member of the Board of Directors by virtue of his job as head of the National Federation for Safeguarding the Constitution; he now took on the additional job of running the secretariat.

[67] Interview with Minaguchi Kōzō, December 21, 1961.

Minaguchi stated in an interview that he was a supporter of the Socialist Party, and that he had never belonged to the JCP, having broken with the Communists at the time of the abortive strike of February 1, 1947.[68] One of his associates described Minaguchi as a weak leader but a superb coordinator (*matome-yaku*). He had an uncanny knack of finding points of agreement in conflicting opinions, and invariably settled arguments with a minimum of ruffled feelings. An intellectual, he was a rapid, brilliant speaker and was excellent at planning and coordinating overall tactics; on practical details, however, he lacked experience and knowledge.[69] Minaguchi's ability to settle arguments was to be sorely taxed over the coming months.

The two assistant-directors represented the JSP and Sōhyō respectively. Itō Shigeru, a junior staff employee of JSP headquarters in Tokyo, was a graduate of the Faculty of Economics, Tokyo University. Iwatare Sukio was a thirty-one-year-old employee at Sōhyō headquarters in Tokyo. He had been involved in the student movement at Chūō University and was a typical Sōhyō "activist" in the anti-treaty demonstrations, standing on top of a loudspeaker truck in the thick of the battle. Iwatare was a member of the Sōhyō delegation that traveled to Communist China in October 1959 for the 10th Anniversary Celebrations of the People's Republic of China. The other members of the secretariat were former Zengakuren students and two female secretaries.

The council printed a small news bulletin, *Kyōtō Nyūsu*, every week or ten days from April 18, 1959, to April 30, 1960, when the staff became too busy to put it out. The paper published its final edition on July 10, 1960.[70] Issues were a single sheet, 10 by 14 inches, with easy-to-read characters printed on both sides. About 3,000 copies of each issue were printed and circulated, free of charge, to local joint struggle councils and labor union

---

[68] *Ibid.*

[69] Interview with an associate of Minaguchi Kōzō.

[70] A complete collection of these bulletins was available in 1961 at the People's Council headquarters in the House of Councillors Annex. The bulletin was originally published under the name *Kokumin Kaigi Nyūsu*, but later changed to *Kyōtō Nyūsu*.

115

headquarters. A typical issue contained news of previous "struggles," the general line for the next demonstration, slogans, anti-government news items, and exhortations by various left wing leaders to fight still harder in the next battle.

Expenses for headquarters' activities were met by contributions from the participating organizations. According to Director Minaguchi, a total of 6,500,000 yen ($18,055) was spent from March 1959 to July 1960.[71] Another source states that between February and June 1960, 1,650,000 yen ($4,600) was laid out.[72] Of course there is no way to document these figures. Conservatives charged that far more than this was spent and that some of it came to Japan from Communist Bloc countries (these charges are discussed below). The main expenses, according to members of the secretariat, were the printing of the news bulletins, handbills, and posters, renting halls for rallies and meetings, and paying the salaries of the two secretaries.

Some of the council's most important work went on in the countryside during 1959. The prefectural and district joint struggle councils formed rapidly in the spring of 1959, with Sōhyō playing a major rôle. By July 1959, 45 of Japan's 46 prefectures had set up joint struggle councils, and it is noteworthy that the headquarters for 31 of these councils were in Sōhyō offices, while 8 were in JSP offices.[73] These councils varied in name and composition, depending on the relative strength of the local leftist groups. Participation on the boards of directors of the local councils was sometimes determined by the amount of money (per capita) contributed by each member-group. Organizations, rather than individuals, were the units of membership in all the councils. Some of the types of organizations included were peace committees, women's associations, farmers' and teachers' unions, mothers' groups, child protection societies, and the like. A few new local elements, such as a civic group in Nerima Ward, Tokyo, and a shopkeepers' group in the city of Maebashi, at-

[71] Interview with Minaguchi Kōzō, December 21, 1961.

[72] Ide Busaburō, *Ampo Tōsō*, p. 54.

[73] Japan Socialist Party, Secretariat for the Anti-Security Treaty Struggle, People's Movement Committee, "Situation of the Nation-wide Joint Struggle Against Security Treaty Revision," July 25, 1959.

tracted attention for their unprecedent participation in the leftist movement, but most of the organizations were long-time advocates of left wing causes. The councils printed handbills and posters, arranged for anti-treaty speeches by scholars and famous people in factories, and ran small meetings in the towns and villages. Most important of all, they helped organize and stir up enthusiasm in the local rallies and demonstrations and arranged for the sending of local delegates to Tokyo to join in the larger protest demonstrations.

The most important regional council was unquestionably the Tokyo Joint Struggle Council for Safeguarding Peace and Democracy. This council sat on the Board of Directors as one of the thirteen original sponsors, and also on the five-member Strategy Committee. It included Sōhyō's regional chapter, Chihyō, in Tokyo, which played a leading role in furnishing manpower for the demonstrations.[74] The council's headquarters were provided by Sōhyō. On its Board of Directors were Sōhyō's Okamoto Ushitarō, well-known leftist intellectual, Nakano Yoshio, and China-expert Uchiyama Kanzō.

One of the most striking features of the People's Council, the one that really distinguished it from the council against the Police Bill, was the extent of Communist influence among its members. We have seen that the JCP was made an "observer" on the Board of Directors, but this does not tell the whole story. At the inaugural on March 28, 1959, JSP Secretary-General Asanuma Inejirō and JCP Secretary-General Miyamoto Kenji stood side by side on the rostrum, and *Akahata* subsequently reported that this was an "epochal" event.[75] Each time delegates gathered from all over Japan to attend meetings of the National Representatives Council, the JCP delegates would meet separately on the previous day to coordinate their strategy. At the second meeting of the council on September 16, 1959, 70 of the 300 national delegates were JCP members.[76] Though the Communists were supposed to be "observers" only, their influence grew steadily during the course of the movement, and they came to

[74] Kōan Chōsa Chō, *Ampo Tōsō*, p. 56.
[75] Ide Busaburō, *Ampo Tōsō*, p. 54.
[76] Kōan Chōsa Chō, *Ampo Tōsō*, p. 75.

have a powerful voice in the important Strategy Committee in April 1960.[77] Kamiyama Shigeo, the JCP representative on the Board of Directors, made this boast in the April 1960 issue of *Zenei*: ". . . it may have been natural for the Socialists, including Sōhyō, to have *appeared* to hold the leadership at the center. But looking at the actual situation throughout the past year's struggle, the JSP, JCP and Sōhyō have come to form the backbone (of the movement), a fact which is openly admitted by the activists." [78]

Communist influence ranged far beyond the formal party structure into the unions and the hundreds of "democratic" and "progressive" organizations that had sprung up in postwar Japan. These groups consisted of thousands of well-intentioned Japanese people who rallied to the call to protect newly won democratic rights, and to express their loathing of militarism and war. Famous names adorned the boards of these organizations, lending authority and prestige. But a remarkable number were controlled or heavily influenced by a relatively small number of JCP members who infiltrated the key executive organs, issued statements, and ran the daily activities.

A typical example of Communist penetration of "peace organizations" was found in Gensuikyō, which was originally set up to be an anti-nuclear weapon organization and which sponsored nationwide rallies at Hiroshima each year to commemorate the first atomic bombing. Gradually the Communists seized the key positions; Gensuikyō openly accepted money from Communist China and Russia to help it stage rallies, which were strongly anti-American in tone,[79] and its Director was Yasui Kaoru, winner of a Lenin Peace Prize. According to Ishihara Kanichirō, Chairman of Japan's National Public Safety Commission, 121 of Gensuikyō's 1,164 local branch directors were

[77] See *Tokyo Shimbun*, June 25, 1959, for an example of the quarrels and dissension within the People's Council.

[78] Kamiyama Shigeo, *Ampo Tōsō*, p. 10, italics added.

[79] Yasui Kaoru admitted that groups in the Soviet Union and Communist China had contributed about $5,000 each in 1958 and 1959. The Japanese Government alleged that Communist China gave $20,000 and the Soviet Union $11,000 in 1958. *New York Times*, July 26, 1959.

Communists in 1959.[80] According to the PSIA, 13 of the 71 standing directors and 9 of the 17 members of the secretariat were JCP members.[81] Yet the surprising fact was that famous non-Communists such as Nobel Prize-winner Dr. Yukawa Hideki and LDP Diet member Kitamura Tokutarō let their names be used as directors of Gensuikyō, though they rarely attended meetings, and gave the Communist activists a free hand in speaking on all issues. The truth is that it was as hard for the Japanese man of letters or science to oppose this sort of anti-bomb group (or even to withhold cooperation) as it was for an American to attack the Boy Scouts, and the Communists took advantage of this fact.[82]

While the Communists were only observers on the Board of Directors, they controlled at least three of the thirteen original sponsors (Japan Peace Committee, Japan-China Friendship Association, and Gensuikyō) and exerted a powerful influence in others. PSIA figures illustrate this point. Of the Japan Peace Committee's 45 standing directors, 18 were JCP members and one of these was a JCP Central Committee member. Of the Japan-China Friendship Association's 50 standing directors, 18 were JCP members; of its 166 directors, 27 were JCP members, and on its 13-man secretariat, 7 were JCP members.[83]

Communist participation in the local councils was even more pronounced, a fact admitted privately by JSP officials after the crisis was over. Though the JCP was denied full membership on

[80] *Japan Times,* July 29, 1959.

[81] Kōan Chōsa Chō, *Ampo Tōsō,* p. 46.

[82] See *Asahi Shimbun,* September 15, 1961, for details on the JCP activities in Gensuikyō; also see Paul F. Langer, *op. cit.,* pp. 64–69, for a description of JCP infiltration into these organizations.

[83] Kōan Chōsa Chō, *Ampo Tōsō,* pp. 45–46. It should be observed here that the Public Security Investigation Agency (Kōan Chōsa Chō) was set up in July 1952 for the primary purpose of investigating Communist activities, and that its opinions and interpretations, therefore, might tend to exaggerate the nature of the Communist threat. Indeed, *Ampo Tōsō* does overemphasize the Communist rôle (both domestic and international) in the anti-treaty movement in its overall interpretation; this does not, however, invalidate its statistics and facts. I have used the PSIA materials advisedly, checking them against leftist sources where possible, and indicating the points on which there is serious disagreement.

the central Board of Directors, it gained full admission to 64 percent of the local councils, was an observer in 3 percent, and failed to participate in only 29 percent.[84] The JCP staffed the offices of these councils with 1,781 of its members.[85] The JCP itself agreed with PSIA's conclusion that it played an important rôle in the local councils. Kamiyama Shigeo presented a chart showing the JCP analysis of its own success in moving into the councils; as of June 15, 1959, the party was formally participating in 41 of the 46 prefectural councils either under its own name (34) or some other name (7).[86]

The Communist Party and the JSP clashed over the naming of the prefectural councils, as they had at the center. In the end, the Socialists succeeded in naming 26 of them "Councils for Preventing Revision of the Security Treaty" (Ampo Jōyaku Kaitei Soshi Kenmin Kaigi), while the Communists managed to name 22 of them "Councils for abolishing the Security Treaty" (Ampo Jōyaku Haiki [or Haishi] Kenmin Kaigi). Nine of the councils compromised and included both slogans in their names.[87]

Another local issue between the Communists and Socialists was the question whether to make these councils permanent organizations (perpetuating the united front at the local level) or to make them *ad hoc*, single campaign coalitions. The Communists favored the permanent type in order to retain the new united front and they succeeded, over Socialist objections, in making 484 of the 1,686 councils permanent in nature. During the course of the movement, 122 more changed to permanent status.[88] The Socialists, even as they were being dragged deeper into the movement, insisted that the alliance with the Communists was not a real united front based on broad policy agreement, but at best only a "rudimentary" front for the limited

[84] Kōan Chōsa Chō, *Ampo Tōsō*, p. 51.

[85] *Ibid.*, pp. 62–66, contains charts with statistical breakdowns of Communist participation at each level.

[86] Kamiyama Shigeo, *Ampo Tōsō*, pp. 10–13. Page 12 contains a chart showing a prefectural breakdown of JCP participation.

[87] Kōan Chōsa Chō, *Ampo Tōsō*, pp. 54–55.

[88] *Ibid.*, p. 53.

purpose of struggling against Kishi and the new treaty. The Communists thought otherwise and sought everywhere to expand the front and strengthen their own hand within it.

During the early days of the anti-treaty movement, the chief attacks on the treaty were made on scheduled "united action" (tōitsu kōdō) days, on which all participating bodies on the People's Council augmented strikes and workshop rallies by Sōhyō unionists with demonstrations, auto parades, sit-down protests, and public rallies. The activities were centered in Tokyo, but they were also carried out in the major cities and even in some towns and villages throughout the nation. Ten of these united action days were held in 1959, the ninth being the climactic November 27, 1959 Incident of which we shall speak in Chapter 5.[89] In general, the slogans and aims of each united action day were tied in with particular labor demands and left wing causes during that period: the spring labor offensive, support for the Sunakawa decision, support for the coal miners' battle against rationalization and dismissals, demands for higher year-end bonuses. The point of all this activity, according to Director Minaguchi, was twofold: to serve as a method of expressing (hyōgen hōhō) the people's will and to be an "educational activity" (keimō undō) to enlighten the nation on the dangers of war in the new treaty.[90] The tone of the campaign in 1959 was similar to other "peace movements" in emphasis, stressing the dangers of nuclear holocaust and aggressive militarism. It was not until May 19, 1960, that the issue of "democracy" and parliamentarianism became prominent, and then the themes dwelt on the hardships which the new treaty would bring to the daily lives of the people.

The demonstrations did not reach major proportions until November 27, 1959. One leftist writer noted that the 100,000 people across the nation who demonstrated in the 3rd United Action on June 25 were exceeded in number by those who

[89] The People's Council has put out a mimeographed chronology of all major events from February 1959 to July 1960 entitled, "Ampo Jōyaku Kaitei Soshi Tōsō Nenpyō." The size of the crowds on each united action day is given in Sayoku Dantai Jiten, pp. 20–22.

[90] Interview with Minaguchi Kōzō, December 21, 1961.

watched the all-star baseball game at Korakuen Stadium or on TV at home on the same day.[91] The main participants in the rallies and demonstrations were organized laborers, with a smattering of hard-core Zengakuren followers. On the surface, at least, the Council did not succeed during 1959 in giving the movement a broadly based grass roots following. It was not until the treaty draft was in its final stages and violence broke out around the Diet that the public seemed to wake up to the growing crisis and take an interest in the specific issues of treaty revision.

Summary and Conclusions

The People's Council was a loose coalition of preexisting left wing forces.[92] It represented the closest approach to unity that had ever been achieved in postwar Japan among leftist groups, but it did not weld together the whole of the left wing into a genuine united front. Mistrust and suspicion which had originated in prewar days could not be removed even for so important an issue as the security treaty, and there were deep differences in the ultimate objectives of the member groups.

More than anything else, the People's Council was a labor protest movement in origin and nature. Sōhyō's organized unionists gave the council its influence and its strength. Sōhyō's turn to the left and new congeniality with the Communist Party was met by a switch in the JCP line toward peaceful revolution, neutralism for Japan, and a broad united front. This new alignment drove Zenrō and Shinsanbetsu from the movement and opened up a deep crevice in the Socialist Party; the loss of the democratic socialist elements deprived the movement of the voices of moderation and non-Marxist reformism which had prevailed in the Police Bill affair.

The Socialist Party, torn by the split between its Sōhyō-backed

[91] Hidaka Rokurō, ed., *Gogatsu Jūkunichi*, Tokyo: Iwanami Shinsho, 1960, p. 27.

[92] The few fresh elements that appeared at the local levels, such as the Nerima-ky civic group and the Maebashi shopkeepers' organization did not exert much influence over the dominant older organizations such as Sōhyō and the JCP.

left wing and Zenrō-backed right wing, seemed paralyzed in the crucial months from December 1958 to March 1959 when the new council was forming. The most it could do was to jump reluctantly onto the rolling bandwagon after the Communists and Sōhyō had seized the initiative and set the tone for the new campaign. The Socialist leaders never really recovered the initiative and proved unable, during the course of the movement, to lend it the kind of mature political leadership that could benefit the party at the polls later on.

The Communists and their allies benefited most from the formation of the new council; for the first time since 1950 they shared the limelight of political respectability with the JSP as they quietly worked in the background to steer the movement into anti-American channels. The Communist strength in the regional councils was testimony to their untiring efforts to control the symbols of "peace, democracy, and independence," in postwar Japan. It also accentuated the weakness of the Socialist Party outside of its union strongholds. While the JCP never gained full control over the People's Council, it was in a position to influence events at crucial moments. Without the experienced personnel and organizational machinery of the Communist Party, it is doubtful that the movement would have gotten as far as it did up to May 19, 1960.

The People's Council had one characteristic common to many Japanese organizations: the diffusion of responsibility. At the center it was a body without a head; in the countryside there were branches with no trunk. This meant that the actions and policies of the various members of the council in demonstrating against the treaty could not be ascribed with precision to any particular leader or office in the organization. Real authority, of course, remained where it had been before the council was formed: with Sōhyō, the JSP, JCP, and Zengakuren.[93] But when violence occurred, the Socialists could blame the Communists who could blame Zengakuren, while sympathizers with the students could attack the older leftists for their faulty leadership.

[93] There were instances, however, when dissident elements even in these groups overrode the orders of the leaders, as we shall see below.

Opinions differ as to the effectiveness of the People's Council on stirring up anti-treaty sentiment in the nation as a whole. Some observers believe that the council had little or no effect in 1959, noting that popular interest in the treaty issues (as recorded by all polls) stayed low throughout the year, and that the demonstrations drew very little "new blood" into the campaign. But there is probably some truth in the observation by Ide Busaburō that ". . . though the movement showed no signs of surging forward on the surface, there was a steady build-up which caused the words "security treaty" to seep down and flow as an underground river toward November 27, 1959, increasing in force as it went along." [94] No one can say, of course, whether the movement turned many minds against the idea of treaty revision—an idea that had been supported by a great majority when it first appeared. But it may well be true that the anti-treaty drive, launched over a year before the treaty came to a vote in the Diet, set up a receptivity to the idea that the treaty meant war and insecurity, which, when combined with the startling world events of 1960, resulted in panic and genuine fear. The machinery for the massive protest was then in place and functioning, and the expectation of conflict was ingrained as a result of the year's advance effort by the council.

Thus the groundwork for the political crisis was firmly laid many months before it reached a climax; the lines of battle were drawn in March 1959, and both sides set out to prove that the other was leading Japan to the abyss. The original impetus for revising the treaty, based as it was on a broad consensus, had now separated and reshaped itself around the polarized left and right political forces in Japan.

[94] Ide Busaburō, *Ampo Tōsō*, p. 55.

 CHAPTER 4

The Approaching Storm

THE STORMY events of May and June 1960 make no sense at all unless the events that went before them are understood: the Socialist split, the Sunakawa trial, the propaganda campaigns, and the state of public opinion—all of which set the stage for dramatic developments.

The Socialist Split

The split of the Socialist Party in 1959 and the appearance in the Diet of a third major party (and a second opposition party) had important political effects on the Diet controversy over the new treaty. We saw in the last chapter how the split was foreshadowed by the rivalry between the two major labor federations, Sōhyō and Zenrō, and by Zenrō's refusal to join the People's Council. There were, of course, other deep and complex causes for the split, such as personal and factional rivalries, ideological differences, and longstanding divisions within the labor movement itself, but we shall touch on the split only to the extent that it affected the security treaty struggle of 1960.[1]

The merger of the left and right wings of the Socialist Party in October 1955 had been at best a patchwork affair; the ambiguous and vague platform of the united JSP could not conceal the deep differences that still existed within the party. The compromises of 1955 had been built upon the expectation that victory was just around the corner, and the alliance of the centrist Suzuki and Kawakami factions was intended to be the basis for a future Socialist Party cabinet. With a disappointing growth rate in 1958 and another clear-cut defeat in the House of Coun-

[1] For more complete accounts of the split and its causes, see the following articles to which I am indebted for the analysis that follows: Naoi Takeo, "Behind the Japanese Socialist Split," *New Leader*, Vol. 42, No. 42, November 6, 1959, pp. 19–20; Seki Yoshihiko, "New Trends in Japanese Socialism," *Japan Quarterly*, Vol. 7, No. 2, April-June, 1960, pp. 142–151; and David C. S. Sissons, "Recent Developments in Japan's Socialist Movement," *Far Eastern Survey*, No. 29, March and June 1960, pp. 40–47, 89–92.

cillors election of June 1959, the smoldering disputes over theory and methods of gaining power flared up again. The LDP's move to revise the Police Duties Law and the security treaty raised in acute form the questions that had always divided the Socialists: defense, foreign policy, and the role of the Diet.

At about this time the right wing Socialists, who had been losing ground to the left since 1951, chose to take the offensive under Nishio Suehirō to regain their former leadership of the party.[2] Sōhyō, meanwhile, was moving gradually to the left, as we noted in the last chapter. The net effect of all this was an explosive confrontation of the left and right wings culminating in Nishio's walkout of the party in October 1959.

One of the decisive factors in bringing about the party split was the growing influence among left wing Socialists and Sōhyō unions of the theories of Professor Sakisaka Itsurō, the leading Marxist theoretician in the left wing Socialist camp.[3] Professor

[2] Nishio Suehirō, a prewar veteran of the right wing (shamin) labor movement, was one of the few Socialists to rise through union ranks to a position of party leadership. He was also one of the few avowed non-Marxists in the party, having rejected Communism as early as 1924 after a visit to Moscow. He served in the Ashida coalition cabinet (1947–1948) but fell under a cloud when he was indicted for accepting bribes in the Shōwa Denkō Scandal of 1948. It was not until November 24, 1958, that he was finally cleared in this case and began a political comeback. In 1959 he launched a series of attacks on the left wing Socialists, accusing them of dancing to the JCP tune, of domination by Sōhyō unions, of overemphasizing the class struggle, and of violating the principles of parliamentarianism.

[3] Sakisaka, a professor at Kyūshū University at the time, was the ideological heir to the Rōnō (Labor-Farmer) circle of Marxist intellectuals and professors formed by Yamakawa Hitoshi and others in the mid-1920's. Known as the Rōnō faction, this group differed from the Japan Communist Party in its belief that the Socialist revolution could be achieved in a single, one-stage class struggle against the Japanese bourgeoisie. Suppressed in the 1930's, the Rōnō theorists reappeared after the war and played an important part in shaping Sōhyō's ideology after 1950. It was no coincidence that the Sakisaka group's bulletin, Shakaishugi (Socialism), had its headquarters in the offices of Sōhyō's chairman, Ōta Kaoru, in 1959. For an interesting description of Sakisaka, see Lawrence Olson, "A Japanese Marxist," American Universities Field Staff Report, East Asia Series, Vol. 9, No. 4 (Japan), March 15, 1961.

Sakisaka reopened the old controversy over the class *vs.* the people's party in December 1958 with an article in *Shakaishugi* that has come to be known as "the Sakisaka thesis." [4] In this article he states that the Socialist Party lost its revolutionary spirit—its very soul—with the merger of left and right wings in 1955. If you are planning to travel from Fukuoka to Tokyo, wrote Sakisaka, you build a party which can go all the way, not a party which will get you only to Osaka.[5] The JSP must set its sights on the immediate, attainable objective of socialist revolution based on the power of labor; this objective must determine the character and composition of the party. Unless the mistaken notion of a broad "people's party" were abandoned and the dominant rôle of labor established, he argued, the party would get no further than Osaka.[6]

Sakisaka went on to say that the socialist revolution could be achieved only by intensifying the class struggle against Japan's ruling bourgeoisie. The Japanese revolution might be a peaceful one but in the final struggle, he wrote, "it is impossible not to contemplate the use of some sort of force." [7] Then, in words which his critics say were highly provocative and his apologists say should not be taken too literally, Sakisaka observed that "if only the transportation and communication workers' unions should strike, they could paralyze Japan's politics and economy. The problem is: can the Socialist Party grasp this power?" [8] Sakisaka concluded that both the objective and subjective conditions were ripe for an immediate revolution, and that the Socialist Party must reorganize itself (i.e., get rid of the right wing) in order to accomplish its historic mission.

Whether or not Sakisaka was advocating violent revolution

[4] Sakisaka Itsurō, "Tadashii Kōryō, Tadashii Kikō" (A Proper Platform and a Proper Organization), *Shakaishugi*, No. 88, December 1958, pp. 46–52.

[5] *Ibid.*, pp. 48–50.

[6] By inference, this argument was aimed at Nishio and his concept of a people's party. There may have been a subtle play on geography as well: Sakisaka himself was teaching in Fukuoka, which he considered the focal point of the labor-management battle, while Nishio was an Osaka man.

[7] *Ibid.*, p. 51.

[8] *Ibid.*

(this has been argued both ways), his words and ideas appeared to have weighed heavily on Sōhyō's decision to resort to force in the security treaty struggle and, concurrently, in the bloody Mitsui Miike coal miners' strike of 1960. No one can say how much a given theory influences action in any human decision, but Sakisaka's thesis seemed to drive the left wing Socialists into the use of political strikes and extra-parliamentary mass action during the 1960 treaty struggle, and his influence overrode the moderate Socialists who wished to use the Diet debate to appeal to the people and who saw the electoral process rather than street fighting as the best means of defeating the conservatives.

The right wing Socialists under Nishio and the left wing under the influence of Sakisaka could not continue for long in the same political party. After a year of open wrangling and fierce competition, Nishio withdrew from the JSP on October 18, 1959, taking with him twenty-four Diet members in his own faction, five "middle right" Socialists, and three rebels from the Kawakami faction.[9] These Socialists then combined in January 1960 to form the nucleus of the new Democratic Socialist Party (Minshu Shakai Tō, hereinafter referred to as the DSP).[10]

The new DSP tried to present a fresh image to the Japanese voters. It stood for gradual reform of capitalism, strict observance of the principles of parliamentarianism, and a neutral for-

[9] The treaty issue provided one of the major charges against Nishio at the Socialists' 16th National Convention in the fall of 1959: Nishio had declared in a speech at Nagoya on July 19, 1959, that the JSP left wing was opposing the new treaty for opposition's sake, and that it should come up with a plan of its own for ensuring Japanese security; the left wing used this charge to claim that Nishio was betraying the anti-treaty drive already underway. Other left wing accusations against Nishio were: (1) that he had been too ready to compromise with the LDP and recognize the Diet extension in the Police Bill struggle; (2) that he favored the teachers' efficiency rating system; (3) that he supported the Chiang Kai-shek Government in Taiwan; and (4) that he tried to woo certain unions away from Sōhyō control.

[10] A dozen more Diet members from the Kawakami faction defected to Nishio in November 1959, so that the DSP was launched on January 24, 1960, with 37 seats in the Lower House, and 16 in the Upper, compared with 128 and 69, respectively, for the JSP.

eign policy.[11] The DSP favored abolishing the security treaty with the United States in stages through negotiations. It admitted, however, that minimum military measures should be taken to defend the country pending a complete disarmament agreement among all nations. Like the rest of Japan, the party was divided over the question of how soon to abolish the treaty and how much to rearm: though the majority favored limited self-defense measures, Katayama Tetsu, one of the party's most distinguished members and the only Socialist ever to become Prime Minister, was opposed to all armaments, and another group led by Nagasue Eiichi believed in strengthening the Self-defense Forces. These and other differences of viewpoint were to emerge during the anti-treaty struggle and blur the image of the new party.

The DSP, which set out to win support from the neglected middle stratum of Japanese society (the small and medium enterprisers, farmers, and fishermen), won immediate support from Zenrō as well as from an impressive list of intellectuals and educators such as college Presidents Morito Tatsuo, Rōyama Masamichi, and Yabe Teiji as well as Professors Inoki Masamichi, Nakamura Kikuo, and Seki Yoshihiko. Even Uemura Kōgorō, Vice-President of the conservative Federation of Economic Organizations (Keidanren) praised the new party, giving rise to JSP charges that the DSP was nothing more than a second conservative party. People spoke of a "DSP–boom" in early 1960, and it is quite likely that the party would have increased its Diet strength had an election been held at that time. Instead, however, the party's bright new image was badly tarnished by its apparent wavering at the height of the treaty crisis, and in the November 1960 elections it was nearly wiped out as a major political force.[12]

[11] The platform of the new party was similar in many respects to the *Bad Godesberg* platform adopted by the West German Socialist Party in November 1959. An English text of the party's provisional platform and policies may be found in a handbook, *The Japan Democratic Socialist Party* (undated), printed by the party around September 1960.

[12] The Japanese texts of the new party's constitution, platform, and policies may be found in the special supplement to the party organ, *Shūkan Shakai Shimbun*, February 1, 1960.

Nishio's walkout removed a major obstacle to the remolding of the JSP into a more revolutionary class party based on the theories of Sakisaka and the power of Sōhyō—and this just a few months before the climactic stages of the treaty battle. It might have led to an even sharper turn to the left by the JSP had there not been the following moderating factors. First, the members of the right wing Kawakami faction who remained loyal had to be rewarded with positions of power and with policy concessions; this gave the right wingers a voice far greater than their small number would command. Second, the very weakness of the JSP in the Diet forced it to seek DSP cooperation on key issues. Third, the new DSP attracted some dissident Sōhyō unionists, notably in the National Railway Workers' Union, and this forced Sōhyō to make concessions to hold together its forces.[13] For these reasons the JSP did not turn further to the left in early 1960 but remained mostly under the influence of the dominant left-center Suzuki faction.

The Socialist Party split was to affect the security treaty battle in several different ways: the loss of Zenrō and the right wing Socialists reduced the total size and effectiveness of the mass demonstrations. The loss of Nishio, Katayama, and others deprived the party of leading non-Marxist supporters of the parliamentary system and made it almost inevitable that the JSP would "take to the streets" to block the treaty. Perhaps equally important, the People's Council found itself unable to claim that it represented *all* "progressive and democratic" elements in Japan, and the strong hand of the JCP behind the People's Council became more and more evident. Finally, the new DSP represented an opportunity and a threat for both the conservatives and the JSP during the Diet debate on the revised security treaty. Both sides needed DSP support for a crucial reason: when the JSP exhausted all other Diet tactics and staged a boycott, the DSP could either join the boycott and support the charge that the conservatives were a "tyrannous majority," or it could stay in the Diet and vote against the treaty, which

[13] Naoi Takeo, "New Course in Japanese Trade Unionism," *New Leader,* Vol. 43, No. 17, April 25, 1960, pp. 20–21.

would have taken most of the steam out of the JSP charges and given Kishi's forceful methods a cloak of respectability. For this reason the LDP and JSP fought hard to win DSP support during the early months of 1960 and the new party was subjected to the most intensive pressures in its very infancy. We shall see below how it reached to these pressures.

The Sunakawa Case

We noted earlier that only one base problem—the Sunakawa case—ever reached major proportions up to 1960. This case created a national furor by calling into question the constitutionality of the security treaty at the very moment when that treaty was being renegotiated and while the left wing was plotting a massive attack on the alliance.

Sunakawa is the name of the small village that lies next to Tachikawa Air Base, a vital air transport center for U.S. Forces in the Far East. In 1955 the Governments of the United States and Japan agreed to lengthen the runway at Tachikawa to take care of the larger jet aircraft then coming into use, and for this purpose the Japanese Government began a survey of the private land at the end of the runway in Sunakawa. Leftist groups, who had long been trying to stir up popular opposition to U.S. bases all over Japan, found Sunakawa well suited to their purpose: it was much closer to Tokyo (eighty minutes by car) than, for example, Uchinada or Asama, and demonstrators could be easily mobilized and taken to the area. The air base was important to the U.S. Air Force, and the Japanese Government was committed to extending the runway.

On November 5, 1955, leftist students and labor unionists tried to block the survey and clashed with police in a rough brawl in which seventy were injured and three arrested. As plans for requisitioning the private land proceeded, leftist groups made a national "cause" out of the affair. They used the theme that the United States was lengthening the runway in order to accommodate larger jet bombers for use in nuclear aggression against Russia and China, and they tried to dramatize the plight of the poor farmers who were being "robbed of their

131

hereditary land" for these militaristic objectives. There were more clashes, and on July 8, 1957, 300 labor unionists and students broke through a barbed-wire fence and onto the runway at Tachikawa. This time seven leaders were arrested and tried.[14] On March 30, 1959, a sensational verdict was handed down by Tokyo District Court Judge Date Akio: the seven were acquitted and the constitutionality of the security treaty itself was denied.

Judge Date held that the law under which the seven were being tried (The Law for Special Measures Concerning Criminal Cases) violated Article XXXI of the Constitution (which contains Japan's "due process" clause).[15] The law, which gave special legal protection to U.S. troops, would be constitutional if the stationing of these troops in Japan were in itself constitutional. But, declared the Judge, U.S. troops in Japan constituted war potential, and Article IX of the Constitution prohibits Japan from maintaining any kind of war potential, even for self-defense. Judge Date referred to the pacific spirit and intent of the Japanese Constitution in his reasoning, and concluded that if the presence of U.S. troops were unconstitutional, then there was no reason for them to enjoy privileged protection under Article II of the Law for Special Measures Concerning Criminal Cases. Such protection, he held, would violate Article XXXI of the Constitution.

Judge Date's decision hit the Japanese Government like a bombshell. Not only did it cast grave doubts on the validity of the security treaty, but it also undermined the entire foreign policy of successive Japanese Governments since the Peace Treaty of 1951. Furthermore, it came at the moment when the conservatives were feuding over the revised treaty draft. The left wing, buoyed up by its success in blocking Kishi's Police Bill in late 1958, and embarking on the anti-treaty Peo-

[14] The seven were indicted under Article II of the Law for Special Measures Concerning Criminal Cases, one of the domestic laws enacted specifically to implement the administrative agreement under the security treaty.

[15] Article XXXI states: "No person shall be deprived of life or liberty, nor shall any other criminal penalty be imposed, except according to procedure established by law."

ple's Council drive in March 1959, was overjoyed with this welcome boost for its publicity campaign against the treaty.

The government lost no time in appealing the decision to the Supreme Court, where a new trial opened in September 1959.[16] The trial was attended by heated discussion in the press and full publicity across the nation; the issues were crucial and without precedent. The government pressed for a quick decision so that the treaty negotiations, which had already dragged on for a year, might be quickly concluded. The seven defendants were aided by a battery of some 280 lawyers led by prominent Socialist Unno Shinkichi, Director of the Japan Civil Liberties Union.

The Supreme Court held six public sessions on the case and handed down its decision on December 16, 1959: it unanimously rescinded the Date verdict and sent the case back to the District Court for retrial. The Supreme Court took the position that Article IX of the Constitution did not prohibit Japan from taking measures necessary to preserve her existence. What Article IX did prohibit, said the court, was war potential maintained by Japan for the purpose of waging wars of aggression. U.S. troops in Japan did not constitute such prohibited war potential, nor did they violate the peaceful intent of Article IX.[17] The court did not rule on the question of whether or not the security treaty was valid; this question, it said, was a political matter that should be determined by the Diet, the cabinet, and ultimately by the people.

With the constitutionality of the treaty thus removed from the shadows, the government pressed forward with final negotiations on the revised treaty, which was ready for signing three weeks later. The Supreme Court's reversal came as a severe blow to the leftists. The momentum they had hoped to create for the anti-treaty movement in 1959 was simply not up to ex-

[16] A useful summary of the trial is found in Alfred C. Oppler, "The Sunakawa Case: Its Legal and Political Implications," *Political Science Quarterly*, Vol. 76, No. 2, June 1961, pp. 241–263. See also John M. Maki, *Court and Constitution in Japan*, Seattle: University of Washington Press, 1964, Chapter 23.

[17] The Supreme Court avoided, however, the sensitive issue of whether or not Japan's own Self-defense Forces were constitutional.

133

pectations, and the unanimity of the Court's decision hurt their cause with the public. It may have helped to convince some leftists that the only way to fight the treaty was to resort to mass violence. The Socialists, who for the first time had fought the conservatives on a major issue through the judicial process rather than in the Diet or in the streets, immediately accused the Supreme Court of political partiality and said that it had betrayed the concept of an independent judiciary. In any event, the trial helped keep the treaty issue on the front pages for much of 1959 and the Date decision of March 30 was a stimulus for the left and a shock for the right as long as it stood. The trial itself probably raised new doubts about the security treaty in the public mind.

The Anti-treaty Forces, 1959

The campaign against the revised security treaty began officially with the gathering of leftist forces under the People's Council in March 1959 and ran through the rest of the year in ten "united action" drives. As we saw in the last chapter, these drives were coordinated with the major Sōhyō campaigns and were almost identical with the traditional labor offensives of postwar Japan. There were two new features, however: a hardening of anti-treaty sentiment among older organizations and the appearance of new groups set up specifically to oppose treaty revision. In both cases, the result was a vast outflow of anti-treaty propaganda. The leftist campaign followed the basic principle that the attack on the treaty must be many-faceted: each leftist organization was instructed to support the attack in ways suited to its special concerns. In other words, pro-Peking groups would stress how the new treaty would damage Sino-Japanese relations; leftist lawyers would bring out the legal "defects" in the treaty; leftist scholars would use their prestige, publications, and influence to alert students and intellectuals to the dangers of the new treaty; and leftist journalists would publicize the anti-government campaign.[18]

[18] Of course the JSP attack in the Diet was an important part of the overall campaign; a discussion of the Diet debate will be found in the following two chapters.

Among the older left wing organizations, Sōhyō led the way. At its 12th National Convention in August and September 1959, Sōhyō took its most radical line in recent years, voting down a motion to give exclusive support to the Japan Socialist Party and pledging to ". . . lead all Japanese workers in their fight to crush the Kishi Government's attempt to revise the Japan–U.S. Security Treaty." [19] At this convention, Sōhyō launched an extraordinary fund-raising campaign, approving a special assessment of 45 yen (about 12 cents) per head which was designed to increase yearly revenue by 150 percent over the 1959–1960 total and bring 114 million yen (about $317,000) into its coffers.[20]

The main theme of Sōhyō's anti-treaty campaign was that the treaty lay at the heart of all the problems of Japan's laboring masses. The foremost labor problem in Japan during 1959 was the displacement of coal miners by the "energy revolution," and Sōhyō therefore used the discontented coal mine unionists in Tanrō as the spearhead of its anti-treaty rallies and demonstrations in the fall of 1959. Politically active unions geared their particular protests into the anti-treaty campaign. The Japan Teachers' Union (Nikkyōsō), for example, staged classroom walkouts on September 8, 1959—the day of the People's Council's 6th United Action—to protest the teachers' efficiency rating system. Other unions, such as those of the journalists and press workers, and railway and public enterprise workers, passed resolutions at their yearly conventions pledging to fight harder against the treaty.

The Socialist Party took steps outside the Diet to stir up anti-treaty sentiment. At a meeting of the Party's CEC on July 4, 1959, it was decided that twenty-two teams of Socialist leaders would tour Japan from July 25 to August 5 making anti-treaty speeches. Seminars for rural party members were also planned and carried out during August. The party did not appear to be overly successful outside of Tokyo and the larger cities, and in

[19] *Japan Times*, August 30, 1959.

[20] This new assessment was large by comparison with the previous assessment of annual dues, which ranged from 1.02 to 3.2 yen per month per head. *Japan Times*, article by Horii Etsurō, September 13, 1959.

late October 1959, a new drive was launched to enlist the help of the farmers. A liaison council was set up to coordinate the various leftist farmers' organizations, and signature drives were begun in all the prefectures. The theme of the JSP campaign was originally the idea that the treaty meant war for Japan, but it gradually shifted during 1959 to the bread and butter issues: the farmers were told, for example, how the treaty robbed them of their livelihood and harmed the Japanese economy in general. On other fronts, the Socialists hounded the conservatives with speeches, press conferences, and rallies, criticizing Kishi's handling of the treaty negotiations, hinting that the LDP Government was "selling out" to U.S. imperialists, and raising the spectre of an unwanted war resulting from U.S. "adventures" in the Far East.

The attack on the treaty came in surprising strength from another quarter—from new "private" (*minkan*) organizations of "men of culture" (*bunkajin*) formed solely for the purpose of resisting treaty revision.[21] Leading these groups were the "progressive intellectuals," including many of the famous professors and writers who had been bitter opponents of the alliance since 1951. These intellectuals had played an important rôle in fomenting the great national debate over the treaty in 1957 when they issued a statement on February 28 of that year (fifth anniversary of the signing of the administrative agreement) calling for a reexamination of the security treaty.[22] As discussion and debate wore on from 1957 to 1959, a great variety of solutions sprang up; the more radical among them favored outright abolition of the treaty, while others were for negotiations with the United States to eliminate the most annoying features of the treaty.

Around mid-1959, however, opinion among the progressive intellectuals began to solidify into uncompromising opposition

---

[21] Though these organizations were newly formed, many of them were directed either overtly or from behind-the-scenes by familiar leftist figures.

[22] This statement, entitled "Ampo Jōyaku Saikentō Seimeisho" (Statement on the Reexamination of the Security Treaty), *Asahi Shimbun*, March 1, 1957, blamed the recent Sunakawa tragedy on the "San Francisco system," and called for a great popular movement for treaty revision.

to treaty revision by the Kishi Government. In December 1959 the influential Peace Problems Symposium (Heiwa Mondai Konwa Kai) issued a new statement opposing treaty revision and alleging that the Japanese Government and people would have to take responsibility for any new treaty in the eyes of the Soviet Union and Communist China, whereas in 1951 they had been forced into signing. The group took the remarkable stand that the existing treaty had no definite term and *was therefore provisional in nature*, while the new treaty had a definite ten-year term and would thus lose its provisional character. Other defects in the new treaty, according to the statement, were that it would strengthen Japan's objectionable social and political structure, damage relations with Communist China, increase the chances of war, and lead to the buildup of the munitions industry in Japan. The group called for Japan to do away with the old game of power politics and rely for her security on the peaceful spirit of the Constitution, thus following in the footsteps of her Meiji Period ancestors and leading Asia on a new path to modernization.[23]

This interesting shift in opinion was typified by the attitude of Professor Nakano Yoshio, a well-known leftist intellectual and a signer of the above statement.[24] In the April 1959 issue of *Sekai*, Professor Nakano wrote that it might not be wise to take an unyielding stand against treaty revision, if the revision were such that it would lead eventually to the treaty's abolition. In the following September, however, Nakano wrote a

[23] Heiwa Mondai Konwa Kai (Peace Problems Symposium), "Ampo Kaitei Mondai ni Tsuite no Seimei" (Declaration Regarding the Security Treaty Issue), *Sekai*, February 1960, pp. 12–17.

[24] Born in 1894 in Ōita Prefecture, Professor Nakano graduated from the Philosophy Department of Tokyo Imperial University and later specialized in the philosophy of education. Long a student of John Dewey, and more recently, of the philosophy of materialism, he has been a leading advocate of educational reform in Japan. With his frequent contributions to *Sekai* magazine and his outspoken views on political matters, Nakano has been typical of many leftist intellectuals in the postwar era. He played a major rôle in opposing the revised security treaty in 1960, serving for a time on the Board of Directors of the Tokyo Joint Struggle Council for Safeguarding Peace and Democracy, one of the thirteen original sponsors of the People's Council.

second article in *Sekai* in which he withdrew even tentative support for the revised treaty: "Unfortunately, my previous conclusion must be changed," he wrote. The revised treaty must be opposed unconditionally, not simply because it originated with the conservatives, but because it embodied the Vandenburg Resolution principle (forcing Japan to rearm), and because the mutual defense area would be expanded to include the whole of the Western Pacific.[25]

Almost all of the progressive intellectuals, excepting those attracted to the emerging DSP, appeared to accept Nakano's reasoning, and the formation of effective action groups against the treaty began. Given the strong Marxist and anti-American leanings of many leading intellectuals in Japan—intellectuals who accepted without question that the U.S. started the Korean War in 1950—it was not surprising that they opposed the LDP move to revise the treaty. Less easy to explain, however, was their almost unanimous agreement that the revised treaty would be worse for Japan than the original one, even though the revised treaty contained a ten-year limit while the original had no provision at all for Japan to get out of the alliance. The partisan reasons for the left wing to oppose Kishi's attempt at treaty revision are clear, but among the progressive intellectuals, who generally claimed independence from the parties, not one (to this writer's knowledge) stood up to say that the revised treaty, with its time limit, offered Japan a better hope than the original for abolishing the military alliance.[26]

The first and best known of the new organizations was the Treaty Problems Research Association (Ampo Mondai Kenkyū Kai). This was originally a symposium of eighty-seven intellectuals (Bunkajin Kondankai) which issued a statement on March 23, 1959, against treaty revision and immediately began a signature drive in support of their statement.[27] It formally organ-

[25] Nakano Yoshio, "Kimyō na Gaikō Kōshō wa Tsuzuku" (The Strange Diplomatic Negotiations Continue), *Sekai*, No. 165, September 1959, pp. 27–28.

[26] An article on intellectuals' groups against the treaty appears in *Mainichi Shimbun*, October 8, 1959.

[27] *Tokyo Shimbun*, March 24, 1959 contains the gist of this statement.

ized itself on July 7, 1959, under the name Treaty Problems Research Association with some 2,000 scholars, teachers, and other intellectuals participating.[28] Among the active leaders were Shimizu Ikutarō and Hidaka Rokurō, while such "figureheads" as Mutai Risaku, Uehara Senroku, and Aono Suekichi lent their prestige by serving on the board. The purpose of the new organization was to publicize the shortcomings of the revised treaty and use the combined strength of many famous intellectuals to turn public opinion against it.

The Treaty Problems Research Association attracted nationwide attention by presenting to Foreign Minister Fujiyama an open letter with eight questions on the new treaty on October 17, 1959.[29] The eight questions summarized the criticisms of the draft treaty first published in October 1959. How did the treaty fit in with the recent relaxation of world tension? Why doesn't Japan take the lead in world disarmament? Isn't ten years too long? The questions also suggested that the new treaty was a collective defense pact prohibited by the Constitution, that neutralism was the best guarantee of Japan's security, that relations with Communist China would be worsened and new obligations placed on Japan. Finally, there was a demand for a specific treaty provision outlawing nuclear weapons in Japan.

Foreign Minister Fujiyama's lengthy reply to these questions on November 7, 1959, drew new criticism from the Treaty Problems Research Association on November 24. Fujiyama stated, in sum, that world tensions still existed despite the recent thaw, that the new treaty was far better than the existing one, self-defense was not prohibited by the Constitution, that neutralism was only a sham by which the Communists hoped to pull Japan into their camp, and that the treaty was entirely defensive. He repeated his earlier points that prior consultations

[28] *Mainichi Shimbun*, July 8, 1959, has an account of the inauguration.

[29] The text and Fujiyama's replies are found in Usui Yoshimi, ed., *Gendai Kyōyō Zenshū Bekkan* (Modern Culture Collection, Special Supplement), *1960: Nihon Seiji no Shoten* (1960: Focus of Japanese Politics), Tokyo: Chikuma Publishing Co., 1960, pp. 33–51. See also *Asahi Shimbun*, October 17 and November 8, 1959.

would give Japan an equal hand in the alliance, and that the new treaty need not bar relations with Communist China. The Treaty Problems Research Association countered that Kishi was leaving Japanese foreign policy in the hands of the United States, accused the government of "anachronistic thinking," and said that growing defense spending was a serious threat to the people's livelihood.[30] In this way the group focused national attention on the new treaty and publicized its opposition. It also worked to collect signatures, influence other intellectuals, and bolster the various united action drives against the treaty.

Two other important groups of intellectuals sprang up in 1959 to oppose the revised treaty. The Association for Criticizing the Security Treaty (Ampo Hihan no Kai) was founded on November 9, 1959, under the energetic leadership of such leftist writers as Nakajima Kenzō and Matsuoka Yōko.[31] This group collected a somewhat broader class of intellectuals, including many of the younger artists, writers, playwrights, critics, and popular performers. The leaders tried to draw "new blood" into the anti-treaty movement by focusing on the treaty issue alone, rather than on the whole range of leftist protests. The leadership, however, remained in the hands of intellectuals who were either pro-Communist or left Socialist in orientation. The Association was closely connected with the Japan Journalists' Congress (Nihon Jānarisuto Kaigi), where it had its headquarters, and the Japan P.E.N. Club, of which Miss Matsuoka was General Secretary. It distributed some 30,000 copies of a pamphlet called *Dangerous Treaty*, written by the Japan Journalists' Congress, which claimed to expose the leaders of the pro-treaty conspiracy within the LDP; the fact that many members of the Congress covered the anti-treaty movement for the large newspapers meant that a strong anti-Kishi flavor would pervade the news.[32] The Association also sponsored its own lectures and rallies and cooperated with the People's Council.

[30] *Yomiuri Shimbun*, November 25, 1959.

[31] See *Asahi Shimbun*, October 15, 1959 and November 10, 1959; also *Sankei Shimbun*, November 9, 1959.

[32] Nihon Jānarisuto Kaigi, "Kiken na Jōyaku" (Dangerous Treaty), pamphlet, Tokyo: Nihon Hyōron Shinsha, 1959.

Another new organization was the Jurists' Congress for Preventing the Revision of the Japan–U.S. Security Treaty (Ampo Kaitei Soshi Horitsuka Kaigi), a group of some 200 leftist law scholars and practicing attorneys led by Unno Shinkichi, who was chief counsel for the defense in the Sunakawa trial.[33] Established on December 5, 1959, the group issued an anti-treaty appeal to some 10,000 lawyers in Japan, pointing out what it found to be the chief legal faults of the revised draft treaty.

Many other official and unofficial groups added to the stream of anti-treaty verbiage. The pamphlet war was opened by a lawyers' group (Seinen Horitsuka Kyōkai, Goken Bengoshi Dan) which in June 1959 sold 70,000 copies of a small tract called *Problems of Treaty Revision (Ampo Jōyaku Kaitei o Meguru Mondai)*. This was followed in July 1959 with a pamphlet called *Block Treaty Revision with the Power of the People, and Restore Japan-China Relations (Kokumin no Chikara de Ampo Kaitei Soshi, Nitchū Kokkō Kaifuku e)* which was put out in an edition of 10,000 copies by the Japan-China Cultural Exchange Association (Nihon Chūgoku Bunka Kōryū Kyōkai). One of the most widely read of all was the "handbook" published by the powerful Iwanami Company as a special anti-treaty appendix to the November 1959 issue of *Sekai*. *Sekai*, which has a regular circulation of around 100,000, printed an extra 50,000 of these handbooks (*Ampo Kaitei Mondai Handobukku*) for labor unions and women's groups.[34]

The flowering of all this anti-treaty activity was not, it seems, accompanied by any massive shift in public opinion against the new treaty. What was significant, however, was the fact that these new organizations were established and functioning well in advance of the actual signing of the treaty in January 1960. They were poised and ready, therefore, to strike at the government from the very moment the Diet ratification debate began. They did succeed, moreover, in enlisting the support and active participation of scholars and intellectuals in a purely political movement to an extent unprecedented in modern Japanese his-

[33] Other prominent members of this group were Nagano Kunisuke, Mizuno Tōtarō, Yasui Kaoru, Satō Isao, and Suekawa Hiroshi.

[34] *Nihon Keizai Shimbun*, November 25, 1959.

tory. The conservatives and Kishi Government got off to a late start in the public relations race.

The Pro-treaty Forces, 1959

Conservative critics of Kishi and Fujiyama have often charged that the government and LDP stood idly by and did nothing to counter the growing leftist offensive against the revised security treaty. This is a charge that will not stand up under close scrutiny. While the effectiveness of their pro-treaty propaganda may be questioned, and despite their shaky start, the government, LDP leaders, and other conservative groups took a number of measures to "sell" the new treaty to the Japanese people.

As early as December 1958 the government, staggering from its failure to pass the Police Bill, appeared to grasp the danger of massive popular demonstrations. At the urging of several business leaders, a group called the National Conference on Security Treaty Problems (Ampo Jōyaku Mondai Zenkoku Konwa Kai) was founded on December 15, 1958. This conservative group had strong support from the government, especially the Foreign Ministry, though it was ostensibly a private organization. Led by Hasegawa Saiji, Managing Director of the Jiji Press, the Conference set up branches in the leading cities and sought members from the upper ranks of business, financial, cultural, press, and publishing circles. A former President of the House of Councillors, Satō Naotake, became Chairman, and the seventeen sponsors included Adachi Tadashi, President of the Japan Chamber of Commerce and Industry, Azuma Ryūtarō, Governor of Tokyo, Itō Masanori, of the editorial board of *Sankei Shimbun*, Fukushima Shintarō, President of the *Japan Times*, Yabe Teiji, President of Takushoku University, as well as noted commentators Mitarai Tatsuo, Muraoka Hanako, Inaba Shūzō, and Sakanishi Shio. The new organization became, in effect, a forum for the views of Foreign Minister Fujiyama, who traveled and lectured on the treaty under its auspices in Tokyo, Osaka, Nagoya, Sendai, Takamatsu, and elsewhere during 1959. The Conference printed a series of eight pamphlets, called *Conference Material* (*Kondan Shiryō*), Nos.

142

1–8 between December 1958 and February 1960. In them were the speeches of Fujiyama and others giving economic, political, and military reasons why Japan should keep its ties with the free world. Complex points in the new treaty were clarified and Socialist arguments rebutted.

Whatever else these efforts proved, one certain result was that Fujiyama gained considerable publicity and projected himself for the first time as a figure of national political stature. Indeed, he was the only high LDP figure to take the government's case before the people until the fall of 1959; Kishi and the others were tied up, as we have seen, with the thorny problem of adjusting factional differences. It is not likely that he scored much success in converting the nation as a whole to his ideas, for the conference seemed to attract only those moderates and conservatives who could be expected in the end to favor treaty revision anyway, and he did not appear to reach the vital "floating vote" sector of the public whose support Kishi would need in time of crisis.

The LDP began discussing ways to combat the People's Council in late June 1959. The main obstacle was that party leaders were still at odds among themselves, and could scarcely launch a publicity drive for a government policy that was still subject to change in important respects. At a meeting of the party's seven top executives on July 21, 1959, it was finally decided that the LDP's Public Relations Committee should distribute between one and two million pamphlets spelling out the party's aims in revising the treaty. It was also decided that challenges from the left for open debates would be accepted.[35] The pamphlet, called "Why Is the Japan–U.S. Security Treaty Being Revised?" (*Nichi-bei Ampo Jōyaku o Naze Kaitei Suru Ka?*) appeared in late July and marked the beginning of the LDP's positive drive to win popular support. Forty-two pages were devoted to arguments stressing the independence, security, and prosperity the treaty would bring to Japan, and the remaining thirty-nine had questions and answers devoted to rejecting left-

[35] For further information on the new counteroffensive, see *Mainichi Shimbun*, July 5, 1959, and *Sankei Shimbun*, July 25, 1959.

ist arguments. The pamphlet did serve to rekindle public debate over the treaty; the Socialists considered it important enough to warrant several heated rebuttals, and the press gave it considerable publicity.[36] Unhappily for the LDP, Kōno Ichirō publicly denounced the LDP pamphlet and continued his attacks on the revised treaty plan while the pamphlet was being distributed.

The LDP's next act was to hold a "National Organization and Information Conference" (Zenkoku Soshiki Kōhō Kaigi) in Tokyo on September 9, 1959, attended by about 200 representatives of regional supporting organizations. At this conference, Kishi, Kawashima Shōjirō, and Funada Naka made speeches in behalf of the revised treaty.

The LDP then accepted a Socialist challenge to a public debate and on October 1, 1959, Prime Minister Kishi and Funada Naka of the LDP clashed with JSP Chairman Suzuki Mosaburō and Katsumata Seiichi at Sankei Hall, Tokyo. The debate, carried to the nation by the Japan Broadcasting Company, brought out familiar arguments on both sides, but revealed a somewhat new approach by the Socialists. Instead of arguing that the treaty would lead Japan to disaster, they now stressed the new "spirit of Camp David" (brought on by Khrushchev's visit to Washington in September 1959) and claimed that the new treaty would run counter to the growing trend toward peaceful coexistence in the world. The conservatives were accused of trying to prevent the new "thaw." Kishi struck back with the assertion that neutralism was "pure illusion" in today's world and that, despite the temporary thaw, many problems remained to be solved before Japan could loosen her alliance with the United States.[37]

There were two other conservative groups that worked to promote the idea of treaty revision in 1959. One was the "Peo-

[36] See, for example, the series of twenty articles on the revised treaty in *Mainichi Shimbun* between August 21 and September 12, 1959; see also *Tokyo Shimbun*, August 17–18, 1959.

[37] For an account of the debate, see *Mainichi Shimbun*, October 2, 1959; see also the round table discussion in *Sankei Shimbun*, October 23, 1959, "Yukidoke to Ampo" (The Thaw and Treaty Revision) by Fujiyama, Sone Eki, and Ōya Sōichi.

144

ple's League for the Revision of the Security Treaty" (Ampo Kaitei Kokumin Rengō) which held its inaugural meeting of 300 people on September 5, 1959. This group was sponsored by forty well-known figures such as Kamikawa Hikomatsu, former Tokyo University professor, Takayama Iwao, Japan University professor, Abe Shinnosuke, journalist and later Chairman of the Japan Broadcasting Company, and Imamura Hitoshi, former general. These leaders, sometimes called "democratic conservatives," seemed to be setting up a counterpart to the leftist People's Council, but never succeeded in gathering the momentum of the latter organization. Branches were set up in all the prefectures, and the organization sponsored lectures for women's groups, distributed 300,000 cartoon-type booklets called *Easy Guide to Treaty Revision* (*Ampo Kaitei Hayawakari*) and printed some 200,000 handbills. The group spread the theme of "peace and prosperity" under the security treaty and branded unarmed neutrality as the first step toward Japan's ruin.[38]

The second new organization was the "Security Research Group" (Anzen Hoshō Kenkyū Kai) consisting of some twenty prominent legal scholars. This group, which was the conservative answer to the leftist lawyers' and scholars' groups, was led by Ichimata Masao, Ōhira Zengo, and Maebara Mitsuo, deans of the respective law departments of Waseda, Hitotsubashi, and Keio Universities.[39] On December 12, 1959, they delivered a statement to Foreign Minister Fujiyama supporting the government's position on treaty revision.[40] The statement observed that diplomatic problems must be seen from a national, nonpartisan, nonideological viewpoint. "Prevention of the revision means the retention of the existing treaty; in other words, no improvement of the *status quo*," it said.[41] The statement went on to point out that the amended treaty would represent several steps of progress over the existing one; it also took the un-

[38] *Nihon Keizai Shimbun,* November 25, 1959.

[39] This group was also referred to in the press as the "Law Scholars' Group" (Hōgakusha Gurūpu).

[40] The statement, "Our Position on the Amendment of the Japan–U.S. Security Treaty," may be found in English in the *Japan Times,* December 23, 1959; see also *Asahi Shimbun,* December 13, 1959.

[41] *Japan Times,* December 23, 1959.

usual (for intellectuals) position that self-defense was permissible under the Constitution. The statement, representing the views of some of Japan's most eminent legal scholars, was notable in that it was the only act by scholars in unconditional support of treaty revision during the entire campaign. Almost all other professors and researchers were either silent or active in support of the opposition. Perhaps sociologists will some day explain why many of Japan's leading experts in international law favored treaty revision while many other scholars, particularly the political scientists, were in the vanguard of the movement against it.

Other smaller conservative groups backed treaty revision. Among these was the Yūshi no Kai, a group of some 200 young university graduates who had originally joined together in 1950 as students to fight the pro-JCP Zengakuren, and later kept their organization alive, despite demanding careers in widely different areas of government, business, teaching, and journalism. They published one of the most convincing pamphlets in favor of treaty revision, entitled, A *Youthful Sound Judgment on Treaty Revision*,[42] and worked hard to persuade their circle of friends that revision was a good idea.

Whatever effect these pro-treaty efforts may have had on the Japanese people, they did not, it is safe to say, succeed in countering the vast leftist propaganda campaign against the treaty. Of course it is always harder to persuade people to take to the streets *for* a cause than *against* it—particularly when the cause is a complicated legal document. But there are other, more basic reasons why the conservatives did not have great success. First, the LDP hurt itself by publicly wrangling over the treaty negotiations at the time when it was trying to sell the new treaty to the people. The arguments used by faction leaders against each other made good ammunition for the opposition. Second, the conservative propaganda did not reach down into lower echelons of society as did the leftists'. It was aimed, characteristically, at the leaders of conservative organizations rather than at the masses. Third, the leading businessmen who provided most of the LDP's funds at election times seemed reluctant

[42] *Ampo Kaitei ni Yoseru Wakaki Ryōshiki no Iken*, supplement to *Keizai Ōrai*, December 1959.

to support a massive "PR" campaign.[43] Fourth, the pro-treaty groups were late in getting started, compared with their leftist counterparts. Finally, the conservatives were somewhat defensive in their treatment of the issues. For example, by continually denying that the new treaty would lead Japan into war, they gave added publicity to JSP charges that the treaty would do exactly that. They could have stressed the positive benefits of the treaty and its deterrent value more fully. It appears that the LDP, though it exerted itself to some degree, was relying heavily on its large Diet majority, and that it did not yet fully appreciate the flammability of the treaty issue among an aroused people.

Public Opinion on the Treaty Issue, 1959

How did all the furor—the pamphlets, handbills, lectures, rallies, debates, broadcasts, and public statements affect the "man in the street" during 1959? Was he living in a state of excitement over the forthcoming Diet debate, or was he bored, apathetic, struggling to understand the issues? To approach this question, we are forced to rely on surveys of public opinion conducted by the major newspapers and the government, for there were no elections between June 1959 and November 1960 that could give a clue to trends in popular thought. Most Japanese adults are avid newspaper readers, and they were bombarded with news of treaty revision almost daily throughout the year. Between April and October, 1959 more than 200 editorials in the leading dailies addressed themselves to the problem.[44] The press told readers again and again that the issue was the biggest of the year and that the nation's future was at stake. Though most newspapers did not openly take sides during 1959, some expressed doubts and reservations about the way negotiations

[43] The "financial circles" (*zaikai*) had already been tapped in 1959 for a reported 550,000,000 yen (about $1,500,000) for the local and House of Councillors elections of April and June. The LDP's request for another 300,000,000 (about $833,000) for a pro-treaty publicity campaign met with "sour faces" (*shibui kao*) among the regular party donors. *Tokyo Shimbun* (evening), November 6, 1959, and *Mainichi Shimbun*, November 11, 1959.

[44] According to a survey conducted by the Japan Newspaper Publishers and Editors Association, whose results appeared in the *Japan Times*, November 17, 1960.

were progressing, and exhorted the government to pursue their "wishes" on specific points.

The first of the important tests of public opinion was run by the *Tokyo Shimbun* in July 1959—some three months after the People's Council launched its offensive against the revised treaty.[45] The following were some of the questions and results:

> Q: Are you well informed on the current treaty revision issues?
> A: Well informed   16.6%
>   Somewhat informed   65.1%
>   Not informed   18.3%
>
> Q: Do you think that the new treaty will involve Japan in war or make Japan more secure?
> A: Likely to involve Japan in war   44.5%
>   Guarantees Japan's security   21.5%
>   Don't know   34.0%
>
> Q: Which course should Japan follow to protect her security?
> A: Side with the free world   45.3%
>   Join the Communist Bloc   1.6%
>   Adopt Indian-style neutralism   36.0%
>   Other   1.8%
>   Don't know   15.3%

(It is notable here that less than half the respondents favored siding with the free world and that almost none wished Japan to join the Communist Bloc.)

> Q: Are you generally in favor of treaty revision, opposed to it, or do you wish to abolish the treaty altogether?
> A: In favor of revision   31.1%
>   Opposed to revision   10.8%
>   Wish to abolish the treaty   16.9%
>   Don't know   41.2%

[45] The poll was run by the *Tokyo Shimbun* in cooperation with the Public Opinion Science Association (Kōron Kagaku Kyōkai) by a random stratified sample, with 79.7% responding. *Tokyo Shimbun*, July 19, 1959.

Here, the "don't knows" are sizable; this may partly be explained by the fact that no version of the new treaty had as yet been made public, and that the LDP was still battling internally. Another question asked in this poll showed that the respondents were overwhelmingly (75.0 percent) in favor of "prior consultations" in any new treaty.

In August 1959 another nationwide poll was conducted by the *Mainichi Shimbun*, which asked somewhat different questions.[46]

Q: Did you know that the government was planning to revise the security treaty soon?

A: Did know 71.2%
Didn't know 24.8%
Didn't know there was a treaty 3.5%
No response 0.5%

Q: Did you know that the JSP, Sōhyō, and others were opposing the government's plan to revise the treaty?

A: Did know 54.1%
Not too familiar 34.0%
Didn't know 9.5%
No response 2.4%

Q: What do you think of the present security treaty?

A: All right as it stands 12.5%
Should be revised right away 7.2%
Should be revised, but not necessarily now 20.6%
Should be abolished now 6.4%
Should be abolished eventually 13.0%
Other 0.4%
No interest 11.4%
Don't know 24.8%
No response 3.7%

[46] This poll was conducted between August 10–12, 1959, by a random stratified sample of eligible voters, with 3,240 responding out of 4,130 approached in 295 localities throughout Japan. The results were published in *Mainichi Shimbun*, August 26, 1959.

149

THE APPROACHING STORM

These answers reveal the great variety of opinion about the treaty in Japan before 1960.

The *Yomiuri Shimbun* conducted its own nationwide poll in late September 1959 with these results: [47]

Q: Are you very interested in the current treaty revision problem?
A: Very interested   14%
    Somewhat interested   43%
    Not interested   43%

Q: Which is the best course for Japan: siding with the U.S. and free world, siding with the Soviet Union and Communist China, or neutrality?
A: Siding with U.S. and free world   26%
    Siding with Soviet Union and Communist China   1%
    Neutrality   50%
    Don't know   23%

Q: If the security treaty were abolished and all military ties with the U.S. cut, would you be worried about aggression from the Communist Bloc?
A: Would worry   28%
    Would not worry   27%
    Don't know   45%

Q: Do you think the Japan–U.S. Security Treaty is necessary or unnecessary?
A: Necessary   46%
    Unnecessary   12%
    Don't know   42%

This poll showed some of the deep uncertainty about the worth of the treaty that existed through all Japan: was there really a threat? Wasn't neutrality safer? Was the treaty needed at all?

[47] This poll was conducted on September 26–27, 1959, by the *Yomiuri Shimbun* in 219 places by a random stratified sample, using the direct interview method with 2,593 responding. *Yomiuri Shimbun*, October 4, 1959.

Less than half the people seemed to be certain that the treaty was serving them well.

The Prime Minister's Office began probing the minds of the citizens in late July 1959 and announced its findings on October 9, 1959.[48]

> Q: Did you know that treaty revision has recently become a problem?
> A: Did know   50%
>   Didn't know   50%

(Only 11 percent of the total could name specific points in the treaty to be revised.)

> Q: Are you in favor of or opposed to the present treaty?
> A: In favor   15%
>   Opposed   10%
>   Can't say in general terms, undecided   25%
>   Unaware of the problem (above)   50%

> Q: Are you in favor of or opposed to Japan's general cooperation with the U.S. in the future?
> A: In favor   53%
>   Opposed   17%
>   Uncertain   30%

> Q: Are you in favor of or opposed to increasing our self-defense strength?
> A: In favor   43%
>   Opposed   30%
>   Undecided   27%

Since public opinion surveys can be used to prove almost anything, particularly in Japan where, one suspects, the press and government appear to suit them to their respective "moods," and where they are still something of a novelty, we should be cautious in jumping to firm conclusions from the above. Cer-

[48] This poll, conducted by the Central Research Company (*Chūō Chōsa Sha*) at the government's request, drew 8,444 responses from 10,000 eligible voters in 137 cities and towns and 147 villages throughout Japan, using the direct interview method. *Yomiuri Shimbun* (evening), October 9, 1959.

tainly the urban-rural split in Japanese politics accounts for some of the apparent apathy in the midst of the political tension; it would have been interesting to poll Tokyo's voters alone on these issues. Even so, it is surprising that the polls showed so little interest in or knowledge of this vital diplomatic problem. It supports the conclusion that the great outpouring of emotion in May and June 1960 owed less to the treaty revision problem itself than to Prime Minister Kishi's handling of it.

The polls do suggest that there was no clear mandate for Kishi to proceed with treaty revision in 1959—that the national consensus of 1957 in favor of treaty revision had broken down along sharp political lines, that the nation was deeply divided over specific issues and unclear on the best foreign policy choice for Japan. Despite the hardening of organizational and ideological lines in the pro- and anti-treaty camps, the giant "PR" campaigns, and the columns and pages of comment on the issue, it appears that the "man in the street"—if such an individual existed—was quietly pursuing his own affairs and suspending judgment until more of the facts were in.

The year 1959 witnessed events that were to have a profound influence on the future: Though the public was not yet aroused or even unified on any particular point, the treaty revision issue had been thrust before the nation as the most crucial policy decision since the end of World War II. The battle lines were drawn and the heat and tension from Japan's longstanding political division had now been tied irrevocably to the fate of the new treaty. Thousands of political ambitions rested on the fortunes of Kishi and his bid for a diplomatic triumph.

CHAPTER 5

November 27 and the Signing of the Treaty

THE STRUGGLE over the revised security treaty was well underway before the final draft was negotiated, with the left wing in Japan "absolutely opposed" not only to the idea of revising the treaty but also to any form of military alliance with the United States. The first major test of strength between the two sides occurred as the People's Council fought to prevent Prime Minister Kishi from signing the revised treaty in Washington. Though it received little press coverage outside Japan, this battle was fought in deadly earnest, and in retrospect we can see that it played an important—perhaps decisive—rôle in shaping the events of 1960.

The Diet had discussed treaty revision periodically since the beginning of negotiations in 1958; but during 1959, this single issue came to involve and overshadow all others. There were, of course, other vital matters before the Diet: a Socialist proposal for renouncing nuclear weapons, the government's decision to buy Lockheed Starfighters, the minimum wage bill, a new defense bill, the fisheries agreement with the Soviet Union, the Vietnam reparations bill, and the perennial problems of Okinawa and Communist China, but all of these somehow became entangled in the controversy over the new treaty. As negotiations drew toward a close in the fall of 1959 the two parties, which had been quite literally at each other's throats all year, prepared for a climactic debate; tempers were short and tension mounted so that normal proceedings in the Diet became nearly impossible.

Under these circumstances the nation had its first look at the draft of the new security treaty on October 6, 1959. After three weeks of commentary by the press and public figures—much of it skeptical—the 33rd Extraordinary Diet convened on October 28 to consider the draft.[1] Kishi, still weakened by his

[1] *Asahi Shimbun* summarized the doubts in its editorial of October 19, 1959 (evening), "Ampo wa Anzen no Hoshō Ka?" (Does the Treaty Really Guarantee Security?).

continuing struggle with Kōno over the question of the duration of the treaty, and by intense personal attacks from the opposition, nevertheless displayed a hardening attitude by turning down opposition demands to dissolve the Lower House prior to ratifying the treaty. Then, on November 9, 1959, Foreign Minister Fujiyama presented his controversial Interim Report to the House of Representatives. In it he summed up the conservative views of the new treaty and made an impassioned plea for quick acceptance by the Diet.

Until now the Socialists had attacked the treaty in the absence of an official draft; now they were able to press the government on the precise wording of each article, and they quickly rose to the offensive.[2] They appeared to catch Kishi and Fujiyama off guard. For example, a great uproar arose over the matter of the scope of the Far East: how far and under what circumstances could the United States dispatch its Japan-based troops under the new treaty? Article VI simply granted bases to the United States ". . . for the purpose of contributing to the security of Japan and the maintenance of international peace and security in the Far East. . . ." When pressed to give an exact definition of "Far East," Fujiyama shifted his position twice in three days. On November 16 he said that U.S. forces in Japan could be sent into combat anywhere, even beyond the Far East. The next day he said that "in general" (ōmune) they could be mobilized only in the Far East. On November 18, he said there would be some exceptions to this but that U.S. forces could not be sent "far away from the Far East."[3] The Socialists seized on Fujiyama's shifting replies to engage in raucous behavior in the committee room; most of the press immediately sided with them and denounced the govern-

[2] Since the next chapter describes the Diet debate of 1960 in some detail, we shall not dwell on the substance of the debate here.

[3] *Japan Times*, November 18–19, 1959; see also Dai-Sanjūsan-kai Kokkai, Shūgiin *Honkaigiroku*, Dai-rokugo (33rd Diet, House of Representatives Plenary No. 6), November 10, 1959, pp. 4–9. Fujiyama also said that in his personal view the Far East consisted of Japan and its vicinity, the area north of the Philippines and the coastal part of the Asian continent. We shall see in the next chapter how these words got him into further difficulties.

154

ment for its evasive stand. The government, thrown onto the defensive, was hard pressed to justify other points in the new treaty: did Japan have a veto in the proposed "prior consultations"? Could U.S. forces bring in nuclear weapons? Was Japan undertaking any new defense obligations? Was ten years too long? The government's answers left the impression of uncertainty and confusion—so much so that some Foreign Office officials were reported to be worried that the treaty would not be ratified by the Diet in 1960.[4]

Another explosive issue came before the Diet just as the draft treaty was being raked over the coals: the difficult Vietnam reparations bill. Although this bill did not appear to be related to the security treaty, the Japanese left wing, with its all-embracing Marxist outlook, immediately saw an intimate connection. In brief, the government had signed a $55,600,000 war reparations and economic cooperation agreement with Saigon on May 13, 1959, and the bill was now before the Diet for ratification. The Socialists objected that South Vietnam did not truly represent all of Vietnam and that the payment would violate the Geneva Agreement of 1954 which provided for the unification of Vietnam.[5]

The reparations bill was hotly debated in the House of Representatives Foreign Affairs Committee for several weeks in November 1959. Then the LDP Chairman, Ozawa Saeki (who later chaired the Special Committee on the Security Treaty), tried to close the debate and bring the bill to a vote in the predawn hours of November 26, 1959. Using the same tactics that became famous in 1960, the Socialists called for a vote of non-

---

[4] *Japan Times*, November 20, 1959, article by Hirasawa Kazushige.

[5] The Socialists characterized the agreement as "20 billion yen for three chickens." Okada Haruo, who had studied the question for three years, led an impressive Socialist attack. His other arguments were: (1) North Vietnam suffered more than South Vietnam from the Japanese occupation; (2) the peace treaty which obligated Japan to pay reparations had been signed for Vietnam by a French citizen who was not a legal representative of the government in Saigon; and (3) the agreement represented the "imperialist ambition of the monopolistic Japanese capitalists to spread their influence to Southeast Asia in cooperation with the U.S. policy of stepping up the SEATO defense framework." *Japan Times*, December 24, 1959.

confidence in Ozawa and the proceedings dissolved into wild disorder: all the LDP members rose and called for the closure vote to proceed. The Socialists heckled the Chairman, whose chair was thrown across the room and whose glass of water was broken on the desk before him. The Socialists then marched out of the room shouting that the closure was invalid, and in the midst of the confusion the LDP members ended the debate, passed the bill and rushed it to the floor of the House. Then, in an early morning plenary session of the House of Representatives on November 27, the LDP forced the bill through to completion.

This sort of Diet scramble was not new in Japanese politics, but its timing was particularly important, for November 27 was the day chosen by the People's Council for the 8th United Action—the largest demonstration of 1959. The fact that emotions were at a high pitch over the treaty draft and the reparation bill, and that the press was giving great play to the "tough" tactics of the conservatives in forcing the bill through, gave the left wing the spark it needed for a climactic protest march on the Diet. Of course, there were careful preparations for the dramatic events of November 27, for almost nothing is spontaneous in Japanese politics and mass demonstrations were carefully planned.

The "November 27 Incident"

The storming of the Diet on November 27, 1959—now known in Japanese annals as the "November 27 Incident"—was the third of its kind since World War II.[6] This incident had its origins in the early stages of the anti-treaty movement during the summer of 1959.[7]

[6] The first was on March 9, 1950, in protest against the budget and the second was on November 1, 1951, against Prime Minister Yoshida. The November 27 Incident has also been called the "Diet Invasion Demonstration Incident" (*Kokkai Ranyū Demo Jiken*) and the "Diet Petition Demonstration Incident" (*Kokkai Seigan Demo Jiken*), depending on the speaker's political viewpoint.

[7] For a variety of discussions of the incident see all the major Japanese newspapers of November 28, 1959, and the following other reports: *Kōan Chōsa Chō* (Public Security Investigation Agency), *Ampo Tōsō no Gaiyō*

It will be recalled that the People's Council plotted a series of ten "united action" drives against treaty revision in 1959, and that none of these drives—at least until November—attracted much public attention. As early as July 1959, younger elements in the People's Council—notably the leaders of Zengakuren and a few of their sympathizers—became restless with their "uninspired" leadership and proposed the staging of some spectacular incident that might arouse the nation, deal a blow to the "ruling circles," and dramatize the treaty issue. These feelings soon crystalized around the slogan "To the Diet!" (*Kokkai E!*). The dominant voices on the People's Council, however, shied away from the idea of a mass movement on the Diet and insisted on orderly marches to invite the broadest possible public participation and support. The Socialist Party, as the major parliamentary opposition party, was hesitant to back an assault on the Diet, symbol of postwar Japanese democracy. The Communists, who were still recovering from their loss of popularity after the "Bloody May Day" episode of 1952, saw no sense in jeopardizing their united front strategy and image of respectability to satisfy the whims of the hot-headed young students, many of whom they had expelled from the party.

During the summer of 1959 the People's Council became involved in the first of many bitter disputes over tactics. Zengakuren, increasingly impatient with its "weak-kneed" leaders, wanted to use the 5th World Conference Against Atomic and Hydrogen Bombs, a leftist-inspired gathering at Hiroshima on August 6, 1959, to pass a resolution against treaty revision, but the JSP, JCP, and Sōhyō refused to go along despite the existence of a significant minority in the leftist camp who sympathized with the students. One writer in this minority said later that the left wing forfeited here a great opportunity to merge

(An Outline of the Security Treaty Struggle), Tokyo: 1960, pp. 133–135; Ide Busaburō, *Ampo Tōsō* (The Security Treaty Struggle), Tokyo: Sanichi Shobo, 1960, pp. 59–64; Saitō Ichirō, *Ampo Tōsō Shi* (A History of the Security Treaty Struggle), Tokyo: Sanichi Shobo, 1962, pp. 131–148; Shinobu Seizaburō, *Ampo Tōsō Shi* (A History of the Security Treaty Struggle), Tokyo: Sekai Shoin, 1961, pp. 64–91; and "Zadankai: Kokkai Demo Jiken o Mokugeki Shite" (Round-table Discussion: Witnessing the Diet Demonstration Incident), *Sekai*, February 1960, pp. 118–131.

the two elements ("peace and democracy") in the postwar leftist movement.[8]

The People's Council agreed at its directors' meeting on August 21, 1959, that the object of the struggle was not merely to prevent revision of the old treaty but also to overthrow the entire security system with the United States. The Socialists held that blocking the revised treaty and overthrowing Kishi were inseparable political objectives; during the autumn, therefore, the debate inside the Diet and the mass movement outside must converge to produce the dissolution of the Lower House and the end of the Kishi Cabinet. The Communists, on the other hand, warned that too much stress on the anti-Kishi aspects of the struggle would weaken the solidarity of the united front and divert attention from the main enemy: U.S. imperialism. This dispute was not resolved, and the statement issued at the directors' meeting of September 5, 1959, simply papered over the differences.[9]

The November action plans were first officially announced at the second meeting of the National Representatives Council in Tokyo on September 16, 1959: the 7th United Action would begin on October 20 and run for 10 days. It would consist of spreading posters and handbills, collecting signatures, holding sidewalk and village rallies, and sponsoring lectures, debates, and research meetings. This was to be climaxed, during the last ten days of November, by the 8th United Action aimed at ending treaty negotiations and overthrowing Kishi.[10] The main

[8] Takane Masaaki, in Kenkyusha Kondankai, ed., *Shin Ampo Jōyaku* (The New Security Treaty), 8th ed., Tokyo: Sanichi Shobo, 1960, pp. 165–197.

[9] Kōan Chōsa Chō, *Ampo Tōsō*, pp. 74–76. The JCP, according to this source, held a special meeting on September 15, 1959, to instruct its seventy delegates to the National Representatives Council meeting (scheduled for the next day) to speak out for its position, which they did. The JCP later changed its mind; soon after Chairman Nosaka Sanzō returned from Communist China in the fall of 1959 a number of reports by regional JCP bodies began to include resolutions calling for the overthrow of Kishi. These reports appeared without explanation in *Akahata*, November 26, 1959. Kōan Chōsa Chō, *Ampo Tōsō*, p. 78.

[10] *Yomiuri Shimbun*, September 17, 1959.

goal, of course, was to prevent the new treaty from being signed.

When the 7th United Action failed to produce nationwide excitement (Zengakuren labeled it a "schedule struggle" (*suke-juru tōsō*), and when the treaty talks seemed to be nearing an end, many leaders in Zengakuren became convinced of the need for radical action and the "To the Diet!" movement gathered fresh momentum.[11] They reasoned that the 8th United Action would be the last chance to prevent Kishi from signing the treaty, and they were disgusted with the uncertain and timid leaders of the People's Council. The whole left wing movement had become stagnant and bureaucratic, they felt, and it was time to draw on the "untapped energy" of the rank-and-file workers to get the movement going again. The only question was, how to get around the older leaders and take direct action?

The People's Council played into Zengakuren's hands by deciding to turn the 8th United Action into a massive petition march on the Diet. The council, apparently disturbed by rumblings within its own ranks, on one hand, and Kishi's rush to sign the treaty, on the other, decided that there would be no attempt to break into the Diet compound, but that petitions would be presented en masse to the Speakers of both Houses. Kishi would waver and fall, it was hoped, by the sheer force of numbers at the Diet walls. Each component of the council now busied itself preparing for what seemed to be the final push in the anti-treaty drive.

Sōhyō, which had earlier decided to merge its annual fall offensive with the anti-treaty campaign, held its 13th Extraordinary Convention on November 19–20 to coordinate member unions. The two major goals adopted were to aid Tanro's struggle against mass dismissals of coal miners and to smash the

[11] At this point Zengakuren was firmly controlled by the extreme leftist Communist League (Kyōsandō) which held eighteen of the thirty CEC seats. Information in this chapter on Zengakuren and its rôle in the November 27 Incident, except as otherwise noted, came from interviews with Communist League members, whose identities are protected here for obvious reasons. They allowed me to draw heavily on notebooks, diaries, and sketches used at the time in their headquarters.

present system based on the security treaty.[12] The People's Council and Sōhyō revealed the importance they attached to November 27 by calling for a maximum "mobilization" (dōin) for that day.[13] The order was for a "Double Five," meaning that 60,000 workers were to be called to the streets. With the expected 10,000 students, it was hoped that some 70,000 demonstrators would mass around the Diet on November 27.

The Socialist Party announced equally ambitious plans: 100,-000 people were to participate in the petitioning, 20,000 petition forms were to be distributed to the unionists, JSP Diet members were to participate in the rallies and marches, and an action squad was to be formed to spread handbills. On the mornings of November 24–25, JSP Diet members were to appear for 90 minutes at Tokyo's station platforms to urge commuters to support the drive. JSP members of the House of Councillors were to divide themselves into eighteen squads and address regional rallies on November 27.[14] General responsibility for the drive was given to Secretary-General Asanuma Inejirō, while three others, Yamahana Hideo, Akamatsu Isamu, and Eda Saburō, were to be his lieutenants.

[12] It is interesting to note that the JCP was critical of Sōhyō's resolution at this convention that a victory in the coal-miners' struggle would assure victory in the anti-treaty struggle. Akahata, November 17, 1959, said that even a victory at Miike would not necessarily mean victory over the treaty; in this way the Communists continued to play down the class struggle in favor of the broad united front strategy. Kōan Chōsa Chō, Ampo Tōsō, p. 78.

[13] Labor demonstrations have been refined to the last detail in Japan. There were five standard classes of mobilization, numbered one through five in order of increasing strength. A "Number Five," for example, meant that 30,000 workers would be called out to the streets and each local enterprise union knew immediately how many workers it would have to provide, quotas having been carefully negotiated in advance. Thus a plant with 100 workers might have to send 30 demonstrators for a Number Five mobilization, but only one worker for a Number One. This quota system was not always reliable, of course; if Sōhyō's high command misjudged the mood of the locals, they quickly discovered that the quotas were not being filled. Sōhyō considered it a good demo if half the overall quota showed up.

[14] This program was laid down by the JSP's People's Movement Committee on November 20, 1959. Sankei Shimbun, November 21, 1959.

Nervous LDP leaders sensed that trouble was brewing and urged the Speaker of the House of Representatives to take steps to curb demonstrations in the vicinity of the Diet. No action was taken, however.

The leftists held their final strategy meeting on November 23, 1959. Present were about fifty of Japan's left wing elite: union strongmen, descended from the feudal labor-boss system, radical intellectuals educated in the post-World War I period of rapid growth and rapid suppression, anarchists, pacifists, workers up from the ranks, and recent college graduates who had earned their stripes in the student movement of the 1950's. Most of them had been educated under the Emperor system, and many had suffered in jails at the hands of the militarists. A curious mixture of tradition and change, these men represented many sources of protest in modern Japan, and it is not surprising that there were conflicting views on how to proceed on November 27.

Under the chairmanship of Asanuma, the meeting finally adopted a plan whereby the demonstrators would be divided into three separate groups: one, under the nominal command of Akamatsu Isamu, would assemble near Chapel Center just below the main gate of the Diet compound.[15] The second group, under Eda Saburō, would gather near the Agriculture Ministry down the hill to the southeast of the main gate. The third group, under Yamahana Hideo, would gather near the Tokyo Grand Hotel on the street running south from the Diet past the Prime Minister's official residence. Akamatsu's Group One, which had the choice position for an attack on the main gate, was purposely assigned workers from the Tokyo Metropolitan Workers Unions (Tororen), who were notoriously "doc-

[15] The Diet Building, at 215 feet the (then) tallest building in Tokyo, stands on a hill just south of the outer moat of the Imperial Palace. It occupies a spacious compound, roughly triangular in shape, surrounded by low walls and iron rail fences. There are three main vehicular entrances but one of them, the main gate, is not open to normal foot or vehicular traffic, being reserved for badged officials or special visitors. Radiating downhill from the Diet compound are nine broader or narrower avenues of approach.

161

ile." Eda's Group Two would get workers from the government enterprise unions, including the National Railways, Postal, and Communications workers, who were considered "medium" in fighting strength. The most militant of all unionists were placed in the third and toughest position under Yamahana. These were the small and medium enterprise workers, whose wage demands were far more acute than those of the relatively more satisfied workers in the modern industries and government enterprises.[16] To approach the Diet they would have to march up a steeper hill and face police barricades flanked by walls on both sides of the street. Zengakuren's expected force of 10,000 was to be divided, under Asanuma's plan, into thirds and stationed at each of the three positions so as to be kept under firm control. The demonstrators would assemble at the three points at 2:00 P.M., hold rallies and pep talks at 3:00, march up and jostle against the police barricades at 4:00, with selected representatives then to be admitted into the Diet compound accompanied by JSP Diet members to present petitions. The plan assumed that the demonstrators would quickly fall back from the impregnable police barriers and reassemble down the hill near the present MITI Building. Here they would have some final congratulatory speeches, then break up and go home.

Zengakuren rightly saw in this plan a plot to weaken or destroy their fighting power, and its infuriated leaders worked overtly and covertly at this meeting to have it changed. They wanted to concentrate all "active elements"—i.e., those willing to clash with the police—at a given point, preferably the main gate, in hopes that they could burst into the Diet followed by masses of workers.[17] Some support for this idea came from Zen-

[16] The fighting elements in this group were workers from the All Japan Metal Industry Workers' Union (Zenkinzoku), the Federation of Synthetic Chemical Industry Workers' Unions (Gōkarōren), and the All Japan Shipbuilding Workers' Union (Zenzōsen); many of these men were experienced in front-line battle against the police.

[17] Zengakuren had decided at its 12th Central Committee Meeting, November 9–10, 1959, that it would attempt to force its way into the Diet compound during the 8th United Action. A message to this effect was issued to its local chapters in Tokyo on November 16, 1959. Kōan Chōsa Chō, *Ampo Tōsō*, p. 133.

162

kinzoku, from workers in the Ministry of Agriculture's union (Nōrinshō Rōdō Kumiai), and from the JSP's Youth Department. The older leaders carried the day, however; the JSP, JCP, and Sōhyō accepted the idea of massing near the Diet to display the strength of anti-treaty sentiment, but they were anxious to keep command over the unruly students and avoid a bloody mob scene. This plan seemed to be the result of one of those unworkable compromises in which those who favored a Diet demonstration and those who wished to avoid bloodshed were both satisfied in the decision-making process and both determined to have their own way in the actual event.

On the night of November 25, 1959, five Zengakuren leaders met with five like-minded representatives of Tokyo Chihyō (Sōhyō's Tokyo Chapter) and decided that Zengakuren would concentrate most of its forces near Chapel Center with Akamatsu's group. If conditions seemed right at the time, a bold attempt would be made to crash through the main gate. This decision was passed on the night of November 26 to the various self-government associations on the local campuses.

By now events were favoring the radical students. For almost a year demonstrators had been called out to protest against the new treaty and yet the talks seemed to be proceeding inexorably to a successful conclusion. The long and frustrating struggle appeared to be in its final stages, and a "now or never" mood prevailed. Just five days before November 27, Fujiyama announced that the pact would be signed in Washington between January 15–23. The forced passage of the Vietnam reparations bill added a fresh sense of outrage against the "high-handed" Kishi Administration. The Diet session was almost over, and the government had not clarified its stand on many disputed points in the treaty. There had been so much talk of "To the Diet!" over the past months that the scheme no longer seemed an affront to the parliamentary system—in fact, the leftist leaders had nearly convinced themselves and their followers that the democratic process *demanded* this sort of action. In sum, conditions were ripe for some radical act, and many workers appeared to be in a more radical mood than their leaders

—or so it seemed to Zengakuren. The students were quick to seize the opportunity.

November 27 was a clear day and the demonstrators turned out in surprisingly large numbers. The People's Council claimed that 80,000 demonstrated in Tokyo alone and that a total of 500,000 people in 620 villages, towns and cities throughout Japan joined the drive. The National Public Safety Council placed the number in Tokyo at 24,200 while the Public Security Investigation Agency said that about 25,000 showed up at the Diet.[18] In Tokyo, the demonstrators poured into the three staging areas around 1:00 P.M. and lined up under the tall red banners of their respective unions or college groups. Loudspeakers blared away and union organizers hurried about issuing last minute instructions and slogans. Five thousand policemen were moved into the Diet vicinity, where they set up barricades of armored cars along the roads they knew would be used.

At 2:00 P.M. the rallies and speeches (*sōkekki taikai*) began, with JSP Diet members (including Asanuma), JCP officials, and Sōhyō leaders exhorting the workers in bold and exciting speeches. "Down with Kishi!" "End Treaty Talks Immediately!" and "Block the Signing of the Treaty!" were the main slogans of the day. Around 2:30 P.M. the demonstrators in Yamahana's third group (near the Tokyo Grand Hotel) began to advance toward the front lines of the police. The police resisted passively, holding their billy-clubs sideways to form a human fence—despite a rain of rocks thrown at them. A fierce shoving battle ensued, and the demonstrators were able to inch their way up the hill to the Prime Minister's residence before the police lines tightened and held.

Meanwhile Zengakuren was moving ahead with its plans. By 3:00 P.M. their main forces were assembled near Chapel Center under the leadership of Shimizu Takeo of Tokyo Univer-

[18] Kōan Chōsa Chō, *Ampo Tōsō*, p. 133. Guessing the size of demonstrations in Japan is akin to the popular sport of reckoning the size of audiences in U.S. presidential campaigns, with political motivation bearing heavily on the statistics. While 80,000 was surely an exaggeration, it is fair to say that the People's Council turned out more people than in any of the other seven united actions of 1959.

sity.[19] At about 3:30, some 1,000 of these students led by the group from Hōsei University charged into and through the right flank of the police, clambering over the armored cars and racing up to the main gate. At this very moment JSP Diet members Asanuma, Okada Haruo, and Kashiwa Masao were at the main gate set to accompany thirty representatives into the compound to present their petitions.

At this point the facts are mired in controversy. The Chief of the Diet Guard Force, Yamano, testified later that Okada Haruo shouted, "Diet members are coming through so open the gate!" and that when he complied with this order the shouting demonstrators poured in along with the petitioners.[20] The Director of the National Police Agency, Kashiwamura Nobuo, and the Chief of the Tokyo Metropolitan Police, Ōgura Ken, also testified on November 30, 1959, before the House of Representatives Judiciary Committee that Asanuma virtually opened the gates for the demonstrators by accompanying the petitioners into the Diet.[21] The PSIA said that the first charge involved only 600 people including 300 students, and that they approached the main gate under pretext of petitioning.[22] The LDP claimed that Asanuma and his cohorts actually led the charge into the Diet compound.[23] The Zengakuren leaders, on the other hand, took full credit for leading the charge through the gate; they specifically denied that Asanuma led the charge, though they admitted that the presence of the JSP Diet members might have inspired confidence in the more timid students.[24]

[19] Among the front ranks of these students were: 600 from Hosei University, 300 from Japan Women's University, 200 from Meiji, 180 from Ochanomizu, 100 from Rikkyō, and 50 each from Keiō, Aoyama Gakuin, and Tokyo Kōgyō. Kōan Chōsa Chō, *Ampo Tōsō*, p. 133.

[20] *Asahi Shimbun*, November 29, 1959.

[21] *Sankei Shimbun* (evening), November 30, 1959.

[22] Kōan Chōsa Chō, *Ampo Tōsō*, pp. 133–134.

[23] *Mainichi Shimbun*, November 28, 1959, statement by Kawashima Shōjirō, Secretary-General of the LDP.

[24] Interview with Zengakuren leaders, December 30, 1961. In this case, from all evidence available I have no reason to doubt the word of the students.

Whatever the truth may have been, about 5,000 exuberant students and workers rushed through the main gate and into the compound, followed immediately by Eda's second group. Minutes later the third group got word of the break-through and charged past the police lines, storming up the hill from the south and into the compound.

By now all order and control had disappeared. About 12,000 demonstrators were in the compound sitting on the ground or milling about, singing songs, shouting slogans, and snake-dancing. Several students even urinated on the walls of the Diet building to show their contempt for the parliamentary system in Japan. The police were momentarily cut off from each other and seemingly powerless.[25] There were no moves to continue the charge into the Diet building itself, and the mood at the time was generally cheerful.

The leaders of the People's Council were thrown into confusion. Minaguchi, Iwai Akira, and Kamiyama Shigeo had been standing in a parked "propaganda truck" near Chapel Center since 2:00 P.M.[26] When the crowds surged up to and through the main gate, ten of the top leaders of the People's Council held a hurried conference in the truck; as they argued, the demonstrators filed past them and into the compound. There was nothing left to do but follow them in, and the truck now drove through the main gate too. Iwai took over and congratulated the workers on their impressive struggle; in almost the next breath he asked them to regroup and withdraw from the area. Some Socialists, including Asanuma and Vice-Speaker Masaki also entreated the demonstrators to leave. Many of the students and workers ignored these requests and it was nearly 6:00 P.M.

[25] They could, of course, have resorted to tougher measures such as the use of billy-clubs, tear gas, or fire hoses, but their orders were to refrain from such steps. These orders were presumably based on the government's awareness of the widespread sympathy that would have been aroused in the event of violence against the unarmed workers or students.

[26] The propaganda truck is a special vehicle used in Japan for running demonstrations and making election speeches. Somewhat larger than a station wagon, it has a raised deck and railing in the back where a speaker can stand and address the crowd over loudspeakers.

before the unionists reformed their lines, shouted *"Banzai!"* three times, and marched out of the compound. Some 3,000 Zengakuren students were the last to go; this group marched down the hill to the Defense Agency Building and continued to perform. It was not until well after 10 P.M. that the last group dispersed at Shimbashi Station and order was restored.[27]

Back at the headquarters of the People's Council a serious assessment of the day's activities was underway, and a turning point in the anti-treaty movement was at hand.

In the Wake of November 27

It quickly became evident that public opinion was running overwhelmingly against the demonstrators; almost all the newspapers and important commentators condemned the assault on the Diet. While Zengakuren came in for some of the blame, the Socialist Party took a major share of the criticism.[28] The LDP moved swiftly to press its advantage; it charged the Socialists with inciting the affair and held hearings (in the absence of the Socialist members) in the Disciplinary Committee of the House of Representatives to see whether Asanuma and the others were guilty of improper conduct.[29] On December 25 the LDP passed a bill in the House of Representatives (again without the Socialists) which would ban all demonstrations in

[27] In the whole affair, some 432 demonstrators and 241 police were injured, according to *Japan Times*, November 28, 1959. Other estimates placed the number of injured somewhat lower. There were no deaths.

[28] *Sankei Shimbun*'s editorial, November 29, 1959, in which the students are more or less dismissed and the JSP blamed, is extremely interesting. See also the editorials of *Asahi*, *Yomiuri*, and *Tokyo*, November 28, 1959. For a cross section of commentary, see: *Mainichi Shimbun*, November 28, 1959, comments by Ōya Sōichi, Aono Suckichi, and Hayashi Kentarō; *Yomiuri Shimbun*, November 28, 1959, comments by Mitarai Tatsuo, Hirabayashi Taiko, and Yabe Teiji; *Sankei Shimbun*, November 29, 1959, symposium by Sakanishi Shio, Nakamura Tetsu, and Ishida Hirohide. There was a widespread feeling now that the anti-treaty struggle had passed its climax. *Yomiuri Shimbun*, December 11, 1959, headline.

[29] These hearings eventually came to nothing as the Diet session ended July 15, 1960, without any action being taken. *Asahi Evening News*, July 16, 1960.

167

the vicinity of the Diet.[30] Although these moves were ineffective, the LDP gained the offensive that the Socialists had held in October and November and made the most of it to rally public opinion around the new treaty.

The Socialists took the position that the demonstrators were exercising their right of collective petition, that nothing illegal had occurred, and that the 8th United Action had been a success. It was unfortunate that the demonstrations had turned into an invasion of the Diet compound, the party said, for it gave the LDP a chance for a political counterblow.[31] Asanuma defended his rôle in the affair as follows:

> As Socialist Diet members our basic policy was to serve as intermediaries to deliver the representatives' petitions to both Houses of the Diet and to the Government. We regret that one group, including Zengakuren, departed from the planned action and entered the Diet compound, and we recognize that this resulted from poor control by the leadership. LDP propaganda has it that we Socialist Diet members led the invasion, but it is absolutely untrue that we instigated the young people to recklessness in our speeches. As planned, we simply served as intermediaries, receiving the petitions of the representatives. When one group of people did enter the Diet compound, I, along with other JSP Diet members, even tried to persuade them to retreat. I want there to be no mistake about this. So that there will be no more situations like this in the future, group petitioners must respect the Diet's authority and have more self-control; at the same time the Diet itself must

[30] This bill passed in the House of Councillors on March 21, 1960, but in the new session (34th Regular Diet) the Lower House was required to redeliberate the bill and it got lost in the shuffle during the frantic days of April 1960. A similar bill was passed in the House of Representatives in 1961, but large-scale demonstrations against it caused LDP leaders to let it die before it passed in the House of Councillors.

[31] These judgments were made by the JSP's Central Executive Committee on December 11, 1959. *Japan Times,* December 12, 1959.

make efforts to increase its authority. I am opposed to the rash passage of legislation curbing demonstrations in the vicinity of the Diet.[32]

Although there was some sympathy for Zengakuren within the JSP, particularly among its younger elements, the party leaders took a stern view.[33] Chairman Suzuki branded its leaders as "arrogant and self-righteous" and the party's Central Executive Committee formally demanded its ouster from the People's Council. From this point on, there was continuous friction between the Socialists and the Zengakuren.

Despite their setback on November 27, the Socialists continued the futile battle to end treaty negotiations and punch holes in the draft text before the Diet. In December they raised new objections to the "prior consultation" provision in connection with the Yoshida-Acheson exchange of notes in 1952.[34] The government floundered a bit on this matter but the Foreign Office finally announced that efforts were being made to win U.S. agreement to prior consultations under any and all circumstances, and this settled the matter for the time being.

The reactions of other left wing elements to November 27 can be summarized briefly as follows. Zengakuren saw it as ". . . an epochal event in the history of the labor and student movements." [35] Despite searches and arrests by the police and a

[32] *Mainichi Shimbun*, November 28, 1959.

[33] Zengakuren leaders claimed that Ōshiba Shigeo and Ioka Daiji on the JSP's People's Movement Committee were in sympathy with their basic aims.

[34] The Yoshida-Acheson exchange of notes committed Japan to support U.S. forces while they were acting as members of the United Nations Forces. The Socialists questioned whether Japan would have the right to prior consultations under the new treaty if the Yoshida-Acheson agreement remained in force and if the U.S. forces again acted as U.N. Forces in the Far East. U.S. Department of State, *Treaty of Peace with Japan and Exchange of Notes*, signed September 8, 1951 (Vol. 3, *United States Treaties and Other International Agreements*, TIAS 2490), Washington: U.S. Government Printing Office, pp. 3326–3328.

[35] *Mainichi Shimbun*, November 28, 1959, comment by Kasuya Hidetake. See also *"Otona Nayamasu Daijin-kyū"* (A Cabinet Level Headache for Adults), *Shūkan Asahi*, December 20, 1959, pp. 3–10.

mounting chorus of criticism within the People's Council, it prepared for further violent action.[36]

Sōhyō, like Zengakuren, was subjected to searches and arrests for its part in the affair.[37] Its leaders tried to shift the blame for violence to the LDP Government and right wing groups. Iwai Akira, Sōhyō's Secretary-General, even hinted that the police themselves had provoked the incident: "Looking at today's [November 27, 1959] police formation, I thought it strange that it was different from usual. Ordinarily the police station their men 10–20 deep in front of the gate and prevent anyone from approaching, but today they used only a barricade of armored cars parked sideways. Leaving only a thin cordon of men in front of the main gate, they were purposely trying to draw the demonstrators inside. My inference is that the Government and LDP were trying to provoke us into making a big incident out of it." [38] This was the first in a series of remarkable accusations that the government somehow provoked the "masses" into violence during the anti-treaty campaign. The falsity of the charge was proved by the testimony of Zengakuren leaders who plotted the assault well in advance.

Minaguchi Kōzō, Director of the People's Council, went even further to obscure the facts: "The purpose of the demonstration was to have as many people as possible petition. For this purpose 20,000 sample petition forms were distributed to the organizations and in the event that we were stopped along the way, it was planned that only the representatives should enter the Diet. However, incited by right wing propaganda trucks brandishing bamboo poles, we were provoked and became excited. There is an opinion that this spur-of-the-moment action

[36] A total of nine students was eventually tried and found guilty of trespassing and violating public safety ordinances. Their sentences, all suspended, ranged from four to ten months with two years of probation. *Asahi Evening News*, December 22, 1961, and *Japan Times*, December 23, 1961. Their subsequent appeal was turned down, *Asahi Shimbun*, July 17, 1963.

[37] On the night of November 28, 1959, police searched Sōhyō's Tokyo headquarters and three other Sōhyō-affiliated organizations: Chihyō and two offices of Zenkinzoku. *Japan Times*, November 30, 1959.

[38] *Mainichi Shimbun*, November 28, 1959.

was a tactical excess, but the extent of the mass mobilization shows how angry the people are about treaty revision."[39]

The Communists reacted sharply against the young upstarts of Zengakuren, calling them Trotskyites, adventurists, and tools of American imperialism, among other things. The JCP worked hard to discredit Zengakuren in the People's Council and to preserve its own image as a patriotic, responsible opposition party dedicated to overthrowing the security system and winning independence for the Japanese people.[40]

The left wing was seriously divided over the theoretical challenge presented by Zengakuren—a cleavage which has continued along more or less similar lines to the present. It was a question whether the movement was to be a truly revolutionary one, led by activist students and the hard core of the labor movement, in which violence might play a part in overthrowing the treaty and unseating the conservatives, or whether it would place equal stress on parliamentary opposition and the "democratic process," accepting the lesser goals of overthrowing Kishi, dissolving the Diet, and discrediting the treaty in the eyes of the world. In some ways, it was a reincarnation of the old *Rōnō-ha—Kōza-ha* argument of the prewar period, though the lines were by no means clearly drawn.

Broadly speaking, Zengakuren now took the *Rōnō-ha* view that conditions favored a one-stage socialist revolution. Thus while the JSP was officially trying to throw Zengakuren out of the People's Council, there were some elements within the party that tended to sympathize, at least in theoretical terms, with the students' position. The JCP and the more "orthodox" Marxists of the *Kōza-ha* lineage took the opposite view. They argued that the objective conditions were not yet right for a socialist revolution and that the first task was to unite the nation in a multiclass, broadly based democratic front, with relatively less

[39] *Ibid.*

[40] See, for example, Iwabayashi Toranosuke, "Torotsukisuto to no Arasoi to Tō Kensetsu" (The Fight Against Trotskyites and Party Construction), *Zenei*, February 1960, pp. 53–60. The writer draws a careful distinction between the extreme left adventurism of the students and the militant revolutionary heroism of the masses.

171

emphasis on overthrowing Kishi and more on the national struggle for independence against U.S. imperialism. Then in a second stage of the revolution, socialist victory might be achieved.

The students posed a particularly acute problem for the progressive intellectuals, who now saw some of their long-held theories being put into practice. Could the professors turn their backs on these young Marxist zealots? One member of Tokyo University's faculty chose to view the Diet invaders as followers of the tradition of Sakura Sōgorō (1604-1645), a peasant hero who was put to death for making an unpardonable direct appeal (*jikiso*) to the Shogun in behalf of his oppressed people and whose martyrdom later inspired peasant uprisings and Kabuki dramas.[41]

There were other interpretations of the November 27 Incident. Shimizu Ikutarō, well-known Professor of Sociology at Gakushūin, was highly critical of the People's Council—particularly the JCP—for what he termed its hypocritical leadership. He saw in the events of November 27 an outpouring of energy, vigor, and intelligence among the workers which had hitherto been unsuspected. These qualities should have been used to oppose the treaty—directly, boldly, and without regard for the respectable image and the united front. He felt that the leaders of Sōhyō and the JCP were contemptuous of the masses, concerned only with preserving their own power, and therefore unable to give correct political guidance to the students and workers who were sincerely interested in blocking the treaty. The People's Council, under the false concept of "broad-basism" (*habahiro-shugi*), was dissipating its energy and wasting its resources. It had allowed the burden of the struggle to fall on the shoulders of the young students—who were correct in their choice of tactics.[42] Though he denies that he played this rôle,

[41] Arase Yutaka, in Hidaka Rokurō, ed., *Gogatsu Jūkunichi*, Tokyo: Iwanami Publishing Co., 1960, p. 29.

[42] Interview with Shimizu Ikutarō, October 13, 1961. Among the prolific Shimizu's better known articles on this subject are: "Ima Koso Kokkai E: Seigan no Susume" (Now to the Diet—On with the Petitions), *Sekai*, May 1960, pp. 18–28; and "Ampo Tōsō Ichinen-go no Shisō" (Thoughts on the Security Treaty Struggle a Year Later), *Chūō Kōron*, July 1961, pp. 45–57. In English, see "The Intellectuals," *New Politics*, Vol. 1, No. 2, Winter 1962, pp. 151–158.

Shimizu came to have the reputation during the following spring as the foremost supporter of Zengakuren among the progressive intellectuals.

There were other leading scholars whose views of Shimizu and Zengakuren were strongly critical. We shall see in later chapters how differences in interpretation of the events of November 27 led to serious dissension among the progressive intellectuals in the spring of 1960, and indeed down to the present time.

The First Haneda Incident: January 16, 1960

After November 27, Zengakuren leaders were flushed with confidence and began to talk of even wilder demonstrations on December 10, the day set for the 9th United Action. It was at this point that the students, in two bizarre episodes, began to show open contempt for the authority of the police. On November 30, one policeman was captured by thirty Zengakuren students on the campus of Waseda University and held for five hours while police officials negotiated for his release. No action was taken against the students, who claimed they were upholding the sanctity of the campus and had caught the policeman trespassing.[43] In the other episode, two Zengakuren leaders involved in the November 27 affair hid out on the campuses of Tokyo University for eleven and thirteen days respectively while the police waited patiently outside with warrants for their arrest.[44]

Incidents of this sort inspired further challenges of the law, and baiting the police became something of a popular campus

[43] *Japan Times*, December 1, 1959.

[44] For the details of this episode, see *Japan Times*, December 7–12, 1959. The two students, Hayama Takeo and Shimizu Takeo, took advantage of the campus immunity first established by a circular in May 1952 from the Vice-minister of Education to university authorities. The siege finally ended when the two left their campuses (Hayama from Hongo, Shimizu from Komaba) voluntarily to join the demonstrations of December 10 and were quickly arrested. President Kaya Seiji of Tokyo University assumed the rôle of "powerless mediator" throughout the affair, and proved totally unable to persuade the students to leave the campus. Hayama and Shimizu were later issued "warnings" by the university after a meeting of the faculty decided against expulsion.

pastime. In early December, Zengakuren began organizing for the December 10 demonstrations, promising that 20,000 students would try to break into the Diet this time. As we have seen, the JSP, JCP, and most of Sōhyō were opposed to further incidents involving the Diet, and they combined to vote down the idea in the People's Council. As a result, the 9th United Action of December 10 was anticlimactic: relatively few students came out and there was no invasion of the Diet. This day revealed clearly the fact that the students were powerless to act by themselves—only with massive Sōhyō support could they carry out their revolutionary work. Only one group petitioned the Diet on December 10; this was the Association for Criticizing the Security Treaty (Ampo Hihan no Kai), which for a time showed a measure of independence from the People's Council.

The great question now was how to prevent Kishi from getting to Washington to sign the treaty. Zengakuren favored the use of force at Haneda Airport.[45] At the third meeting of the National Representatives Council on December 25, 1959, a motion for holding demonstrations at Haneda to coincide with Kishi's take-off was debated. Zengakuren leaders later claimed that a majority of the 300 present agreed with them, but that a JCP representative led a minority against them and carried the day. Within Sōhyō—which originally favored the idea—and the JSP, a heated debate took place: some argued that Kishi's departure could not be ignored if they were intent on preventing the treaty from being signed, while others felt that a repetition of the uncontrolled situation of November 27 would be disastrous for the anti-treaty movement. The issue was finally settled in a series of directors' meetings of the People's Council in early January 1960; Sōhyō and the JSP joined with the JCP and agreed to hold a rally in central Tokyo rather than at the airport.

Zengakuren now found itself completely isolated. Even Sō-

[45] The concept of trying to bottle up the Prime Minister in his own country was not entirely new: in November 1956 some rightists tried to prevent Hatoyama from leaving for Moscow. Ivan Morris, *Nationalism and the Right Wing in Japan*, London: Oxford University Press, 1960, p. 366.

hyō's regional chapter, Tokyo Chihyō, which had earlier supported the students, dropped out of the Haneda plan on January 13 under strong pressure from the JCP and Sōhyō. Prominent leftist writer Nakajima Kenzō, speaking for the Association for Criticizing the Security Treaty, announced that he would support a students' demonstration at Haneda if it were orderly.[46] In the event, however, the Association obeyed the People's Council and left the students to their own devices.

Zengakuren pressed ahead undaunted, for the opportunities seemed irresistible: the airport, nearly an hour by car from downtown Tokyo, had few access roads and these could be blocked off with ease, they thought. Even if they failed, their attempt would, they imagined, give Kishi a black eye in Washington and in the eyes of the world. Perhaps they could force Kishi to take off from the U.S. Air Force Base at Tachikawa —an act that would be loaded with political meaning for the Japanese people. The highly theoretical student leaders also saw Kishi's trip as symbolic; the representative of burgeoning Japanese monopoly capital (now reaching maturity) was taking the initiative in going to America to strengthen the military and economic partnership with the Wall Street imperialists. This was far different from the JCP view in which Japan's bourgeoisie was playing the passive rôle and U.S. imperialism was taking the initiative in revising the treaty in order further to exploit the Japanese people. For Zengakuren, the prime enemy was Kishi and Japanese monopoly capital—not U.S. imperialism—and Kishi's trip must be prevented at all costs.

The government kept the exact time of Kishi's departure a close secret, for rumors were circulating that Zengakuren students might hurl a bomb at the plane or lie down on the runways. The police were now keeping a close watch on the students; on January 13 they issued a demand for the students to drop their plans. The students held nightly strategy sessions in secret places—dormitories, classrooms, and inns throughout Tokyo. Their final meeting took place on the night of January 14, two days before Kishi was to leave. Karoji Kentarō presided

[46] Hidaka Rokurō, ed., *Gogatsu Jūkunichi*, p. 30.

over a group of twenty Zengakuren officers who were mostly from Tokyo, Meiji, and Chūō Universities.[47] Karoji now decided that the students would try to take over the terminal building at the airport and block Kishi's path to the plane.

At noon on January 15 the word leaked out that Kishi was to leave early the next morning, so the students quickly advanced their schedule: they would go to the airport that evening and try to hold out until Kishi's arrival the next day. Karoji and a group of Tokyo University students sauntered casually into the airport lobby around 7:00 P.M. and were soon followed by some 700–800 others, who arrived in tourist buses and trains. At 10:00 P.M. the police were amazed to discover a student rally going on inside the terminal building. A few labor union representatives (notably those from the Nagasaki Shipbuilding Company) appeared on the scene to wish the students well and the ubiquitous rightist, Akao Bin, arrived with four carloads of thugs to mix it up with the students.[48] The police

[47] Karoji was undoubtedly the brain behind the January 16 Incident. A student of literature at Hokkaido University, he had joined the JCP at an early age and had been purged in January 1959 for dissident activities. Raised by his mother in Hokkaido's poverty, and sent to college by her great personal sacrifice, Karoji was extremely popular among his fellow students, was a fan of the theater, movies, and sports, and was well-read on the subject of existentialism. Karoji was the strong, silent type, rare in Zengakuren circles, who was not much interested in theoretical Marxism, but transmitted his deep sense of the injustice of things to other students and inspired them with his sincerity and single-minded devotion to the cause. He was expelled from Hokkaido University in March 1960 for failing to pass the required examinations. Later he turned up in the employ of Tanaka Seigen, a well-known rightist leader with a distinctive philosophy all his own (see below).

[48] Akao Bin, most famous of Japan's current rightist fanatics, and his organization are well described in Morris, *op. cit.*, pp. 187–191 and elsewhere. Two months after this affair he welcomed Chancellor Adenauer at Haneda Airport with banners bearing huge swastikas; ten months later he was seriously implicated in the assassination of Asanuma. Throughout the anti-treaty movement his disciples attempted to thwart the activities of the left wing (see below). In January 1965 he was injured when hit by a motorcycle but recovered in time to lead scuffles against leftists who were protesting the entry of a U.S. nuclear-powered submarine at the port of Sasebo in February 1965.

176

kept Akao outside, and by 11:00 P.M. they had recovered from their surprise and surrounded the building. With that special sense of propriety that bars Japanese from exposing internal disturbances to foreigners, both sides refrained from action until just after midnight when the last of the international flight passengers had cleared the terminal. Then the students poured into the restaurant off the main lobby and erected a barricade of chairs and tables against the door. Just before 3:00 A.M. the police made their move, knocking down the barricade and dragging the students out one by one. There were no serious injuries but the scuffle lasted for an hour and a half as the students put up a strong fight. The police, still embarrassed by their apparent weakness on November 27, were far more businesslike this time and promptly arrested seventy-six of the ringleaders, ejecting the rest from the airport grounds.[49] Among those arrested was a small, quiet girl named Kamba Michiko; in June her death would create dramatic news in all the major capitals of the world.[50]

The Prime Minister's departure was now a simple matter. The ejected students, joined by over 1,000 others and a few unionists, continued to mill around the outer approaches to the airport, but Kishi took no chances. Leaving his Nampeidai residence near Shibuya Station escorted by fifteen motorcycles and twelve truckloads of police (followed by seventy newsmen's cars), the caravan sped along back alleys in Tokyo's early morning darkness and approached the airport from the Tamagawa River while a helicopter hovered overhead to warn of possible ambushes. Kishi drove to the side of the waiting aircraft, dispensed with the normal "*Banzai*" ceremonies, and took off at 8:00 A.M. as the 2,000 demonstrators watched in the wintry rain outside the airport. One small band of students had stood

[49] The students were amazed at how well the police recognized and picked out their leaders on the spot. Of the total of seventy-six arrested, twenty-two were ultimately indicted, tried, and given suspended sentences ranging from four to ten months.

[50] The World Communist movement was caught napping by the young Zengakuren zealots. *Pravda* characterized them for some time after January 16 as struggling patriots, while the JCP's organ, *Akahata*, branded them provocateurs. Gradually the JCP view came to prevail.

up all night in a train from Kyoto with the hope of lying on the runways in front of Kishi's plane; they arrived just in time to see it disappear over the Pacific. Kishi's plane belonged to Japan Air Lines; in September 1951, Prime Minister Yoshida had left for San Francisco in a Pan-American plane. The difference told much about the man and the nation that insisted on revising the security treaty.

The Treaty Is Signed

The final drafts of the treaty and administrative agreement were polished and made ready for signing at the twenty-second official meeting between Fujiyama and MacArthur on January 6, 1960. At this stage the LDP pulled itself together long enough to display a façade of unity toward the public.[51] Aside from the incidents described above, there were no signs that the treaty issue would blow up into a national furor in May and there was actually competition among some LDP leaders for places on the official party to Washington. Kishi and Fujiyama bickered over who should sign the treaty (since Herter would sign for the United States, Fujiyama reportedly claimed the privilege for his side), and many conservative politicians still seemed to feel that their association with it would benefit them in the long run.[52] Kishi now began telling newsmen what he had been thinking all along—that he had no intention of resigning after the treaty was ratified—in fact, he would use the treaty to consolidate his power. His term as LDP President was not due to expire until January 1961, and it was not inconceivable that he could have pitted Kōno and Ikeda against each other once again and held power in the balance.

Kishi's reception in America was a warm one: *Time* placed him on its January 25, 1960, cover and *Newsweek* dubbed him

[51] However, Miki Takeo was still grumbling that Japan should have some kind of veto over the deployment of the U.S. troops, Ikeda was (curiously enough) urging friendlier relations with Communist China, and Kōno was insisting that the treaty should be Kishi's last act in office.

[52] *Japan Times*, December 7 and 30, 1959; *Yomiuri Shimbun* (evening), "*Daimyō Gyōretsu*," December 22, 1959. Kishi persuaded Ishii Mitsujirō to go to Washington, but Ōno Bamboku refused, apparently wishing to keep freedom of action in the forthcoming dogfight for succession.

JANUARY 16 INCIDENT. Police break up the Zengakuren students' barricade in the terminal building at Haneda Airport on the eve of Kishi's departure for Washington, January 16, 1960.

AT HANEDA. Zengakuren students clash with police on January 16, 1960. The placards read "On to Haneda" and "Scrap the security treaty."

DIET DEBATE. Prime Minister Kishi (right) replies to the question of Socialist Diet member Tanaka Minoru in the House of Representatives Special Committee on the Security Treaty, May 3.

MAY DAY, 1960. Cheerful workers and students carry an effigy of Kishi through the streets of Tokyo; the signs say "Scope of the Far East" and "Foreign Aggression."

JUNE 15. Zengakuren students "snake-dance" in front of the Diet's Main Gate as police prepare to defend against their attack.

DIET INVASION. Students prepare to break through police barricade at the Diet's South Gate on June 15, 1960. Photographers at upper left prepare to record the event.

JUNE 15. A police truck is overturned and set on fire by Zengakuren.

DIET DEMONSTRATION. The Main Gate of the Diet is surrounded on June 18, 1960, in a futile attempt to block automatic Diet approval of the treaty at midnight.

MAY 19. House of Representatives Speaker Kiyose Ichirō, having been trapped for five hours in his office, and having fought his way to the rostrum, clutches the microphone and prepares to call the plenary session to order shortly before midnight on May 19, 1960.

INJURED SPEAKER. Kiyose Ichirō is carried to Diet deliberations on May 27, 1960, having injured his ankle during the scuffle on the night of May 19.

LOWER HOUSE APPROVES TREATY. Conservative Diet
members give the traditional "Banzai" for the successful passage
of the security treaty. At right are the empty seats of the Opposition.

VICTORY CELEBRATION. In the early morning hours of May
20, 1960, Prime Minister Kishi celebrates the successful passage
of the treaty with his key strategists. Seated from left to right: Ono
Bamboku, Kishi, Kawashima Shojirō, Fukunaga Kenji, and Fujiyama Aiichirō.

HAGERTY SURROUNDED. The car carrying Presidential Press Secretary James C. Hagerty and U. S. Ambassador to Japan Douglas MacArthur II is mobbed by students and workers as it prepares to leave Haneda Airport on June 10, 1960.

CLOSE-UP. An unknown Japanese photographer took this photograph of Hagerty (right) and Presidential Appointments Secretary Thomas E. Stephens while they were surrounded by the mob.

VIOLENCE AT THE DIET. Injured students are stretched out on the street after the June 15 Diet invasion attempt.

VIOLENCE AT THE DIET. Injured police are aided after clashing with students, June 15, 1960.

FUNERAL PARADE. Students march through the streets of Tokyo carrying a photograph of the deceased Miss Kamba Michiko, on June 24, 1960.

MEETING OF PARTY LEADERS. The strain shows on Kishi as he meets with JSP Chairman Asanuma Inejirō on June 17, 1960.

EXCHANGE OF RATIFICATIONS. Ambassador Douglas Mac-Arthur II and Foreign Minister Fujiyama Aiichirō exchange instruments of ratification for the U.S.-Japan Treaty of Mutual Cooperation and Security on June 23, 1960 in Tokyo.

BITTER END. Kishi is carried from the celebration of Prime Minister Ikeda's election after being stabbed in the leg six times by a rightist assailant.

the "friendly savvy salesman from Japan." [53] All this got back to the Japanese press and Kishi's stock undoubtedly rose from the low point it had reached during 1959.

The revised security treaty was signed by Kishi, Herter, and others in the East Room of the White House at 2:30 P.M. January 19, 1960, with President Eisenhower looking on. The treaty was not, strictly speaking, a mutual defense pact, for though it went beyond the old treaty and explicitly obligated the United States to act "to meet the common danger" in case of an armed attack on either party *in the territories under the administration of Japan* (Article V) it did not obligate Japan to aid the United States in case the latter were attacked outside this area. Okinawa and other islands under the "residual sovereignty" of Japan but administered by the United States were thus excluded from the treaty area by the above language. The response of both parties to an armed attack in the treaty area would be limited by their respective Constitutional provisions and processes. The new treaty, like the old one, granted the use of bases in Japan to U.S. forces for the purpose of "contributing to the security of Japan and the maintenance of international peace and security in the Far East" (Article VI). A new administrative agreement was to govern the use of these bases; this agreement relieved Japan of sharing in the cost of maintaining the U.S. troops (amounting to $30 million annually at that time) and made some of the wording more agreeable to the Japanese, but it did not limit in any essential manner the status of U.S. troops in Japan.[54]

[53] *Newsweek*, January 24, 1960.

[54] U.S. Department of State, *Agreement Under Article VI of the Treaty of Mutual Cooperation and Security: Facilities and Areas and the Status of United States Armed Forces in Japan* (Vol. 11, *United States Treaties and Other International Agreements*, TIAS 4510), Washington: U.S. Government Printing Office, 1961, pp. 1652–1674. The main changes, designed mostly to make the agreement correspond more closely to the NATO status of forces agreements, were in Articles III, XII, XIV, XVIII, XXIV, and XXV of the old agreement. Even though this was the first time the administrative agreement had come before the Diet, its provisions did not figure prominently in the debate and we shall not therefore dwell on these changes.

The new treaty removed two features that had been objectionable to Japan in the old one: it deleted the clause permitting U.S. forces to intervene at the request of the Japanese Government in large-scale riots and disturbances and it eliminated the requirement for Japan to get prior consent from the United States for granting military rights to any third party. It also added an obligation for both parties to settle disputes in accordance with the U.N. Charter (Article I), a major improvement in the eyes of the Japanese Government.

Article III obliged both parties to maintain and develop, subject to constitutional limitations, their capacity to resist armed attack, and Article IV provided for consultations in the event that the security of Japan or peace and security in the Far East were threatened. In the exchange of notes accompanying the treaty the United States agreed to consult with Japan beforehand on major changes in deployment, equipment (i.e., nuclear weapons) and use of bases for military combat operations outside Japan. Either party could terminate the treaty after ten years by giving one year's advance notice to the other.

In the Joint Communiqué after the signing, both sides stressed the economic and cooperative aspects of the treaty, and mention was made of the forthcoming celebration of the centennial of U.S.–Japan relations in the "new era." [55] The next day it was also announced that President Eisenhower and Crown Prince Akihito would exchange visits in 1960, and that the President would arrive in Japan around June 20.[56] Few people—perhaps not even Kishi—were aware at that time of the enormous potential effect of this decision on Japanese politics.

Back in Tokyo the signing was greeted calmly. The treaty

[55] See Appendix E.

[56] There were reliable reports of a behind-the-scenes clash on this matter. According to one account, the Crown Prince's forthcoming visit was originally to be announced by both governments in the Joint Communiqué of January 19, and the date for the visit was to be May 1960. The Imperial Household Agency, in theory an "outer office" in the Prime Minister's Office, objected on the grounds that the trip might be utilized politically. I.H.A. Director Usami Takeshi apparently won the day, for the trip was postponed until the autumn of 1960. *Japan Times*, March 9, 1960, article by Murata Kiyoaki.

text and entire administrative agreement were carried in the newspapers. The People's Council rallied at Hibiya Park on the day of Kishi's departure and Sōhyō called for strikes and workshop rallies on the day of the signing. The Socialist Party made a statement on January 19 to the effect that the hand that countersigned the Imperial Rescript to begin the Pacific War had now signed the new pact which might drive Japan into a new abyss. Sōhyō said that the government was going against the times and the new Democratic Socialist Party observed that the treaty added to the apprehensions of the Japanese people and was unconstitutional. Zenrō deplored the treaty and urged the government to dissolve the House of Representatives.[57]

No untoward incidents marred Kishi's return to Tokyo on January 24, 1960. The LDP saw to it that he received a "hero's welcome" and the nation settled back for the long and bitter debate over ratification in the Diet. The People's Council spoke ominously of large-scale strikes and demonstrations in mid-April, near the climax of the debate, but for the moment, at least, there were no new outbursts.

With the signing of the treaty, the protest movement entered a new phase. November 27 marked the climax of the "older" left wing's attempt to block the new treaty. The efforts of organized labor, with its not entirely welcome spearhead of extremist students, had not been enough to upset the government's plans on the streets outside the Diet. The Socialists, in spite of their strong verbal attacks, were too weak in numbers to block the treaty inside the Diet. New blood—an aroused nation—would be needed if ratification were to be blocked in the Diet.

[57] *Japan Times*, January 20, 1960.

CHAPTER 6

The Great Debate of 1960

THE YEAR 1960 will be remembered in Japan for its unprecedented political turmoil, but behind the disturbances were economic developments of high significance. To balance this account of a nation in political crisis, we should note at least briefly the remarkable economic growth that occurred in spite of the troubled political scene. One needed only a few hours in Tokyo of 1960 to see the nation moving forward: buildings, bridges, roads, and subways sprang up almost overnight; giant cranes, earth-movers and dump trucks tore into whole city blocks even as thousands of demonstrators marched the streets in political protest. The figures below tell an impressive story of a land weak in capital and raw materials but rich in energy, resourcefulness, and ambition.[1]

In the five years between 1955–1960, Japan's per capita income increased by 80 percent. The gross national product in 1960 alone increased by an incredible 16 percent to $38.7 billion—the highest growth rate of any nation in the world that year. In fiscal 1960 (April 1, 1960–March 31, 1961) per capita income rose to $352 a year, roughly equal to that of Greece, Mexico, or Cuba; this made it the highest ever in Japan and highest in Asia, but it was still only one-seventh the level of the United States and considerably below that of Great Britain ($1,082) and West Germany ($965). Nevertheless Japan led the world in shipbuilding, produced 24 million (short) tons of steel and 115 billion kilowatt hours of electricity, ranking fifth in the world in both. She made nearly 2 million cameras, 3½ million television sets, and 13 million radios. The population

[1] Statistics quoted below are taken from the following sources: *Britannica Book of the Year*, 1962, pp. 229, 363, 370–371; Japan, Office of the Prime Minister, Bureau of Statistics, *Japan Statistical Yearbook, 1961*, Tokyo: Japan Statistical Association, 1962, pp. 166, 190; *Asahi Evening News*, December 8, 1960, November 28, December 12 and 27, 1961; *Japan Times*, November 22, 28, and December 12 and 26, 1961, and September 17, 1964; *New York Times*, April 29, 1962.

continued to grow, though at a declining rate, and there were almost 94 million Japanese on these crowded islands whose total area equaled that of Montana.

One may well ask why this nation suffered its worst political crisis since the war in this year of rapid economic progress. To this legitimate question one can only point to some of the shadows that lay behind the hopeful statistical profile. Not all Japanese were sharing in the new wealth, and workers in the large modernized industries were leaving those in medium and small enterprises far behind. This gap has been called the "double-decker economy" (*nijū keizai*).[2] It will be recalled that unionized workers in the small and medium enterprises were among the most militant in the November 27 Incident.

Another problem was that expenditures in the public sector were lagging, prompting the *Asahi Shimbun* to observe that the Japanese economy had the appearance of "an obese body supported by weak legs."[3] The gap between rural and urban incomes was increasing, meaning that second and third sons were moving from farms to the cities to find new jobs and face difficult social readjustment. One-third of the entire population was concentrated in the two metropolitan areas of Tokyo and Osaka, and one out of ten Japanese lived in Tokyo, which exercised a commanding influence over all aspects of the nation's life. A new middle class was forming, with rising expectations and sharp demands on the old order. With its new attachment to television sets, electric rice-cookers and heaters, and with the new "leisure boom" (*reja būmu*), all based on precarious installment buying and hard-earned savings, this group was in no mood for political and diplomatic events that might "rock the boat." In sum, Japan faced economic and social problems common to all rapidly modernizing nations—some of them in their most acute form.

[2] For an interesting and relevant work on this subject, see Allan B. Cole, *Political Tendencies of Japanese in Small Enterprises,* New York: Institute of Pacific Relations, 1959.

[3] *Asahi Shimbun,* editorial, August 15, 1960.

The Communist Bloc and the Treaty

Is it not clear to everyone today that in conditions of a modern rocket-nuclear war all Japan with her small and thickly populated territory, dotted moreover with foreign war bases, risks sharing the tragic fate of Hiroshima and Nagasaki in the very first minutes of hostilities? [4]

This message arrived three days after Kishi's return from Washington, and though the world was still basking in the warmth of the "spirit of Camp David," it was clear that the Russians intended to put up a strong fight against the new treaty. It is not possible to understand the mood of anxiety in Tokyo during the Diet debate without mention of this dark cloud on the Western horizon.

Since the San Francisco Peace Conference of 1951, the Soviet Union had condemned the security treaty as a provocative threat to itself and Communist China; in December 1958 the new Soviet line urged Japan to adopt neutrality and abandon the treaty; in return, the Soviet Union would guarantee Japan's neutrality and create a nuclear-free zone in East Asia.[5] Using diplomatic, economic, and psychological pressures, the Soviets made a strong appeal to public opinion. On the diplomatic front, they warned that the small islands of Habomai and Shikotan, which were to revert to Japan with the signing of a peace treaty, would not be given back as long as the new treaty remained in force.[6] In the annual spring negotiations over fishing rights they took a stiffer attitude. And, in a bit of "missile diplomacy" that was not lost on the Japanese people, they fired rockets almost directly over Japan in January 1960—missiles that reportedly hit within a mile of their mark down range in the

[4] "Soviet Memorandum handed by Foreign Minister of the U.S.S.R. A. A. Gromyko to Japanese Ambassador in the U.S.S.R. S. Kadowaki, in connection with the signing of the U.S.–Japan Treaty of Mutual Cooperation and Security, January 27, 1960," *Contemporary Japan*, Vol. 26, No. 3, May 1960, pp. 593–595.

[5] This differed from the earlier line in that it accepted for the first time the idea of a neutral (though capitalist) Japan.

[6] *Ibid.*

Pacific Ocean. Finally, they directed a constant stream of propaganda directly to the Japanese people, all with this important message: whereas the 1951 pact had been "forced on Japan," the act of concluding a new treaty would be a voluntary one by Japan and one for which she would have to accept the consequences. The new treaty, with its aggressive designs against the Russian and Chinese people, could only expose Japan to fresh nuclear calamities.[7]

In Communist China a special reservoir of hatred for the Kishi Government had been growing since Kishi became the first Japanese Prime Minister to visit Chiang Kai-shek in Taiwan and subsequently opened the "new era" in Washington. "We have no objection to Japan's friendship with the United States," said Chou En-lai, "but the point is, Kishi went to the United States to curry favor from his American masters by slinging mud at the New China." [8] For this and other reasons Communist China broke off trade and other contacts with Japan in May 1958; apparently the Chinese gave up all hope of doing business with Japan while Kishi remained in office.

Like the Soviet Union, Communist China began a propaganda campaign against the new treaty in the fall of 1958.[9] Foreign Minister Ch'en Yi, in a note dated November 19, 1958, accused Kishi of plotting against China and warned him to come to his senses or face disaster.[10] With the signing of the revised treaty, the Chinese opened up a barrage of propaganda on the theme that Japanese reactionaries, in collusion with U.S.

[7] For samples of the Soviet propaganda, see: *Izvestia* cartoons, reprinted in *Japan Times*, February 9, 1960; speech by Khrushchev to Indonesian Parliament, reported in *Japan Times*, February 28, 1960; *Izvestia*, March 25, 1960, article entitled "Neutrality or the Road to Catastrophe"; statement by Ambassador Fedorenko of March 4, 1960, reported in *Japan Times*, March 5, 1960; and Khrushchev's letter to members of a Japanese women's association, reported in *Japan Times*, March 9, 1960.

[8] Statement by Chou En-lai to visiting Japanese correspondents, July 25, 1957. *Japan Times*, July 31, 1957.

[9] For a discussion of Soviet and Chinese policies toward Japan at this time see Paul F. Langer, "Moscow, Peking and Japan: Views and Approaches," *RAND Corporation Paper* P-2098, September 12, 1960.

[10] *Japan Times*, November 20, 1958.

imperialists, were preparing for new aggression and menacing peace in the Far East; the Kishi clique was intent on reviving the Greater East Asia Co-prosperity Sphere. The Chinese fully supported the JCP's united front efforts and sent many telegrams of encouragement on the occasions of the People's Council's united action drives.[11]

One cannot tell precisely how much this Communist pressure affected the thinking of the Japanese people. Sometimes, as in May 1958 when the Communist Chinese tried to influence the general elections in Japan, the attempt seemed to backfire. But in equating the new treaty with war and nuclear holocaust, the Communist propagandists appear to have scored a major victory. They found ample support among Japanese leftists, and were able to reach the minds of many neutralists and non-Communists who had become convinced that the treaty was a dangerous and unwarranted risk at a time when the balance of world power appeared to be leaning toward the Communist Bloc. Mao's thesis that the East wind was prevailing [12] had taken root among significant elements in the Japanese political scene and this contributed to the worried mood as the Diet began the great debate over ratification of the new treaty.

Political Strategies in the Great Debate

The signed treaty confronted the Japanese political system with a challenge that it was not prepared to meet. To be ratified the treaty needed the approval of a simple majority in both houses, then the signatures of the cabinet members and finally

[11] For samples of the Chinese position, see Kuo Mo-jo, "Resolutely Crush the Military Alliance Between the U.S. and Japanese Reactionaries," *Peking Review*, No. 4 (January 21, 1960), pp. 14–19; statement by Ch'en Yi in *Japan Times*, January 15, 1960; and *Hung Ch'i*, article by Ch'en Yi, February 1, 1960. Two books in English on the security treaty were also published in Communist China in 1960: *Support the Just Struggle of the Japanese People Against the Japan–U.S. Treaty of Military Alliance* (Peking: Foreign Languages Press, 1960), and *Oppose the Revival of Japanese Militarism: A Selection of Important Documents and Commentaries*, Peking: Foreign Languages Press, 1960.

[12] *Jen-min jih-pao*, November 20, 1957; Survey of the China Mainland Press, No. 1656, November 21, 1957.

the attestation of the Emperor (as a formality). With the exchange of instruments of ratification with the United States, it would enter into force, replacing the existing security treaty. The Lower House was the key, for treaties were approved automatically thirty days after passage there even if the Upper House failed to act—provided that the Diet remained in session during that period.[13] Kishi, as President of the majority party and Prime Minister of Japan, had originated the negotiations and signed the revised treaty; his party still held a commanding majority in the Lower House in January 1960 (LDP-288; JSP-128; DSP-37; JCP-1), having won 57.8 percent of the vote in the general elections of May 1958. Why then was the system unprepared for the challenge?

One basic factor was the difference between the treaty and other forms of legislation: there could be no political compromise on its contents. Negotiated entirely by the leaders of the majority party, it had either to be accepted or rejected as it stood. Despite the existence of contrary opinion, it was ruled that the Diet could not amend the treaty; the most the opposition could do was win a majority for rejection and then send it back for renegotiation with recommendations for improvements. During the previous eighteen months, the issue had become totally partisan; ratification would therefore mean total victory for the LDP and total defeat for the opposition. Kishi, with his political career staked on ratification, could not afford a compromise at this point. No face-saving amendments could be added.

Total defeat is total disgrace in Japan, and complete rejection of the minority opinion goes against the customary process of making decisions—a process which rests on real or imagined consensus. This is why the treaty issue was so crucial for the parties, and why a breakdown in the parliamentary process was virtually inevitable in the spring of 1960.

Behind this collision course were the complicated factional struggles in all the parties. In the LDP, Kishi and his brother, Satō, were the mainstream leaders, with Ikeda, Ishii, and Ōno

[13] Articles LX, LXI of the Constitution.

the wary "middle-of-the-roaders," and Kōno, Ishibashi, and Miki-Matsumura in opposition as the debate got under way.[14] By now, all the factions outside the mainstream had accepted the "*hanamichi* theory"—a unique Japanese political concept. A *hanamichi* (flowery way) is a ramp leading through the audience from the Kabuki stage to the rear of the theater where dramatic entrances and exits are made. Actors customarily perform the *roppō* (literally: six directions) or "bold gesticulations" as they make their grand exits along the *hanamichi*. All these factions agreed that the treaty should be Kishi's "last act" in office—that he would make the same sort of grand exit that Hatoyama had made after signing the Japan–Soviet Union Joint Statement in 1956.

Kishi had other plans. He intended to let the debate in the Diet proceed for several months and then bring the issue to a vote, with the least possible disorder; he would later share in the warm afterglow of President Eisenhower's June visit and, in effect, charge back down the *hanamichi* (as Kabuki heroes sometimes do) to win a third term as President of the LDP. Though the other factions were growing increasingly restless, Kishi still had two factors in his favor: first, with Satō, he controlled the largest single bloc in the LDP; whoever aspired to succeed him would need his support; second, the Kōno-Ikeda rivalry continued to cancel out the strength of these two leading candidates for the office. On these two factors he built his plans.

Ikeda Hayato now had the full support of Yoshida Shigeru, who, as we have seen, had reemerged as a leading power in the LDP. Their strategy was to give limited aid to Kishi on the treaty issue, but to make sure that he got into enough trouble so that he would be forced to retire after ratification. To this end Ikeda gave tacit backing to the treaty itself but refused to take a public position in favor of any tactics that might anger the press or tarnish his "image." Yoshida also worked from Oiso to reunite the old "Yoshida faction" by bringing Satō back into the fold. It appears that he was able to strike a bargain with the

[14] See chart, next page.

CHART 1

ACTIONAL COMPOSITION OF THE LIBERAL DEMOCRATIC PARTY, BY NUMBER OF HOUSE
ʳ REPRESENTATIVES' MEMBERS AND PRINCIPAL SUPPORTERS, JANUARY 1960 *

"Main Stream"	"Middle Current"	"Anti-Mainstreamers"
ʳSHI FACTION—63	IKEDA FACTION—39	KŌNO FACTION—34
	Yoshida Shigeru	Hiratsuka Tsunejirō
ʳSHI SUB-GROUP—44	Masutani Shūji	Kitamura Tokutarō
awashima Shōjirō	Hayashi Jōji	Takasaki Tatsunosuke
ıkuda Takeo	Kosaka Zentarō	Matsuda Takechiyo
˂agi Munenori	Kogane Yoshiteru	Nakasone Yasuhirō
ıiina Etsusaburō		
ʸabe Kentarō	ISHII FACTION—18	MIKI-MATSUMURA FACTION—28
˪orishita Kunio	Tanaka Isaji	Takeyama Yūtarō
⍺rahashi Wataru	Nadao Hirokichi	Ide Ichitarō
	Kobayashi Kanae	Kawasaki Hideji
ᴶᴶIYAMA SUB-GROUP—13	Katō Ryōgorō	Furui Yoshimi
ᴢawa Saeki		Shiga Kenjirō
ʳafune Seijirō	ŌNO FACTION—32	
ᴢaki Masumi	Murakami Isamu	ISHIBASHI FACTION—10
	Kuraishi Tadao	Ōkubo Tomejirō
˻YA OKINORI SUB-GROUP—4	Mizuta Mikio	Katō Jōtarō
ᵉki Kōshirō	Aoki Masashi	Shimamura Ichirō
ᴢzukida Yoshitomo	Funada Naka	
ᴛŌ FACTION—28		
ʳatanabe Yoshio		
⍺shimoto Ryōgo		
˪chi Kiichi		
ᵒri Shigeru		
˻kunaga Kenji		

* *Japan Times*, January 4, 1960, article by Ikeda Hajime; these figures must be con-
ʳdered approximate only as the factions changed frequently and no one source could be
ʳthoritative. For factional breakdowns on other dates see Robert A. Scalapino and
ⁿnosuke Masumi, *Parties and Politics in Contemporary Japan* (Berkeley and Los An-
˪es: University of California Press, 1962), Appendix, Chart 10.

Kishi-Satō forces whereby Ikeda would help Kishi get the treaty through the Diet and then Kishi and Satō would step down and throw their weight to Ikeda for the next party presidency. The vital question was: would Kishi actually step down after a victory in the Diet and Eisenhower's visit? If the middle factions could have been sure of this, they might have combined with the mainstream to make short work of the Socialists' opposition. But they could not be sure, and they therefore stayed aloof, allowing the political crisis to expand and engulf Kishi for a time. In this way the power struggle among the conservatives added to the crisis.

Ishii and Ōno, the other "middle-of-the-roaders," each had ambitions of his own. Essentially, their chances depended on getting Kishi out and moving to the top through a stalemate between Kōno and Ikeda. Kōno, since June 1959 the leading anti-Kishi force in the LDP, appeared to reach some sort of vague understanding with Kishi on March 17, 1960, and for a time lessened his public criticism of the treaty.[15] Kōno's strategy was to force Kishi out after ratification and win support from all who objected to Kishi's tactics in "ramming through" the treaty. He also tried to ally himself with his old colleague, Ōno Bamboku. Ishibashi, who, for reasons of health, was not a contender, nevertheless made life difficult for Kishi by choosing this time to advocate closer relations with the Soviet Union and Communist China.[16] Miki and Matsumura remained critical of Kishi and the treaty throughout the debate, lending support to certain of the JSP objections to the treaty.

Kishi had the option of dissolving the Diet immediately after his return from Washington in January 1960, and there were many who felt he should have done so. If he had survived the attempt by conservative faction leaders to form a coalition against him, and if the LDP had returned to power with a reasonable majority—as it almost surely would have—Kishi might well have stayed in office for a third term. Why did he not at-

[15] For an account of this remarkable "understanding," see *Yomiuri Shimbun*, March 18, 1960.

[16] See, for example, his interview with Sōhyō's Iwai Akira, *Yomiuri Shimbun* (evening), March 9, 1960.

190

tempt this course of action? He answered the question in an interview with the writer:

> QUESTION: As you look back on the events from January 19, 1960 when you signed the treaty in Washington to July 1960, when you resigned, is there anything you would do differently if you had it to do over again?

> KISHI: Yes, I now know that I should have dissolved the Diet immediately after my return from Washington and sought the nation's opinion in February. The LDP would have been returned to power and there would have been no trouble with the passage of the treaty.

> QUESTION: Did it occur to you at that time to dissolve the Diet?

> KISHI: Yes it did, but I simply lacked the courage [*yūki ga tarinakatta*]. You see, it is very hard on Diet members to hold an election; elections cost each member a great deal of money, and no one likes them. So when the question arose within the LDP, the mood [*kūki*] was against it. Therefore I did not press it. I see now that I should have.[17]

Given Kishi's need for support from at least some of the other LDP factions, in order to press ahead with the treaty, it is clear that he could not ignore the prevailing sentiment against an election and dissolve the Diet on his own. Such were the considerations behind the LDP strategy in the battle to ratify the treaty.

The Socialists, too, had internal party problems to solve before they could give full attention to the debate. In the wake of Nishio's defection in the fall of 1959, there was a move to replace Chairman Suzuki Mosaburō by Kawakami Jōtarō, leader of the loyal right wing faction. Suzuki, who had been Chairman for nine years, announced in March 1960 that he was ready

---

[17] Interview with Kishi Nobusuke, January 10, 1962.

to retire, and threw all his influence behind Asanuma Inejirō for the post. Ideology, which normally plays a rôle in JSP factional alignments, seemed almost lacking this time as the left wing Wada faction and important leaders of Sōhyō backed Kawakami while the far-left Nomizo and Matsumoto factions were split on the issue. Asanuma, nominally a member of the Kawakami faction, had risen in party esteem since the November 27 Incident, and he narrowly defeated Kawakami (228-209) at an extraordinary party convention on March 25, 1960. Eda Saburō, representing a rising group of younger intellectuals in the Suzuki faction, became the new Secretary-General.[18] That the Socialist Party had moved leftward since 1951 was clearly shown in this election of Asanuma, who continued to voice his famous statement of March 1959 that U.S. imperialism was the common enemy of the Japanese and Chinese people. Whether they agreed with this statement or not, the Japanese people accorded Asanuma a greater measure of popular affection than any other Socialist politician since the war; the burly, flamboyant leader, who was assassinated only six months later by a rightist fanatic, was closer to the "common man" than any of the others, and he shared in their passions and their excesses during the anti-treaty crisis.

With its factional problems settled for the moment, the JSP prepared to carry out its policy of absolute opposition (*zettai hantai*) in the Diet—even at the cost of physical violence. There were two important features of the Socialist strategy: first, the process of deliberations was to be delayed and obstructed in every possible way so that the treaty could not be brought to a vote in the regular Diet session, scheduled to end on May 26. Second, the "weak points" in the treaty were to be attacked with maximum publicity in the debate itself. The JSP had lost its psychological offensive as a result of the November 27 Incident, and it badly needed to restore its image as a responsible opposition party if it wished to gain the support of the press

[18] The newly elected CEC consisted of six members from the Suzuki faction, three from the Wada faction, and two each from the Kawakami, Matsumoto, and Nomizo factions.

and moderate anti-Kishi elements. A skilled attack in the Diet might swing the situation in their favor.[19]

The new Democratic Socialist Party (DSP) occupied the pivotal position. Because it stood for strict parliamentarianism, the party was virtually obligated to see the ratification debate through to the end—even though this might indirectly help Kishi to isolate the JSP. The LDP knew that it could escape the charges of "single-handedly ramming the treaty through" if only the DSP would refuse to join the anticipated Diet boycott by the JSP, and it made every effort to be conciliatory toward the DSP in March and April. The JSP, which had at first blasted Nishio's party as "traitors to Socialism" and as a "second conservative party," realized the need for a total boycott of the Diet, leaving the LDP to debate the treaty alone in the final stages. From March 11, 1960, therefore, the JSP held open the possibility of a "joint struggle" with the DSP.

The new party hoped, more than anything else, for an early dissolution of the Diet to capitalize on the supposed *"Minshabumu"* that it felt would win it from seven to twelve new seats in the next election. With only thirty-seven (later thirty-eight) seats in the Lower House, the party's vote was not crucial in the ratification battle; what mattered was its moral endorsement of either Kishi's forceful tactics or JSP obstruction. The DSP tried in vain to take a middle course, making its support for the treaty conditional upon certain procedural and substantive concessions, and Nishio asserted that he stood ready to play the time-honored rôle of mediator between the two parties in the final stage of the debate.[20] This might have worked on other

[19] A *Tokyo Shimbun* poll in February 1960 revealed that nearly 40% of the voters had not made up their minds on the treaty issue, and the competition for this vital "floating vote" shaped the debating tactics of both parties. According to this poll, 24.9% were for ratification, 36.0% were against, and 39.1% didn't know (quoted by Fukuda Kanichi in "The May-June Incident," *Far Eastern Survey*, Vol. 29, No. 10, October 1960, p. 148n.

[20] The DSP clarified its opposition to the treaty on April 23, 1960, as follows: (1) Article III accepts the Vandenburg Resolution and therefore infringes on the Japanese Constitution; (2) Article V would require Japan to enter a war between the United States and a third country; (3) U.S. forces

legislation (Nishio did in fact mediate in the Police Bill affair), but, as we have seen, there was nothing left to mediate in the last cold choice of either accepting or rejecting the new treaty.

The Debate in the Diet

The Japanese Diet entered its seventieth and most tumultuous year in 1960. The 34th Ordinary Session, which was scheduled to sit until May 26, ran into an early snarl when the Socialists demanded that House of Representatives Speaker Katō Ryōgorō resign for his part in the November 27 Incident and afterward. The LDP, ignoring Katō's reasonable question as to what he could have done to prevent the incident, pressured him into resigning in line with their strategy of giving the Socialists no pretext for trouble at this stage. His place was taken by 75-year-old Kiyose Ichirō, veteran of many parliamentary battles.

The revised security treaty was presented to the Diet on February 5, and after a week of wrangling, it was decided to form special *ad hoc* committees in both Houses which would have exclusive control over the deliberations. The House of Representatives Special Committee on the Japan–U.S. Security Treaty, etc., was established on February 11, 1960, with twenty-eight LDP members, thirteen JSP members and four DSP members under the chairmanship of LDP "strongman" Ozawa Saeki.[21] This Committee met thirty-seven times between February 13 and May 19, 1960, and was the major forum for the great debate. The House of Councillors similarly set up a Special Committee of thirty-five under the chairmanship of Kusaba Ryūen, with nineteen members from the LDP, ten from the

---

might stay in Japan for a limited period, but an indefinite stay was not permissible; (4) Japan should have a veto in prior consultations regarding the equipment and deployment of the U.S. troops and the treaty should contain a specific prohibition against the United States' introduction of nuclear weapons into Japan; (5) Revision of the treaty should be possible at any time after one year's notice. *Asahi Shimbun*, April 24, 1960.

[21] Ozawa, already unpopular with the Socialists for his rôle in "forcing through" the Vietnam Reparations Bill the previous November, was a close associate of Fujiyama's, and a former Cabinet Minister under Yoshida. He was reportedly chosen because of his reputation for toughness in the Diet.

JSP, and two each from the DSP, Dōshikai, and Independents.[22] Debate on the treaty also took place in the Budget Committees of both Houses and was probably the most exhaustive one in the postwar period.[23] Public hearings were held from May 13 to May 16, in Tokyo, Osaka, Sendai, and Fukuoka, with important figures testifying on both sides before nationwide radio and TV audiences.[24]

The Socialists began to delay proceedings from the very beginning. Since the budget had to be passed before April 1, they attacked the treaty in the two Budget Committees and postponed the start of serious work in the Treaty Committees on the grounds that the budget took precedence. They twice arranged to invite Kishi and Fujiyama to appear simultaneously in different committee rooms (March 3 and 22) in order to delay one or the other committee. Then they launched a major controversy by asserting that the Diet had the power to amend the language of treaties, and by refusing to discuss the contents of the security treaty until this question was resolved. Hearings were held in the House of Representatives Steering Committee on the matter, and it was finally decided that the Diet could not amend treaties; this dispute, however, tied up the Special Treaty Committee in the Lower House from February 19 to March 8.[25] The result of these delays was that the important interpellations on the treaty did not begin until after the budget had been passed at the end of March. There was much ground

[22] This Committee played a far less significant part in the debate, meeting only nine times between March 16 and June 20—the last seven times under boycott by the JSP and DSP (June 8–20, 1960).

[23] An idea of the comparative length of the deliberations may be gotten from the following rough survey by the writer: the proceedings of the above two Special Committees took over 200 hours and filled 851 pages of the Diet record; the whole peace treaty debate took 130 hours and 677 pages, and the Japan-Soviet Joint Statement took 25 hours and 142 pages.

[24] Witnesses for the LDP included Fukushima Shintarō, Ōi Atsushi, Ōhira Zengo, Tamura Kōsaku, Taoka Ryōichi, and others; for the JSP, Ōuchi Hyōe, Matsuoka Yōko, Suekawa Hiroshi, and Nishi Haruhiko; and for the DSP, Inoki Masamichi, and Tabata Shigejirō.

[25] The LDP was moving cautiously at this point, seeking to convey the impression of infinite patience. Kōno Ichirō aroused the mainstream by agreeing with the Socialists on this point on February 20.

to be covered: the revised treaty and attached minute, the exchanges of notes, the long administrative agreement, and thirty-two related domestic legal amendments all required the Diet's approval. Kishi was still hoping in late March to vote on the treaty in the Lower House by April 20, but it was already clear that the debate would drag on to the May 26 deadline—when there would have to be a dramatic showdown.

It would take a thick volume to touch on all the important and interesting aspects of the Diet debate, for it probed into every phase of Japan's foreign policy.[26] Here we can discuss only the highlights, hoping to impart some of the flavor—the extraordinary bitterness and tension—that prevailed throughout. Two warnings should be made at this point. First, though we deal here only with the substantive aspects of the debate, it should be remembered that it all took place against a highly emotional background, with noisy demonstrations on the streets outside, with the press growing ever more hostile to Kishi and the government, with Soviet and Chinese threats rumbling off the continent, and with high tension in world affairs culminating in the U-2 incident and the summit breakup in May. Second, we have stressed here the more effective JSP arguments, and the weaker government responses, in order to explain how the debate actually contributed to public unrest outside the Diet. This approach is based on the belief that, though the government scored a number of debating points, the Socialists did mount an effective attack and were successful in stirring up real doubts about the treaty in the public mind during the course of the debate.[27]

[26] A useful summary in Japanese may be found in Nihon Kokusai Mondai Kenkyūjo (Japan International Problems Research Institute), *Shin Ampo Jōyaku no Shingi* (Diet Deliberations on the New Security Treaty), *Kokusai Mondai Shirīzu Dai-nigo*, Tokyo: Nihon Kokusai Mondai Kenkyūjo, 1960.

[27] We have not dealt with the more frivolous Socialist arguments which were designed to waste time or blur the issues. There were many of these, but the most amazing was that of Ishibashi Masashi (JSP) who told the House of Representatives Special Committee on May 6 that the old treaty already contained two features that the government was claiming for the new one: the obligation for the United States to defend Japan and to remain faithful to the United Nations Charter. Ishibashi, quoting Yoshida

Kishi led off for the government with a speech to the House of Representatives on February 2, 1960, in which he declared that the treaty opened up an entirely new relationship with the United States. Fujiyama followed on February 9 with a speech listing what the government considered the major advantages of the new treaty: it was defensive in character, compatible with the U.N. Charter, obligated the United States to defend Japan, provided for prior consultation, included a time limit, and rested on a broad basis of economic and political cooperation.

The Socialists, led by Okada Haruo, Yokomichi Setsuo, and Asukata Ichio, had done considerable homework. On the first day of substantive discussions in the House of Representatives Special Committee, JSP member Matsumoto Shichirō passed around two photographs of Kishi: in one he was shown wearing formal clothes in an official portrait of the Tōjō Cabinet; in the other he was wearing workers' clothes and was being hustled off to Sugamo Prison by U.S. soldiers. How could Kishi, a member of the Tōjō Cabinet on Pearl Harbor Day, insist that the new treaty was entirely defensive in character, asked Matsumoto. He then continued:

> Does not the new treaty serve to defend the United States rather than the homeland?
>
> KISHI: As you will clearly understand if you look at this treaty, Japan will as a matter of course repel any invasion against her territory using her right of self-defense, and the United States' obligation to cooperate in this respect is clearly defined here. Nowhere is it stipulated that Japan must take action in American territory or in a foreign country. Rather, I think the distinctive feature is that the United States is now clearly obligated to cooperate in the defense of Japan.[28]

to prove his point, was thus undercutting the very arguments originally used by Socialists and others to obtain a revised treaty. *Japan Times*, May 7, 1960.

[28] Dai-Sanjūyon-kai Kokkai, Shūgiin, Nichibei Anzen Hoshō Jōyaku Tō Tokubetsu Iinkai, *Giroku*, Dai-shichigo (34th Diet, House of Representa-

Other personal attacks on Kishi were to follow.[29]

The most widely argued point surrounded the meaning of "Far East" as used in Article VI, which stated (in part):

> For the purpose of contributing to the security of Japan and the maintenance of peace and security *in the Far East*, the United States of America is granted the use by its land, air and naval forces of facilities and areas in Japan.[30]

The Socialists tried to trap the government into defining the precise limits beyond which Japan-based U.S. troops might not be sent; their purpose was to show that both signatories had aggressive military designs and they hoped to reveal the dimensions of those designs. On November 10, 1959, Fujiyama had gotten into trouble when he included coastal China and part of Siberia in the "Far East" of the draft treaty; on November 17 the top seven LDP leaders had confirmed this interpretation. Now, however, the government was forced to retreat. On February 8, 1960, after some vacillation, it declared that its "unified view" (*tōitsu kenkai*) of the Far East included the general area north of the Philippines and around Japan, including the Southern Kuriles, Habomai, Shikotan (occupied by the Soviet Union), as well as South Korea and the Chinese offshore islands of Quemoy and Matsu. This view excluded the China mainland and Soviet Siberia.[31] Concerning North Korea and the offshore islands, Kishi had this to say:

> KISHI: I do not think that the whole of North Korea is included. But on the question of whether the bound-

---

tives, Special Committee on the Japan–U.S. Security Treaty, etc., *Proceedings*, No. 7), March 15, 1960, p. 6. This Committee will hereinafter be referred to as the HR Special Committee.

[29] See HR Special Committee, *Proceedings*, No. 15, April 8, 1960, p. 2.

[30] Appendix D, italics added.

[31] Dai-Sanjūyon-kai Kokkai, Sangiin, Yosan Iinkai, *Giroku*, Dai-Yongo (34th Diet, House of Councillors, Budget Committee, *Proceedings*, No. 4), February 8, 1960, pp. 10–13. This Committee is hereinafter referred to as the HC Budget Committee.

ary at the 38th parallel will ever be moved, I do not think one can make a clear statement. . . .

Awaya [Yūzō, JSP]: Well then, we cannot get a definite answer as to whether or not North Korea is included, but what about Quemoy and Matsu?

Kishi: In the sense that the maritime area is included, I think the interpretation must be that they are within it.[32]

The Socialists then tried to pin Kishi down on the question of whether U.S. troops were restricted to the area in Kishi's definition of the Far East, or whether they could go beyond that area for combat operations. The following long passage illustrates the kind of response by Kishi that the Socialists and the press later termed "bureaucratic, arrogant, and evasive."

Imazumi [Isamu, JSP]: I think this is a grave statement by the Prime Minister. When the U.S. troops mobilize to defend the peace and security of the Far East, suppose that the U.S. military should happen not to agree with our view of the term "Far East" in this treaty, even though the Prime Minister has said that the scope of the Far East as expressed in the treaty is generally synonymous with his own views as to the area in which the U.S. troops stationed here may operate. . . . This is the most crucial part of the treaty and I demand from the Prime Minister a response that will make the issue absolutely clear to the nation.

Kishi: I think I am being extremely clear. As I stated a moment ago, the point of concern in the past several days involves the meaning of "Far East" in relation to the purpose of stationing U.S. troops in Japan. . . .

[32] Dai-Sanjūyon-kai Kokkai, Shūgiin, Yosan Iinkai, *Giroku*, Dai-Rokugo (34th Diet, House of Representatives, Budget Committee, *Proceedings*, No. 6), February 10, 1960, p. 6. This Committee is hereinafter referred to as the HR Budget Committee.

On the question of the area within which the U.S. military could operate in order to deter an invasion from outside, the U.S. is an independent, sovereign nation and its Constitution, unlike Japan's, does not place limitations on its operations to repel an invasion. . . . As to the question of the extent of the area, as I explained earlier, it is the Far East in general [ōmune]. As I clearly explained a moment ago, it is impossible from a practical standpoint to discuss military operations in terms of drawing a line. As far as we are concerned, when we use the term "in general," we have a different sort of concept in mind. To Mr. Imazumi's question whether there is exact agreement over the scope of the Far East, for the reasons I have just mentioned, we are proceeding on the strength of a feeling that in the prior consultations we will have a veto over the operations of the U.S. military. Therefore the agreement "in general" that we are now talking about is an entirely proper interpretation, I think.

HIROSE [DSP]: This word, "in general" is incomprehensible. . . .

KISHI: As I have been saying, they [the area where U.S. forces may take action and the LDP's unified view of the Far East] are in general agreement. I am not saying that there are not the slightest differences between them.

HIROSE: Well then, the area of the Far East as set forth in the unified view is not an absolute thing. In fact, the Far East can be changed again?

KISHI: The area of the Far East is not at all changed by this. The problem up to now has been the import of "Far East" as it is used in Article VI of the treaty to describe the purposes in providing Japanese bases. The question you asked a moment ago was, if the U.S. forces were attacked from outside, how far could they go in repelling this attack. According to the U.N. Char-

ter and the U.S. Constitution, they are free and un-
limited in this respect. Those U.S. troops stationed in
Japan, however, will be the subject of prior consultations and Japan will accordingly restrict their sphere of
operations in general to the area that I have mentioned.
This is not the sort of thing where there can be complete agreement and no slight shifts at all.[33]

Kishi was saying, in essence, that Japan would use the prior consultation clause to veto Japan-based U.S. military operations going beyond the Far East as defined in the "unified view"—a
claim that would embroil him in a fresh dispute as to whether
or not Japan had the veto power in prior consultations.[34]

On the question of including Quemoy and Matsu, the Socialists argued that even the treaty between the United States
and the Republic of China failed to include these islands, and
charged that the government was dragging Japan to the brink
of war.[35] After considerable debate, Kishi shifted his position
again and refused to say whether or not the islands were included: "As I have said repeatedly, the concept of the Far East
is intrinsically vague and abstract, and it is not appropriate for
me to state concretely in this debate whether every island is or
is not included in the area." [36] With this "abstract theory"

[33] HR Budget Committee, *Proceedings*, No. 7, February 11, 1960, pp.
5–6.

[34] Kishi recapitulated this view in the so-called unified interpretation
(*tōitsu kaishaku*) in the HR Special Committee, *Proceedings*, No. 4, February 26, 1960, pp. 9–10; here he said that the U.S. forces in Japan were
restricted by (a) the U.N. Charter and (b) the requirement for prior consultations with the Japanese Government.

[35] U.S. Department of State, *Mutual Defense Treaty Between The
United States of America and The Republic of China* (Vol. 6, *U.S. Treaties
and Other International Agreements*, TIAS 3178), Washington: U.S. Government Printing Office, 1956, pp. 433–454. Article VI of this treaty states
that: "For the purposes of Articles II and V, the terms 'territorial' and
'territories' shall mean in respect of the Republic of China, Taiwan and
the Pescadores; and in respect of the United States of America, the island
territories in the West Pacific under its jurisdiction. The provisions of
Articles II and V will be applicable to such other territories as may be
determined by mutual agreement" (p. 437).

[36] HR Special Committee, *Proceedings*, No. 10, March 25, 1960, p. 6.

(*bakuzen-ron*) as it came to be called, Kishi put an end to naming specific areas in the Far East. When the Socialists challenged him to admit that he had changed his position, however, Kishi refused to do so, and all JSP and DSP members stomped out of the committee room, charging him with contempt of the Diet and saying that deliberations could not continue until he showed "more sincerity." [37] It was not until April 1 that deliberations resumed, and from Kishi's standpoint, a precious week had been lost. The LDP stuck to the "abstract theory" from this point on and was roundly condemned by the press for its shiftiness on the issue.[38]

Basic to the whole debate was the question of whether or not the treaty would drag Japan into an unwanted war in some other part of the Far East. Kishi responded to this question as follows:

"It is true that under the present treaty American troops can use Japanese bases [to counter threats to the peace in the Far East] and that at present, the Japanese Government cannot influence the operations of the U.S. military stationed here. America can operate just as it pleases. Under these circumstances there is a danger that Japan might be involved in a war without its prior knowledge.

"But if such a case should arise under the new treaty, the American troops would have to get Japan's consent in prior consultations in order to move, and thus a limitation has been imposed. This is one of the points wherein the new treaty has been improved over the old one with a logical revision." [39]

Sharp disagreement then arose over the intent of the "prior consultation" clause in the exchange of notes; the United States had promised in the exchange to consult with Japan on major

[37] *Japan Times*, March 26 and April 2, 1960.

[38] For an example of the criticism of the government on this point, see Hoshino Yasusaburō, "Kokkai Ronsō Kara—Kyokutō no Han'i, Jizen Kyōgi, Kempō" (From the Diet Controversy: Scope of the Far East, Prior Consultation and the Constitution), *Sekai*, April 1960, pp. 52–64. For the final adjustment of the U.S. and Japanese opinions, see *Asaki Evening News*, June 8–9, 1960.

[39] HR Special Committee, *Proceedings*, No. 6, March 11, 1960, pp. 9–10.

changes in deployment of troops, equipment and use of facilities for military combat operations.[40] The Joint Communiqué of January 19 also referred to this promise; President Eisenhower assured Prime Minister Kishi that the United States had no intention of acting in a manner contrary to the wishes of Japan in matters involving prior consultation.[41] The government used these two provisions as its major selling point for the treaty; because of them, it claimed, the fear of being dragged into war could be laid to rest, and no nuclear weapons or ICBM's would enter Japan. But skeptics both within the LDP (Miki, Matsumura, and Kōno) as well as the opposition were not satisfied that Japan's influence in the consultations would suffice.[42]

The Socialists were quick to demand a clarification on this point, and Fujiyama appeared reluctant, in 1960, to take his former stand:

> Kōno [Mitsu, JSP]: The matter of prior consultations is the key to whether or not Japan is going to be dragged into war by this dangerous treaty. First of all, does Japan have the veto power in these prior consultations . . . ? In the actual text there is no provision for prior consultation; neither the exchange of notes nor the minute has any provision for prior consultation. The only thing to base them on is the Joint Communiqué, but in the news conference following the signing, Mr. Kishi said that legally there is no power of veto. Is this true?

> Fujiyama: On the matter of consultation, in order for this consultation to be effected, mutual discussions

[40] Appendix D.

[41] Appendix E.

[42] As long ago as July 23, 1959, Fujiyama had stated unequivocally that Japan would have the right of veto in prior consultation over the deployment and equipment of U.S. forces, and that the U.S. Government would be violating the treaty if it overrode this veto (*Japan Times*, July 24, 1959). He reiterated this point in replying to the Eight Questions of the Security Treaty Problems Research Association in November 1959 (above, pp. 139–40).

must be carried out, and so I think that there will be times when "yes" will be said and times when "no" will be said. In cases where we persist in saying "no" we have the power of veto. The particular reason for adding "prior" to "consultation" is that the consultation is to take place before the problem arises. That the consultation must reach settlement beforehand is clearly indicated by the meaning of the words "prior consultations." From the very beginning, therefore, we have held to the interpretation that if as a matter of course the consultation fails to reach a settlement, unilateral action cannot be taken. This is also affirmed in the recent Kishi-Eisenhower Communiqué.[43]

Kishi, when confronted by the same question on the following day, introduced his own interpretation of the word "veto":

I think that the government has been consistent on this point. The reason I do not explicitly use the words "veto power" [*kyohiken*] is that, as I was saying, I consider the term veto power to have special meaning in international law. But speaking from common sense on the question whether Japan can exercise a veto— whether the United States can take action in the face of this veto—whether the United States is bound by this veto—in this sense Japan has the veto and the United States may not take action in opposition to this veto. With this meaning, speaking from the common sense point of view, I am stating clearly that Japan has the veto power. We in the government have from beginning to end consistently maintained this position and in no way is there any inconsistency.[44]

The opposition refused to accept Kishi's "common sense" version of the veto power and doubted the legal validity of the

[43] HC Budget Committee, *Proceedings*, No. 2, February 5, 1960, p. 17. (Kōno erred in saying that there was no reference to prior consultation in the exchange of notes; he may have meant to say no reference to veto power.)

[44] HR Budget Committee, *Proceedings*, No. 3, February 6, 1960, p. 5.

Joint Communiqué. Why, asked Yokomichi Setsuo, did the Communiqué not say "reaffirmed" instead of "assured" with respect to President Eisenhower's statement of intention not to act contrary to the wishes of the Japanese Government if Japan's veto rights were already implicit in the exchange of notes? Kishi responded that the "problem is one of interpreting the treaty and exchange notes together. The Joint Communiqué by President Eisenhower and me was, by legal interpretation, a 'reaffirmation.'" [45] Eleven days later, Hōzumi Shichirō (JSP) asked Fujiyama about the legal validity of the Joint Communiqué and received this answer: "Basically it is not a legal document. It is a Communiqué declaring the mutual intent of the highest authorities in both governments. With this sort of political validity, it is thus mutually binding. I do not know what you mean by 'legal,' but as I have been saying, it is not an international agreement and does not have the same binding force as an international treaty." [46] What would happen, the Socialists demanded to know, if the United States disregarded a Japanese objection in prior consultations? Kishi said that, in case of a serious breach of faith, the treaty could be abolished, but in the following exchange, he argued that both parties were entering this treaty in good faith:

> TAKEYA [Gentarō, DSP]: I would like to ask this: I suppose there are a number of legal opinions as to whether the Japanese Government could abrogate the treaty if the United States mobilized troops here in the face of a Japanese veto, to cope with a problem arising in Quemoy or Matsu. . . . But leaving this theoretical question aside, does the government, if such a case should arise, plan to declare that the treaty is abrogated because of a serious violation? Or will the government throw up its hands and say, "It's no use—they have broken their promise but it can't be helped. We are a subordinate country and we must keep quiet, do as they say, and wait and see what happens." You may

[45] HR Budget Committee, *Proceedings*, No. 4, February 8, 1960, p. 10.
[46] HR Special Committee, *Proceedings*, No. 2, February 19, 1960, p. 14.

say this is hypothetical and therefore meaningless, but I think that since this area is where problems are most likely to occur, we must clear up these questions now. I would like your answer on this point.

KISHI: As I have been saying, we may have different opinions on this point, but I am entering this treaty on the basis of complete trust between Japan and the United States. In the problem you have just raised, you are arguing from the assumption that the United States will violate the treaty. . . . I do not think it is proper for me to assume responsibility for saying what Japan will do in case the treaty is violated at the time when both countries are entering this treaty on a relationship of absolute good faith. . . .

Then, in an exchange of high significance:

UKEDA [Shinkichi, DSP]: . . . if Quemoy and Matsu were attacked, have you definitely decided at this stage to use a veto in prior consultation?

KISHI: . . . when trouble arose at Quemoy and Matsu several years ago, U.S. troops based in Japan were not dispatched; furthermore, if such a situation should recur, and if U.S. troops were about to be launched from here, I would apply the veto.[47]

It is clear from the above that Kishi was committed to two debatable propositions: first, that Japan in effect had a veto power in prior consultation even though this power was not explicit in the revised treaty or related documents before the Diet; and second, by employing the veto, Japan could prevent such military moves of the Japan-based U.S. troops as might be distasteful to the nation—as, for example, dispatch of troops directly to Quemoy.

Seizing this opening, the Socialists went on to raise a number of concrete situations whereby the veto power, if it existed

[47] HR Special Committee, *Proceedings*, No. 25, April 28, 1960, pp. 4, 7, 9.

206

at all, might be rendered meaningless. (1) Granting that consultations would take place when the U.S. used its bases in Japan for military combat operations and not merely when troops or supplies were moved, suppose that the U.S. Seventh Fleet were convoying troops to combat in Quemoy but that it stopped over at Okinawa for supplies on route, or suppose that it moved troops from Japan to Okinawa and then later from Okinawa to the combat zone; Japan would then be a staging area for war, subject to enemy reprisals, yet the United States would be relieved of its obligation to consult.[48] (2) Who would be the judge of whether a troop movement constituted part of military combat operations? [49] (3) The U.S. Fifth Air Force in Japan had by its own admission the capability of carrying nuclear weapons, and the movement of its planes in and out of Japan did not require prior consultation; if such aircraft took off from Japan, picked up nuclear weapons elsewhere, and then proceeded into military combat, this action would not be subject to prior consultation.[50] (4) The Fifth Air Force had its Headquarters at Camp Fūchū in Japan with a base at Taegu, Korea; if fighting should break out in Korea and the Fifth Air Force began combat operations under orders from Camp Fūchū, should not the movements of the United States air units in Korea also be the subject of prior consultations? [51] (5) Prior consultation, when it occurred, would be carried out in secret, and the Diet and public would not have a voice in the key decisions involving war and peace.[52] (6) If United States bases were attacked in Japan, the government could not, in any prior consultation that might take place, prevent the United States from exercising its right of self-defense.[53] (7) The U.S. Seventh Fleet was already carrying nuclear weapons into Yokosuka despite the government's declared intention to veto the introduc-

[48] HR Special Committee, *Proceedings*, No. 17, April 13, 1960, p. 18.
[49] HR Budget Committee, *Proceedings*, No. 3, February 6, 1960, p. 7; and HR Special Committee, *Proceedings*, No. 17, April 13, 1960, p. 19.
[50] HR Special Committee, *Proceedings*, No. 20, April 19, 1960, p. 2.
[51] HR Special Committee, *Proceedings*, No. 20, April 19, 1960, pp. 14–16.
[52] HR Special Committee, *Proceedings*, No. 20, April 19, 1960, p. 11.
[53] *Asahi Shimbun* (evening), April 27, 1960.

tion of such weapons; thus the prior consultation clause had already been rendered meaningless.[54]

The government met these and other objections with legal and technical responses (see references), but the burden of its case lay in the contention that the United States would act in good faith, consult whenever appropriate, and respect the wishes of the Japanese Government in all cases. But the Socialists' forceful arguments had created an image of a weak Japan being pushed around by its powerful ally in the prior consultations, and the government's case in favor of the new treaty was seriously undermined in the press and among articulate critics.

The problem of self-defense under Article V of the new treaty stirred up longstanding constitutional questions (discussed in Chapter 1). In short, the Socialists said that the Japanese Constitution ruled out the right of self-defense and prohibited the maintenance of self-defense forces. The new treaty, which called for the exercise of the right of self-defense, possibly in conjunction with United States forces, violated Article IX of the Constitution. The government's answer was that Japan had the inherent right of self-defense, but that the Constitution placed certain limitations upon the exercise of that right, and deployment of the Self-defense Forces was limited basically to the area under Japanese administration. Nothing in the new treaty called for Japan to exceed this limitation.[55]

The Socialists stressed that Japan would be exercising the right of *collective* self-defense under Article V—a right they claimed she did not have under the Constitution:

> DŌMORI [JSP]: If an attack is made against an American Air Force base in Japan, this would be both an attack against the American Air Force and an attack against Japan. Thus Japan would undertake military action with the Self-defense Forces. That is the right of individual self-defense. But this would also be the right

[54] *Ibid.*

[55] HC Budget Committee, *Proceedings*, No. 10, March 8, 1960, p. 5; and HR Special Committee, *Proceedings*, No. 12, April 5, 1960, pp. 4–5.

of collective self-defense by my interpretation. I would like to hear the Foreign Minister's opinion on this point.

FUJIYAMA: Any attack would have to violate Japan's land, sea or air space and in this case Japan could exercise its right of self-defense.

DŌMORI: Is it self-defense if the American Army and Japanese Self-defense Forces undertake joint military action to meet the attack? I think this must be interpreted as the right of collective self-defense. What about this?

FUJIYAMA: When the Japanese Self-defense Forces take action, it will be at a time when Japan has been attacked, as I have just said, so that it will be exercising the right of individual self-defense.[56]

This bickering over definitions had a deeper significance. The Socialists argued that the treaty called for collective self-defense because they wanted to convince the nation that the United States was planning to set up a NEATO (Northeast Asia Treaty Organization) similar to NATO. According to their reasoning, United States strategy called for a set of interlocking treaties linking Japan with the Republic of Korea, the Republic of China, and the Philippines; in this way the United States would use its bases in Japan to support military actions in the other areas. As proof of this plot, the Socialists cited a number of ways in which the ties were being established. The following exchange is typical:

OKADA [Haruo]: Recently, from March 16 [1960] for a period of 12 days the Army, Navy and Air Force of Taiwan and the U.S. were scheduled to hold "Operation Blue Star." Do you know about this, Director-General Akagi?

AKAGI [Munenori, Director-General of the Defense Agency]: Yes, I know about this.

[56] HR Budget Committee, *Proceedings*, No. 9, February 13, 1960, p. 13.

OKADA: Did U.S. Forces in Japan participate in these maneuvers?

AKAGI: I shall reply after looking into the matter.

OKADA: The Japanese Government doesn't even know about this sort of thing. It has been completely blindfolded by America so that it doesn't know what is being done. Even if a nuclear bomb were brought in it would not know. Mr. Akagi, don't you even know about this matter? They did participate, I imagine, Mr. Katō, please reply; the matter is very clear, is it not?

KATŌ [Yōzō, Director of the Defense Bureau]: Operation Blue Star was carried out by the Taiwan–U.S. Forces from March 23–27. As for the U.S. forces in Japan, the First Marine Air Division from Oppama participated in these maneuvers.

OKADA: Mr. Akagi, you really must remember these things. Well, what about this, Mr. Prime Minister? Even on maneuvers between America and Taiwan U.S. troops stationed in Japan are used. . . . If this is not NEATO, what is it . . . ?

KISHI: That was a case of maneuvers, of course; as you know, in the present treaty these are not covered. Thus for the time being there may be some things that the Director-General of the Defense Agency does not know. This is precisely one of the reasons for wanting to amend this treaty. . . .

Kishi went on to say that under the new treaty the provision for consultations under Article IV would keep Japan aware of U.S. military moves. Okada insisted, however, that this use of U.S. troops in Japan for joint U.S.–Taiwan maneuvers "clearly exposes America's intention to establish NEATO through the security treaty." [57]

[57] HR Special Committee, *Proceedings*, No. 23, April 26, 1960, pp. 13–15; see also Okada's charges that Japan cooperated in building a microwave network in Taiwan (*Asahi Shimbun*, evening, April 27, 1960).

Another government claim that came under fire was the argument that the new treaty obligated the United States to defend Japan for the first time while Japan undertook no new obligations to the United States. The Socialists disagreed violently. By the language of Article V, they said, the United States was obligated only to exercise its right of individual or collective self-defense in case of an armed attack in the treaty area; where and how it exercised these rights were not defined. The implication was that a Communist attack against Japan might be met by a U.S. thrust elsewhere, while Japan would be abandoned to her fate. Furthermore, Japan was committing herself to the exercise of her right of individual self-defense (if indeed she had one) whereas previously the exercise of this right had been optional.[58] Another new obligation was buried in Article III, according to the Socialists. Based on the Vandenburg Resolution this article would oblige Japan to rearm even faster and the consultations under Article IV would give the U.S. a strong voice in the process.[59]

The Socialists went to great lengths to point out what they considered dangerous weaknesses in the language of the treaty: what constituted an armed attack under Article V? Was Japan to be bound by the United States' broad definition? Who would ultimately decide whether an attack had occurred? [60] Supposing the attack were provoked by the United States? [61] What is the meaning of "threatened" in Article IV? [62] Was the treaty a military alliance? If not, what was it? [63] Did not the treaty violate the concept of regional security organizations

[58] Exchange between Sone Eki (DSP) and Kishi, HC Budget Committee, *Proceedings*, No. 8, March 5, 1960, pp. 8–9.

[59] HR Special Committee, *Proceedings*, No. 21, April 20, 1960, pp. 30–31; HR Budget Committee, *Proceedings*, No. 4, February 8, 1960, pp. 14–15; HC Budget Committee, *Proceedings*, No. 7, March 4, 1960, p. 12; and HC Budget Committee, *Proceedings*, No. 10, March 8, 1960, p. 27.

[60] HR Special Committee, *Proceedings*, No. 7, March 15, 1960, pp. 19–23.

[61] HC Budget Committee, *Proceedings*, No. 18, March 21, 1960, p. 19.

[62] HR Special Committee, *Proceedings*, No. 11, April 1, 1960, pp. 8–9; and HR Special Committee, *Proceedings*, No. 13, April 6, 1960.

[63] HR Special Committee, *Proceedings*, No. 15, April 8, 1960, p. 13.

envisioned in Article LII of the U.N. Charter? [64] Space does not permit us to go into the detailed reasoning behind these questions and answers; it suffices to show that no aspect of the treaty was overlooked in the vigorous opposition assault on the question of self-defense.

The remaining points in the dispute may be listed briefly as follows. Until the return of international tension in May 1960, an important Socialist argument had been that the new treaty ran against the current of the times—that it threatened the chances of peaceful coexistence and violated the "spirit of Camp David." Kishi, while admitting that a thaw had taken place in the Cold War, nevertheless maintained that many problems remained to be settled and local wars were still possible—hence the continuing need for the alliance with the United States, which was strictly defensive in character.[65] The Socialists eyed Article II with unconcealed suspicion; the "economic cooperation clause" was nothing more than a guise for joint U.S.–Japan weapons production and it traded Japan's economic independence for United States military aid.[66] Nagasue Eiichi of the DSP declared that Japan would be unable to remain neutral if the United States used its Japanese bases to support combat operations against a third country.[67] The Socialists charged that the "internal disturbance clause" of the old treaty had reappeared in new clothing under Article IV— the "consultation clause." [68] The legality of United States bases in Japanese territory not under the administration of Japan was doubted; Takeya Gentarō (DSP) argued that Japan's prior per-

[64] HR Special Committee, *Proceedings*, No. 15, April 8, 1960, p. 13.

[65] HR Special Committee, *Proceedings*, No. 4, February 26, 1960, p. 2; No. 7, March 15, 1960, p. 3; and No. 21, April 20, 1960, pp. 5–6; HC Budget Committee, *Proceedings*, No. 2, February 5, 1960, p. 14; and No. 8, March 5, 1960, pp. 1–2.

[66] HC Budget Committee, *Proceedings*, No. 7, March 4, 1960, p. 10.

[67] *Japan Times*, March 22, 1960 (from the HC Budget Committee, March 21, 1960).

[68] HR Budget Committee, *Proceedings*, No. 9, February 13, 1960, p. 11. The government did say elsewhere that an internal disturbance supported from outside might result in action under Article V, however.

mission under Article VI applied no less to bases in Okinawa than to the others.[69]

The ten-year time limit was the subject of much debate; the opposition sided with dissident LDP members in arguing that ten years was too long a commitment in this rapidly changing world and together they advocated a one-year term with an option to terminate by one year's notice.[70] The opposition tried to prove that the treaty assumed hypothetical enemies in the Soviet Union and Communist China, and held that relations with the bloc would suffer badly if Japan took this step which would be considered aggressive by her Communist neighbors. Kishi, pressed by Okada Haruo on this point, denied that the treaty was aimed at specific "enemies" and answered that "security systems are set up precisely because peace is desired, and I don't think peace and security are mutually contradictory." [71]

A final word should be said of the strong implication in many of the Socialists' arguments that the United States had ulterior motives in the treaty ranging from gradual economic exploitation to outright treachery. One example was the suggestion by Ōnuki Daihachi that in case hostilities should break out elsewhere in the Far East, the United States might suddenly and unilaterally return Okinawa to Japanese administration, thus bringing the island into the treaty area, exposing it to enemy attack, and pulling Japan into the war.[72] There was much excitement when Asukata Ichio (JSP) produced Self-defense Force maps of Kamchatka Peninsula, the Northern Kuriles, Eastern Siberia, Manchuria, and Chungking, and declared that Japanese

[69] HR Special Committee, *Proceedings*, No. 17, April 13, 1960, pp. 28–29.

[70] HC Budget Committee, *Proceedings*, No. 4, February 17, 1960, p. 30; No. 8, March 5, 1960, p. 12; and No. 10, March 8, 1960, p. 27.

[71] HR Special Committee, *Proceedings*, No. 21, April 20, 1960, p. 9.

[72] HR Special Committee, *Proceedings*, No. 13, April 6, 1960, p. 13. Other attempts were made to undermine confidence in the United States Government; old incidents such as the alleged U.S. effort to set up a "secret Japanese Navy" during the Korean War were brought out in order to reveal the United States' dishonorable intentions (HR Special Committee, *Proceedings*, No. 30, May 7, 1960).

planes were currently flying over these areas.[73] The government denied these charges and rested its case on the need for trust in the United States; this was why the U-2 incident was to have such a tremendous impact on Japan just as the great debate was reaching its climax in May.

The Debate Outside the Diet

While the debate raged on inside the Diet, a campaign of gigantic proportions was being waged outside in the newspapers, magazines, books, radio, and television. Never since the war had a foreign policy issue so absorbed the nation; the Diet deliberations were carried by TV and radio into private homes, bars, and coffee shops, and phrases such as "scope of the Far East" and "prior consultation" became popular topics of conversation among housewives and office clerks. Between February and June 1960, hardly a day passed without some newsworthy development in the debate.

Both the older left wing organizations and the new anti-treaty groups intensified the attack they had begun in 1959 (Chapter 4). Pamphlets, handbills, and posters poured off the presses carrying arguments that are by now familiar to the reader: the risk of war, the danger of alienating the Soviet Union and Communist China, the infringements on Japan's sovereignty, and the violation of the Constitution. The parties added to the flow with pamphlets, "white papers," and articles stating their positions.[74] What really distinguished this period from the earlier debate was the shift of moderate or "neutral" opinion against the treaty. This could be seen clearly in the attitudes of the major newspapers in Tokyo which claimed to

[73] HR Special Committee, *Proceedings*, No. 18, April 14, 1960, and No. 19, April 15, 1960.

[74] See, for example, "Ampo Hijun Kokkai o Mae ni Shite" (The Diet Before the Ratification of the Treaty), interview with Narita Tomomi (JSP) and Sone Eki (DSP) by Arase Yūtaka, *Sekai*, March 1960, pp. 36–51; Mikami Masayoshi, *Gyōsei Kyōtei Hakusho* (White Paper on the Administrative Agreement), *Chūō Kōron*, June 1960, pp. 71–83; pamphlet (title not available) published by the LDP's Political Affairs Research Council, April 4, 1960; Minshu Shakai Tō, *Shin Ampo Jōyaku no Shotai* (pamphlet), published by the DSP, March 30, 1960.

be independent: until January 1960 the press, despite some misgivings, had generally welcomed treaty negotiations, but in that month the tone changed to one of outright hostility. The *Asahi Shimbun* editorial of January 14, 1960, made four demands that, if they had been accepted, would have changed the basic character of the treaty. They sought to (1) replace the "prior consultation" clause with "prior agreement"; (2) limit the purpose of United States bases in Article VI to the maintenance of Japan's security only; (3) delete all clauses incurring doubts as to constitutionality (the meaning here is not clear); and (4) drastically reduce the ten-year term of the treaty.[75] With Japan's leading daily thus opposed to core provisions of the treaty, and with the rest of the supposedly nonpartisan press growing more critical of the government by the day, Kishi was clearly headed for trouble.

Throughout the Diet debate the press remained critical of the government's handling of the interpellations and dubious of the treaty itself. The *Asahi's* editorial of April 15, for instance, accused the government of not showing sufficient "sincerity," and complained that the issues were not being "clarified." All the papers called on Kishi to "satisfy" the nation's doubts: "Even though the world outlook of the several political parties may be different, the nature of the problem is such that, for the sake of the nation and the people, the parties must get together and forge a mutually satisfactory policy." [76]

To the Western reader, the *Asahi's* insistence on a "mutually satisfactory policy" seemed incredibly naive in the context of the bitter partisan rivalry, the Cold War, and serious ideological gap between the parties in Japan. It can be explained in part, however, by the traditional belief that all disputes may be settled harmoniously by mutual accommodation of conflicting interests—that each side must yield slightly to preserve the unity of the whole. The press was also motivated in part by growing impatience with Kishi, by nationalist feelings that the treaty was too restrictive, and by its long history of opposition

[75] *Asahi Shimbun*, editorial, January 14, 1960.

[76] *Asahi Shimbun*, editorial, May 13, 1960. See this editorial for a summary of Asahi's objections to the revised treaty.

to the party in power which had become the measure of its "objectivity."

This was also an active season of books by scholars for popular consumption. One of the best known anti-treaty books was that of Ishimoto Yasuo, *Treaties and the People* (*Jōyaku to Kokumin*), an Iwanami publication discussing the treaty in terms of the United Nations and international law.[77] By June 1960 this book had climbed to the list of top ten best-sellers. Another was *The Nature of the Security Treaty Problem* by Terasawa Hajime, an Assistant Professor of International Law at Tokyo University. Terasawa, who stated in his first sentence, "I am a specialist in international law and I would like to give my opinion on the various problems from the standpoint of international law," went on to make the extralegal judgment that Article II on economic cooperation was really a disguised bargain whereby Japan would increase her military production while the United States would allow her to capture new markets in Southeast Asia.[78] A number of other books claiming scholarly or legal approaches to the treaty problem followed these two.[79]

The treaty was not without its scholarly defenders, though they were voices in the wilderness of Japan's emotional publishing world. The two best known scholars to support the revised treaty were Ōhira Zengo of Hitotsubashi University and Tanaka Naokichi of Hosei University. Ōhira had written two books in 1959 arguing generally for treaty revision, and had been instrumental in forming the Security Research Group in 1959. In January 1960, under the editorship of Ōhira and Tanaka, this group published *Research on the Security System*, a two-volume series of essays by prominent scholars.[80] The editors

[77] Tokyo: Iwanami Shinsho, 1960.

[78] Terasawa Hajime, *Ampo Jōyaku no Mondaisei* (The Nature of the Security Treaty Problem), Tokyo: Yūshindō, 1960, pp. 3ff.

[79] Among them were, Tabata Shigejirō, *Ampo Taisei to Jieiken* (The Security System and the Right of Self-defense), Tokyo: Yūshindō, 1960; and Kenkyūsha Kondankai, *Shin Ampo Jōyaku* (The New Security Treaty), Tokyo: Sanichi Shobo, 1960.

[80] Anzen Hoshō Kenkyū Kai, *Anzen Hoshō Taisei no Kenkyū* (Research on the Security System), 2 Vols., Tokyo: Jiji Press, 1960. Ōhira Zengo's

called for an end to emotional opposition to the new treaty and an objective comparison of the old and new treaties. Their book contained essays by such respected scholars as Yokota Kichisaburō (later Chief Justice of the Supreme Court), Rōyama Masamichi, and Hayashi Kentarō. These scholars were by no means entirely satisfied with the new treaty but most of them agreed that it was an improvement over the old one and that it was as good as could realistically be expected in the present state of world affairs. Another scholar who actively supported the treaty was Tamura Kosaku, who wrote a pamphlet called "Defense of the Free World and the New Japan–U.S. Security Treaty." [81]

The weekly and monthly magazines overflowed with articles on the treaty in the spring of 1960, with *Sekai* leading the opposition as usual. As in the Diet debate, every aspect of the treaty was examined. Professor Irie Keishirō of Aiichi University wrote in *Sekai* that Japan must heed Soviet feelings about the new treaty and called for general elections.[82] Tsuji Kiyoaki of Tokyo University also desired a national referendum on the new treaty.[83] Tsūda Tatsuo, a Kyōdō reporter, wrote that the new administrative agreement had many dubious provisions, including a basic labor supply contract under which Japanese employees of United States forces could engage in espionage.[84] Kuwabara Takeo, specialist in French literature, cited a secret poll of 2,500 Japanese leaders in all fields taken in 1959; the results, he said, showed that 539 were in favor of revision, 341 favored keeping the old treaty, 206 were for abrogation, and 63

---

two books were: *Nihon no Anzen Hoshō to Kokusai Hō* (Japan's Security and International Law), Tokyo: Yūshindō, 1959 and *Shūdan Anzen Hoshō to Nihon Gaikō* (Collective Security and Japanese Diplomacy), Tokyo: Hitotsubashi Shobo, 1959.

[81] Tamura Kosaku, *Jiyū Sekai no Bōei to Nichibei Shin Ampo Jōyaku*, Tokyo: Hōkoku Shimbunsha, 1960.

[82] Irie Keishirō, "Kyokutō no Han'i to Soren Oboegaki" (The Scope of the Far East and the Soviet Memorandum), *Sekai*, April 1960, pp. 29–35.

[83] Tsuji Kiyoaki, "Mushiro Kokkai Tōhyō-hō no Seitei o" (Instead of the Diet Election Law Should Be Changed), *Sekai*, April 1960, pp. 12–15.

[84] Tsūda Tatsuo, "Shin Jōyaku e no Arata na Giwaku" (New Doubts About the Security Treaty), *Sekai*, June 1960, pp. 80–88.

had no opinion.[85] Takeuchi Yoshimi, specialist in Chinese Studies, warned that the new treaty would deprive Japan of her last chance to make amends and prove her sense of responsibility for the damage she had done to the Chinese people.[86] Saionji Kinkazu, leftist son of the great *genrō* and Japan's only important permanent resident in Peking, described in the April *Sekai* the hostility of Communist China toward the new treaty.[87] Fujiwara Hirotatsu of Meiji University called the new treaty the "most humiliating in history" and Fukushima Shingo of Senshū University invoked George Washington's Farewell Address to emphasize that any mutual defense pact or alliance between two nations would be detrimental to peace with other nations.[88] Ryū Shintarō, the influential head of *Asahi's* editorial staff, accused the government of weakness and incompetence in negotiating the treaty and urged a shorter time limit.[89]

While one might have expected this outburst from Japan's vocal left wing and suspicious press, the remarkable new factor in the controversy was the appearance of important nonpartisan "moderates" on the side of the opposition. Of these, the most famous was Nishi Haruhiko, a retired career diplomat, former Ambassador to Great Britain (1955–1957) and an adviser to Shell Sekiyu KK. Nishi wrote articles critical of the new treaty in the February and April issues of *Chūō Kōron*, was quoted by the Socialists in the Diet debate, and appeared as a JSP witness in the Special Committee public hearings on May 14, 1960; a significant number of members of the Foreign Office

[85] Kuwabara Takeo, "Shin Ampo ni Interi wa Hantai Da" (Intellectuals Are Against Security Treaty Revision), *Sekai*, April 1960, pp. 26–28.

[86] Takeuchi Yoshimi, "Nitchū Kankei no Yukue" (Future of Japan-Communist China Relations), *Chūō Kōron*, March 1960, pp. 77–87.

[87] Saionji Kinkazu, "Ampo Kaitei to Chūritsu Kankei" (Security Treaty Revision and Neutral Relations), *Sekai*, April 1960, pp. 36–41.

[88] Fujiwara Hirotatsu, "Shijō Kūzen no Kutsujoku Jōyaku" (The Most Humiliating Treaty in History), *Bungei Shunjū*, April 1960, pp. 62–68; and Fukushima Shingo, "Jijō Oyobi Sōgō Enjo no Na no Moto ni" (In the Name of Self-defense and Mutual Assistance), *Chūō Kōron*, February 1960, pp. 30–45.

[89] "Ampo Kaitei o Dō Shitara Yoi Ka?" (What to Do About Treaty Revision?), *Bungei Shunjū*, June 1960, pp. 64–72.

were reported to be in agreement with his views, which made them even more interesting.[90] The gist of Nishi's arguments was that Japan should not annoy the Soviet Union by concluding this new treaty on her own initiative and taking responsibility for it in the eyes of the Soviet Union; it would only hamper peace treaty negotiations with the U.S.S.R. for another ten years. Nishi, drawing on his experience in Moscow at the time of the anti-Comintern Pact of 1936, thought it better to keep the old treaty and respect historical Russian anxieties for her Eastern flank.[91] Nishi also subscribed to the not uncommon view that "should a war break out, the United States will certainly make the utmost efforts to defend Japan, whether or not she is bound to do so under the existing Security Treaty. . . ." [92] Nishi told this writer that he was motivated in all these writings not as a member of any party but as a "patriot and lover of peace." [93]

Looking back on the public debate over the treaty in the spring of 1960 one is impressed less by the intensity of the attacks of the left wing than by the shift of moderates like Nishi Haruhiko to the opposition and by the relatively weak fight put up by those who claimed to believe in the treaty. There is no question that important segments of public opinion changed from apathy to opposition as a result of the debate in this period, and though a majority of the nation still probably favored the treaty, the vigorous and determined minority, with its new allies from the center, became resolved more than ever to avoid a humiliating defeat in the Diet.[94]

[90] Nishi Haruhiko, "Nihon Gaikō o Ureeru" (Worrying About Japan's Diplomacy), *Chūō Kōron*, February 1960, pp. 92–104; and "Nihon Gaikō o Ureete Futatabi" (Worrying Again About Japan's Diplomacy), *Chūō Kōron*, April 1960, pp. 30–45.

[91] Soviet writers later called Nishi a member of the "more far-sighted political circles." V. Smolensky and S. Bykov, "Japan's Realities and Her Military Alliance with the U.S.," *International Affairs* (Moscow), May 1960, p. 44.

[92] Nishi Haruhiko, "Some Comments Upon the Projected Revision of the Japan–U.S. Security Treaty" (mimeographed), February 11, 1959, p. 4.

[93] Interview with Nishi Haruhiko, September 20, 1961.

[94] Public opinions polls taken during the spring of 1960 indicated a

Before leaving the great debate, we should cite one opinion which was of more than usual interest during this period. This was a letter to the Osaka *Asahi Shimbun* [95] from ex-Lieutenant General Endō Saburō, once a staff officer in the North China Expeditionary Army (1937) and former member of the ultra-nationalist Sakura Kai (Cherry Blossom Society) in the 1930's. Addressing his letter to Kishi, Endō referred to the recent riots in Korea and went on to point out that, just as Japan had been unable to control her own militarists, so now she would be unable to check the movements of United States forces under the new treaty. Endō then wrote: "Mr. Kishi: You know that I have a long experience [*sic*] of military affairs, and I can say without any hesitation that today, when we have such highly developed weapons, the defense of a nation cannot be based upon the use of military strength." He then warned of the dangers of making an enemy of Communist China and closed with this appeal: "You may have your own commitments, but which do you think is more important—saving your face or the welfare of the nation? Mr. Kishi, please listen to the voice of the people, pay some attention to the unsavory comments [*sic*] made by the Soviet Union and Red China, and take advice from an old friend of yours who worked with you in the Ministry of Munitions. Be courageous enough to correct your mistakes."

Kishi, besieged on one side by leftists who had been jailed by the militarists during the war, now faced resistance from nationalists who had helped him pursue the war in East Asia. He had correctly diagnosed the mood of the nation in 1957 when he first pushed for treaty revision, but in the final days of debate the mood was swinging against him. Moderates and conservatives were joining the left and the issue was not so much the treaty now as the man who tried to use it for his own political future.

lessening of support for the revised treaty. Hidaka Rokurō, ed., *Gogatsu Jūkunichi*, p. 33.

[95] Reprinted in the *Asahi Evening News*, May 4, 1960.

 CHAPTER 7

Kishi's Gambit: May 19

In May and June 1960 the "mood" of the nation made itself felt as never before on Japan's postwar democratic process, unseating a Prime Minister and preventing the President of the United States from visiting Tokyo. The events of May 19–20 changed the character of the treaty dispute from a struggle by the left wing to an emotional outburst by ordinary citizens ranging far beyond the legal and political implications of the treaty itself. To understand the depth and intensity of the reaction to Kishi's move, we should examine first the immediate context in which it occurred.

Outside the Diet: The Left Wing Before May 19

Following the excitement of the November 27 Incident and the airport battle of January 16, 1960, the left wing was relatively calm until April; rallies and parades continued, but the nation's attention was drawn primarily to the debate within the Diet.[1] During the calm, the People's Council laid plans for a climactic program to coincide with what it imagined would be the end of the Diet debate around April 26.

The Socialists, though chiefly concerned with events inside the Diet, found time for speeches, signature drives, demonstrations and parades; their prefectural Assemblymen took an active rôle during this period. Sōhyō devoted its "annual spring offensive" to the anti-treaty campaign and supplied much of the manpower for demonstrations from its Government Enterprise Workers' Unions (Kōrōkyō) in Tokyo.

Sōhyō was embroiled in three other thorny problems at this time. First, in the Miike coal miners' strike, it was committed to a last-ditch battle against the Mitsui colliery; the "Sakisaka

[1] In this period United Actions 12 (February 25) and 13 (March 19) were held without incident; the 4th and 5th meetings of the National Representatives Council were also held on January 28 and March 18 respectively, to coordinate future strategy and plan massive petition and signature drives.

221

thesis" in action resulted in fierce picketing, bloodshed, and one death. Second, it faced new competition from Zenrō and the DSP and the loss of some workers who were attracted by Zenrō's current emphasis on economic over political struggles. Sōhyō actually feared that the DSP and Zenrō might try to cause splits within its unions. For this reason, the anti-treaty movement after May 19, with its appeal to nationalist sentiment, came at an opportune moment for Sōhyō. It seemed to justify Sōhyō's politically oriented struggle as opposed to the more moderate economic offensive of the DSP and Zenrō.[2] The third problem was that larger year-end bonuses in 1959 and spring wage increases in 1960 as well as the upswing of the economy had taken some of the "fight" from important unions; Kōrōkyō, for example, dropped out of the April 15 demonstrations as the result of a mediation proposal on wage demands. For these reasons, Sōhyō could not mount enormous demonstrations at will; it was not until the stimulating events of May 19–20 that it could really flex its muscles and propose a nationwide political strike.

The JCP worked to strengthen the united front with the JSP and at the same time to discredit the mainstream of Zengakuren. In the April Zenei, Kamiyama Shigeo, JCP representative on the People's Council, used Mao Tse-tung's "paper tiger" thesis to explain his party's policies. The enemy must be taken seriously at the tactical level, wrote Kamiyama, because the JCP was still too weak to provide vital political leadership to the masses. Some compromises might be made with the JSP in order to achieve an effective united front; it was not possible, however, to cooperate with sectarians (Zengakuren) who opposed the will of the party.[3] In the same article, Kamiyama

[2] To meet the threat from the DSP and Zenrō, Sōhyō took a conciliatory but ambiguous stand: its main current "Labor Comrades Group" (Rōdōsha Dōshikai) stated publicly that more emphasis should be given to economic problems and to the political parties. For an interesting discussion of this stand, see "Sōhyō to 'Nihonteki Kumiaishugi'" (Sōhyō and Japanese-style Unionism), Asahi Jiyanaru, February 14, 1960, pp. 8–13.

[3] Kamiyama Shigeo, "Dai-jūniji Tōitsu Kōdō no Yoru" (Night of the 12th United Action), Zenei, April 1960, reprinted in Kamiyama Shigeo, Ampo Tōsō to Tōitsu Sensen (The Security Treaty and The United Front), Tokyo: Shindokusho Shinsha, 1960, pp. 22–25.

detailed the JCP charges against the students. They were guilty, he wrote, of "extremist" and "divisive" tactics, and they failed utterly to appreciate the need for a united front in the struggle for independence. Kamiyama made it clear, however, that he was attacking only the mainstream leadership of Zengakuren: "Therefore we are claiming that only the Trotskyites—not the whole of Zengakuren—are agents of imperialism. We shall fight hard against their impulsive extreme leftism [*kyokusateki mōdō*] and factionalism, and we appeal to all peace-loving and democratic forces to adopt a correct and proper attitude in this regard." [4] In singling out the leadership for attack, the party gave a hint of its behind-the-scenes activities to create a separate student movement that would follow its directions. The JCP recognized the students' value as demonstrators, and it now redoubled its efforts to build up the "anti-mainstream" of Zengakuren.

With the arrests of key leaders in the January 16 affair, Zengakuren became temporarily paralyzed. In the People's Council it was isolated and even the thirty-member panel of lawyers formed through Sōhyō to give legal aid to arrested students disbanded in disgust on April 16, 1960, over the students' continuing extremism.[5] The students continued to show complete contempt for their critics.[6] They found some support from a handful of prominent intellectuals such as Shimizu Ikutarō (as noted above) and from a small group calling itself the "New Left" (Shinsayoku).[7]

Financial support came also from a new and surprising quarter: from Tanaka Seigen, prewar member of the JCP and more recently a convert to active right wing movements against Com-

[4] *Ibid.*, pp. 18–19. See also *Akahata*, editorials of January 14 and February 18, 1960, for further criticism of Zengakuren.

[5] Zengakuren had again tried to invade the Diet on February 25, 1960, and had caused other clashes with the police.

[6] See "Torotsukisuto to Iwarete Mo" (Even If We Are Called Trotskyites), *Chūō Kōron*, April 1960, pp. 126–145 (a panel discussion).

[7] This group included Takei Akio, critic; Asada Mitsuteru, Assistant Professor of Economics, Shizuoka University; Yamada Soboku, philosopher; and Sekine Hiroshi, poet. Though the students claimed many younger members of the "Old Left" were attracted by this movement, there is little evidence to support them on this point.

munism. A wealthy businessman, Tanaka disclosed in 1963 that he began supporting Karoji Kentarō and other student leaders because of his admiration for their brave struggle against the JCP. Tanaka claims to have given five million yen (nearly $14,000) to Zengakuren leaders between January and June 1960 and the students involved have confirmed it.[8] The disclosure would seem to solve the mystery of how the mainstream students paid for the expenses of running demonstrations: the handbills, placards, leaflets, and so forth. Both Tanaka and the students he supported claim that Tanaka did not influence their day-to-day tactics in the struggles, however.

Pandemonium reigned at Zengakuren's 15th Extraordinary Convention (March 16–17) when a pro-JCP delegation was refused admission and finally boycotted the convention. This marked the final split between pro-JCP and anti-JCP elements that had begun in 1958. The mainstream, meeting alone, adopted a radical action program; in defiance of the People's Council, they scheduled new Diet invasions for April 15 and 26 to coincide with the beginning and end of the 15th United Action. The anti-mainstream, now closely controlled by the JCP, resolved to hold "orderly" demonstrations under the guidance of the People's Council.

April 26 was an important date because it was the last day the LDP could push the treaty through the Lower House and have it automatically ratified by the Upper House before the regular session ended on May 26. If it failed to win approval before April 26, it would face an additional battle to extend the Diet session—another opportunity for the Socialists to obstruct the voting. The People's Council, half expecting the LDP to meet the April 26 deadline, planned for all anti-treaty activity to reach a climax on that date.

[8] This disclosure, which caused a minor sensation in Tokyo, was made during a taped broadcast and printed in "Rokuon Kosei: 'Yuganda Seishun' no Hamon" (Repercussions from the Taped Broadcast, "Warped Youth"), *Shūkan Asahi* (from TBS Broadcast), March 22, 1963, pp. 12–20. See also Tanaka Seigen, "Ima Koso Iu: Ampo Tōsō to Watakushi" (Now I Speak Up: The Security Treaty Struggle and I), *Bungei Shunjū*, May 1963, pp. 220–231.

During April the tempo of left wing activities increased. In addition to rallies and demonstrations, two Buddhist monks began a well-publicized three-week fast against the treaty in Asakusa; the Association for Criticizing the Security Treaty sold fancy paper to collect money for the drive; and Tokyo Chihyō sponsored a lantern parade.

By far the most important activity was the individual petitioning at the Diet. Professor Shimizu Ikutarō is generally given credit for starting this movement; in the May edition of *Sekai* (appearing in early April) his article "Now to the Diet!" (*Ima Koso Kokkai E!*) urged people to ignore the neatly printed petition forms put out by the People's Council. Write out your own petition, wrote Shimizu, and bring it to the Diet yourself. Shimizu envisioned a long stream of Japanese people marching several abreast from Hokkaido and Kyushu toward the Diet to exercise their constitutional right of petition; this was the only remedy, he said, when the Diet had lost its original function of representing the popular will. Stacks of paper would not impress the government, but masses of people, using the historical right of individual petition under Article XVI of the Constitution, would restore the Diet to its proper rôle.[9] Shimizu himself, along with Professor Uehara Senroku, led a group of 300 scholars from nine universities in Tokyo to petition the Diet on April 19, 1960, and many other scholars' groups followed their example, gaining considerable publicity in the press.

The People's Council was torn on the question of tactics for the April 26 action. Zengakuren, which ridiculed the calm petition marches as "*oshōkō seigan demo*" (incense-burning petition demonstrations), urged as usual a massive assault on the Diet. The JSP representative, Ōshiba Shigeo, did not go that far but insisted that the demonstrations be held in the Diet vicinity. Suzuki Ichizō, JCP "observer," stood alone in counseling against action near the Diet on the ground that there was no guarantee against a repetition of November 27. Ōshiba and Suzuki exchanged sharp words at the April 12 Directors' Meeting, but on April 13 secret meetings between JCP Secretary-General

[9] *Sekai*, May 1960, pp. 18–28.

Miyamoto Kenji and Sōhyō's Iwai Akira on one hand, and between Asanuma and Shiga Yoshio (JCP) on the other, resolved the matter.[10] The result of these meetings was the new "Strategy Committee" (Senjutsu Iinkai) consisting of the following five members: JSP, JCP, Sōhyō, Chūritsu Rōren, and the Tokyo Joint Struggle Council.[11] A compromise was reached whereby the JCP would sit on this committee as an "observer" but its opinions would be "respected." What this meant, in fact, was that the JCP would exert a strong voice in all matters of tactics from now on, giving official recognition to an actuality that had existed for some time. The JCP yielded on the issue of the April 26 demonstrations but successfully kept the Zengakuren representative off the Strategy Committee.[12]

In this way the decision was finally reached that the demonstrations on April 26, though they would take place near the Diet, would be calm and quiet; there would be petitioning only —no songs, flags, or placards. Five different groups, staggered to avoid overlapping, would parade calmly past the House of Councillors reception area and hand petitions to Diet members. The People's Council informed Zengakuren it would take no responsibility for any violence that might occur, and the assembly area of Tōrōren was moved from Chapel Center to Shiba Park to avoid any implication of cooperation in Zengakuren's plans. The police also warned the students against violence, but Zengakuren responded on April 22 that nothing could stop it from carrying on its fight.

Much publicity preceded the April 26 affair: the JSP hired planes to drop 500,000 leaflets over Tokyo on Sunday, April 24, and the Association for Criticizing the Security Treaty

[10] From a source who was present at the Directors' Meeting of the People's Council on April 12, 1960.

[11] See above, p. 112.

[12] Kamiyama Shigeo, whether for his defeat on the April 26 tactics issue or for his quarrels with Miyamoto Kenji or for other reasons, was replaced as JCP representative to the People's Council by Suzuki Ichizō in April 1960. In October 1964 Kamiyama was finally expelled from the JCP on charges of "anti-party activities." It appears that he opposed the subsequent pro-Chinese Communist stance of the JCP, along with Shiga Yoshio and Suzuki Ichizō.

226

posted such well-known figures as Miss Matsuoka Yōko, Mrs. Asakura Setsu, and Hani Susumu at important railway stations in Tokyo to pass out handbills. Sōhyō prepared for a mobilization of 100,000 workers.

The demonstrations of April 26 turned out to be even larger than those of November 27, though no accurate figures are available. The vast majority of demonstrators were from Sōhyō, but a record number of students—about 13,000—added to the crowds.[13] The students had been under great pressure from the two factions of Zengakuren, and it appears that the anti-mainstream (pro-JCP) group was able to win a majority to the side of "orderly demonstrations."[14] The crowds under the People's Council marched by the west side of the Diet in an orderly fashion, presenting petitions to the waiting JSP Dietmen who applauded in return.

On the opposite side of the Diet, however, Zengakuren mainstream leaders under Karoji Kentarō led some 4,000 students in a charge against the main gate. They were met by reinforced police barricades of armored cars and men. The students threw stones and the police used clubs and in this vicious fight the students were beaten back before reaching the compound. Some 600 rightists also got into minor scuffles with the demonstrators. By nine o'clock that night, after a series of sit-downs and snake dances, the students finally retired. Eighty-three policemen and forty-one students had been injured; almost all of Zengakuren's CEC had been arrested, including Karoji.

Between April 26 and May 19 the left wing continued its pressure against the government, but without further violence. On May Day, a record 600,000 workers, many of them with their families, gathered in the outer gardens of Meiji Shrine in a generally peaceful atmosphere. Though effigies of Kishi and Eisenhower hanging together on the gallows were displayed, the mood was cheerful and there was no further bloodshed. The

[13] Many of the students were reportedly excited during this period by the recent student riots in Korea which were about to overthrow Syngman Rhee.

[14] Police said that the anti-mainstream had 7,200 and the mainstream had 5,500. *Asahi Shimbun*, April 27, 1960.

JSP announced that day that its signature drive would be climaxed between May 10 and 15 with a goal of 15 million; Sōhyō announced that the 16th United Action would run from May 9 to 26, with a minimum of 5,000 demonstrators to be called out each day. Zengakuren's mainstream, under new threats of expulsion by the People's Council, softened its stand and announced in early May that it would give up plans for another Diet attack and accept direction from the Council. The mainstream was chastened by its beating on April 26 and worried that JCP opponents would win over most of the students if they went on with their extremist tactics.

Minaguchi Kōzō led a delegation to the U.S. Embassy on May 13 to present a message of protest to President Eisenhower calling for the U.S. Senate to reject the treaty, return Okinawa, and withdraw all U.S. troops from Japan. On May 14, some 24,000 demonstrators braved the rain to petition the Diet; the number of petitioners had now reached 13.5 million, according to the Socialist Party. This large demonstration was also well behaved; the only notable violence was an attempt by thirty rightists to invade the Diet and petition *for* the treaty.

In these last few weeks of Diet debate, leftist intellectuals played an important part in the growing chorus of warnings to Kishi against a forced vote. Perhaps the most influential group was the Constitutional Problems Research Association (Kempō Mondai Chōsa Kai) formed in 1958 to combat the LDP–sponsored Constitution Research Council. It included former Tokyo University Presidents Nambara Shigeru and Yanaihara Tadao as well as the prestigious Nobel Prize winner, Yukawa Hideki. Choosing May 3, Constitution Day, for a statement they termed "nonpolitical," these fifty-five leading scholars declared that it would be very unfortunate for both Japan and the United States if the government forced the treaty through the Diet before public opinion had become convinced of its merits. They urged caution and a thorough debate.[15] Because of this and other statements by prominent groups, the stage was set

[15] *Asahi Shimbun* (evening), May 3, 1960.

for an outpouring of indignation whenever Kishi made his final move to bring the treaty to a vote.

The U-2 and Rising Tension

The spring of 1960 seems to have been one of those moments in history when authority everywhere is defied and attacked. In this period the world leapt from the relative optimism of the "spirit of Camp David" to the brink of a new war over the U-2 affair, but there were also the following other incidents in the news: On March 15, 1960, rioting by students and others in Korea led to the overthrow of Syngman Rhee on April 27; on April 9, the Prime Minister of the Union of South Africa was shot and nearly killed; on April 29, student rioting in Turkey led to an Army *coup d'état*; and on May 6, Indonesian students demonstrated against the Dutch. Even in the United States there was a stir when Caryl Chessman was executed on May 2; and 200 students were driven by fire hoses from San Francisco City Hall when they heckled the House of Representatives Sub-committee on Un-American Activities on May 13. Though these incidents were unconnected, they were interpreted by young radicals in Japan as evidence of an inevitable uprising against the older order by the postwar generation.[16] Professor Maruyama Masao's observation that "modern Japan . . . developed an unusual sensitivity to changes in the climate of international politics" was strikingly evident in May 1960.[17] In addition there was violence at Miike in late March and early April, resulting in a worker's death and many injuries. Even before the U-2 revelation, then, there was unrest in Japan.

On May 1, 1960, Francis Gary Powers, U.S. pilot of a C.I.A.–launched photo reconnaissance plane parachuted to earth near

[16] The question of how much the Korean students' revolt influenced the Japanese students has been much debated; some observers felt it contributed significantly to the charged atmosphere while others thought it unlikely that Japanese students would identify themselves with the Koreans, who were seen as an unruly lot, incapable of governing themselves anyway.

[17] Maruyama Masao, Introduction to Ivan Morris, *Nationalism and the Right Wing in Japan*, London: Oxford University Press, 1960, p. xxvii.

Sverdlovsk in the Soviet Union. On May 7, after the United States had denied sending the "spy-plane" over Russia, Premier Khrushchev disclosed that Powers was alive and that the U.S. Government had been caught in a major intelligence operation. The events that followed are well known: the U.S. admission, Soviet threats to U.S. allies, the statement that Washington would continue aerial reconnaissance and stand by its allies, the summit debacle in Paris on May 16, the trial of Powers in Moscow later in the summer, and finally the exchange of Powers for Soviet agent Colonel Rudolph Ivanovitch Abel on February 10, 1962. Japan was stunned more than any other nation by the revelation of the nature of the U-2's, and there were special reasons for this.

First, the Japanese had already experienced a U-2 incident of their own in September 1959, when a U-2 made a forced landing near Fujisawa. The event was not publicized until the *Mainichi* "scooped" the story in late November 1959, and Asukata Ichio (JSP) brought it up in the Diet (November 26 and December 1, 1959). The Socialists claimed the plane flew sinister missions and, as a civilian aircraft, violated Article III of the administrative agreement; government leaders stated that the plane was used for high altitude weather observation only and that it was under contract to the U.S. Air Force, bringing it under the purview of the agreement.[18] Asukata strongly endorsed the words of the *Mainichi Shimbun* editorial of November 28: "We begin to wonder in whose hands Japan's sov-

[18] According to Asukata's account in the Diet, an unmarked (except for a tailfin number) plane with long wings and a dark, lusterless coat of paint, made a forced landing at 3:15 P.M. September 24, 1959, at Fujisawa Airport. A group of Japanese glider enthusiasts gathered about the plane, but the pilot did not get out. Within five minutes a U.S. helicopter arrived, followed by an L-20 plane and another helicopter. The pilot, who had no markings on his flying suit, then alighted while American civilians, holding pistols blocked off the area, prohibited picture-taking, questioned spectators, and prevented Fujisawa Police and Procurement Agency personnel from approaching. The plane was then dismantled and taken in pieces to Atsugi Air Base. Dai-sanjūsan-kai Kokkai, Shūgiin Honkai, *Giroku*, Dai Jūyongo (33rd Diet, House of Representatives Plenary Session, *Proceedings*, No. 14), December 1, 1959, pp. 1–2.

230

ereignty actually lies. . . . In actual fact, we are still subordinate." [19]

Though no great public outcry arose at this time, there was some discussion in the press of the "black jets," and the Socialists continued to use it in the Diet as another example of U.S. bad faith under the treaty.[20] Thus when the Socialists' allegations proved true—by U.S. admission—the government's case for placing faith in the United States was shattered. This was a severe blow for Kishi and Fujiyama, who had argued for over a year that the U.S. would not engage in provocative activity under the treaty.

Another reason for the shock in Japan was the then current rash of "exposés" of U.S. intelligence activities in the popular journals. *Bungei Shunjū*, for example, was running a serialized version of Matsumoto Seichō's *Dark Mist Over Japan* in twelve monthly installments during 1960.[21] Matsumoto, a popular detective story writer, "solved" a number of mysteries of the occupation era: the murder of President Shimomura of the National Railways Corporation, looting of diamonds confiscated during the war in Japan, derailment of a train at Mitaka, overturning of a locomotive at Matsukawa, and the testing of a deadly poison on Japanese employees of the Imperial Bank to perfect germ warfare techniques. The writer linked all these crimes and others to a secret U.S. intelligence plot which had as its ultimate purpose the launching of war in Korea. Matsumoto's book was at the top of the best-seller list in May 1960 and he had a wide circle of ardent admirers. It is impossible to understand Japanese reactions to the U-2 without an awareness of these popular suspicions about U.S. intelligence; for

[19] *Ibid.*

[20] See for example, "Rokkido, Baishō, Kuroi Jiettoki" (Lockheeds, Reparations, and Black Jets), *Chūō Kōron*, February 1960, pp. 116–128 (panel discussion with Usui Yoshimi and JSP Diet members Asukata Ichio, Ishibashi Masashi, Okada Haruo, and Matsumoto Shichirō).

[21] Matsumoto Seichō, *Nihon No Kuroi Kiri* (Dark Mist Over Japan), 3 vols., Tokyo: Bungei Shunjū Shinsha, 1960. According to the *Bungei Shunjū* office in Tokyo, about 55,000 copies of Volume 1 were sold between May and October 1960.

many, the U-2 was the only evidence needed to prove all the other tales of horror.

With this background, the panic of May and June can be appreciated. The Socialists had their moment of triumph in the Diet on May 9–10, when they accused the United States of flying over the Soviet Union and China from Japan and demanded the immediate removal of all black jets from the country. They also insisted that any new security treaty give Japan the right to inspect U.S. bases. The government persisted in the story that the U-2's at Atsugi were for weather study, not espionage, but promised to press the U.S. Government for further information. Other LDP Diet members tried to counterattack by charging that Soviet aircraft had often violated Japan's air space.[22] From this point on the Socialists took full advantage of the United States' embarrassment and hammered away on the theme that the treaty was likely to drag Japan into war—precisely the theme that the Soviet Union and China had been pressing for the past eighteen months. Morishima Moritō (JSP) even went back to the U.S.–Japan Treaties of Commerce of 1894 and 1911, giving instances of U.S. bad faith and alleging that Washington was not to be trusted.[23]

The United States assured Japan on May 10, 1960, that "U-2 aircraft flying from American bases in Japan have been and will continue to be utilized only for legitimate and normal purposes and not for intelligence overflight missions," [24] and promised to support its allies in case of a Soviet attack. For the moment, however, Japan had suffered a serious loss of faith; even the friendliest critics sat back in silent dismay as the wave of shock swept the nation.[25] The popular columnist Aramaki Hideo summed up much of the popular feeling in his front page

[22] HR Special Committee, *Proceedings*, No. 31, May 9, 1960, p. 8; No. 32, May 10, 1960, pp. 10, 24; No. 33, May 11, 1960, p. 11. On May 8 a U.S. Air Force spokesman in Japan stated that three U-2's had been in Japan for the last few years and that they were now grounded.

[23] *Japan Times*, May 18, 1960.

[24] *Asahi Evening News*, May 11, 1960.

[25] See for example the column of the normally friendly Hirasawa Kazushige, *Japan Times*, May 13, 1960.

column in the *Asahi:* "The Japanese Government in its responses to Diet interpellations acts like an American branch store, and like a child, sent on an errand, answering, '*Hai, sō desu ka?*' whenever America speaks. . . . We are tired of hearing that 'America is clean and trustworthy.' We must face this problem from the standpoint of Japan's interests, and we would like to see it ironed out properly." [26]

Throughout May and June the Soviet Union chilled the blood of the Japanese people with official notes and horrendous propaganda broadcasts on Radio Moscow. The theme was Japan's responsibility for the provocative spy planes and the new treaty; terrible consequences would befall U.S. accomplices in this aggression. On May 15 the Soviets gave new evidence of their skill in rocketry by placing a four-and-one-half ton space-ship in orbit. Two weeks later Soviet Defense Minister Malinovsky sent the Tokyo stock market into a tailspin with the announcement that he had ordered Soviet rocket installation commanders to strike back at bases used by planes that violated Soviet air space.[27] The *Asahi* commented on June 1 that "the danger involved in this statement is truly horrifying. We wonder if the Soviet Government itself is aware of it." [28] Communist China added to the tension by charging that U-2's had repeatedly violated her air space and by holding huge rallies between May 9 and 13 in Peking, Nanking, Wuhan, Shanghai, and elsewhere.[29]

The Kishi Cabinet thus faced an aroused left wing and an apprehensive nation as it prepared for a showdown on the treaty in May 1960.

Party Strategies for the Ratification Vote

Kishi's original plan to secure passage of the treaty in the Lower House before April 26 had to be dropped because of the

[26] *Asahi Shimbun,* "Tensei Jingo," May 13, 1960.

[27] *Asahi Shimbun,* May 31, 1960.

[28] *Asahi Shimbun,* editorial, June 1, 1960.

[29] NCNA claimed that more than 12 million people demonstrated in thirty-three cities, making it the largest popular demonstration in Chinese history, *Asahi Evening News,* May 16, 1960.

intransigence of the Socialists and the foot-dragging of his rivals in the LDP. He made one effort to hold public hearings—a final step in deliberations—on April 22, but JSP Diet members created such disorder in the committee room that Chairman Ozawa Saeki was prevented from reaching his seat to open the meeting.[30] Then Kishi tried to circumvent the Special Committee and bring the treaty to a vote on the House floor by having Ozawa present an interim report on April 24. At this point, however, the LDP anti-mainstream factions (as well as Ikeda) refused to cooperate and advised Kishi to act "softly" (*odayaka ni*) in the face of mounting public unrest. Kishi was forced, therefore, to accept a mediation plan offered by Speaker Kiyose under which the treaty would remain in committee for further debate, the scheduling of meetings would be increased to include weekends, and all parties would henceforth refrain from disorderly conduct.[31]

In this way the April 26 deadline passed, and Kishi was faced with the double problem of extending the Diet session and pushing through the treaty.[32] Kishi and his strategists now aimed to bring the treaty to a vote by May 10 or, at the very latest, by May 15; this would assure automatic ratification by June 15 and allow a "cooling off" period before President Eisenhower's arrival on June 19.[33] To this end they tried to schedule

[30] On April 22 the Socialists laid siege to the House of Representatives Special Committee Room in the early morning and when Ozawa appeared, they formed a defensive cordon around his seat. Diet guards lifted Ozawa to their shoulders and charged into the defenders, but the Socialists held firm and the meeting ended in shouting, punching and lost tempers.

[31] This plan was first put forward by the DSP's Mizutani Chōzaburō, who reportedly made a vague bargain with Kishi whereby the DSP would agree to end debate by May 15 if Kishi would abandon his interim report plan.

[32] This was an interesting example of the somewhat independent rôle of the House of Councillors. Even though Kishi could plan on pushing the treaty through the Lower House, he could not be sure the Upper House would follow suit, despite its large LDP majority. For this reason he based all calculations on the passage of the thirty-day automatic ratification period.

[33] Kishi's chief lieutenants at this time included his brother, Satō Eisaku, Kawashima Shōjirō, Fujiyama, Arafune Seijirō, Fukunaga Kenji, Ozawa Saeki and Funada Naka. Their final choice of May 19–20 for the vote was

public hearings in Tokyo alone on May 11, but they were again thwarted by the Socialists, who succeeded in postponing the hearings until May 13–16 and in spreading them to Osaka, Sendai, and Fukuoka. Kishi was again forced to move slowly for two reasons: the anti-mainstream faction heads were arguing strongly against "railroading" the treaty through and even joined the Socialists in hostile interpellations in the Special Committee.[34] Secondly, DSP support for closure and a treaty vote was now vital to the LDP if it wished to avoid isolation in the Diet.

The DSP, only five months old, was already rent by factionalism. A senior "parliamentary faction" headed by Chairman Nishio and Sone Eki insisted that the party see the debate through to the end, while the younger and more numerous "Diet-members' Group" led by Mizutani Chōzaburō, Kasuga Ikko, and former members of the Kawakami faction asserted that the party must prove its progressive character by joining the JSP in boycotting the final vote.[35] Kishi could not be sure which side would win out, but he modified his tactics in hopes that the "parliamentary faction" would prevail and keep the party in the Diet. On May 2, however, the DSP reversed its "promise" of April 24 to support an end to debate by May 15 on the grounds that many points remained to be clarified and

---

not made, according to Kishi, until the Socialists turned down Kiyose's mediation proposal of May 17 which would have put off the treaty vote but admitted a thirty-day extension of the Diet. In other words, the timing of the treaty ratification to coincide with Eisenhower's arrival was not a long-planned stratagem but a last-minute decision. Interview with Kishi Nobusuke, January 10, 1962.

[34] On May 12 Furui Yoshimi of the Miki-Matsumura faction urged the government not to rush ahead with ratification while such provisions as the scope of the Far East and prior consultation were unclear to the public, and before the "understanding" of Communist China and the Soviet Union had been reached. HR Special Committee, *Proceedings*, No. 34, May 12, 1960.

[35] For a complete summary of this controversy, see *Asahi Evening News*, May 19, 1960 (translation from *Asahi Jiyanaru*). The party's position at this stage on the treaty question can be found in Minshu Shakai Tō, Kyōsen Kyoku, *Shin Ampo Jōyaku no Shotai* (The True Character of the New Security Treaty), pamphlet, March 30, 1960.

opinions were still too far apart between the LDP and JSP. Nishio said on May 7 that the Lower House should be dissolved before a vote was taken on the treaty but that he would not object to extending the Diet beyond May 26. Two days later the party's CEC directly contradicted him: it would oppose any extension of the Diet and it hinted that it might join the JSP boycott.

Kishi faced a real dilemma at this point. He could not retreat and hope to remain in office, yet he could not treat the Socialists too roughly even when they resorted to physical measures to prevent the vote.[36] It was becoming clearer that neither the LDP anti-mainstream nor the DSP was going to cooperate. The press was hostile and poised to attack any forceful steps. The middle factions in the LDP were still playing hard to get. Outside the Diet the demonstrations were growing larger each day. The world situation appeared more and more ominous; the May 26 deadline was approaching; the Eisenhower visit was impending; and there seemed to be no hope of avoiding a physical clash with the Socialists. Thus, on May 15, the LDP announced its firm intention to extend the Diet session by forty-five to fifty days, and the vote was tentatively scheduled for May 20. The party did not, however, say how it would bring about the vote, and there were intense and complex factional disputes on procedure.[37] A caucus of LDP Diet members on May 17 left the final decisions on tactics to the government leaders. Details were worked out in meetings between Ozawa Saeki and Kawashima

[36] A public opinion poll taken in mid-February 1960 revealed the nature of the dilemma: when asked their attitude on whether the Opposition should use "preventive tactics" to block the treaty in the Diet, 57.8% thought this wrong and only 12.5% thought it permissible. But asked whether the government, confronted with an Opposition boycott, should take the final vote in their absence, 59.9% thought this wrong and 19.7% thought it permissible. *Tokyo Shimbun*, cited by David C. S. Sissons, "Recent Developments in Japan's Socialist Movement," *Far Eastern Survey*, Vol. 29, No. 2, June 1960, p. 91n.

[37] The anti-mainstream reportedly agreed to extend the Diet session but opposed the use of police to overcome Socialist tactics. Miki at this point was urging the government, as the price for his support, to attach a rider to the treaty stating Japan's determination not to be drawn into outside conflicts through the treaty.

Shōjirō on the night of May 17 and between Kawashima, Ozawa, and Fukunaga Kenji on the night of May 18, with Kishi calling the shots from behind the scenes.

The Socialists began preparing for Asanuma's "emergency declaration" on May 16. They were determined to use physical steps if necessary to block either the extension of the Diet or approval of the treaty itself. The DSP's position was not made entirely clear at this stage, but the party turned down a JSP offer to pool resources in opposing the LDP. Kawakami Jōtarō suggested that all JSP Lower House members resign to bring about dissolution, but the party's CEC decided to save this move for a last resort. As a final delaying tactic, the JSP decided that all its Lower House members would address the Special Committee and present anti-treaty petitions.

On May 17 Speaker Kiyose Ichirō (LDP) and Vice-Speaker Nakamura Takaichi (JSP) formally resigned from their respective parties as a gesture of impartiality. Kiyose then appealed to the heads of the three parties for order in the Diet. This gesture won praise from normally anti-government columnists.[38] The more realistic Diet members of both parties began bringing blankets and toothbrushes to the Diet; husky "secretaries" and "staff members" began to swarm in the hallways, and a tense atmosphere prevailed.

May 19

May 19, 1960, along with December 8, 1941, will become an unforgettable date for the nation. It is well known that on December 8, 1941, the surprise attack against Pearl Harbor touched off the Pacific War which cost the lives of 1,200,000 of our countrymen, but May 19, 1960, was the day when the government, under Kishi Nobusuke, who had been involved in planning the surprise attack, delivered a surprise political attack against the nation and against democracy.[39]

[38] See for example *Asahi Shimbun*, "Tensei Jingo," May 18, 1960.

[39] Hidaka Rokurō, ed., *Gogatsu Jūkunichi* (May 19), Tokyo: Iwanami Shinsho, 1960, p. 46. It will be recalled that December 8, not 7, was the date in Japan of the Pearl Harbor attack.

These were the words of one of Kishi's intellectual critics; though overly dramatic, they reflect the surprise and shock in Japan over his handling of the vote in the Diet. They also reflect the general preoccupation with war during this period. Since the events of May 19–20 had more to do with the subsequent furor than the treaty itself, it is worth examining them in some detail. The main facts were not in dispute, but the manner of the voting and the validity of the procedures became subjects of a roaring controversy.[40]

On Thursday morning, May 19, 1960, the LDP formally proposed a fifty-day extension of the regular Diet session. House of Representatives Speaker Kiyose referred the matter to the Steering Committee, whose approval was required prior to a vote in plenary session. At about the same time (10:41 A.M.) the House of Representatives Special Committee opened its 37th meeting, with the Socialists carrying out their plan to present petitions and to stall. The LDP members tried to close the debate and vote on the treaty, but the session fell into disorder and the Chairman had to call for a recess at 12:37 P.M. All afternoon the Directors of the Steering Committee wrangled about the proposed extension and it was not until 4:30 P.M. that Chairman Arafune Seijirō could open a meeting.[41] At this session there was further shoving and confusion, as JSP and DSP Committeemen stomped out shouting that the meeting was improper. The LDP members, now meeting alone, quickly ap-

[40] The following account has been pieced together from the Diet *Proceedings,* newspapers, articles, and interviews. For a JSP-sponsored version, see "Minshushugi no Genri wa Kō Shite Yaburareta" (How Democratic Principles Were Violated), *Gekkan Shakai Tō,* July 1960, pp. 11–21. LDP views of JSP behavior can be found in "Shakai Tō wa Gikaishugi Seitō ka?" (Is the JSP a Parliamentary Party?), *Gekkan Seiji,* No. 101, Summer 1960, pp. 50–62. Speaker Kiyose's justification for his own actions can be found in "Gichō no Tachiba Kara" (From the Speaker's Standpoint), *Jiyū,* July 1960, pp. 59–63.

[41] Arafune was a key man in the Kishi-Fujiyama camp, having been made Chairman of the Steering Committee by virtue of his strong stand as LDP floor leader in the Police Bill Affair. Born in 1911 in Saitama Prefecture, he had been a bank president and local assemblyman before the war; he was elected to the Diet for the first time in 1947.

proved the extension motion and an announcement was made that a plenary session would begin at 5:00 P.M.

Socialist Diet members and their burly male "secretaries" then staged a mass sit-down (*suwarikomi*) outside Speaker Kiyose's office to prevent him from reaching the rostrum. At this stage they were still unaware of Kishi's plan to vote on the treaty as well, and were seeking only to block the extension vote. There were skirmishes in the hallways as LDP members and their "secretaries" brushed with the Socialists. Kiyose, literally trapped in his office, used his telephone to call for mediation talks with party leaders.[42]

The People's Council sent out an "emergency mobilization order" at 2:30 P.M. and assembled some 15,000 demonstrators around the Diet by early evening. The crowd, mostly Sōhyō unionists, chanted "Ampo Hantai" (Down with the Treaty) and "Kishi Taose" (Overthrow Kishi) as rain began to fall. About 5,000 policemen were on hand to guard the Diet Building. At 6:00 P.M. Kiyose and House of Councillors Speaker Matsuno Tsuruhei ordered 2,000 police into the Diet compound, but not into the building itself. More wrestling took place between Diet members outside the Speaker's office. Just after 9:00 P.M. Kiyose began a series of appeals to the Socialists over the public address system: "Please stop the sit-down demonstration as it will only cause confusion and disorder." The LDP withdrew its

[42] In the seventy-five-year-old Kiyose the LDP had a seasoned parliamentary fighter whose experience went back to the "Secret Expense Incident" involving Tanaka Giichi on March 24, 1927, when blood was shed in the Diet. Born in 1885 in Hyogo, Kiyose graduated from the Law Department of Kyoto Imperial University, began practicing law in 1910, ran successfully for the House of Representatives in 1920, vigorously opposed the Peace Preservation Law in 1925, and made headlines as a lawyer in the Shimpeitai Case (1933). After the war he was purged from public office but helped defend Tōjō in the International Military Tribunal for the Far East; returning to politics in the Progressive Party under Shigemitsu in 1953, he became Minister of Education in the third Hatoyama Cabinet (November 1955 to December 1956). Kiyose was part of the braintrust behind the LDP's "Political Philosophy of Neo-Conservatism" (Ardath W. Burks, *The Government of Japan*, New York: Thomas Y. Crowell Co., 1961, p. 79). In early 1964 he rejoined the LDP, from which he had resigned on May 17, 1960.

members from the scene. Nishio and other DSP leaders stood by, hoping for a chance to "mediate."

At 10:25 P.M., with Speaker Kiyose still imprisoned in his office, the first bell rang for the plenary session. At this point, in the first surprise move of the day, Chairman Ozawa called for the Special Committee on the Treaty to reconvene, with members of all parties present. Nishimura Rikiya and Matsumoto Shichirō (both JSP) stood and presented nonconfidence motions to the Chairman, and at the same time, Shiikuma Saburō (LDP) proposed that the debate be ended and a vote taken. For the next two minutes there was so much confusion that the Diet proceedings do not record the events. The Socialists, shouting and harassing the Chairman, walked out of the room as Ozawa announced closure, took the vote, and declared that the treaty and related bills were approved. The *Proceedings* contain only this brief notation:

> 10:25 P.M.
> Chairman Ozawa: Before the intermission . . . (Many people talk and leave their seats, confusion reigns, impossible to hear). . . .
> 10:27 P.M.[43]

Minutes later Kiyose issued a warning: "Break up the sit-down within fifteen minutes or I shall be forced to ask the police to enter the Diet Building." At 10:35 P.M. the last bell for the plenary session sounded and LDP Diet members filed into the Diet Chamber. Ozawa had on his desk the Special Committee's favorable report on the treaty. The anti-mainstream factions, claiming that this was the first time they had heard of Kishi's plan to vote on the treaty that night, left the Chamber for hurried discussions; they decided to vote for extension but not for the treaty. Ishii, Ōno, and Ikeda kept their factions in the Chamber and voted for both measures.

At 10:48 P.M. Kiyose issued his final warning, but the Socialists, who were arrayed with locked arms on the floor between the Speaker's office and the rostrum in the Diet Chamber, re-

[43] HR Special Committee, *Proceedings*, No. 37, May 19, 1960, p. 13.

fused to budge. At 11:00 o'clock Kiyose ordered 500 police officers to break up the blockade. During the next forty-five minutes each Socialist was carried bodily by three or four policemen (a process known in Japanese slang as *"gobōnuki"* or uprooting) out of the area amid popping flash bulbs and the glare of movie camera lights. This was the second time in the history of the Diet that police had actually entered the Chamber.[44] At 11:48 P.M., Kiyose, flanked by a squad of Diet guards, made his way through the melee to his seat on the dais; a minute later he opened the plenary session in the presence of LDP members only.[45] The fifty-day extension was quickly approved, and Kiyose then announced that a new session would be convened "tomorrow"—just after midnight. The session ended at 11:51 P.M. and exactly fifteen minutes later, at six minutes past midnight, a new plenary session opened. Ozawa made his report, and Kiyose called for a rising vote on the treaty and related bills. The *Proceedings* record that "all present arose." [46] Then there were the traditional "Banzai's" and the stormy session adjourned at 12:19 P.M. This meant, of course, that without any action by the House of Councillors, the new treaty would automatically receive the Diet's approval exactly thirty days later, on June 19, 1960.

Outside, the crowds, which had dwindled to some 5,000, heard the news in darkness and went home. The next morning banner headlines in all the major papers proclaimed that the LDP had

[44] The first was on June 2, 1956, in a House of Councillors dispute over education bills. On June 3, 1954, police had entered the Diet Building but not the Chamber. (Information furnished by the House of Councillors Secretariat, January 11, 1962.)

[45] It should be noted here that the Police did not prevent the Socialists from attending the session; the JSP and DSP members absented themselves by choice to build a case of "unilateral voting" (*tandoku saiketsu*) against the conservatives.

[46] Dai-Sanjūyon-kai Kokkai, Shūgiin, Honkai, *Giroku*, Dai-Sanjūsango (34th Diet, House of Representatives Plenary Session, *Proceedings*, No. 33), May 20, 1960, pp. 553–554. There is no official record of how each member voted because it was a rising vote, but Hidaka Rokurō, ed., *Gogatsu Jūkunichi* contains a chart on pp. 69–72 purporting to show who voted for the treaty; this chart was based on assumed factional alignments.

"unilaterally" approved the treaty; photographs showed LDP Diet members raising their arms for the "Banzai" next to rows of empty Socialist seats. The JSP declared on May 20 that the extension and treaty passage were null and void and began a boycott of all Diet proceedings. Japan was thus plunged into her worst crisis since the war.

Reactions to Kishi's Surprise Maneuver

The Japanese people were well enough accustomed to rousing battles among their elected representatives, and they had long been aware of the impending clash, but the rapidity of Kishi's move, coming as it did after the disturbing events of the past few months, produced genuine surprise and shock. The *Asahi Shimbun's* morning edition for May 20 had gone all the way from Tokyo to Kamakura with a front page editorial warning the parties against violence, when it had to be recalled, overtaken by events. The People's Council, which had planned a major rally for May 20 to block the treaty in the Lower House, had quickly to change its placards and slogans to protest against Kishi's "undemocratic" actions.

Surprise is odious in Japan, and people go to extreme lengths to avoid it. It was not so surprising that Kishi resorted to force, but the "slick" way in which he arranged to have the treaty pass the Diet automatically on the day of Eisenhower's arrival was more than many could take. These had been rumors, for several days before May 19, that he might try such a maneuver, but the stark accomplished fact was still a shock. After all, Kishi had specifically stated in the Diet on May 4 that there was no connection at all between Eisenhower's visit and ratification.[47] Some felt that it was a neat trick and that the Socialists had been outwitted, but many more were repelled by what seemed to have been unnecessary deception in approving the treaty hard on the heels of the Diet extension vote. The column "Tensei Jingo" expressed a widespread opinion on May 21: Kishi might think he is presenting Ike with a bouquet on June 19 but "that is the thinking of a petty bureaucrat concerned with

[47] HR Special Committee, *Proceedings*, No. 28, May 4, 1960, p. 2.

242

protocol. It is like a retainer performing tricks before his master. He seems to be forgetting the importance of the loyalty he owes to the people."[48] Or, as Ryū Shintarō, chief editorial writer for the *Asahi* stated later: "If only . . . Prime Minister Kishi had shown a little more honesty and sincerity toward the nation in dealing with the question, and if only he had shed his tough, autocratic skin to reveal just a little more humanity, the split between left and right in the nation would almost certainly have been much less severe."[49] Others, such as Matsumoto Shigeharu, wrote that if only Kishi had waited three or four days before breaking up the Socialists' sit-down, public opinion might have swung against the Socialists for their obstructionism.[50] Three former Prime Ministers (Higashikuni, Katayama, and Ishibashi) joined in a growing chorus of voices calling for Kishi to resign.

The press quickly and uniformly condemned Kishi as if with one voice.[51] The *Asahi* editorial for May 20, "The LDP and government's Undemocratic Act," said that the LDP's mainstream had placed a great strain on Japan's parliamentary democracy, and called on Kishi to "reflect" on his acts. It made no mention of the Socialists' prior use of force.[52] The *Mainichi* said, "In view of the fact that doubts about the new treaty continue to exist despite more than 100 days of deliberations and that practically no debate had been held on the new administrative agreement which is so closely tied in with the daily lives of the people, we had repeatedly called for thorough deliberations through extension of the session and for the dissolution of the Lower House thereafter to ascertain the public's

[48] *Asahi Shimbun*, May 21, 1960.

[49] Ryū Shintarō, "What Happened in Japan?—A Symposium," *Japan Quarterly*, Vol. 7, No. 4, October-December 1960, p. 413.

[50] Matsumoto Shigeharu, "Reisen no Naka no Daisanji Demokurashii" (Third Democracy in the Cold War), *Fujin Kōron*, August 1960, p. 53.

[51] Edward P. Whittemore, *The Press in Japan Today: A Case Study*, Columbia: University of South Carolina Press, 1961, pp. 28–37, discusses the press's early reactions to the May 19–20 incidents; the appendix (pp. 88–91) has an interesting comparison of the "Big Three" newspapers' coverage of the events.

[52] *Asahi Shimbun*, editorial, May 20, 1960.

opinion." [53] *Tokyo Shimbun* said that Speaker Kiyose should have called a "summit meeting" of the three party heads to avert the disaster.[54] The *Yomiuri* was indignant that hundreds of policemen had been called into the Diet: "When the government and government party so easily take such extraordinary measures, the prestige and power of parliamentary government cannot be preserved." [55] Even the conservative *Nihon Keizai Shimbun* censured the LDP for taking "single-handed action." [56] The theme of "tyranny of the majority" was common to all the discussions of LDP behavior.

On May 21, the attack on Kishi was even more severe. The *Asahi*, putting its editorial on the front page in place of the news lead, demanded Kishi's resignation and general elections. Branding the LDP's forced approval as "violence of the majority" (*tasū no bōryoku*), the editorial said: "It is because deliberations and debate are held only superficially and attempts are made to decide the issue from the beginning on the strength of numbers that the strange phrase which is peculiar to Japan, 'violence of the majority' is used." Identifying itself with "the great majority of people," *Asahi* went on to say: "If the people should learn the truth of the issue, the great majority of them would support an opinion that would occupy a large place halfway between the two extremes. This is because the great majority of the people are not satisfied with the existing security treaty which has no time limit and which does not provide for prior consultations." [57] Behind these remarks, and indeed running through all the commentary, was the special Japanese faith in consensus and harmonious "adjustment" of conflicting opinions. *Asahi*, typically, searched for middle ground in the dispute through some form of *ad hoc* compromise, disregarding entirely the numerical strength of the parties and the ideological divisions between them.

The other papers were almost as critical of Kishi. *Tokyo*

[53] *Mainichi Shimbun*, editorial, May 20, 1960.
[54] *Tokyo Shimbun*, editorial, May 20, 1960.
[55] *Yomiuri Shimbun*, editorial, May 20, 1960.
[56] *Nihon Keizai Shimbun*, editorial, May 20, 1960.
[57] *Asahi Shimbun*, May 21, 1960.

Shimbun described May 20 as "an unprecedented day of shame in the history of the Diet," and added that "the offense is more heinous in that it was obviously carefully thought out." [58] *Nihon Keizai Shimbun* noted that it was Kishi's duty to take steps to restore the situation, and said, "Prime Minister Kishi is again showing a two-faced attitude, but such shameful shilly-shallying and lack of dignity cannot be permitted." [59] *Mainichi Shimbun* said flatly that the LDP had placed an "indelible blot" on parliamentary government in Japan and that the responsibility rested with Kishi alone.[60]

Kishi, who had never enjoyed the best of relations with the press, and was less than loved for his remark of January 16, 1960, that the only parts of Japanese newspapers worth reading were the sports pages, aggravated the press again by canceling his May 20 news conference on grounds that the situation was "too delicate." Then on May 25–26, he publicly censured the papers for their presumption that they alone represented public opinion. When he finally met reporters on May 28, he upheld his party's moves of May 19–20 and said he had no intention of resigning. "If we succumbed now," he added, "Japan would be placed in great danger." When a questioner suggested that the demonstrations against him were receiving very little public criticism, Kishi made a reply that was to become famous: "I think that we must also incline our ears to the voiceless voices. What we hear now are only the audible voices, that is all." [61] No sooner had Kishi mentioned the "voiceless voices" than Tsurumi Shunsuke and other intellectuals began forming an anti-government demonstration group known as the Voiceless Voices Society (Koe Naki Koe no Kai). We shall see in

[58] *Tokyo Shimbun*, editorial, May 21, 1960.

[59] *Nihon Keizai Shimbun*, editorial, May 21, 1960.

[60] *Mainichi Shimbun*, editorial, May 21, 1960.

[61] "Watakushi wa 'koe naki koe' nimo mimi o katamukenakereba naranu to omou. Ima no wa 'koe aru koe' dake da." *Asahi Shimbun* (evening), May 28, 1960. One of Kishi's secretaries told this writer later that Kishi's remark was prompted by the great volume of mail he had received in favor of the treaty; some of the letters had even been written in blood, according to this source.

the next chapter how this group attracted attention during the June demonstrations.

Kishi's personal responsibility for almost everything that happened in Japan after May 19 was a theme that ran through much of the commentary. In Japan it is rare that personal responsibility is fixed and clear because of the organizational entities in which individuals submerge themselves, but there was, nevertheless, a preoccupation with fixing the blame somewhere, and Kishi, as an unpopular and declining Prime Minister, became a personal symbol of the anti-government, anti-authoritarian feelings among the press and many of the people. One Tokyo University professor told this writer, "If you are not Japanese, you cannot understand why Kishi was so unpopular. The pent-up resentment and jealousy towards all bureaucrats exploded at this time against Kishi, whose insolence (*gōman*) typified the worst aspects of prewar bureaucracy." [62]

There is no other way to explain the intensity of the attack against Kishi at this time, as well as the general dismissal of the Opposition's responsibility. It led to almost ludicrous extremes. On May 26, for example, the column "Tensei Jingo" complained of the noise and disturbances created by demonstrations outside Kishi's private residence: the old and sick could not rest, babies were missing their afternoon naps, children's education was being interrupted, the area was littered with handbills, and fences and hedges were being damaged. "It was thoughtless of Mr. Kishi to have established his official residence in the middle of a quiet residential area in the first place. It is not fair to the neighbors." The column closed with this appeal: "Mr. Kishi, the public has deserted you. Resign! Then we shall get some peace and quiet." [63] Another editorial bemoaned the inability of the Diet to deal with the damage from the actual tidal wave of May 24 and said, "Prime Minister Kishi should listen to the 'voiceless voices' of the sufferers." [64] In this way the press helped switch the issue from the treaty itself to the question of Kishi's competence to lead the government and

[62] Interview with Professor Tsuji Kiyoaki, December 28, 1961.
[63] *Asahi Shimbun*, May 26, 1960.
[64] *Asahi Evening News*, June 7, 1960.

played an important rôle in setting the tone for the great protest demonstrations of May and June.

Kishi's claim that public opinion was really behind him infuriated the press (see all editorials, May 30, 1960), and polls were quickly published to show that this was not true. The most widely quoted of these polls were those of *Asahi Shimbun* taken on May 25–26 and published on June 2–3, 1960. Large headlines on June 2 announced the politically significant results: "50% Say Government and LDP Not Good, 32% Also Criticize JSP," and "56% Lack Confidence in Present Diet." [65] On June 3, even more potent headlines appeared on *Asahi's* front page: "What Do You Think of the Kishi Cabinet? 58% Favor Change." [66] This page also had a cartoon of two men reading newspapers; Asanuma was reading that 50 percent disapproved of the LDP, while Kishi was looking at the sports section and saying that the matches had come out 100 percent right. The *Asahi*, both in its news emphasis and editorials, stressed that public opinion was against Kishi, and that Kishi was ignoring the popular will by failing to resign.[67] If the newspapers were critical of the government, the weekly and monthly journals were outraged.[68] Most

[65] *Asahi Shimbun*, front page headlines, June 2, 1960.

[66] *Asahi Shimbun*, front page headlines, June 3, 1960.

[67] Whether the *Asahi* polls truly reflected national opinion remains open to question. Though the "mood" of Tokyo was running against Kishi, placid rural areas must have had far different feelings, as shown by the LDP's success at the polls in the general elections of November 1960. In the emotional climate of May 1960, to ask the question whether the cabinet should be replaced was to imply the answer. In any case, the *Asahi* was joined by many others in condemning Kishi for trampling on the true feelings of the nation.

[68] For a sampling of anti-government articles, see the following: Itō Masami, "Gikaishugi no Hametsu o Fusegu Tame ni" ('To Prevent the Collapse of Parliamentarianism), *Jiyū*, July 1960, pp. 44–51 and "Kyōkō Saiketsu to Kempō (Forced Passage and the Constitution), *Asahi Jiyanaru*, June 12, 1960, pp. 7–10; Kawakami Jōtarō, "Giketsu e no Gigi" (Doubts About the Approval), *Jiyū*, July 1960, pp. 64–68; "Kishi Shushō no San Dai-misu" (Prime Minister Kishi's Three Great Misses), *Seikai Orai*, preface, July 1960, p. 1; Matsuoka Yōko, "Gijidō o Kakonda Hito no Nami" (The Wave of People that Surrounded the Diet), *Sekai*, July 1960, pp. 44–45; Matsuyama Zenzō, "Kono Bōkyo Yurusumaji" (This Outrage Is Not to Be Tolerated), *Shūkan Asahi*, July 3, 1960, pp. 18–21; Nakano Yoshio,

of the articles contained emotional, personal attacks against Kishi himself; the latent hostility toward some aspects of his personality and background (discussed in Chapter 2) now burst into the open: his alleged arrogance, bureaucratism, contempt for the masses (*kanson minpi*), and cringing subservience to the United States were widely noted and bitterly denounced.

What of the Opposition? Had not the Socialist Diet members violated parliamentary rules? There is no question that this aspect of the controversy received far less attention from the press and public. Many editorials and articles stated that the Socialists had been wrong too, but once mentioned, this fact was either forgotten or dismissed as a "lesser evil." Only Kishi was asked to take responsibility for the impasse, and nothing short of his resignation would be acceptable. One line of reasoning behind this attitude was expressed by Professor Tsuji Kiyoaki in an article called, "The Easy 'Both Sides Were Wrong' Theory," in which he warned against falling into the trap of considering both sides equally at fault.[69] Tsuji granted that the Socialists had exceeded permissible limits for obstructing debate, but their *purpose* was what counted, he wrote. All they were doing was seeking to postpone the vote and force the conservatives to reflect. The LDP, on the other hand, used tactics which resulted in binding the whole nation to the treaty; the consequences of their action were graver, and therefore their behavior in the Diet more reprehensible.[70]

"Gogatsu Hatsuka o Miushinau na" (Don't Forget May 20), *Shūkan Asahi*, June 25, 1960, pp. 9–12; Shinohara Hajime, " 'Gikaishugi' no Kokufuku" (Conquest of "Parliamentarianism"), *Jiyū*, July 1960, pp. 52–58; Tanikawa Tetsuzō, "Mattaku Mucha Da" (It Was Really Outrageous), *Sekai*, July 1960, pp. 35–36; Yanaihara Tadao, "Minshushugi o Mamoru Yūki o" (Have Courage to Safeguard Democracy), *Shūkan Asahi*, July 3, 1960, pp. 22–23; and "Minshushugi no Genri wa Kō Shite Yaburareta" (Thus Were Democratic Principles Trampled Upon), *Gekkan Shakai Tō*, July 1960, pp. 11–21.

[69] " 'An'i na Ryōseizai-ron' ni Tsuite," *Sekai*, July 1960, pp. 36–38.

[70] The logic here is open to question. If *purpose* and *presumed consequence* are the criteria by which to judge parliamentary tactics, then it would be fairer to judge the JSP by their overall purpose, which was not merely to postpone a vote but to end the alliance with the United States

Only a few writers gave serious attention to the question of precisely how Kishi had violated the rules of parliament.[71] The legal case against the government in their articles may be summarized as follows. (1) The Speaker failed to consult the Steering Committee in a proper manner (under House of Representatives Rule 92) before the Committee approved the Diet extension motion. (2) It was questionable whether a bill as important as the treaty could be presented to the House of Representatives as an "urgent motion" (*kinkyū dōgi*). (3) Though Diet Law Number 115 gives the House of Representatives Speaker the right to ask the cabinet to send in police to maintain order, the National Public Safety Commission (NPSC) *may* have a veto right in such cases and on May 19 it was not given an opportunity to exercise that right. (4) House of Representatives Precedent Number 4 states that extensions of the Diet shall be voted within two days of the end of the regular session, but Kishi forced through the extension seven days before the end. (5) Motions of nonconfidence must take precedence over other motions, but there was no record of how Nishimura's motion was disposed of in the House of Representatives Special Committee. (6) The Steering Committee's vote for extension was not recorded in the *Proceedings* because of confusion and disorder; the same was true of the Special Committee's vote on the treaty.[72]

---

entirely. This would be a fairer basis for comparison with LDP purposes. But even the premise is doubtful.

[71] The most important of these were: Hidaka Rokurō, ed., *Gogatsu Jūkunichi*, pp. 46–49; Hashimoto Kiminobu, "Hōteki Nimo Mukō de Aru (It Was Legally Invalid Too), *Chūō Kōron*, July 1960, pp. 42–46; Ukai Nobushige, "Kyōkō Saiketsu no Mondaiten" (Problems in the Forceful Passage), *Shisō*, July 1960, pp. 124–128, and Itō Masami, "Kyōkō Saiketsu to Kempō" (Forced Passage and the Constitution), *Asahi Jiyanaru*, June 12, 1960, pp. 7–10.

[72] These points are all debatable, though space does not allow a thorough discussion here. Regarding Numbers 1, 2, 5, and 6 it is legitimate to ask whether any other procedure could have been followed in view of the disorder created by the Socialists. Regarding Number 3, there is no agreement among Japanese legal scholars that the NPSC has such a veto, nor is there any written provision or precedent for the same. Number 4 depends on precedent which of course carries less weight than law or Diet regulations.

The same articles contained many nonlegal, political arguments against the government. They held, briefly, that Kishi had trampled on minority rights, ignored the press, public opinion, and petitions, ended the debate before all the issues had been "clarified," voted in the absence of the Opposition, sent the treaty to the floor in a surprise maneuver, filled the Diet galleries with sympathizers, hired thugs for secretaries, showed contempt for objections within his own party, and generally violated the "spirit" of parliamentary democracy.

The case for Kishi—though few made it—was that the Opposition had trapped the Speaker in his office, brought in an "action squad" of strong men to help block the vote, tied up committee meetings with shouting and shoving, resorted to delaying tactics in place of serious debate, argued for more thorough deliberations but refused to extend the Diet session, and, posing as representatives of the voice of the people, tried to impose the will of the minority on the nation. While Kishi cut procedural corners, the Opposition was first to violate the "spirit" of parliamentary democracy; they left him no choice but to call in the police to execute the will of the elected majority. The Opposition, though it objected loudly to Kishi's methods, was seeking first of all to abolish the whole alliance with the United States, and this alliance was supported by a majority of the Japanese people.

These were the two sides to the dispute, put without their many ramifications. Neither side had a totally convincing legal case against the other, and judgment of right and wrong in the end had to be based on political or other considerations. If Kishi made a serious political error, it lay in his miscalculation of the strength of public antipathy against him even before May 19. It appears that he had no conception of the anger his maneuver would evoke. His attempt, moreover, to boost his political fortunes through President Eisenhower's prestige was in flagrant disregard of the new nationalism in Japan. Five years earlier, his tactics might have succeeded; in Japan of 1960, the appearance of servility in "presenting" the ratified treaty as a welcoming gift for Eisenhower was simply intolerable.

Outside the Diet the daily demonstrations became noticeably

larger and angrier after May 19. On May 20, Zengakuren students attacked the Prime Minister's official residence and surrounded his home in Nampeidaimachi, as 20,000 were mobilized around the Diet by the People's Council.[73] The Council now found new and willing volunteers for the demonstrations, and from this time until June 22, it had no trouble mustering large forces. Moderates—non-Communists, Christians, Buddhists, young office clerks, and artists—found themselves in demonstrations for the first time in their lives. The issue was no longer simply the treaty, which many of the new demonstrators had never read; it had become inextricably tied to Kishi's personality, President Eisenhower's visit, Japanese national pride, and the question of war or peace in the strained aftermath of the U-2 and the summit debacle in Paris.

[73] The mainstream of Zengakuren reportedly mobilized 10,000 students on this occasion. Some students threw mud, stones, shoes, and bottles at the policemen, and at 6:20 P.M. 300 of them attacked the official residence, some scaling the wall and others breaking down the main gate; 66 students and 149 policemen were hurt. *Japan Times*, May 21, 1960.

251

CHAPTER 8

The Crisis

FOR ALMOST two months Japan drifted along without an effective Diet—the supreme organ of the State. As students, laborers, and ordinary citizens massed about its walls and politicians bargained inside, Japan's parliamentary democracy faced its most severe test since the war. These were days of high emotion in Tokyo—one young man said they reminded him of the time of the B-29 raids—so tense was the atmosphere.

Yet, in the discussion that follows, it is important to keep in mind that this was essentially a crisis for Tokyo—that almost half the people in Japan were absorbed in transplanting rice seedlings into wet paddy fields or in other farm work. There were demonstrations in a few other large cities, but none to compare with those of Tokyo; the rural areas remained placid throughout. Even in Tokyo one could find large, happy crowds at baseball games; coffee shops were filled as usual, pachinko parlors active, and the May *sumō* tourney packed with ardent fans. On May 22, a Sunday, thousands toured United States air and naval bases in a friendly and orderly manner. Business went on as usual, though Tokyo's commuters were sometimes delayed by transportation strikes or traffic tie-ups from the demonstrations. Tokyo's citizens could choose whether or not to involve themselves in the political crisis and most chose not to do so; on the other hand, they tolerated the disturbances with surprising equanimity. Thus there was the strange situation of a nation going calmly about its affairs even as the Prime Minister was trapped nightly in his official residence by angry crowds. These were the conditions that allowed both sides in the controversy to find evidence that (1) the nation was overwhelmingly opposed to the new treaty and to Kishi, or (2) the nation was politically apathetic and only a small minority of hard-core leftists were behind all the trouble. The weakness of the parties, as they tried to take advantage of the furor, has never been more apparent.

Impasse in the Diet

From May 20 until July 18, 1960, the Opposition parties refused to participate in Diet proceedings. The Socialists held that the vote on extension had been invalid, and that the Diet session officially ended on May 26. They insisted on general elections before ratification and demanded that Kishi resign and postpone the Eisenhower visit. Before a nationwide television audience on May 30, Asanuma said that the fundamental issue was not the extension of the Diet itself, but the way in which the nation's affairs were to be handled and the fate of constitutional government in Japan.[1] Nishio again tried to mediate, but his position was much closer to that of the JSP: he offered to recognize the extension vote as valid if the LDP would (1) declare the treaty vote invalid, (2) dissolve the Diet, and (3) bring about Kishi's resignation.[2] Other members of the DSP, however, declared that the extension vote was invalid and that Nishio was speaking for himself, not the party. Nishio went out of his way to deny reports that he favored the treaty itself. By seeking to stand between the disputants, he alienated both and the DSP "image" suffered badly in consequence. Kishi maintained his "high posture," holding that the extension and treaty votes had been proper, that he would not yield to violence from minorities outside the Diet, and that he would neither resign nor dissolve the Lower House.

Despite continuing rounds of meetings between top party leaders, no compromise could be reached. Given Kishi's determination to remain in office and the unalterable language of the treaty, there were no points for "adjustment" in the usual Japanese sense. The LDP forged ahead alone, voting to extend the session in the House of Councillors on May 26, and discussing measures to deal with tidal wave damage on May 27. Elderly Speaker Kiyose, still recovering from an ankle injury suffered on May 19, presided in the Diet on May 27 after being carried to the rostrum on the back of a colleague.

[1] *Asahi Evening News*, May 31, 1960.
[2] *Ibid.*

Kishi's new plan was to push the treaty through the Upper House rather than wait for "automatic approval" after thirty days; he wished to undercut charges that the LDP mainstream was isolated and powerless within the party. After two weeks of fruitless negotiations to win over the Independents and Dōshikai, who held fourteen and eleven Upper House seats respectively, the LDP began "singlehanded" negotiations in the House of Councillors Special Committee on June 8, intending to press for a vote on the floor by June 16. Thus the stigma— now almost a cliché in the press—of a tyrannical majority fell more heavily than ever over the LDP mainstream. Meanwhile, JSP Upper House members openly discussed new physical steps to block passage on the floor.

The real drawback to a vote, however, was the anti-Kishi movement within the LDP. Had all the factions, or even the middle group of Ikeda, Ishii, and Ōno, joined Kishi in a positive, forthright stand for quick treaty approval in the Upper House, the ratification process could have been completed several days before the Eisenhower visit and the domestic crisis could have been settled. The artificial thirty-day period would have been removed, and the left could not have capitalized on the sense of anticipation and climax it created. That the middle factions did not do so, but allowed tension to mount toward the deadline of midnight, June 18, revealed their true intention to embroil Kishi in so much trouble that he would be forced to bargain with them to get the treaty through. The treaty and the question of Eisenhower's visit were mere pawns in this power struggle; the key questions were: When would Kishi announce his resignation plans? When would he actually retire? And how could they maneuver to best advantage in forming the new cabinet? [3]

The anti-mainstream factions thwarted Kishi's attempt to win a quick vote in the Upper House by refusing to cooperate until the "confusion" had been cleared up. Ishibashi asked Kishi to resign immediately, while the others insisted that he should

[3] For a discussion of the complicated LDP struggle at this time, see "Jimintō no 'Jitsuryokusha-tachi'" (Strongmen of the LDP), *Shūkan Asahi*, June 26, 1960, panel discussion, pp. 16–20.

at least announce a future date for his resignation before ratification.[4] Kōno changed his position several times but held generally that Kishi should take responsibility for the situation; he should resign soon but avoid dissolving the Diet until the treaty was ratified.[5] Kōno's "indignation" over Kishi's tactics may have been real enough, but it contrasted strangely with his insistence in the Police Bill Affair that Kishi ride roughshod over the Opposition and push that bill to completion. Sixteen members from the three rebel factions began discussions on the night of June 1 on a formal break with the LDP; they set up a four-man committee to call dissident LDP members to an anti-Kishi rally on June 3.[6] On June 2, however, this plan foundered as the three middle factions withheld their support; in the end, the rally of June 3 was canceled. Lacking the strength to overthrow Kishi without help either from these middle factions or from moderate leftists, the anti-mainstream had to content itself after June 2 with warnings that pushing the treaty through the House of Councillors might further irritate the public and provoke strong anti-American demonstrations during the Eisenhower visit.[7] Such statements had the desired effect of harassing Kishi, for leftists seized upon them to show that the Kishi-Satō fraction of the LDP was totally isolated, even in the conservative camp.[8]

The significant factor holding the LDP together in these hectic days seems to have been the tacit alliance between the Kishi-Satō forces, on one hand, and the Ikeda faction on the other, with Ishii and Ōno also cooperating to a lesser extent. Without this coalition a party split might well have occurred; with

[4] *Asahi Evening News*, May 28, 1960.

[5] *Ibid.*, May 31, 1960.

[6] The four were: Kawasaki Hideji, Mori Kiyoshi, Katō Tsunetarō, and Hirano Saburō. *Asahi Evening News*, June 2, 1960.

[7] *Asahi Evening News*, June 6, 1960.

[8] It has also been reported that certain financial circles refused to help Kishi finance a PR campaign for the revised treaty owing to their disappointment over the results of previous campaigns and their disapproval of his tactics on May 19. Frank C. Langdon, "The Political Contributions of Big Business in Japan," *Asian Survey*, Vol. 3, No. 10, October 1963, p. 467.

it, Kishi was able to ride out the storm until ratification. It is probably a sound conjecture that Ikeda's support stemmed from the original "Yoshida Plan" whereby Kishi would pass "his treaty" and then yield to Ikeda (with Satō next in line) in return for Ikeda's support for the treaty. Ikeda was careful, however, to dissociate himself from Kishi's unpopular tactics; he told reporters that he had not "clarified his stand" to Kishi and Kawashima prior to the controversial treaty vote.[9] Ishii and Ōno took somewhat clearer stands: Ishii said flatly that he opposed the use of police to carry out the vote, and Ōno said he was opposed to "forceful action" and that it could not be helped if the cabinet had to be replaced. In inner party councils, however, all three turned down rebel invitations to join an anti-Kishi coalition, and this was decisive in keeping Kishi in power.[10] There were reports that the Ishii and Ikeda factions were split internally as to whether to (1) play along with Kishi, support the treaty vote, and succeed to power "from inside" or (2) to pin the responsibility for May 19 squarely on the Prime Minister, form a coalition against him, and battle for the succession in the party convention to follow. In both factions the first opinion had won out by June 2, but not without heated argument.[11]

The Socialists, in addition to their boycott of the Diet, used two other forms of pressure to bring about Kishi's resignation and dissolution of the Diet. The first was their direct support of the mass demonstrations and strikes—of which we shall speak in a moment; the second was their threat to resign en masse from the House of Representatives—a move that the Kawakami faction had favored since April for this contingency. At a spe-

[9] *Asahi Evening News*, May 21, 1960. Yoshida, though away from Japan from May 12 to June 14, 1960, talked every day with LDP leaders by telephone. Interview with Yoshida's private secretary, Shirahata, May 6, 1962.

[10] There is some evidence that Miki's defection from the anti-mainstream on June 2 also played a part in weakening the movement to oust Kishi; Miki allegedly wished to avoid a revolt that would give Kōno the upper hand in the next cabinet. Shinobu Seizaburō, *Ampo Tōsō Shi* (A History of the Security Treaty Struggle), Tokyo: Sekai Shoin, 1961, p. 279.

[11] Interview with Endō Kōsuke, *Asahi Shimbun* political reporter, January 13, 1962.

cial meeting of JSP Diet members on June 1, 1960, all 125 Lower House members handed their resignations to Chairman Asanuma, who was entrusted with the decision to resign at the proper moment. Backers of this move hoped it would lead to the immediate dissolution of the Lower House and lend support to the popular campaign outside the Diet.[12] An Extraordinary Party Convention supported the plan on June 6. The press and commentators, however, were highly critical, pointing out that the move would forfeit public confidence; they said it would be irresponsible, ineffective, suicidal.[13] The LDP denounced the idea as a "flamboyant gesture" and said it would "not affect in the least our party's determination to ratify the Security Treaty as quickly as possible." [14] Deterred, perhaps, by these adverse reactions, Asanuma backed away from the plan, and on June 7, the party canceled its earlier order for Lower House members to return to their constituencies to "broaden the struggle." Instead, they were told to remain in Tokyo to assist in the campaign.[15]

Another political movement at this time is worth noting, even though it failed. This was a plan in late May to form a coalition between the LDP anti-mainstream and moderate Socialists. The idea was based on the well-known friendship between Kōno and Katsumata Seiichi of the JSP's Wada faction, and it had the enthusiastic support of the Young Japan Society (Wakai Nihon no Kai), a group of 400 young writers, artists, and intellectuals.[16] Its backers thought they saw an exciting opportunity to break down the polarized Japanese political forces around a new, moderate axis; it could, they thought, serve to

[12] "Naze Wareware wa Giin Sōjishoku o Ketsui Shita ka" (Why We Diet Members Decided to Resign En Masse), *Shakai Shimpō*, June 6, 1960. See also Miyazawa Toshiyoshi, "Tadachi ni Kaisan ga Hitsuyō" (Immediate Dissolution Is Necessary), *Mainichi Shimbun*, June 2, 1960. Miyazawa was a well-known authority on the Constitution and administrative law from Tokyo University.

[13] See, for example, *Asahi Shimbun*, editorial, June 6, 1960.

[14] Statement by Kawashima Shojirō, *Asahi Evening News*, June 7, 1960.

[15] *Asahi Evening News*, June 8, 1960.

[16] *Asahi Shimbun*, May 31, 1960.

overthrow the hated Kishi without seriously disrupting political and economic stability. The proponents of this scheme were aided by such figures as Tsurumi Kazuko (daughter of former LDP Diet member Tsurumi Yūsuke), who arranged meetings with anti-mainstream faction leaders, and by younger political scientists at Tokyo University. The movement seemed to be coming to a head on June 11, when a meeting was held at the Toshi Center Hotel attended by, among others, Utsunomiya Tokuma (LDP, Ishibashi faction Diet member), Kasuga Ikko (DSP) and Katsumata Seiichi (JSP); it collapsed, however, in the mounting tension after the Hagerty episode when cooperation between left and right seemed out of the question. It is not known whether the principals, Kōno and Katsumata, ever seriously entertained the idea, but the fact that the movement simmered on for several weeks suggests that there were actual tendencies toward a political realignment at this time—tendencies that could be important in some future crisis when LDP unity might prove to be less solid.

As the politicians quarreled inside the Diet, the focus of Japanese politics moved for a time to the streets outside, where the fifteen-month campaign against the new security treaty was reaching a climax.

Strikes and Demonstrations

In the period of turmoil after May 19, major events followed in quick succession: Sōhyō's nationwide strike of June 4, the arrival and mobbing of James Hagerty on June 10, the fierce battle at the Diet on June 15, the cancellation of Eisenhower's visit on June 16, the statement of the "Big Seven" newspapers on June 17, Diet approval of the treaty at midnight on June 18, ratification of the treaty and Kishi's resignation announcement on June 23. Whole books have been written on these events in Japan, and here we can only touch on the highlights of the struggle.

The general strike of June 4, largest up to that time in the history of Japan's labor movement, was organized by Sōhyō and fully supported by the People's Council and connected left wing elements.[17] Sōhyō claimed that 5.6 million unionists and sympathizers participated throughout the nation on June 4, in labor's first major action against the government since November 27, 1959.[18] In calling for the strike, Sōhyō leaders were pitting themselves against an ingrained mistrust of purely political strikes among many unionists, the fear of reprisals among government workers, apathy among the rank-and-file, and possible resentment by the press and public. These leaders correctly reckoned, as it turned out, that the national reaction against Kishi's moves of May 19–20 was so great that such objections could be overcome.

The strike of June 4 centered on the national and private railway workers' unions; in Tokyo, commuter trains stopped between 4:00 and 8:00 A.M. and streetcars, buses, and over half of Tokyo's 12,000 taxis also stopped operating in these key rush hours. At Shinagawa Station, Zengakuren students sat on the tracks and for a time the police made no effort to remove them. One can readily imagine the impact of all this on the world's largest city, where millions of citizens are totally dependent upon public transportation. Elsewhere, teachers, government workers, and other Sōhyō unionists joined in various types of work stoppages; a smattering of intellectuals and students showed up in the picket lines. There were few outbreaks of violence.[19]

[17] For a variety of discussions of the strike, see: Hidaka Rokurō, ed., *Gogatsu Jūgonichi*, pp. 121–139; Ide Busaburō, *Ampo Tōsō*, pp. 155–166; Saitō Ichirō, *Ampo Tōsō Shi*, pp. 239–251; and Shinobu Seizaburō, *Ampo Tōsō Shi*, pp. 296–312. There had only been two previous waves of political strikes in postwar Japan since General MacArthur called off the famous February 1 (1947) affair; these were in 1952 (*Rōtō-sutō*) against the Subversive Activities Prevention Bill and in 1958, against the Police Bill revision (above, pp. 101–105).

[18] This figure, according to Sōhyō's reckoning, included 3.6 million Sōhyō unionists, 1 million workers from nineteen independent unions, 500,000 students and leftists, and 500,000 unorganized workers in small and medium enterprises (*Asahi Evening News*, June 4, 1960). Hidaka Rokurō, ed., *Gogatsu Jūkunichi*, p. 124, places the total at 4.6 million.

[19] The left gave particular attention to a shop-keepers' strike in Maebashi, Gumma Prefecture, led by a small cleaning-shop operator; see Iwata

The June 4 strike had been well advertised in advance; Sō-hyō formed special committees to appeal to the public and prevent unnecessary disturbances. Leftist intellectuals, educators, and writers, as well as most of the press, had endorsed the strike and called on the nation to show its approval. Government leaders had warned that disciplinary measures would be taken, and Kishi himself, appearing on television on the eve of the strike, said that this was "a political strike not permitted under the labor union laws." [20] Sōhyō, in its public statement of June 2, stopped short of calling for a "political strike" but claimed that it was a "protest going to the limits permitted to the public and workers when democracy is on the brink of a crisis." [21] Sōhyō's avowed purpose was to unseat Kishi and achieve dissolution of the Lower House before the treaty was ratified.

Both sides claimed to take comfort from the orderliness of the whole affair.[22] The left saw it as a major triumph; the lack of disturbances was evidence of public support. Government leaders, on the other hand, interpreted the orderliness as proof of public indifference and good sense; they took the somewhat foolish position that since there were no disturbances, there was no real upsurge of feeling (*moriagari wa nai*).[23] The Socialists were elated by the size and calmness of the strike, and the JCP

Tōichi, "Kurininguya no Keiken" (The Experience of a Cleaner), *Sekai*, August 1960, pp. 179–181. For a description of the activities of participating unions, see Hidaka Rokurō, ed., *Gogatsu Jūkunichi*, p. 124.

[20] *Asahi Evening News*, June 4, 1960.

[21] *Asahi Evening News*, June 3, 1960. At issue were Articles XVII and XVIII of the Public Corporations Labor Relations Law (*Kōrōhō*) which deprived workers in public corporations of the right to strike; Article XXXI of the National Railway Corporation Law; and Article XXVIII of the Constitution, which guaranteed the right to organize, bargain, and act collectively. Hidaka Rokurō, ed., *Gogatsu Jūkunichi*, p. 120.

[22] For a variety of statements on the strike, see: "Roku-yon Sutō to Kongo no Seijō" (The June 4 Strike and the Subsequent Political Situation), *Shūkan Asahi*, June 19, 1960, pp. 86–87, statements by Kawashima Shōjirō, Kawasaki Hideji, Eda Saburō, Sone Eki, and Shiga Yoshio.

[23] This was an invitation to trouble: it could only strengthen the extremists who were already arguing that nothing short of violence would convince Kishi of the strength of the opposition.

called it "a tremendous success" (*idai na seika*).[24] The press, which had warned against violence on both sides, generally supported Sōhyō and evaded the question of legality; it held that the strike was a justifiable defense of democracy in the face of a clear challenge, and that it was supported, moreover, by a majority of the people.

The strike of June 15, known as the "Second May Day," was arranged to coincide with the expected vote on the treaty in the Upper House. It featured work stoppages by unions in private industry and affected some 5.8 million workers, according to Sōhyō. There was violence at Hamamatsu Station when workers had to be physically removed from the tracks by police, and the massive strike set the stage for Zengakuren's assault on the Diet. Leftists considered this strike somewhat less effective than that of June 4, because the majority of the railway workers were not involved, and because unionists in the important iron and steel industries (Tekko Rōren) refused to cooperate. The June 22 strike, labor's last effort to bring down Kishi before ratification, involved a record 6.2 million workers (according to Sōhyō) and paralyzed the Tokkaidō trunk line for the first time in history.

These strikes, though unprecedented in size, were not enough in themselves to force Kishi to resign, but the degree of worker-participation—even after some union treasuries had been depleted—was impressive. Sōhyō tested and proved what some leftists had long argued: that purely political action can be useful and successful—at least in terms of public tolerance—in times of high political tension. In future crises, the general strike would almost certainly be an important weapon in Sōhyō's arsenal. On the other hand, disciplinary measures by the government as well as the failure of the movement to prevent ratification or improve their economic position, may have sobered some of the rank-and-file.[25]

[24] *Akahata*, June 5, 1960.

[25] Government discipline, which was postponed until after the crisis in July 1960, included the following: 221 postal workers received pay cuts and 100 were reprimanded (*Asahi Evening News*, July 7, 1960); the National Railways Corporation dismissed 13 workers (including two union chair-

Demonstrations in postwar Japan—known in Japanese as *"demo"*—have become part ritual, part recreation, and part protest, the mixture varying with the occasion and the participants. Contrary to some reports, they are not "riots," though they have led to riots; neither are they "spontaneous," being carefully organized and tightly disciplined. There were 223 *demo* involving an estimated 961,000 people in Tokyo between April 1959 and July 1960.[26] Their size ranged from several hundred to a maximum claim by leftists of 330,000. After May 19, daily *demo* in Tokyo ranged from a few thousand to upwards of 135,000.[27] The popular *demo* were known legally as "group demonstration marches" (*shūdan jii kōshin*) and required prior approval from the Tokyo Public Safety Commission. Approval was usually granted as a matter of course after negotiations on the time, place, and routes of march. The Commission regularly refused to allow *demo* near the Diet, however, so that after May 20 the People's Council stopped applying and the daily Diet *demo* were, strictly speaking, illegal.[28]

Various kinds of *demo* were used in May and June. The more radical mainstreamers of Zengakuren favored the "snake-dance" (*jigu-jagu*) for important occasions; in these, ranks of six abreast locked arms and careened from side to side down the street in long columns; the flankers brushed aside all obstacles, causing skirmishes with the police who resented being bumped or swatted with placards. Other *demo* were more relaxed, with long columns of workers or students simply walking or jogging, singing songs or shouting slogans, and carrying signs and banners. The new "French-style" *demo* appeared on the Ginza on

men), suspended 151, cut the pay of 134, gave official reprimands to 343, and admonished 630 (*Asahi Evening News*, July 9, 1960).

[26] Figures from the Tokyo Metropolitan Police, cited by Fukui Fumio, "What Happened in Japan? A Symposium: The 'Demo' in Japan," *Japan Quarterly*, Vol. 7, No. 4, October-December 1960, pp. 425–427.

[27] *Demo* also took place in Sapporo, Nagoya, Kyoto, Osaka, Fukuoka, and elsewhere, but since they did not greatly affect the political situation in Tokyo, we have been forced to omit a discussion of them here.

[28] A group march (*shūdan kōshin*) without flags and placards was always permissible at the Diet, however.

June 22, as participants joined hands with arms outstretched and paraded down the middle of the street, blocking all traffic. In addition, there were auto caravans and lantern parades at night.

The more violent *demo* resembled village festivals when portable shrines (*mikoshi*) bearing the local deity are carried about the streets by nearly naked young men chanting "Wasshoi Wasshoi!" As in these rituals, when the god is supposed to impart direction to the bearers, some participants in the *demo* of May and June said later they found satisfaction in merging themselves in the throng and losing all sense of identity and responsibility. The rhythm in these marches was a left-right, left-right pair of double beats; in place of "Wasshoi Wasshoi!" were the new sounds, "Ampo Hantai!" (Down with the Treaty!), "Kokkai Kaisan!" (Dissolve the Diet!), "Kishi Taose!" (Overthrow Kishi!) and sometimes "Kishi Korose!" (Kill Kishi!). The *demo* leaders trotted like drill sergeants at the side of the main body, leading the chants and songs, and using megaphones and whistles to keep order. A leader on the left would blow two short blasts for the challenge: "Ampo" and a leader on the right would give two corresponding blasts in lower pitch: "Hantai!" A long blast on the whistle would bring the column to a halt. At night, leaders used paper lanterns with identifying characters to keep order. In this way the larger groups stayed together and kept firm marching discipline.

Almost all the demonstrators came to the central rallies in groups: workers with their factory locals, students with other members of their faculty (*gakubu*)—and there were few instances of casual or "spontaneous" participation from the sidewalks.[29] A typical student *demo* group might include 700–800 students, five or six leaders, and one sub-leader for each thirty to fifty marchers. Most of the students within each sub-unit knew each other well, and this contributed to order in the ranks. The sub-groups would meet daily on the college campuses (or in workshops or government offices), just after noon, ride to-

[29] The Voiceless Voices Association was a special case; the fact that it drew so much attention was evidence of its exceptional nature.

gether by subway or bus to the major assembly points (Hibiya Park, Shimizu-dani Park, Yotsuya Sotobori Park) and merge with larger crowds. Professional organizers from Sōhyō, the JCP, and the People's Council would direct them to assigned positions over loudspeakers. There, Diet members from the JSP and JCP would try to arouse enthusiasm with pep talks and *"sprech-call"*; placards and banners would be unfurled for the march.

The demonstrators would then march for several hours, generally to the Diet, and sometimes beyond, to the Prime Minister's residences, the U.S. Embassy, or government offices, often dissolving near Shimbashi station in the early evening. Great physical stamina was required for these grueling marches; on June 12, one group of students jogged all the way from the Diet to Kishi's Nampeidai residence—a distance of over three miles —to prevent a rumored meeting between Kishi and Hagerty. Mainstream Zengakuren *demo* often lasted on into the night around the Prime Minister's official residence; a face-saving "out" (*kikkake*) would have to be arranged between student leaders and the authorities so that students could catch the last trains home around midnight. The mainstreamers argued daily for "break-ins" (*totsunyū*) and "sit-downs" (*suwarikomi*) while others in the People's Council called for dissolving the marches (*nagare kaisan*) in the early evening; these slogans came to identify the warring factions within the left wing.

It is important to note that there were differences among the student demonstrators. The case of Tokyo University—which, ironically, had educated Kishi and many of the prewar elite— illustrates these differences, for "Todai" was at the heart of the movement. The University's Komaba Dormitories were unheated, squalid, concrete buildings, housing about 800 first- and second-year students who paid $10.00 a month to live six-to-a-room. Almost all the students here were poor, from rural areas, and above average in intelligence. They were closely knit, easy to mobilize, and extremely radical in outlook. It was here that mainstream Zengakuren leaders plotted tactics late at night after a frantic day's demonstrating; from Komaba, the word of the next day's program would go out to the other mainstream strongholds.

By rough calculation, there were four major categories of students at Tokyo University: first, there were about 5 percent who seldom attended classes and devoted almost full time to "the revolution"—the Zengakuren activists. The next 20 percent were students keenly interested in Marxism and politics and aggressively involved in the anti-treaty campaign but not necessarily as Zengakuren officers. These two groups formed the hard core of anti-treaty sentiment at the University. A third group of about 40 percent was politically apathetic most of the time, preferring the movies, jazz and coffee houses to politics for their recreation; this group became highly aroused after May 19, however, and revealed an unsuspected zest for the excitement of the *demo*. Untutored in *demo* discipline and quick to lose their tempers, this group actually exceeded the others in violence and, once aroused, could easily be manipulated by the theoreticians of the first group, as happened on June 15. The fourth group of some 35 percent did not participate at all, and were either conservative, disinterested, or concerned about jobs after graduation. Another distinction was that first- and second-year students, who were younger, more impressionable, and further away from job-hunting, were more active than their older colleagues on the Hongo Campus. Among juniors and seniors, students in the respected Law Faculty were the least radical, having promising careers laid out before them, while those in the Economics, Literature, and Science Faculties were considerably more active.[30]

Competition between Zengakuren's mainstream and anti-mainstream was fierce in May and June. In general, newcomers joined one side or the other for reasons other than ideology: for convenience, to be with friends, preference for tactics, or because their leaders had already committed them. We have seen that the pro-JCP anti-mainstream seemed to have the edge on April 26; by June 15, when the tension reached a climax,

---

[30] These observations stem from talks with students at Tokyo University while the writer was enrolled there from 1960 to 1961. The generalizations might also apply in a rough way to other universities in Tokyo.

it appeared that the mainstreamers held the advantage. Mainstream strongholds were at Tokyo University (especially at Komaba), Meiji, Chūō, and part of Waseda; anti-mainstreamers were concentrated at Tokyo Education University, Tokyo Metropolitan University, Waseda's First Literature Faculty, part of Hosei, and in Chūō's night school. The more easy-going students, and those from the Christian and women's universities, tended to demonstrate with the more orderly anti-mainstream, even though they were led by the JCP. This gave a false impression of Communist strength to uninformed observers.

A great variety of motives brought new blood into the movement after May 19: in addition to those who were seriously shocked by Kishi's handling of the treaty, there were some who came simply to ride with the tide; some came for the fun of it, and some were simply curious.[31] Wealthier students, who normally attended classes in sports jackets and slacks, switched to the more spartan student uniforms to prove their solidarity with the masses. Some of the younger demonstrators said later they felt they were upholding the new social ideals in Japan by joining in; to stay home would be reactionary. Others enjoyed for the first time a sense of mission: a conviction that their direct action was right, "pure," and effective. Some looked back later on the *demo* with nostalgia: there had been a sense of heroism and *camaraderie* that was lacking in their daily lives. All kinds of people participated in the more peaceful *demo*: sons and daughters of wealthy financiers, Christian groups, office girls, young businessmen—even a few high school students.[32] We would not attempt here to say which motive was dominant, but it was clear at least that the central issue was not, for many of the newcomers, the security treaty itself. The long campaign and the troubled international situation set the stage for emotional outpouring and the resurgence of nationalist feel-

[31] For an interesting discussion by a leftist Japanese sociologist, see Hidaka Rokurō, ed., *Gogatsu Jūkunichi*, pp. 74–140.

[32] To keep the numbers in perspective, though, it should be recalled that even the large *demo* were equalled in number by those simultaneously watching ball games, or swimming at the beaches, or hiking in the mountains.

ings made Kishi and Eisenhower—both associated with war and Japan's defeat—the worst possible symbols for the new alliance. On top of this were the frustrations of the younger generation and the confusion of ideals among the old; the *demo* served as an outlet for their unarticulated protest.

New songs were written for the *demo* of May and June; one that was popular among newcomers was "Tachiagare!" (Rise Up) a stanza of which ran as follows:

> *Tachiagaru toki da, taisetsu na toki wa ima,*
> *Kodomo-tachi no mirai no tame ni,*
> *Nikushimi no hi ga moeagaranai uchi ni*
> *Hitoashi hayaku keshitomete shimau no da.*
> *Tate, tate, tachiagare, tachiagare!*

> Now is the time to rise up, now is the vital moment,
> For our children's future,
> Before the flames of hatred flare up
> Let us quickly extinguish the fire.
> Stand up, stand up, arise, arise! [33]

Students also sang the song of the pro-Communist International Student Federation (*Kokusai Gakuren no Uta*) and of course, the *Internationale*. The slogans most frequently seen on their placards were: "Kishi Naikaku wa Taijin Seyo!" (Kishi Cabinet Resign!), "Aiku no Hōnichi o Soshi Seyo!" (Stop Ike's Visit to Japan!) and "Ampo Jōyaku o Funsai Seyo!" (Smash the Security Treaty).

The war of handbills and leaflets reached a new level of ferocity as the *demo* swelled in size; a conservative handbill passed to sidewalk onlookers branded the Socialists "labor aristocrats" (*rōdō kizoku*) and accused them of buying demonstrators (*arubaito demotai*) with funds from the Communist Bloc, of playing on the emotions of innocent housewives and students, of squeezing money from the poorer workers and of riding around in fancy cars. The JSP countered with handbills detailing the

[33] By Hayashi Hikaru and Sekine Hiroshi. Other new songs were: "Ajia ni Heiwa o" (Peace in Asia), by Ishikawa Tatsuzō and Kinoshita Chūji, and "Koe Naki Koe no Kōshinka" (Voiceless Voices Society Marching Song), by Yasuda Takeshi and Nakada Yoshinao.

government's "fascist methods" and the "brutality" of the police. Communist propaganda stressed opposition to the Eisenhower visit, racial oppression of Japan, and U.S. support for the Kishi Cabinet.[34]

The People's Council offices became a whirlwind of activity, coordinating *demo*, directing the regional joint struggle councils, issuing statements and arguing tactics. There was continuing friction on the Strategy Committee between the JSP and JCP; the Socialists emphasized the goal of overthrowing Kishi (*Kishi Dato!*) while the JCP played down this slogan as destructive of national unity. The Communists threw all their energy into directing the *demo* toward the U.S. Embassy and toward blocking the Eisenhower visit.[35] The Zengakuren mainstream kept up its fight for violent attacks on the Diet, but it was largely ignored by other council members during this period. Sōhyō was the dominant voice on the Strategy Committee, selecting the dates for the major *demo* and ordering up the manpower from its member unions.[36]

Kishi was so harassed at this time that some advisers suggested he leave Tokyo for Hakone or "rest" elsewhere in the mountains; this idea was finally rejected as inappropriate for the head of a government in time of crisis. On many June nights he was forced to wait until the last Zengakuren students went home after midnight before returning to his home in Nampeidaimachi. It is probably not an exaggeration to say that his life would have been in danger had he come out any earlier.[37]

[34] From the collection of handbills on the treaty movement at the Social Science Research Institute, Tokyo University.

[35] Interview with Katō Senko, JSP liaison man during May-June with the People's Council, November 9, 1961.

[36] Hidaka Rokurō, ed., *Gogatsu Jūkunichi*, pp. 114–115 and Ide Busaburō, *Ampo Tōsō*, p. 54.

[37] It is interesting that, although Kishi and his circle of close advisers felt extreme personal danger, others in the conservative camp did not feel threatened in the slightest by the extreme left. Businessmen did not have the least fear of an impending revolution; some were angry at Kishi and others were slightly amused by the whole affair ("Boys will be boys"); where concern existed, it was mainly over the prospective damage to U.S.–Japanese trade.

A notable aspect of the *demo* was the lack of overt anti-Americanism (except in the Hagerty affair which we shall discuss in a moment). American reporters and tourists mingled freely among demonstrators, and one American student even participated in the *demo*. Linda Beech, the attractive wife of reporter Keyes Beech, recalls standing on the sidewalk watching a *demo*, with shoes in hand, her feet aching after a long day, when one snake-dancing student broke from the ranks and handed her a newspaper to stand on. A U.S. Embassy official remembers a large crowd of students pounding on the Embassy gate as he approached to enter; they stepped politely aside as he passed through the open gate, and waited for the gate to be locked again before resuming their pounding. Many other similar episodes could be cited. This is not to deny that anti-American feelings existed among some, but only to show that a remarkable degree of order and restraint prevailed throughout.

The often-heard charges that the demonstrators were mostly hired should be disposed of before leaving this subject. Available evidence points overwhelmingly to the fact that most of the demonstrators were not on the streets primarily because they were paid to be there. It is true that there were handouts on both sides: unions gave out expense money (*nitto*) and *dō-inhi* (mobilization money) until their treasuries ran dry; it was common parctice in all strikes and *demo* to reimburse workers for lost wages and expenses to the extent possible. Conservative groups also arranged for people to demonstrate at certain times and places, and spent a large sum preparing for Eisenhower's welcome. But most of the demonstrators in June were not hirelings; the workers and students who participated were so emotionally aroused that cash incentives were not required.[38]

The other side of this coin was that the *demo* did cost a great deal of money: the handbills, posters, placards, loudspeakers, trucks, newsletters, flags, office and hall rentals, stamps, lanterns, airplane leaflet drops, and the professionals who

[38] People's Council officials, however, admitted wryly that some demonstrators who had been brought from as far away as Aiichi Prefecture at the rate of $5 and $10 dollars *per* individual, spent their time in Tokyo not at the Diet but in Asakusa amusement centers or visiting relatives.

269

manned the staffs of the various organizations were a few of the expenses. Where did the money come from? The People's Council claims it spent a total of 6.5 million yen (about $18,055) in 1959–1960—all of it donated by member organizations.[39] Shinoda Kosaku, Chairman of the LDP's Public Relations Committee, stated on June 15, 1960, that he knew from "reliable sources" that the demonstrations were being led "both financially and spiritually" by the Communists.[40] Fujii Heigo, Executive Director of Yawata Iron and Steel Company, estimated that the JSP and Sōhyō alone spent 600 million yen (about 1.67 million dollars) with "international financial aid." [41]

Some foreign correspondents were quick to jump on such statements to show that the *demo* were the handiwork of an international Communist conspiracy, which was far from the truth. Certainly some of the money was provided by Sōhyō's member unions; we know that Sōhyō conducted an extraordinary fund-raising drive in 1959.[42] We have noted that the Zengakuren mainstream received at least five million yen from Tanaka Seigen, a rightist businessman. The JCP and JSP undoubtedly contributed substantial sums to the movement. Did Communist China or the Soviet Union also contribute? The answer is that we simply do not know. We can presume that advice and perhaps money flowed into Japan from the bloc, in view of its intensive propaganda drive to block the treaty and embarrass the United States; in fact, from the Communist standpoint, it would have been foolish not to fish in these troubled waters. It is this writer's guess, though, that the protest *demo* of May and June were essentially domestic in origin, and that material aid from abroad did not significantly affect their size and character.

The Intellectuals Mobilize

We have seen that Japan's progressive intellectuals were outspoken critics of the original security treaty and of the govern-

[39] Interview with Minaguchi Kōzō, December 21, 1961.
[40] *Mainichi Daily News*, June 16, 1960.
[41] *Asahi Evening News*, June 30, 1960.
[42] *Japan Times*, September 13, 1959, article by Horii Etsurō.

ment's revision policies, and that they formed a variety of organizations to conduct their campaign. In May and June they not only wrote and spoke against the treaty, but also joined in demonstrating and in urging students and colleagues to action. Their unprecedented participation gave the protest movement its unique flavor.

Though these *interi* had spoken with one voice in earlier times, they were divided on goals and tactics during the crisis. Broadly speaking, two main tendencies emerged among the activists: one, represented by Shimizu Ikutarō, saw the main issue as the treaty itself and favored forceful action by a nucleus of laborers and students to prevent ratification. The other, more prominent, group saw May 19 as the beginning of a new struggle transcending the treaty issue and becoming a defense of parliamentary politics itself. They favored maximum popular participation and frowned on extremism that might drive the moderates away. The former group felt that Kishi's actions on May 19–20 were not much worse than previous LDP maneuvers—that the important thing was to block the treaty, and that no intermediate goals, such as overthrowing Kishi, could justify the struggle. The latter group, while firmly opposing the treaty, dwelt more on Kishi's "crime" against the parliamentary process, and gave greater weight to the goal of bringing him down. Their basic argument was that the Diet had closed its ears to expressions of the popular will, and had thus lost the function for which it had been created. They tried to alert the ordinary citizenry—the *"shimin"*—to this threat to democracy, and they therefore came to be called the "Shimin-ha" or Citizen Faction.[43]

It was the Shimin-ha that gave the intellectuals their dominant voice after May 19.[44] The Shimin-ha embraced scholars of

[43] For a description of the *shimin* concept, see Hidaka Rokurō, ed., *Gogatsu Jūkunichi*, pp. 97–100. There were of course overlapping memberships as between the two tendencies noted here; this division oversimplifies to some extent the multiplicity of intellectual approaches to the issues.

[44] The former group continued to be active, however, in the older anti-treaty organizations: Ampo Mondai Kenkyū Kai (above, pp. 138–140) and Ampo Hihan no Kai (p. 140). Other intellectuals' organizations active

many disciplines and viewpoints, and was not tightly knit, but its theoretical leadership derived primarily from Professor Maruyama Masao, whose preeminence as a theoretician on present and past Japanese politics projected him into the rôle. Maruyama, though not himself a political activist, had a small group of younger followers at Tokyo University and elsewhere who carried his ideas into action. This group, which had been involved in the older anti-treaty campaign as well, launched its organizing activities on May 24, 1960, when the two leading anti-treaty intellectual groups sponsored a meeting of scholars and *bunkajin* (men of culture) to demand Kishi's resignation and nonrecognition of the treaty vote.

Professor Maruyama addressed an overflowing crowd of some 2,500 professors, critics, and graduate students in Kanda's Kyō-iku Kaikan. He called for unity from an entirely new point of departure: "For example, even those who up to now have been sincerely in favor of revising the treaty, if they have a fragment of reason and conscience, have no choice but to join with us and rise up to erase this stain from Japan's political history." [45] He said that all the issues since the war—the Constitution, military bases, the teachers' efficiency rating system—which had hitherto been fought separately, had been condensed at one stroke on May 19; the question now was not whether one believed in the new treaty but whether the democratic process would survive: "If we sanction the events of the night of May 19–20, it is tantamount to admitting that the authorities are omnipotent in the sense that they can use any forceful methods they wish. If you admit that the authorities are omnipotent, you cannot at the same time accept democracy. To affirm one is to deny the other and *vice versa*. This is the choice that has been placed before us." [46] Maruyama then closed his emotional

---

in the protest movement were the Ampo Kaitei Soshi Hōritsuka Kaigi (above, p. 186), Koe Naki Koe no Kai (below, pp. 343ff.), Ampo Mondai Rekishika Kondankai (Symposium of Historians on the Security Treaty Problem), a Marxist group formed on December 21, 1959; and Tokyo Daigaku Kyōkan Shūkai (Tokyo University Staff Rally).

[45] Maruyama Masao, "Sentaku no Toki" (Time for a Choice), *Tokyo Daigaku Shimbun*, special issue, July 11, 1960.

[46] *Ibid.*

speech with these words: "At this moment in history let us transcend our differences and join hands so that the security of our nation may be ensured, not against any foreign country but first of all against the authorities." [47]

After this rally, many of these scholars staged a *demo* at the Diet—perhaps the first of its kind in Japanese history—and sent representatives to remonstrate with Kishi. The representatives waited for five hours without seeing Kishi, but the others outside resolved to create a new organization called the National Society of Scholars and Researchers for the Protection of Democracy (Minshushugi o Mamoru Zenkoku Gakusha Kenkyūsha no Kai) which came to be known by its short form, Mingakken. The new organization was officially launched on June 2 as a loose association of local branches tied at the center to a liaison council (Zenkoku Renraku Kyōgi Kai) located in the office of Professor Kitagawa Ryūkichi, of Hosei University. About 15,000 members in 120 colleges and research institutes eventually enrolled; the organization printed an organ paper, *Mingakken Niyūsu* and encouraged new faces to join *as individuals* in the protest.

The basic purpose of Mingakken—as conceived by the young political scientists at Tokyo University—was to divorce itself from the older, formalistic, and bureaucratic organizations and devote itself specifically to the new and crucial issue of democracy in Japan.[48] In its efforts to bring the apathetic or previ-

[47] *Ibid.*, Professor Maruyama has confirmed the accuracy of my translations. His speech was not made from a prepared text. Asked for a more precise definition of "rise up" (*tachiagaru*), he said he meant that citizens should not remain silent or apathetic in the face of clear danger to the parliamentary process, but should exert their rights as citizens. Interview with Maruyama Masao, March 9, 1962. For another expression of his views at the time see "Kono Jitai no Seijiteki Mondaiten" (Political Problems in the Current Situation), *Asahi Jānaru*, June 12, 1960, pp. 11–17.

[48] This organization invites further attention by scholars interested in Japanese intellectuals and organizations. As in most other Japanese organizations, Mingakken had its stable of powerless elder "figureheads" at the top, and a small core of younger men who directed its activities from behind the scenes. For additional material on Mingakken, see the five issues of *Mingakken Niyūsu*, dated June 10, 16, and 24, July 16, and August 15, 1960; Hidaka Rokurō, ed., *Gogatsu Jūkunichi*, pp. 89–100, and Tokyo Dai-

ously unorganized intellectuals into the movement, the prestige of Tokyo University helped Mingakken overcome the apprehensions of scholars who were plunging for the first time into political waters. The organization also sponsored lecture meetings, rallies, and auto parades, village discussion groups, poster-hanging, and later on, a "Back-home Movement." It encouraged each of its branches to issue statements and set up its own *demo* group to cooperate with the People's Council. (This was the Gakusha Bunkajin Shūkai that was attacked by the police on June 15.) Soon after Mingakken was launched, however, the "regular" leftist intellectuals, such as Kitagawa Ryūkichi and Hidaka Rokurō, gained the upper hand and used Mingakken to further the older campaign against the treaty. This caused friction with the newer elements who had joined out of anger at Kishi rather than dissatisfaction with the treaty or opposition to the Eisenhower visit. In practice, therefore, a discrepancy grew up between the Shimin-ha ideal of nonpartisan citizen participation to defend democracy and the partisan struggle that had been going on for months before.

The Voiceless Voices Association (Koe Naki Koe no Kai), formed after Kishi's famous press conference of May 28, attracted the attention of many leftist scholars as an embryonic version of a new kind of organization in Japan: one in which ordinary citizens would have no connection with each other except their shared voluntary participation in a "spontaneous" protest against the government.[49] Since Japanese organizations are characteristically closed groups with intricate rules for entry and mobility, this group would indeed have been a "breakthrough" had it been what it purported to be. Behind the façade of spontaneity, however, was the guiding hand of the Institute of Science of Thought (Shisō no Kagaku Kenkyū Kai). This was an association of highly theoretical and idealistic social scien-

gaku Shokuin Kumiai, ed., *6:15 Jiken Zengo: Ichō Namiki kara Kokkai E* (Before and After the June 15 Incident: From the Row of Gingko Trees to the Diet), Tokyo: Tokyo Daigaku Shokuin Kumiai, 1960.

[49] See " 'Koe Naki Koe' Yo Te o Musube!" (Let the Voiceless Voices Join Hands), *Shūkan Asahi* (July 3, 1960), pp. 11–17; and Hidaka Rokurō, ed., *Gogatsu Jūkunichi*, pp. 80–81 and 106.

tists and others—some of them trained in the West, and many Marxist-oriented—who were generally considered to be a left-of-center element in the Shimin-ha. These intellectuals had previously been aloof from politics, but liked to think of themselves as masters of *ninjutsu* (occult art), working invisibly to improve the lot of the oppressed classes.[50] In May and June they organized *demo* by appealing literally to the "man in the street" and began publishing a newsletter called *Koe Naki Koe no Tayori*, which contained the personal impressions of individuals during the *demo*. It also set up branches in many Tokyo wards and launched a letter-writing campaign to explain the "true" situation in Japan to the American people. The *demo* could not be considered a success, since only a few hundred people joined in on any one day, but the attempt to break down old patterns of organization was significant both for its conception and for its failure to attract sizable numbers of "*shimin*" to its cause in the crisis.

One of the prime movers behind Koe Naki Koe no Kai was Tsurumi Shunsuke, a leading member of the Institute of Science of Thought. Tsurumi, a graduate of Harvard (1942) and son of former Cabinet Minister Tsurumi Yūsuke, distinguished himself on May 30, 1960, by dramatically resigning from his teaching position at the Tokyo Institute of Technology on grounds that he could no longer work as a public servant (at the metropolitan college) so long as the top public servants, Kishi and Kiyose, remained in office.[51] His resignation followed that of Takeuchi Yoshimi, of the Tokyo Metropolitan University, who also stirred academic circles with this statement on

[50] See this group's publication *Shisō no Kagaku, Kinkyū Tokushū: Shimin to Shite no Teikō* (Science of Thought, Special Emergency Supplement: Protesting as Citizens), No. 19, July 1960. The Institute of Science of Thought has been described by R. P. Dore as very conscious of the rôle of intellectuals in Japanese society and interested in studying the philosophy of the common man, in "The Tokyo Institute of Science of Thought —a Survey Report," *Far Eastern Quarterly*, Vol. 13, No. 1, November 1953, pp. 23–36. For studies by its members, see also Katō Hidetoshi, ed., *Japanese Popular Culture*, Rutland: Charles E. Tuttle and Co., 1959.

[51] Tsurumi's statement of resignation may be found in *Asahi Shimbun*, May 31, 1960, p. 11.

May 21: "Because of the outrageous acts of Prime Minister Kishi and Lower House Speaker Kiyose Ichirō, who are the chief servants of the nation, parliamentary government has been abandoned and the constitution flouted. As a protest against their actions, I feel bound to resign my chair at the Metropolitan University, where I am employed by the government." [52]

The cases of Tsurumi and Takeuchi pointed up an interesting trend among the intellectuals at this time: in general, those most active in the protest movement were specialists in fields other than law, politics, and diplomacy. Besides Takeuchi (Chinese literature) and Tsurumi (philosophy), there was Nakajima Kenzō, a "critic" trained in French literature, who played a major rôle in Ampo Hihan no Kai. A second notable feature was the part played by intellectuals who had been educated in the United States and were considered "authorities" on the U.S.; among these were Minami Hiroshi, a social psychologist who attended Cornell, Tsurumi Shunsuke from Harvard, Matsuoka Yōko from Swarthmore and the Fletcher School of Law and Diplomacy, and Saitō Makoto from Harvard and the University of Pennsylvania. All of these were outspoken opponents of the treaty and President Eisenhower's visit. Many others, normally considered "pro-American," such as the Y.W.C.A. leaders or the student and faculty members of International Christian University, joined in the protest movement; one suspects they were under strong pressure to prove their "Japaneseness" in this time of nationalistic ferment, but there were doubtless other causes for their feelings which are well worth pondering.

Where were the conservative or moderate intellectuals at this time? Professor Nakamura Kikuo of Keio University believes there were many silent and unorganized scholars in the universities who, though they may have objected to Kishi, were basically in favor of the new treaty and Eisenhower's visit, and

[52] Takeuchi's full statement may be found in his book, *Fufukujū no Isan* (A Legacy of Disobedience), Tokyo: Chikuma Shobo, 1961, pp. 106–107, which also contains his other essays and speeches on the treaty and related issues.

opposed to the street *demo* and trends toward violence.[53] Why, it may be asked, were there no vocal scholars or "critics" to articulate the views of other members of the intelligentsia—the professional classes—who normally voted conservatively? One reason was the reluctance of the press to print anything but the views of the Opposition during this period (see below). Another, surely, was the general mistrust of Kishi. Still a third reason for their apathy or defensive silence was the pressure on all campuses by younger and more radical faculty members. In this climate of "reverse-McCarthyism," scholars who dared to criticize the mass protest movement were showered with abuse. As liberals during World War II were called *"hikokumin"* (traitors), those who dared buck the tide were branded *"goyō gakusha"* (scholars in the employ of the government) or *"jinmin no teki"* (enemies of the people). Very few outside the conservative camp had the courage to oppose the general "mood" and criticize aspects of the left wing movement; among them were Fukuda Tsuneari, Etō Jun (both specialists in literature) and Inoki Masamichi, a professor at Kyoto University.[54] Some professors said later that their names had been "utilized" by unscrupulous leftist colleagues; at least one was hounded into leaving his faculty because of his unwillingness to join in the protest.

It would be impossible to touch here on the variety of ways in which the progressive intellectuals stimulated popular feelings during the crisis. Almost daily, new statements of protest were issued by teachers, scholars, and writers, so that the ordinary newspaper reader could easily get the impression that the

[53] Nakamura Kikuo, *Gikai Seiji to Taishū Kōdō* (Parliamentary Politics and Mass Action), Tokyo: Yūshindō, 1960, p. 91.

[54] For examples of their writing, see Fukuda Tsuneari, *Jōshiki ni Kaere* (Return to Common Sense), Tokyo: Shichōsha, 1960; Etō Jun, *Hizuke no Aru Bunsho* (Certain Dated Essays), Tokyo: Chikuma Shobo, 1960; and Inoki Masamichi, "Seijiteki no Kiki no Soko ni Aru Mono" (At the Bottom of the Political Crisis), *Chūō Kōron*, August 1960, pp. 73–79. Hirabayashi Taiko, proletarian novelist of the 1930's, might also be included in this group; in *Asahi Shimbun*, June 5, 1960, she criticized the "gap" between Sōhyō leaders and the masses. When she subsequently criticized the Matsukawa Trial decision—which was highly popular with the left—in the following August, her house was wrecked by unknown assailants.

entire intellectual establishment—including playwrights, artists, poets, and other *"bunkajin"*—were united in protest against the government. The activities of the intellectuals created a new "nonpolitical" image in the struggle, and gave it a kind of inevitability and dignity that the labor movement alone could not have achieved. Whatever their effect on the general public (and it was probably large), there is no question that the *interi* played a major rôle in inspiring the students and younger generation to demonstrate. They were, in effect, a political force of considerable strength. As one girl student put it, "When I saw Professor X (an elderly, highly respected professor at Tokyo University) joining in the protest, I knew that something important was wrong and I felt I had to demonstrate myself." But in addition to their traditional rôle of inciting others to action, the intellectuals for the first time stepped down into the grimy arena of political action. For many, it was a frustrating and unhappy time; others drew hope from the experience. We shall discuss in the next chapter the interpretations and conclusions they gave to the affair.

Attitudes in the Mass Media

Both the left and the right were critical of the rôle played by the mass media during the treaty crisis. If nothing else, this censure revealed the importance of the mass media in postwar Japanese politics. This study would not be complete without brief mention of the influence of radio, TV, and the press on the treaty crisis.[55]

[55] A detailed study in English by Edward P. Whittemore, *The Press in Japan Today: A Case Study*, Columbia: University of South Carolina Press, 1961, contains some useful insights. Other relevant articles in English on the Japanese press are: William Lange, "Some Remarks on the Japanese Press," *Japan Quarterly*, Vol. 7, No. 3, July–September 1960, pp. 281–287; Murata Kiyoaki, "The Newspapers of Japan," *Japan Times*, October 1, 1958; Nabeyama Sadachika, "The Press," *New Leader*, Section Two, "Japan Today," November 28, 1960, pp. 36–42; Ryū Shintarō, "What Happened in Japan? A Symposium: On the Security Treaty," *Japan Quarterly*, Vol. 7, No. 4, October–December 1960, pp. 412–417; Edward Seidensticker, "The Japanese Press," *Japan Times*, October 1, 1959. In Japanese

Radio and television carried the political events to all parts of the nation as never before in history. In 1960, 69.1 percent of all households had radios and 33.4 percent had television sets.[56] Almost daily, live broadcasts or taped summaries of the turbulence around the Diet were seen and heard in private homes; the debates, comments, and analyses of the treaty and other issues took up many more hours of broadcast time. In this way, the facts, opinions, and immediate sense of tension were carried in an intimate way to millions of listeners and viewers. TV trucks, manned by helmeted cameramen, worked their way into the midst of excited demonstrators and gave vivid on-the-spot coverage. Radio and television could not give perspective to the events; concentrating on the dramatic and the detailed, they broadcast accounts of students and police slugging it out with each other without conveying how and why the battle had started. One cannot document the point, but it appears that radio and television did much to add to the momentum of "mood" after May 19.

The weekly and monthly magazines, which in 1960 reached new heights in popularity, were also important in carrying the crisis to millions of avid readers.[57] The weeklies, selling for about 11 cents apiece, normally avoided politics and dwelt on gossip, human interest stories, cartoons, and photographs for weary commuters. During May and June, however, they turned to the treaty struggle and startled their readers with such stories as "Is It All Right for Ishihara Yūjirō [a teen-age matinee idol] to Die?" (*Yū-chan o Shinasete mo Ii no ka?*) in *Shūkan Heibon*, and "Contract for Widowhood" (*Mibōjin e no Keiyakusho*)

---

see: Gendai Seiji Kenkyū Shūdan, "Nihon o Bunretsu Saseta Ninenkan: Masu Komi no Iken to Ugoki" (Two Years that Split Japan: Opinions and Trends in the Mass Media), *Jiyū*, July 1960, pp. 22–27; and Tsukamoto Jūichi, "Ampo Seikyoku ni Hatashita Masu Komi no Yakuwari" (The Role of Mass Media in the Current Political Situation), *Seikai Orai*, July 1960, pp. 72–75.

[56] Japan Newspaper Publishers and Editors Association, *The Japanese Press, 1961*, Tokyo: Dai-Nippon Printing Company, 1961, p. 8.

[57] In 1960 there were 1,601 monthlies and 71 weekly magazines in Japan. The booming weeklies sold a record 598 million copies; four of them each sold over half a million *per* week. *Shuppan Niyūsu*, June 1960.

in *Josei Jishin*.[58] The big three "general" monthlies (*Bungei Shunjū, Chūō Kōron,* and *Sekai*) also bulged with articles on the crisis—almost uniformly anti-government in tone—during this period. *Sekai's* publisher, the Iwanami Company, was the leading anti-treaty force in Japan's publishing world.

The Japanese press, with its circulation of 24 million copies (or 37 million if evening editions are counted separately) in 1960 played an enormous if controversial part in the treaty crisis. Both left and right have attacked the press for selling out to the other in the crisis, while leading journalists have stubbornly defended their "political neutrality" throughout.[59] After condemning Kishi and almost ignoring the Socialists' part in the affair, the newspapers followed the Shimin-ha line that "our overriding concern in the present political situation is for the fate of parliamentary democracy." [60] The press generally supported the strikes of June 4 and 11 (only *Nihon Keizai Shimbun* called them illegal), but condemned the Socialist plan to resign from the Lower House.[61] It constantly cautioned against violence in any form [62] but warned at the same time that violence was unavoidable unless Kishi resigned. *Asahi* said on May 21, "If time is allowed to pass with nothing done, new violence will break out in the vicinity of the Diet." [63] This was a case of what Professor Ishida Takeshi has termed (in another context) "closed pragmatism." Only two courses were possible, according to this

[58] Arase Yūtaka, "Hatashite Genron wa Jiyū de aru ka?" (Is the Press Really Free?), *Sekai,* August 1960, p. 205.

[59] Twelve million readers were claimed by the national dailies alone, whose detailed coverage of the crisis in Tokyo reached all corners of the land on the same day as it reached Tokyo. Each newspaper sold was read by an estimated 3.89 readers. *The Japanese Press,* 1961, *op. cit.,* pp. 4, 7, 11.

[60] Statement by the Editor, *Asahi Evening News,* June 4, 1960. In describing the trends in the press, we have paid most attention to the *Asahi Shimbun* which, with its leading circulation of 3.8 million readers, sets the pace for the others.

[61] See editorials in the *Asahi Shimbun, Yomiuri Shimbun, Nihon Keizai Shimbun,* and *Sankei Shimbun,* June 2, 1960, and in the *Asahi Shimbun,* June 8, 1960.

[62] See, for example, *Asahi Shimbun,* May 26, 1960.

[63] *Asahi Shimbun,* editorial, May 21, 1960.

reasoning: if Kishi refused to accept *Asahi's* demands by re-signing, then violence must ensue—even though the *Asahi* counseled against it. Somehow this position seemed to exonerate the individuals who engaged in violence. Some editorials also argued against "angering the demonstrators," as if the demonstrations embodied the generalized public will. Taking these positions, the papers did little to prevent the violence, and may even have encouraged it.

Most of the press began opposing the Eisenhower visit in late May 1960, while cautioning that anti-American feelings and anti-Kishi feelings must not be allowed to merge.[64] They argued in terms of preserving good relations with the United States and urged Americans to understand the true nature of the protest movement.[65] On June 9, Kishi met with several publishers, including Murayama Nagataka of the *Asahi Shimbun*; Murayama was reported to have promised his cooperation in making the Eisenhower visit a success.[66] On June 10, however, the *Asahi* issued another call for the cancellation of Eisenhower's visit.[67] Then, after the Hagerty affair, the mood of the press shifted noticeably and on June 14, the *Asahi* reluctantly called for a welcome for Eisenhower.[68]

After the bloodshed on June 15, the "Big Seven" newspapers of Tokyo published their famous statement, "Wipe Out Violence, Preserve Parliamentary Democracy," which was carried in more than forty of the nation's seventy major newspapers.[69] "Never before have we been so deeply disturbed as we are now about the future of Japan," it declared. "If a social trend permitting violence should once become general, we believe that democracy will die. . . ." The statement asked the government to "respond to the sound judgment of the people" (presumably meaning for Kishi to resign) and called on the Opposition to return to the Diet. This was the first time that Japanese news-

[64] *Mainichi Shimbun*, May 26, 1960, and *Asahi Shimbun*, June 1, 1960.
[65] *Asahi Shimbun*, June 7, 1960.
[66] *Asahi Evening News*, June 11, 1960.
[67] *Asahi Shimbun*, editorial, June 10, 1960.
[68] *Asahi Shimbun*, editorial, June 14, 1960.
[69] See Appendix F for the complete text.

281

papers had ever joined in such a declaration, and it revealed their serious concern over the turn of events. The statement appeared to exert a major influence in checking further violence on the climactic night of June 18 and in taking the heat out of the expanding demonstrations.

When the Eisenhower visit was finally postponed (i.e., concelled) on June 17, most papers called it "regrettable" but necessary. They continued to attack the government but were increasingly critical of extremism and of the Socialists.[70] On June 22, the *Asahi* began to call for deep "soul-searching" on violence: "Rejection of violence is the air and water needed for the life of democracy." [71]

A valid criticism of the press at this time was its acceptance of leftist statistics on the size of the *demo*, which were often more than twice those of the police and NPSC officials.[72] Another defect was its tendency to stress inaccurate news stories about police brutality and rightist provocation both on the front and "social" pages. Political coloring was left to the discretion of individual reporters and there was little apparent effort to arrive at unified editorial policy within each newspaper. Another problem was the failure of the press to print views of moderates or pro-treaty elements during the heat of the crisis. Almost exclusively, it devoted its column space to the emotional *bunkajin* whose views suited the mood of the day. Professor Nakamura Kikuo has said: "If one were to cite the most outstanding thing about journalism's discussion of the revised security treaty, it would be the opposition on the part of amateurs. By amateur, I am not referring to statements by ordinary citizens, but rather to the scholars of literature, philosophy and history who are skilled in fields other than politics and diplomacy." [73]

[70] See, for example, *Asahi Shimbun*, editorial, June 17, 1960. Still, the major blame for the trouble belonged to Kishi, they said, and the clamor for his resignation went on.

[71] *Asahi Shimbun*, editorial, June 22, 1960.

[72] See, for example, the statement of Ishihara Kanichirō, Chairman of the NPSC, *Asahi Evening News*, May 27, 1960.

[73] Nakamura Kikuo, *Gikai Seiji to Taishū Kōdō* (Parliamentary Politics and Mass Action), Tokyo: Yūshindō, 1960, p. 90.

There were several probable causes for this lack of balance. Historically, the press had opposed the party in power; it also had a special sensitivity to suppression of any sort, and Kishi, because of his prewar record, was vulnerable on this score. Furthermore, the intensive competition for readers made the temptation to print sensational stories almost irresistible. Finally, 67 percent of all employees in Japanese newspapers and news agencies belonged to unions in the National Federation of Press Workers' Unions (Shimbun Rōren), which was a Sōhyō affiliate.[74] This meant that reporters and employees up to the level of section chiefs (*buchō*) were Sōhyō unionists. To the extent that there was a strong (and sometimes admitted) sense of identification with Sōhyō's anti-treaty and anti-government objectives, unbiased and factual reporting was bound to suffer. The front-line reporters, often younger and more radical, were particularly susceptible to Sōhyō's influence.

The rôle of the Japan Congress of Journalists (Nihon Jānarisuto Kaigi) should not be overlooked. This was a leftist organization of some 1,700 members from the press, radio, and television, belonging to the Communist-supported International Organization of Journalists (IOJ) in Prague. It was, of course, an avowed opponent of the treaty. In October 1960, it circulated a special issue of its organ, *Jānarisuto*, to the Vienna Conference of the IOJ, which stated:

> Japanese journalists who participated in the great struggle worked through such organizations as labor unions of the press, radio, and TV, holding numerous protest shop rallies, advocating petitioning of the Diet, or participating directly in the demonstrations. . . . At the same time, the democratic journalists fought to report the truthful picture of the people's struggle and anger. They pointed out the dangers of the military pact and wrote many articles, editorials and commentaries pointing out the wrongdoing of the government and government party.[75]

[74] *The Japanese Press*, 1961, p. 40.

[75] "The Press: Taking Due Credit," *Time*, Vol. 76, No. 17, October 24, 1960, pp. 71–72. See also *The Japanese Press*, 1961, p. 7.

Even if their claims were extravagant, these journalists probably accounted for some of the biased reporting.

Time magazine angered Japanese journalists by its critical comments on June 27, 1960;[76] it was doubly annoying to Japanese journalists to come under severe attack by the Japanese left wing as well as by American conservatives during and after the crisis.[77]

No one can measure exactly how much influence the mass media exerted on the political situation in May and June, but they clearly had a part both in setting off the rolling bandwagon of emotionalism and then in slowing it down again. The conformity of most of the newspapers in time of crisis—newspapers which were among the most independent in the world—was surprising. Their emotionalism probably owed less to the hard-working Marxists than to the public tension created by the dramatic domestic and international events of May and June. A more responsible press might have been swayed less by the mood it helped to create; it certainly would have foreseen the eventual upsurge of violence whose consequences could only be self-defeating in the end.

[76] See Shimada Tatsumi, "What Happened in Japan? A Symposium: Free Press Gone Wrong," *Japan Quarterly*, Vol. 7, No. 4, October-December 1960, pp. 417–421.

[77] For a variety of critical discussions, see Arase Yutaka, "Hatashite Genron wa Jiyū de Aru ka?" (Is the Press Really Free?), *Sekai*, August 1960, pp. 203–216; Gendai Seiji Kenkyū Shūdan, "Nihon o Bunretsu Saseta Ninenkan: Masu Komi no Iken to Ugoki" (Two Years that Split Japan: Opinions and Trends in Mass Communications), *Jiyū*, July 1960, pp. 22–27; Hidaka Rokurō, ed., *Gogatsu Jūkunichi*, pp. 200–231; Kano Tsuneo, "Ampo Hantai Tōsō Kiji no Naiyō Bunseki" (An Analysis of the Contents of the Anti-treaty Struggle Articles), *Shimbun Kenkyū*, No. 119, June 1961, pp. 16–20; "Nihon no Seiji Kiki to Shimbun Ronchō" (Japan's Political Crisis and the Tone of the Press), *Shimbun Kenkyū*, special edition, No. 110, September 1960; "Shimbun wa Shinjitsu o Hōdō Shita ka?" (Did the Newspapers Report the Truth?), panel discussion, *Jiyū*, August 1960, pp. 77–92; Matsuoka Yōko, "Yureru Shakai to Yuruganu Shihyō" (Wavering Society and an Unwavering Barometer), *Gendai no Me*, Vol. 2, No. 9, September 1961, pp. 24–28; and "Ampo o Meguru Shimbun Ronchō" (The Tone of the Press on the Security Treaty), a series of three articles by Yoshida Kazundo, Takagi Noritsune, and Kouchi Saburō in *Tokyo Daigaku Shimbun*, June 15, 22, and 29, respectively.

Hagerty Is Mobbed

The issue of President Eisenhower's visit turned the domestic struggle into a serious crisis for U.S.–Japanese relations. The visit had been planned in January 1960 as part of an exchange in which Crown Prince Akihito would visit the United States to celebrate 100 years of relations between the two countries; Eisenhower was to become the first incumbent U.S. President to visit Japan. He was to arrive on June 19 after a goodwill trip to Moscow, and most Japanese had welcomed the idea while the spirit of Camp David prevailed. But the U-2 incident and the summit breakup, as well as Khrushchev's scathing denunciation of the President, raised doubts in Tokyo, and the doubts were deepened when it was announced that the President would also visit the Philippines, Taiwan, Okinawa, and South Korea on the same tour. The trip now came to be regarded in Japan as a Cold War tactic to strengthen the major U.S. military bastions in the Far East. Its new complexion clashed headlong with the mood of many Japanese who would otherwise have been prepared to welcome "Aiku" as an emissary of world peace.

When Kishi arranged for treaty approval to coincide with the day of Eisenhower's arrival, moreover, the domestic quarrel became inextricably tied to the question of whether and how the President should be greeted. The predicament was difficult for many Japanese who were friendly to the United States but had serious reservations about the treaty and genuinely loathed Kishi.

For the United States, and particularly for the Republican Party in this election year, the successful presidential tour of the Far East took on new importance after the rebuff from Khrushchev in Paris. In Japan, where anti-Kishi sentiment was mounting daily, the visit appeared to Kishi's adversaries to be clumsy interference in Japan's internal affairs. The United States faced the dilemma of either backing out as gracefully as possible with the result that Kishi would be further weakened and the passage of the new treaty jeopardized, or waiting out the crisis and breasting the wave of anti-Kishi emotion. Kishi had the choice of canceling the invitation, which was certain to force his retirement, or of risking the visit and hoping to prolong his

285

career in office. In the end, Cold War and political pressures in the United States and political ambitions in Tokyo kept both sides from retreating and postponing the visit.[78]

It was precisely the fear that Eisenhower would receive a rousing welcome—one that would negate much of the mood of protest—that stirred the left wing into action to prevent the visit. The pro-JCP members of the People's Council welcomed the linking of the visit and the treaty, for it gave them new opportunities to steer the protest movement directly against "U.S. imperialism." Since April 4, the council had discussed ways to mount anti-American demonstrations at the time of the visit; on April 26, Zengakuren leaders had promised to mobilize thousands of students against Eisenhower, and Hayama Takeo had even said they should stone him as the "brave Venezuelan students" had stoned Nixon.[79] JSP Chairman Asanuma personally delivered an "open letter" to the U.S. Embassy on May 24 urging the President to cancel his trip; [80] though he was criticized in many editorials for this direct approach to a foreign government, appeals for postponement began to flow in from all quarters. Sōhyō's Iwai Akira supported the *Asahi's* June 1 editorial urging postponement; [81] the JCP proclaimed that preventing the visit was a "just and patriotic

[78] For discussions of this issue, see in English, Richard Rovere, "Letter from Washington, June 18, 1960," *New Yorker*, June 25, 1960, pp. 85–90; and Saitō Makoto, "Reflections on American-Japanese Relations," *Far Eastern Survey*, Vol. 29, No. 10, October 1960, pp. 151–153; in Japanese, see: Hidaka Rokurō, ed., *Gogatsu Jūkunichi*, pp. 142–170; Saitō Makoto, "Aiku Hōnichi Chūshi no Imi" (The Meaning of the Cancellation of Ike's Visit) in *Amerika Gaikō no Ronri to Genjitsu* (Logic and Reality in American Diplomacy), Tokyo: Tokyo Daigaku Shuppan Kai, 1962, pp. 129–134 (compare this with Saitō's article in English above for an interesting example of the use by intellectuals of the Japanese language as a refuge); Takeda Taijun, "Kishi San wa Kangei no Shikaku ga Nai" (Mr. Kishi Is Unqualified to Greet Ike), *Shūkan Asahi*, June 26, 1960, pp. 6–9; and Takeuchi Yoshimi, *Fufukujū no Isan* (A Legacy of Disobedience), Tokyo: Chikuma Shobo, 1961, pp. 148–150.

[79] *Japan Times*, April 26, 1960.

[80] The text of this letter and Ambassador MacArthur's pungent reply can be found in *Asahi Evening News*, May 25, 1960.

[81] *Asahi Evening News*, June 3, 1960.

struggle against U.S. imperialism." [82] Even the moderate DSP said it would welcome a visit from Eisenhower, but not at this time.[83]

An unexpected surge of opposition came from moderates, conservatives, and others who had special relationships with the United States.[84] Most of them argued that the visit at this time could only harm U.S.–Japanese relations, and denounced reports in the U.S. that opposition to the movement was the work of a small handful of Communists. Especially surprising were the active efforts of a U.S. Specialists Scholars Group (Chibeiha Chishikijin) composed of ten specialists in U.S. affairs, and another organization of fifty-nine professors from five Christian Universities around Tokyo.[85] The latter group sent an open letter to President Eisenhower on June 10 calling his visit at this time "singularly unpropitious." Blaming the widespread protest movement on Kishi's "undemocratic procedure," they appealed to the President as "those who cherish special friendship with your people" to postpone the visit.[86] Members of this group later participated in *demo* at the Diet as the "The Association of Faculty Members and Students at Christian Schools for the Protection of Democracy." The organizers behind this group had close ties with the Shimin-ha at Tokyo University; some of its members were long-time opponents of the treaty while others were indifferent to the treaty but angered by Kishi.

[82] *Aikoku to Seigi no Tōsō o Hatten Saseyo!* (Develop the Patriotic and Just Struggle), JCP handbill, June 10, 1960, from the handbill collection on the treaty struggle at the Social Science Research Institute, Tokyo University.

[83] *Asahi Evening News*, June 6, 1960.

[84] For example, some members of the Mikka Kai (Third of the Month Society), a group of top business executives, suggested on June 3 that ways be found to postpone the visit (*Asahi Evening News*, June 4, 1960). Within the Foreign Office, it was rumored that a "postponement faction" was growing. Even Adachi Tadashi, President of the Japan Chamber of Commerce and Industry and a signer of the new treaty, suggested on June 8 that the visit be put off.

[85] The five were: Aoyama Gakuin, Meiji Gakuin, Tokyo Theological University, Tokyo Women's Christian University, and International Christian University.

[86] From a copy of the letter in the author's possession.

287

Individual members wrote personal letters to American friends to explain the "true situation." [87]

A significant attempt to have the visit postponed was made by two individuals with a long record of interest in U.S.–Japanese relations; shortly after Asanuma's approach to the Embassy, Matsumoto Shigeharu (Director of the International House of Japan) and Takagi Yasaka (Professor Emeritus of Tokyo University) appealed to Ambassador MacArthur to find a way to put off the visit.[88] By now, however, the decision rested with the Japanese Government, or so it was thought by the U.S. Government. Such was the climate of opinion when the Kishi Cabinet resolved on June 7, 1960, to proceed with the arrangements and the White House the same day confirmed the President's determination to visit Japan.

James C. Hagerty, the President's Press Secretary, was sent to Japan on June 10 to make final preparations for the visit. The People's Council decided to greet him with a small-scale *demo* at the airport and hand him a letter protesting the visit. The Zengakuren mainstream stayed out of the picture at this point, resolved not to let the Eisenhower issue sidetrack the movement. The Communist-led anti-mainstream, however, under Kuroha Sumihisa of Tokyo Education University, appeared at Haneda in large numbers; in addition, workers from the pro-JCP unions of the Kawasaki Steel Company, as well as local and national JCP officials, showed up to greet Hagerty. When Hagerty's plane

[87] A strong measure of naiveté in international relations must have motivated these efforts. In view of their declared interest in preserving close 'people-to-people" relations with the United States, they were strangely oblivious to the fact that the 35 million Americans who voted for Eisenhower and the millions of others who resented Japanese objections to his visit (as Japanese would have resented an American protest movement against Prince Akihito, regardless of the U.S. political situation) could scarcely be receptive to their *demo* against Ike's visit. Private polls taken by the U.S.–Japan Society of New York soon after the crisis revealed a sharp decline in Japan's popularity in the U.S.

[88] For the views of these two, see the article by Takagi in *Asahi Shimbun*, June 12, 1960; and Matsumoto Shigeharu, "What Happened in Japan? A Symposium: The Cancellation of Eisenhower's Visit," *Japan Quarterly*, Vol. 7, No. 4, October-December 1960, pp. 403–409.

landed around 3:30 P.M. on June 10, about 8,000 to 10,000 demonstrators were gathered around the two access bridges near the airport.[89] Leftist and rightist "representatives" were jammed into the terminal building, separated by a row of police. Hagerty got out of the plane and, with Ambassador MacArthur and Thomas E. Stephens, Presidential Appointments Secretary, jumped into the waiting limousine and headed for the exit, omitting the usual airport formalities and ignoring a U.S. Marine helicopter that could have carried him over the crowds to the Embassy.[90]

As the car emerged from the tunnel and approached Benten Bridge, it was enveloped by the crowds of students and workers who were surging toward the terminal building.[91] When the car stopped, the disorganized crowd mauled it badly, cracking windows, denting fenders, and rocking it back and forth; several leaders jumped onto the roof and led the singing of the *Inter-*

[89] Japanese students liked to point out the neat contrast between the two Haneda episodes: on January 16, the mainstreamers, who saw Japanese monopoly capital with Kishi as its representative as the main enemy and prime mover behind the new treaty, demonstrated at the airport; on June 10, the anti-mainstreamers who believed that U.S. imperialists were forcing the new treaty on Japan came out to meet Hagerty, an emissary sent by the imperialists to see that the treaty got through the Diet.

[90] Hagerty subsequently told this writer that he knew trouble was brewing since he had heard in Okinawa that the students were threatening to wreck his visit and had seen the waiting crowds from his airplane. Still, as a representative of the President, he felt he could not back down before Communist pressure and take the helicopter. He denied, however, leftist allegations that he was serving as a kind of "guinea pig" for Eisenhower's arrival, to test the strength of popular feeling. Hagerty did not recall having been asked by the Japanese police to give them an hour to clear up the *demo* before leaving the airport as some reports have claimed; he also denied that his car drove "full speed into the demonstrators" as leftists later reported. Interview with James C. Hagerty, July 19, 1962.

[91] It is not entirely clear whether this was planned or accidental. A number of reports say that the demonstrators expected Hagerty to leave in the helicopter and were surprised when his car came out of the tunnel; others, including the police, maintained that certain JCP elements, including the anti-mainstream Zengakuren leaders, had carefully planned the trap several days earlier. The exact rôle of the JCP leaders in this affair is not known, but it is of interest to note that almost all the students who led this *demo* defected from the party with Kasuga Shōjirō in the summer of 1961.

nationale and the chanting of *"Hagachi Go Homu!"* and "Don't Come Aiku!" No one tried to open the door or attack Hagerty, but at one time both right wheels were lifted off the ground. "An uncomfortable experience," Hagerty said later, "especially because we couldn't understand what they were yelling." [92] Standing nearby, ostensibly waiting to petition Hagerty, were a group of thirty to forty Socialist Diet members and a number of high JCP officials, including Iwama Masao and Hakamada Satomi. One Socialist, Tanaka Toshio, Chairman of the Party's National Movement Committee and member of the far-left Heiwa Dōshi Kai, gave his namecard to an American reporter on the scene, who later passed it on to MacArthur; Tanaka, who claimed he was merely trying to "mediate," was later the object of much criticism. [93]

Around 4:00 P.M. police worked their way to the car and attempted to break up the mob; a U.S. Marine helicopter hovered overhead but was pelted with rocks and unable to find a place to land near the scene. The crowd, somewhat dazed and wondering what to do next, began to fall back, and by 4:30 the helicopter was able to land, pick up the beleaguered officials, and whisk them downtown. [94]

As usual, the People's Council blamed the trouble on provocation by the police and right wingers; Minaguchi Kōzō said that responsibility must rest on the "suppressive attitude" of the government and police, and called the *demo* "an explosion of public resentment." [95]

[92] Interview, July 19, 1962. For Japanese accounts, see Hidaka Rokurō, ed., *Gogatsu Jūkunichi*, pp. 142–170 and Etō Jun, "Hagachi Shi o Mukaeta Haneda Demo" (The Haneda *Demo* that Greeted Mr. Hagerty), *Asahi Jiyanaru*, June 19, 1960, pp. 4–6.

[93] See Tanaka Toshio and others, "Watakushi no Mita Haneda Demo Jiken" (The Haneda *Demo* as I Saw It), *Shūkan Asahi*, June 26, 1960, pp. 12–13.

[94] In the end, twenty-two men, including Hasegawa Hiroshi, head of the JCP's Youth Department, and Nakanishi Kō, Chairman of the JCP's Kanagawa Prefectural Committee, went on trial before the Tokyo District Court for this incident on December 12, 1960. On April 27, 1965, the court found all twenty-two guilty but gave them suspended sentences ranging from eight months to a year and a half.

[95] *Asahi Evening News*, June 11, 1960.

The Hagerty Incident had several important results. The press turned against the demonstrators and many editorials expressed the fear that Japan's standing in the eyes of the world had dropped sharply. "Unless the Japanese people start behaving as adults," warned the *Akita Sakigake Shimbun*, "they will never be allowed to make their appearance on the international stage." [96] Businessmen showed new concern over the effect on trade with the United States. Moderates and friends of the U.S. who had opposed the Eisenhower visit were caught in a dilemma: on one hand they wished to prove that the anti-Kishi mood had broad national backing (which it did), and on the other, it was hard to deny that the Hagerty mobbing had been caused by a relatively small minority under strong Communist influence. This was a major but short-lived triumph for the Communists; once again they had taken advantage of the general disorder to exploit the energy of the anti-treaty and anti-Kishi movement for their own ends. The general distaste for such discourtesy to a foreign guest, however, probably hurt them more than it helped them in the long run.

There were reliable reports at this time that some members of the non-Communist left were seriously worried for the first time since the formation of the People's Council that the JCP might take over the movement. From this point on, the cooperation between the JSP and JCP deteriorated even further, and the rest of the struggle saw the gap widen between them.[97]

June 15: Day of Bloodshed

The Hagerty affair did not shake Prime Minister Kishi's determination to greet President Eisenhower on June 19. Between June 11 and 14, with public opinion swinging against leftist extremism, the LDP took steps to discredit the Opposition and assure a warm welcome for the President. On June 11, Chief Cabinet Secretary Shiina Etsusaburō accused the Socialists of "marching in step" with the Communists, and Kishi warned

[96] *Asahi Evening News,* summary of press comments, June 13, 1960.

[97] On June 13, a majority of the People's Council Directors beat down a JCP proposal to give financial aid to those arrested in the Hagerty Incident.

that the airport mob had seriously harmed Japan's good name abroad; the people must try to repair this damage, he said, with a warm welcome for Eisenhower.[98]

Kishi called for a "summit meeting" with Asanuma and Nishio on June 13 and hinted at a political truce whereby the Diet would recess for six days surrounding the state visit. Nishio attended the meeting and agreed that the DSP would welcome the President; Asanuma, however, refused to attend unless Kishi promised to resign, dissolve the Diet, and shelve the new treaty. The JCP, meanwhile, branded the truce idea as a new plot to get the treaty through the Diet. On June 13, the JSP's CEC criticized the DSP for joining Kishi in welcoming Eisenhower and turned down an offer of a meeting between Nishio and Asanuma; it resolved to support a peaceful *demo* on June 19. Despite the trend toward moderation, however, Kishi did not attempt to push the treaty through the Upper House, as planned, on June 15, probably because he feared setting off a new wave of protest.

The LDP rushed forward with plans to give the President a rousing reception, announcing that one million well-wishers would be mobilized through the "National Committee for Welcoming President Eisenhower" and scoffing at all talk of untoward incidents marring the visit. Prominent names, such as Abe Yoshishige (President of Gakushūin), Shimonaka Yasaburō (President of Heibonsha), and Mrs. Hatoyama Kaoruko (widow of the former Prime Minister) were enlisted on a committee to support the welcome.[99] On June 14, even the rebel LDP faction leaders fell in line and Zenrō became the first labor organization to support a friendly reception.

Meanwhile, Japan's overworked security officials were showing signs of uneasiness. There is considerable evidence that friction developed between the Prime Minister and the security officials at this time: Kishi reportedly felt that he was not getting their full support in quelling the demonstrations, while police authorities resented the criticism both from the left and the right over

[98] *Asahi Evening News,* June 11, 1960.
[99] *Asahi Evening News,* June 14, 1960.

their handling of the crowds.[100] They felt they were being used to keep an unpopular politician in office at the cost of tarnishing their hard-won postwar image of restraint and courtesy.[101] Furthermore, in view of the widespread unrest, the job of protecting the President and the Emperor from fanatics along the 11.6-mile ride from Haneda Airport to the Palace was a large order.[102] Even during the Crown Prince's wedding parade the previous year, a man had slipped through police lines and jumped on the royal carriage; there seemed no way to assure against similar dashes by Zengakuren or other fanatics. For these reasons, police officials told Kishi after the Hagerty Incident (for which they were roundly condemned) that they could not guarantee the President's safety. Kishi ignored this advice, however, and called for the fullest possible protection.[103] Thus the police conducted practice airport parades and raided likely agitators to snuff out all sources of trouble.[104]

Once the government's intention to go ahead with the visit was made clear on June 13, the People's Council held a heated debate: the JCP and its followers insisted on massive anti-Eisenhower demonstrations, while the JSP and others feared the consequences of a second Hagerty affair, involving the President of the United States. A decisive blow to the JCP came on June

[100] Kishi said later that Occupation-sponsored reforms which gave the Prime Minister only indirect control over the police through the NPSC were at the root of the trouble (interview, January 10, 1962). Another fact was that the incumbent NPSC Chairman, Ishihara Kanichirō, was not a Kishi appointee.

[101] Asahi Evening News, May 30, and June 6, 1960, gave hints of this attitude but not the full story.

[102] The task would indeed have been formidable, even after the open car idea was dropped. Police plans called for 3,800 men at 10-meter intervals along the route with 11,200 others at key points around the city. This meant calling in several thousand police from neighboring prefectures. Normally, state visitors were accorded only 600 policemen along the same route. Asahi Evening News, June 9, 1960.

[103] Asahi Evening News, June 13, 1960.

[104] On the night of June 13, they raided the anti-mainstream Zengakuren headquarters at Tokyo Education University, causing scuffles with students and storms of protest from the academic community.

14 and 15 when Ōta and Iwai of Sōhyō stated that they opposed a *demo* at the airport and along the arrival route on June 19. It appears that this decision met resistance among unions where JCP influence was strongest; Sōhyō had to schedule a closed-door meeting of its Directors on June 16 to resolve conflicting views.[105] The People's Council, over JCP objections, resolved to continue the movement in an auti-government, not anti-American vein, and by the eve of Sōhyō's second major strike of June 15, the mood was shifting toward a warm welcome for Eisenhower. It is likely that his visit to Japan would have been highly successful had not Zengakuren mainstream extremists— now at a fever pitch of excitement over the impending ratification—chosen once again to use senseless violence at the Diet.

Since June 11, mainstream leaders had discussed ways to give the anti-treaty and anti-Kishi movement a final "lift" (*moriagari*) and prevent it from falling under JCP control; led by Tokyo University's Komaba Campus, they decided to launch a major assault on the Diet on June 15, in conjunction with *Sōhyō's* strike and the *demo* of the People's Council. Moderate students argued strongly against the plan, but the extremists won out and final preparations were made late at night on June 14. With many of its leaders in jail, the mainstream was now directed by the twenty-four-year-old Kitakoji Satoshi, a fourth-year economics major at Kyoto University, who had rushed to Tokyo to take over on June 12.[106] As we mentioned above, many of the students under his control were inexperienced in demonstrating and far more excitable than the hardened Zengakuren leaders.

On the afternoon of June 15, with Sōhyō's strike and *demo*

[105] *Mainichi Daily News*, June 16, 1960. This plan was overtaken by events on June 15.

[106] Kitakoji's chief lieutenants at this time were Nishibe Shinobu and Banno Junji of Tokyo University and Katō Noboru of Waseda. This was one of the rare instances in the protest campaign, however, that a single individual—Kitakoji—assumed full responsibility for major decisions. His father, a JCP member, had been fired as a teacher in the Asahigaoka Incident of March 1954; he himself had long been active in leftist campaigns. A JCP member until his purge with other mainstreamers in 1958, Kitakoji later served as Zengakuren National Chairman (July-December 1961). Interview with Kitakoji Satoshi, January 9, 1962.

by some 70,000 already underway, the students began to gather near the main gate of the Diet.[107] The police brought in 5,000 men and blockaded the entrances with rows of trucks. With Kitakoji giving orders from the top of a loudspeaker truck, the students snake-danced wildly around the outside of the Diet compound. Around 4:30 P.M. a group from Meiji University produced wire-cutters and began ripping away the reinforcing wire at the South Gate (Minami Tsūyō Mon); some students began throwing rocks and placards toward the police, who waited silently inside the gate.

At 5:15 P.M. on the opposite side of the compound, a scuffle broke out between a demonstrating Modern Drama Group (Shingekidan) and 200 rightists in the Renovation Action Corps (Ishin Kōdōtai) when the rightists drove their truck into the midst of the marchers.[108] By 6:00 P.M. the students had smashed

[107] This description is based on press accounts and interviews; an excellent summary may be found in "6:15 Ryūketsu Jiken no Kiroku" (Record of the Bloody Affair of June 15), *Asahi Jānaru*, July 3, 1960, pp. 4–21; many other accounts have been written, including: Unno Shinkichi and others, eds., *Rekishi e no Shōgen: 6:15 no Dokyumento* (Evidence for History: Documents of June 15), Tokyo: Nihon Hyōron Shinsha, 1960, a collection of leftist accounts. See also: "Chi ni Somatta Kokkai" (The Diet Soaked in Blood), Radio Kantō Broadcast, *Shūkan Asahi*, July 3, 1960, pp. 30–32; Ōe Kenzaburō, "Rokugatsu Jūgonichi" (June 15), *Nihon Dokusho Shimbun*, June 12, 1961; and "Tatakai no Kiroku" (Record of the Fight), *Tokyo Daigaku Shimbun*, special supplement, July 11, 1960. The police's version is given in a pamphlet called *6:15 Kokkai Totsunyū Jiken o Chūshin ni Shite* (Focusing on the June 15 Diet Invasion Incident), June 1960.

[108] This incident has been widely and wrongly understood by many writers in Japan and the U.S. as provoking the subsequent violence. For example: "On June 15, however, violence erupted in the vicinity of the Diet. It was initiated by a right wing extremist group who apparently drove a truck into a line of demonstrators, most of whom were women. Students witnessing the spectacle stormed the Diet gates and clashed with the police. Six hundred students were injured and one woman was trampled to death in the ensuing struggle" (Scalapino and Masumi, *op. cit.*, p. 140). Or, for another example: "The unleashing of terrorism on the right can also stimulate a reactive terrorism on the left, a cycle already visible during the May-June riots" (Herbert Passin, "The Sources of Protest in Japan," *American Political Science Review*, Vol. 56, No. 2, June 1962, p. 394). Some Japanese leftists have used the incident to justify the students' violence,

the South Gate and were attempting to drag police trucks out onto the street with ropes. Then they launched a fierce rock-throwing charge, ignoring fire hoses and driving the police back into the compound. By 7:00 P.M., about 1,500 students swarmed through the South Gate and into the compound. During the following half-hour, the police counterattacked, wielding wooden clubs and pressing the students back toward the gate. It was in this period that Miss Kamba Michiko, a twenty-two-year-old coed from Tokyo University, was crushed to death.[109]

When word of the death of a student flashed about the Diet and across the nation, the atmosphere became charged: as one student newspaper later put it, "The Treaty Struggle Finally Produced a Martyr." [110] Some erroneous reports had it that four students were dead, and for days afterward, some students believed that the police were hiding the bodies. The wail of am-

---

but in fact there was no causal connection between the two. Zengakuren had begun its attack on the South Gate at 4:30 P.M.; Kitakoji told this writer in an interview on January 9, 1962, that, being on the other side of the Diet compound, he had neither seen nor heard of the rightest attack when he gave his own orders to attack. The Zengakuren invasion had been well planned in advance, and the fact that students came equipped with wire-cutters, ropes, and other tools bears this out. The point is important because Zengakuren must be given full credit for this final episode that persuaded Kishi to cancel Eisenhower's visit and resulted ultimately in Kishi's resignation. For a discussion of the rightists' rôle during the anti-treaty campaign, see below, pp. 319ff.

[109] The cause of her death became a major controversy: leftists claimed the police had purposefully strangled her while conservatives said she had been trampled by her retreating colleagues. The 20,000-word autopsy report presented to the Tokyo District Procurator's Office on July 21, 1960, by Dr. Nakadate Kyūhei of Keio University said she died from "suffocation resulting from pressure on the chest and stomach. However, there were also signs that pressure had been applied to the mouth, nose, and neck. Death due to choking can be 30% ruled out" (Asahi Evening News, July 7, 1960). Dr. Sakamoto Akira, a JSP member of the House of Councillors, after examining the body himself, claimed she had died from pressure on the throat or suffocation—with the strong implication that she had been strangled (Asahi Evening News, July 26, 1960). See also Sakamoto Akira, "Michiko San no Shi" (Miss Michiko's Death), Sekai, August 1960, pp. 123–126.

[110] Waseda Daigaku Shimbun, front page headlines, June 22, 1960.

bulances carrying off the injured lasted long into the night as the battle continued. By about 8:30, some 4,000 students were inside the compound, seven police trucks had been overturned and set on fire, and hundreds of bleeding demonstrators were straggling about the Diet compound. Inside, a group of thirty JSP Diet members clamored at Kishi's office door, challenging him to issue a statement that would "pacify" the students; when Kishi later emerged to go to the men's room, they trapped him in the hallway and members of his staff had to fight to get him back to the safety of his office. Outside, a number of JSP Diet members tried to reason with the students and get them to leave the compound. At about 10:00 P.M. the scene of the battle shifted to the main gate, where once again the students hailed rocks on the police and overturned trucks.

By midnight, the front of the Diet was illuminated by burning police trucks and was strewn with rocks, shoes and broken placards. Around 1:15 A.M. the students began to regroup at Chapel Center for a new attack, and this time the police received orders to use tear-gas for the first time in the anti-treaty struggle. About forty bombs were thrown and those who remained in the area were forcibly ejected. This was the famous moment when the police used clubs on demonstrating professors from Mingakken as well as on reporters and "innocent bystanders," giving rise to heated charges of brutality and excessive violence.

After a few more sporadic outbursts—the Yūrakuchō *kōban* was sacked by angry students—the last demonstrators broke up about 4:30 A.M. and went home. In all, 18 police trucks had been totally destroyed, hundreds of students and police hurt, 196 students arrested, and one girl killed.[111]

[111] Of the 196 arrested, 100 were released within 48 hours, 63 after ten days; in the end, 23 Zengakuren students received suspended sentences of from six to eighteen months from the Tokyo District Court. *The Yomiuri*, August 10, 1965. Ishii Kazumasa, leader of the rightist Ishin Kōdōtai, was sentenced on December 21, 1961, to eighteen months in jail; eighteen others in his squad received sentences of from eight months to a year in jail (twelve of these sentences were suspended). *Asahi Evening News*, December 21, 1960.

297

A word should be said at this point on the conduct of the police on June 15 and throughout the demonstrations. Every day for more than a month they had endured insults as well as rocks and clubs wielded by radical students. It is hard to conceive of any other police force in the world—including New York's finest—behaving as well under similar attention. There was some discontent, it is true, over having to fight Kishi's political battle, but in general they followed their orders and used their weapons in accordance with the law. Though they carried live ammunition, not a shot was fired during the entire movement. Captured students reported no ill treatment at their hands.[112] Between June 11 and 19, 815 policemen were injured, compared with 591 students and unionists; in the whole campaign, the figures were 1,782 and 620 respectively.[113] By June 15 the front-line mobile units were frustrated and short-tempered. The Number Four Mobile Unit of 1,800 men, known throughout the force for its supremacy in *jūdō*, *kendō*, and overall *esprit de corps*, had been used in most of the battles with the students and on June 15, it was stationed at the main gate. Many of its members were the same age as their student adversaries, and there was resentment and envy over the "wise college kids" who had nothing better to do than throw rocks and attack the Diet. "Quite frankly," one police official admitted, "they were like dogs straining at the leash on June 15, eager to get in a few blows of their own." Tired and hungry—the students had burned their supply truck so they had gone without supper— the orders after midnight to disperse the rioters came as a welcome relief, and were probably carried out with excessive zeal.

Into this situation walked the group of college professors car-

[112] Interview with Tanaka Manabu, December 31, 1961, a former Zengakuren chairman at Komaba Campus of Tokyo University who had been jailed three times during the anti-treaty movement.

[113] Keishichō, "Ampo Kaitei Hantai Tōsō: Keibi no Genjō ni Tsuite." (The Struggle Against Security Treaty Revision: On the Current Status of the Police, Internal Use Only), August 1960, Appendix 2, p. 200. The students contested the figures, claiming many unreported injuries of their own, but in any event the number of injured police was sizeable. For students' claims, see *Tokyo Shimbun*, December 13, 1960.

rying placards and attempting to "mediate" in the battle. The inevitable happened, and a number of professorial skulls felt the stored-up wrath of the frustrated police.[114] One must question the wisdom of their attempt to stage a "peaceful" *demo* after the riotous events of that day; there may even have been some sort of crude justice in their sharing of the students' fate, for they had most assuredly helped to incite the students to action.[115] On the other hand, the incident was traumatic for intellectuals participating actively in the "political process" for the first time; some, at least, were confirmed in their preference for the ivory tower. The major leaders of Mingakken were not, as it turned out, among the attacked demonstrators that night.

This incident hurt the postwar image of the police in Japan. "The police have never been less popular with the public than now," commented *Tensei Jingo* on July 11.[116] A flood of literature was produced by the left to show their reversion to prewar brutality,[117] and except for two small pamphlets,[118] they were forced to take the criticism in defensive silence. The evidence available does not bear out the charges against them.

[114] The professors, who later filed charges of attempted murder and abuse of authority leading to injury, claimed that sixty-five of their members had been injured, thirty-five of these seriously (*Asahi Evening News*, July 22, 1960). The case was dropped by the Tokyo District Procurator's Office on November 11, 1962, but the group appealed to the Tokyo District Court and on June 19, 1964, twenty-four of the professors won a total of 6,300,000 yen ($17,500) in damages from the Tokyo Metropolitan Government.

[115] Shimizu Ikutarō makes a similar point in "Ampo Tōsō Ichinengo no Shisō" (Thoughts on the Security Treaty Struggle One Year Later), *Chūō Kōron*, July 1960, pp. 45–47.

[116] *Asahi Shimbun*, July 11, 1960.

[117] See, for example: "Gakusei to Keikan" (Students and the Police), *Tokyo Daigaku Shimbun*, June 15, 1960; "Kedamono no Yō na Kenryoku no Bōgyaku" (Atrocities by the Beastlike Authorities), *Jānarisuto*, June 20, 1960, p. 3; *Mingakken Nyūsu*, No. 3, June 24, 1960, and No. 4, July 16, 1960; Yamaguchi Keiji, "Gozen Reiji no Bōkō" (Violence at Midnight), in Tokyo Daigaku Shokuin Kumiai, *6:15 Jiken Zengo*, pp. 64–75.

[118] Keishichō, "Shōwa 35-nen Kamihanki no Keibi Jiken o Kaerimite" (Looking Back over the Police Incidents in the First Half of 1960), October 1960; and "Ampo Tōsō o Megutte" (Concerning the Security Treaty Struggle), June 1960.

The Treaty Is Ratified and Kishi Resigns

The treaty struggle was anti-climactic after June 15. Kishi met with advisers at midnight and again on the next morning, and then told a news conference on the afternoon of June 16 that "this was not the appropriate time to welcome a state guest"; with this, the feverish preparations for the Eisenhower welcome were called to a halt.[119] He said it was clear that international Communism was behind the violence on June 10 and 15 and deeply regretted the need to cancel the visit. Asked when he would retire, Kishi refused to comment, but promised to stay in office at least until the treaty was ratified.

The JSP said on June 16 that Kishi's decision should be regarded as a victory for the Japanese people who "desired true peace and friendship with the United States."[120] The party added that if Kishi should try to remain in office, it would intensify the campaign to overthrow him. Sōhyō hailed the "people's unified campaign" which won the cancellation of the visit and threatened even larger demonstrations against the treaty itself. All the leftist organizations (except Zengakuren) took pains at this time to point out that "the people" had won the day; they became extremely sensitive to Zengakuren's claim that it alone deserved credit for blocking the visit.

President Kaya Seiji of Tokyo University stirred up a storm on June 16 with his statement (just before Kishi's announcement) that as long as the political situation remained unchanged, "not only is it impossible for the universities to carry out their educational tasks but it is completely ineffectual to appeal to the students for moderation through persuasion and other means of education."[121] Kaya's remark was taken to mean that the students could not be held responsible for their acts until the political situation was restored to normalcy—a strong

---

[119] It was reported later that the Foreign Ministry and high security officials, as well as some cabinet members and Yoshida had all advised against the visit. *Asahi Shimbun*, August 3, 1960, also said that the Imperial Household Agency had expressed its concern through an intermediary on June 15.

[120] *Mainichi Daily News*, June 17, 1960.

[121] *Asahi Evening News*, June 20, 1960.

hint that Kishi should resign. Matsuda Takechiyo, Minister of Education, and others were highly critical of Kaya's statement, and on June 18, Kaya made a public apology to Matsuda.[122] Though there were no further riots, an uneasy atmosphere hung over Tokyo as midnight of June 18 approached. Massive *demo* continued around the Diet, now supplemented by funeral parades and orations at Tokyo University and elsewhere for the new martyr. Students boycotted classes and were joined by faculty members in a new round of protest rallies. Then, on the evening of June 17, Kawakami Jōtarō was stabbed and lightly wounded by a twenty-year-old mechanic as he stood on the Diet steps receiving petitions.[123]

The Socialist Party was shocked on June 17 to find a letter in all the major evening papers from Mrs. Katō Shizue, a prominent JSP member of the Upper House, who had been the highest vote winner in the country in the 1956 Upper House Elections. The letter, entitled "Let Us All Rise Up With Courage," expressed shock over the outbreak of violence: "I feel deeply ashamed that we have come to the point where the democracy of Japan is being exposed to the danger of destruction by such violent action. As a Socialist Party member I wish to apologize deeply to the nation for having been too cowardly these past weeks to say what I knew was right. . . . The Communists, with extremely active backing from Red China and Russia, have tried to destroy the government by creating a popular front. Not only that, they have tried to lead the whole country into anti-American rioting just before the visit of Pres-

---

[122] Edward Seidensticker was prompted to observe that Kaya's statement was "ludicrously similar" to a statement made by General Araki twenty-five years ago. "Both gentlemen said that the miscreants were angry, and that we should not reprove them." "An Eastern Weimar Republic?" *New Leader*, No. 34, September 5, 1960, p. 8.

[123] The JSP immediately accused the police of gross negligence and said "the incident may be regarded as a conspiracy between the Metropolitan Police Board and rightist terrorist organizations" (*Asahi Evening News*, June 18, 1960). There were no subsequent revelations of such a conspiracy; Kawakami was released from the hospital on July 6 and later went on to become Chairman of the JSP. He died of a brain hemorrhage on December 3, 1965.

ident Eisenhower, so that they could isolate Japan from America. . . . The real question now is what kind of ideology we want for ourselves and our children." [124] The far left in the JSP called for Mrs. Katō's immediate expulsion from the party, but Asanuma reportedly urged leniency and the Disciplinary Committee ultimately took no action on the matter.

A huge crowd—numbering up to 330,000 according to leftist sources—massed at the Diet on June 18 to await the climactic moment at midnight. Twelve thousand police were on hand around the Diet, Kishi's residences and the U.S. Embassy in case rumors of a "showdown" proved true. Midnight passed without incident, however, and the controversial treaty finally gained automatic Diet approval. Many demonstrators remained in the streets outside all night to register their disapproval, but there was no further appetite for violence.

On June 20 the treaty passed its last parliamentary hurdle as the House of Councillors (LDP members only) passed the bill revising 32 domestic laws in accordance with the new treaty. On the night of June 21, Kishi sent messengers secretly to the homes of cabinet ministers to collect the necessary signatures. Then, on the morning of June 23, the instruments of ratification were exchanged in a short, unheralded ceremony at Fujiyama's residence in Shirogane, Tokyo. On the same morning, a wan and tired looking Kishi announced his decision to resign: "On the occasion of the coming into effect of this historically significant new security treaty, I keenly realize the need for a change of government to change completely the thinking of the people and aggressively to carry out new policies in line with both the domestic and the international situation. I have therefore decided to resign as Prime Minister." [125] The decision did not actually take effect until July 15, 1960, following the choice of Ikeda as his successor, but it effectively put an end to the crisis in Tokyo and changed the political climate, almost overnight, from high tension to the relative calm that has prevailed to the time of this writing.

[124] *Asahi Shimbun* (evening), June 17, 1960.
[125] *Asahi Evening News*, June 23, 1960.

 CHAPTER 9

The Calm

WITH the treaty ratified and Kishi's resignation plans announced, the inflamed public mood shifted abruptly from outrage to apathy. The *demo* and rallies subsided; a new conservative Prime Minister took office and immediately became popular; parliamentary debate resumed and, in November, general elections were held. Students returned to classes and coffee shops, and scholars, after their brief encounter with raw politics, set about the difficult search for meaning in the confusion. Except for ominous outbursts of rightist terrorism, the political situation was as "normal" a year afterward as if the crisis had never happened. Yet it would be wrong to conclude that the struggle left no mark on the political scene; in this chapter, we shall make some preliminary observations on the seemingly significant after-effects of the crisis.

The Liberal Democratic Party and the Struggle for Power

With the end of the crisis, business leaders exerted strong pressure on the LDP to stabilize the political situation and restore the "image" of responsible government in Japan.[1] Negotiations began immediately within the party for an agreed candidate; as usual, the battle for succession was fought less on issues and policies than on personal loyalties and factional bargaining.[2] The three middle faction leaders, Ōno, Ishii, and Ikeda were the leading candidates with Matsumura (runner-up in 1959) and Fujiyama (prominent because of his rôle in negotiating the treaty) entering the race later on. Kishi, though virtually driven from office by the protest movement, had lost

[1] An example of their thinking may be found in "Aiku Hōnichi Enki: Kinkyū Tokuhō" (Postponement of Ike's Visit: An Emergency Report), *Daiyamondo*, June 25, 1960, pp. 4–10.

[2] This account is based on press reports and interviews with *Asahi Shimbun* Political Section reporters, as well as on the summary in Scalapino and Masumi, *op. cit.*, pp. 142–144 (which, however, differs in some details).

little of his power *within* the party; the Kishi-Satō bloc of 110 followers was the largest single coalition in the LDP.[3]

According to reliable reports, each of the three leading candidates had received, or felt he had received, assurances of Kishi's support at some earlier date, which was surely a measure of Kishi's mastery of political *sumō*. If our earlier conjecture was correct, however, Kishi and Satō were committed to Ikeda under the "Yoshida Plan" whereby Ikeda and then Satō would move to the top. This plan assumed a five-faction alliance among Kishi, Satō, Ikeda, Ōno, and Ishii which would have left the anti-mainstream, with the "dangerous" Kōno, out of party and government posts altogether. Yoshida publicly backed Ikeda on June 24 and Satō did the same on July 11. Kishi, presumably because of previous bargains, did not openly back Ikeda until the eve of the party convention.

When Ikeda received the open support of Yoshida and became the obvious front-runner, Ōno, Ishii, and Kōno banded together to support Ōno and "stop Ikeda." Thus the party was divided roughly between the ex-officials (known also as the "bureaucratic wing") and the party politicians (bred in prewar politics). Kishi and Satō had hoped to choose a successor through "talks," but a deadlock forced the party on July 8 to call a national convention.[4] The day before the convention, Matsumura withdrew his candidacy and the party politicians regrouped around Ishii. At this point Kishi came out openly for Ikeda, who proceeded to beat Ishii on the second ballot on July 14, by 302-194 votes, and became Japan's eighth Prime Minister since the war.

That afternoon, at an LDP reception for the new party President, a prewar rightist fanatic with a record of mental illness

---

[3] According to the *Asahi Jānaru* (June 26, 1960), Lower House members were divided roughly as follows: Kishi: 70; Satō: 40; Ikeda: 50; Ishii: 20; Ōno: 35; Miki-Matsumura: 35; Kōno: 30; Ishibashi: 10. Some of Kishi's 70 were in the process of breaking away to form the new Fujiyama faction at this time.

[4] Kishi reportedly feared that a convention vote would split his and Satō's factions among the various contenders, reducing his power to influence the final choice.

—Aramaki Taisuke—stabbed Kishi six times in the thigh. The wound was not serious (Kishi left the hospital after two weeks), but the question of the man's motivation, and of how he had gained access to the gathering (along with other prewar rightists) remained something of an official mystery.

Prime Minister Ikeda, who took office on July 19, immediately adopted a "low posture" (*teishisei*) in obvious contrast with Kishi.[5] Ikeda pledged, upon becoming President of the LDP, to "promote parliamentary government through mutual cooperation with the Opposition."[6] In his first major clash with the Socialists over the Political Violence Prevention Bill (with now *demo* brewing outside the Diet), Ikeda backed down and allowed the bill to be shelved in the House of Councillors. His ten-year income-doubling plan quickly attracted the nation's attention and perfectly suited the post-treaty mood of conservatism and stability. Other steps, such as appointing the first woman cabinet minister, eating "curried rice" (a cheap and popular dish), and denouncing golf and *geisha* parties also improved his public standing. The press, in a complete somersault from its anti-government stance during the crisis, was sympathetic to the new cabinet.[7] An *Asahi Shimbun* poll taken on August 1–2 showed that 51 percent supported the new cabinet—the highest rate of support for any new Prime Minister since the war.[8] It appeared that Kishi's unpopularity had not seriously damaged

[5] This despite a reputation for bluntness of speech; as Finance Minister under Yoshida he had said publicly that the poor could eat barley if they could not afford rice (1950). In 1951 he had said, in connection with economic retrenchment policies that it could not be helped if five or ten small businessmen went bankrupt (*Asahi Evening News*, July 20, 1960). See also Chalmers A. Johnson, "Low Posture Politics in Japan," *Asian Survey*, Vol. 3, No. 1, January 1963, pp. 17–30.

[6] *Asahi Evening News*, July 15, 1960.

[7] One of the most significant changes after the crisis was the trend in the "Big Three" newspapers toward more constructive criticism of the government. Sweeping changes of personnel in the political section of the *Asahi Shimbun* and elsewhere partly accounted for the difference.

[8] Support for the Socialists fell to 17% compared with 23% in May 1960, 26% in February 1959, and 30% in August 1956 (*Asahi Evening News*, August 8, 1960). As in the crisis, however, the polls must be treated with caution.

the conservative party in the public mind, and that the Socialists had actually *lost* ground during the struggle. Ikeda retained his personal popularity down to the time when illness forced him to retire in the fall of 1964, and his death at the age of 65 on August 13, 1965 was genuinely mourned by the whole nation.

Ikeda set up a Party Modernization Committee in July 1960 to renovate party machinery, curb the excesses of factionalism, and increase grass-roots strength in the party. To strike at one root of factionalism (money), the party incorporated a "People's Association" in 1961 to pool political contributions in one central fund. Miki Takeo led a movement in the fall of 1963 to abolish factions completely, but the factions remained deeply rooted in the political system, and were not likely to disappear soon. It appeared, though, that the crisis aroused concern among some conservatives over the gap between the party and the people, and conservative leaders, particularly the younger ones, devoted more time to improving the party's image throughout the nation. As early as February 1965, the LDP launched a public relations campaign, with "national movement chapters" in each prefecture, to create a more favorable image of the security treaty by 1970. It appeared that the party was determined not to lose a second time in the arena of public opinion.

Though factionalism continued, Ikeda's policy of bringing "strongmen" from all factions into his successive cabinets including members of the old anti-mainstream, lessened the threat of a party split. By reshuffling his ministers three times during his first two years, moreover, Ikeda distributed power among all the factions with delicate timing and balance. Kōno reportedly made one attempt to form a new party in August 1960, but when Ōno and Matsumura refused to join, he gave up the idea.[9] From July 1961 until November 1964 he was a powerful member of Ikeda's Cabinet.

The venerable Kiyose Ichirō, who was rumored to be "ex-

[9] *Asahi Evening News*, August 11–13, 15, 19, 1960. Kōno's sudden death, shortly before Ikeda's in 1965, removed two key figures in the conservative camp and set the stage for the emergence of new, younger leaders in the LDP.

pendable" as the conservatives sought to recast their post-treaty image, was nevertheless elected again on December 8, 1960, as Speaker of the House of Representatives, a job he held until late 1963.

Kishi, recovering quickly from the stabbing, remained a power in the LDP. Of the three top party positions filled in July 1960, for example, his own man, Shiina Etsusaburō became Chairman of the Policy Board and later Foreign Minister, while Satō's follower, Hori Shigeru, took over the Executive Board; four cabinet posts went to followers of Kishi and Satō as compared with three for Ikeda. With continued backing from some financial quarters, Kishi took special interest in the problems of restoring relations with the Republic of Korea and friendship with the Republic of China on Taiwan.

Kishi's younger brother, Satō Eisaku, became Japan's ninth brother to the job) when Ikeda was forced to resign. Though relations between Ikeda and Satō had become strained when Satō tried to defeat Ikeda in the LDP presidential elections of the previous July, it was reportedly Ikeda himself who broke the deadlocked discussions between faction leaders and named Satō as his successor. In this way the two "prize pupils" of the Yoshida School managed the transfer of power and the "Yoshida Plan" was brought to fruition. Kishi's faction dispersed after 1960 and regrouped around Fujiyama, Kawashima, and Fukuda Takeo, but Kishi himself, as former Prime Minister, brother of the Prime Minister, and expert politician, was far from finished as a powerful voice in party councils.

In an interview with this writer on January 10, 1962, Kishi would not admit to continuing political ambitions, but was willing to express his views on the crisis. He was bitter over the treatment he had received from the press and also admitted that LDP propaganda had been insufficient. He felt the Occupation had erred badly in weakening the police and in opening up education to the possibility of infiltration by the Communists—errors which had been flagrantly exposed in the treaty struggle. He said he had been surprised by the size and scope of the popular demonstrations, and expressed a belief that international Communism had played a major part in foment-

307

ing them. Did he fear repetition of such movements in the future? No, he said, he did not, and added the expression "Ame Futte Ji Katamaru" (After the Rain the Earth Hardens).[10] When asked to give advice to his brother, Prime Minister Satō, in January 1965, Kishi wrote that "it is important to win the support of the younger people. It is the young generation that will reconstruct the nation. . . . He should have some political vision which will attract young people." [11]

In the long run, it seemed that this new and sober awareness on the part of the conservatives of the ideals and energies of Japan's younger generation—educated under an entirely different set of assumptions about government, democracy, and freedom—might prove to be the most lasting effect of the treaty struggle.

The cohesive power in the conservative alliance from July 1960 rested on the personality and philosophy of Yoshida Shigeru. The philosophy could be summed up simply as letting sleeping dogs lie, or not poking the hornet's nest. There was a strong presumption that ultimate goals could best be achieved by patience—that time was on their side. No gratuitous opportunities for arousing public unrest should be given to the left in the meanwhile. The test would come, of course, if less patient conservatives pressed the issues of atomic armament, constitutional revision, or strengthening the police, or if the Opposition found fresh support for treaty revision, return of Okinawa, or relations with Communist China. Meanwhile, as long as the Yoshida philosophy dominated the LDP, it was not likely that a new May 19 Incident would again disrupt the nation.

The Left Wing After the Crisis

The brief coalescence of Japan's left wing under the People's Council—at best an unstable merger of mutually suspicious elements—did not maintain its façade of unity after Kishi's resignation. Between June and August, the Socialists and Commu-

[10] For other expressions of Kishi's views, see "Ima ni Shite Omou" (Thinking Back on It Now), *Sandei Mainichi*, August 28, 1960, pp. 12–16.

[11] "Ototo Eisaku o Kataru" (On Satō Eisaku, My Younger Brother), *Seikai Ōrai*, January 1965, p. 81.

nists fought over the correct interpretation of the crucial events, in terms of their previous goals and tactics. The council, in its official evaluation,[12] papered over the differences; it described Kishi's resignation and the discrediting of the treaty as major victories, but warned against retaliation from reactionaries worse than Kishi. It took note of the defects of the political parties, which had failed to provide proper leadership for the radical students, on one hand, and for the apathetic rural elements on the other. It resolved to spread the struggle from Tokyo to the nation as a whole, under the new slogans "Nonrecognition of the Security Treaty" and "Oppose Unwarranted Oppression."

A movement to disband and replace the council got under-way in late 1960; the JSP suggested that it be reformed to en-compass the broader purpose of protecting the Constitution as well as opposing the security treaty. After several months of controversy over the status of the JCP, which demanded full membership on the executive board, the council was formally dissolved on March 29, 1961—two years after its birth—and re-placed by the National Council for Opposition to the Security Treaty and for Safeguarding Peace and Democracy. The new body had the same thirteen directors and the JCP participated once again as an "observer." As in other instances where in-terest subsides and management is left to the "professionals," the council's pro-Communist orientation seemed to grow after this time. For example, when the Soviet Union resumed nuclear tests in September 1961, five of the thirteen Directors were able to defeat a JSP proposal that the council condemn all nuclear tests; the five argued from the JCP line that Soviet tests were "in the interests of peace." [13]

In any event, the council continued to sponsor mass actions in line with "regular" leftist objectives: to block relations with South Korea, oppose the Political Violence Prevention Bill, and keep U.S. nuclear submarines out of Japanese ports. It served the purpose of coordinating expressions of protest by the frag-mented left on specific issues; retaining its offices in the House

[12] Kokumin Kaigi, *Kyoto Niyūsu*, July 10, 1960.
[13] *Japan Times*, September 14, 1961.

of Councillors Annex, its machinery remained intact against the time when some new explosive issue might drive the left into united action.

The Socialist Party, while claiming officially that the treaty struggle must be "highly evaluated" in terms of the development of the movements for peace and democracy, and calling Kishi's overthrow a major victory, nevertheless admitted publicly and privately that its political control over the movement had not been adequate. It criticized the JCP for giving the struggle an anti-American tone and for playing up the theme of racial independence. The party admitted that it had not converted the massive energy of the anti-government struggle into political gains—that it had stressed emotional sloganeering instead of constructive alternatives to conservative rule. The Socialists tried to persuade intellectual leaders of the protest movement such as Nakajima Kenzō, Nakano Yoshio, and Takeuchi Yoshimi to run for the Diet, but the latter reportedly refused to run for office.[14] As a consequence, the party salvaged no long term gains from the struggle; much to its despair, it admitted that Kishi simply "passed the bucket" (tarai-mawashi) to Ikeda and that there had been no fundamental changes in the political order.[15]

One outgrowth of these Socialist appraisals was the "structural reform theory" (kōzō kaikaku ron) advocated by former Secretary-General Eda Saburō.[16] Under this concept, the party

[14] Asahi Evening News, August 27, 1960.

[15] For JSP views and evaluations, see: Asanuma Inejirō, "Ima Koso Tatakai no Kajitsu o" (Now for the Fruits of the Struggle), Gekkan Shakai Tō, August 1960, pp. 4–5; and Tanaka Toshio, "Ampo Tōsō no Seika to Atarashii Mokuhyō" (Achievements of the Security Treaty Struggle and New Objectives), Gekkan Shakai Tō, July 1960, pp. 4–5; the party's official evaluation, a resolution of the 32nd Central Committee Plenum on July 5, 1960, may be found in Nihon Shakai Tō, Kōzō Kaikaku no Riron (Theory of Structural Reform), 3rd ed., Tokyo, March 10, 1961, pp. 364–369.

[16] Narita Tomomi, another advocate of the theory, affirmed in an interview on December 11, 1962, that structural reform was a direct result of the JSP evaluations of the struggle. A useful discussion may be found in R. P. Dore's "The Japanese Socialist Party and Structural Reform," Asian Survey, Vol. 1, No. 8, October 1961, pp. 3–15.

would bring about the revolution by gradual, peaceful, and piecemeal reforms of the evils of monopoly capitalism, aiming ultimately at the creation of conditions for the assumption of power by a Socialist government. The idea was attacked by the older and more doctrinaire theoreticians, including Suzuki Mosaburō, Sasaki Kōzō, Sakisaka Itsurō, and Sōhyō's Ōta Kaoru, who denounced it as rightism, opportunism, and a betrayal of the class struggle. Eda and others defended it as a method of capturing and directing the revolutionary energy of the masses that had been manifested in the treaty struggle; it was a positive, constructive, fighting program to replace the party's sterile and essentially negative programs of the past. The concept, though couched in Marxist terminology, appeared to represent a groping toward a realistic and attractive election platform along lines adopted by the British Labor Party and the West German Socialist Party in recent years. It also represented a rebellion by the younger, postwar generation of JSP leaders against the domination of the Marxists of the prewar period. Using structural reform both as an ideology and a tool in the intraparty power struggle, Eda defeated Sasaki Kōzō for the post of Secretary-General in January 1962.[17] Eda was replaced by Narita in November 1962, and for a time the party's policies were based on a delicate balance of views between the older theoreticians and the younger pragmatists. With the retirement of Chairman Kawakami Jōtarō and his replacement in May 1965 by Sasaki, however, the more doctrinaire left wing of the party seemed clearly to have gained the upper hand.

For a time after the crisis, the JSP remained aloof from the JCP; it cooperated with the conservatives in the Diet, disapproved of JCP attempts to dominate Gensuikyō in 1963, and bitterly denounced the JCP for its last-minute withdrawal from a general strike on April 17, 1964. The JSP also leaned tempo-

---

[17] Eda gave further evidence of the new movement toward pragmatism in the party with his controversial four-point program unveiled at the party convention of July 1962; the final goal of Socialism under the "Eda Vision" was to be a combination of the U.S. standard of living, the Soviet social security system, British parliamentarianism, and the peaceful Constitution of Japan.

311

rarily toward a more balanced version of "positive neutralism" in which friendly relations with the United States as well as with Socialist countries were stressed. The party had always swung toward moderation before elections and radicalism before its own conventions, however, and this vacillation continued after the treaty struggle. The party did appear to recognize its need for better grass-roots support, launching membership drives toward a goal of 200,000; in June 1961, however, its membership was only 42,975, and in late 1964 the claimed membership was only 50,000. Later, the positive neutralism gave way to new affirmations of the "Asanuma statement," by Suzuki in January 1962 and Narita in February 1963, so that its left-leaning foreign policy was not basically changed by the crisis. With regard to the treaty itself, the Socialists continued a policy of "nonrecognition" and attempted to discredit and ultimately to abolish it. JSP leaders gave assurances, however, that although the treaty was "invalid" they would not abrogate it unilaterally; upon coming into power, they would seek to end the pact by negotiations with the United States Government.

Narita Tomomi, then Chairman of the Policy Deliberations Board, and at this writing the party's Secretary-General, said in an interview on December 12, 1961, that future united fronts with the Communist Party should be built upon broad national movements involving all elements of the nation—not on narrow working arrangements between the two parties. He also affirmed that "outside-the-Diet struggles" (ingai tōsō) were the sine qua non of parliamentary democracy when the Diet majority failed to represent the true will of the people. Thus it appeared that the JSP, despite changes in leadership, had not lost faith in "parliamentarianism-plus" [18] when other methods failed inside the Diet. The party announced the launching of a new nationwide drive for the revision of the treaty at a rally of workers in Tokyo on April 26, 1965. And though it kept up its feud with the JCP, it continued to join forces with the Communists in local "joint struggles," such as the demonstrations against the entry of a U.S. nuclear-powered submarine into Sa-

[18] A phrase used by Scalapino and Masumi, op. cit., p. 144.

sebo in February 1965 and the campaign to oppose the Japanese Republic of Korea normalization treaty and agreements.

Sōhyō, which tried in vain to carry the struggle on into July 1960, held its 15th National Convention in August and evaluated the struggle as follows.[19] The use of force and mass action had raised the struggle to a national scale and sharpened the political consciousness of the workers, and the three major strikes had received unprecedented national support. The blocking of the Eisenhower visit struck a blow at the fifteen-year-old policy of Japanese ruling circles to subordinate Japan to America and at their policy of strengthening the alliance. The "irresistible force of the movement" had led to Kishi's resignation. Sōhyō admitted the following weaknesses, however: the council's poor leadership in the early stages resulted in failure to bind the working class closely with the people and organizational and propaganda activities had not been adequate to meet the threat from the DSP.

The treaty struggle and the concurrent strike at Miike seemed to result in a trend toward moderation in Sōhyō, as in the JSP. Ōta and Iwai were sharply criticized by pro-JCP elements at the 15th National Convention for calling off the *demo* along Eisenhower's arrival route. They responded that the strength of the campaign lay not in the united front with the JCP but in the reactions among the people to Kishi's threat to democracy; for this reason they rejected anti-American moves in the struggle. They were reelected Chairman and Secretary-General respectively, and their policy of giving exclusive support to the JSP—which had been beaten down in 1959—won the approval of thirty-one of the fifty-six affiliated unions. Since 1960, Sōhyō has tended to play down purely political action and has given new emphasis to improving wages and working conditions.

The JCP concluded that the "patriotic struggle for independence" had shaken the U.S.-Japan alliance, prevented Eisenhower's visit, overthrown Kishi, and driven the U-2's from Japan. Furthermore, the struggle had developed the political con-

[19] See summary of Sōhyō's "1960-Nendo Undō Hōshin" in Kōan Chōsa Chō, *Ampo Tōsō no Gaiyō*, pp. 236–238.

sciousness of broad segments of the people, clarified the "two-enemy concept," produced new struggle tactics (petitioning, the signature drives, and general strikes), and increased national solidarity. Despite JSP disclaimers, the movement had taken place within the framework of a united front, the party averred.[20] According to the Resolution of the 11th CC Plenum, June 29–July 1, 1960, the failure to block ratification could be ascribed to the following factors: (1) An insufficient grasp of the two-enemy concept by the democratic forces; (2) the fact that only one-third of Japanese wage earners were organized and, even within that fraction, there lurked divisive elements; (3) the lack of a proper relationship between labor and the parties; (4) failure to curb leftist and rightist deviation during the struggle; and (5) faulty cooperation between the JSP and JCP in the united front.[21]

The long anti-treaty campaign succeeded in boosting JCP membership; between 1958 and 1961, the total rose from 40,000 to 90,000, according to police reports. *Akahata's* daily circulation rose from 56,000 to 141,000 in the same period, according to the party.[22] Reliable observers noted that new and vigorous blood poured into the party at the lower and middle levels, but that some of the older intellectual faithful dropped out in disgust over its tactics during the crisis. The party reportedly gained blue-collar workers during this drive, while the proportion of its rural membership dropped.

Though relations with the JSP worsened after June 1960, the party continued to work to "strengthen the united front," which meant, in effect, keeping a strong hand in all mass efforts with Sōhyō and the JSP. Faced with hostility from some JSP elements, the party distinguished between the "well-intentioned"

---

[20] JCP evaluations can be found in: Kamiyama Shigeo, "Ampo Tōsō to Puroretaria Kokusaishugi" (The Treaty Struggle and Proletarian Internationalism), *Zenei*, November 1960, pp. 19–29; Miyamoto Kenji, "Waga Tō no Tatakatta Michi" (The Way Our Party Fought), *Zenei*, September 1960, pp. 15–27.

[21] As summarized in Kōan Chōsa Chō, *Ampo Tōsō no Gaiyō*, pp. 231–234.

[22] In 1964 the police estimated the party's membership at 140,000.

JSP members and others. The party also moved closer to the Communist Chinese line in the Sino-Soviet dispute, and found itself bitterly at odds with the Socialists on the issue of nuclear testing (the Socialists condemned *all* nuclear tests while the Communists denounced only those of the West). A pro-Soviet splinter group headed by Kasuga Shojirō left the party in July 1961, and new internal dissension arose when veteran leader Shiga Yoshio defied party orders and voted in the Diet in May 1964 in favor of the nuclear test ban treaty. By 1965 Shiga and other splinter groups from the JCP, including Kamiyama Shigeo, had formed a second Communist Party which called itself the JCP (Voice of Japan). This party generally reflected the Moscow line in the Moscow-Peking dispute.

The Moscow line on the new security treaty, as expounded by Mikoyan on his visit to Tokyo in August 1961, was that Japan had voluntarily entered into the revised pact and should now be held responsible for it; this raised problems for party theorists who held that U.S. imperialism had forced the treaty on Japan.

The Communists kept up a bitter attack on the mainstream of Zengakuren, and appeared to have gained the upper hand in March 1963 when it was disclosed that the students had accepted financial aid from Tanaka Seigen.[23] The question whether Kamba Michiko was a "people's hero" (*jinmin no eiyū*) or simply another Trotskyite *provocateur* has been a constant thorn in the flesh of all leftists in Japan; attempts to capitalize on the only "martyr" in the struggle degenerated into sordid political controversy. On June 23, 1960, 250 mainstream students attacked the Yoyogi headquarters of the JCP demanding an apology for the article in *Akahata* of the previous day which blamed Miss Kamba's death on student "adventurism"; the students were also annoyed over their exclusion from the committee that arranged for a "People's Funeral," and they accused the JCP of pocketing 1.8 million yen ($5,000) in condolence offerings. After a short battle with local unionists, they were repulsed.[24] When memorial services were held on June 15, 1961,

[23] See, for example, *Akahata*, March 6, 1963.
[24] *Asahi Evening News*, June 24, 1960.

a year after the tragedy, the JCP and its sympathizers denounced and boycotted the ceremonies, and the presence or absence of the leftist elite became a significant gauge of ideology. Some mainstream student leaders made much of Miss Kamba's death, prevailing upon her parents to keep her room at home intact as a kind of shrine; others have openly dismissed her death as "meaningless" and have argued that the student movement should look forward, not backward.[25]

Behind this dispute, of course, was the need to evaluate the movement in Marxist terminology: if Zengakuren's claim that *its* violent Diet invasion (and Miss Kamba's death) were alone responsible for blocking Eisenhower's visit and overthrowing Kishi—the only tangible fruits of the campaign—what meaning could be attached to the fifteen-month struggle by the "democratic forces" prior to June 15? It was absolutely necessary for the JCP to prove that the accumulated force of the workers in the struggle had achieved the successes and that other, less tangible victories, such as heightened consciousness and the discrediting of the treaty, had also been gained.

Zengakuren quickly lost its attraction for most students after June, and the student movement reverted to the hands of a few thousand hard-core radicals. Several hundred mainstreamers rushed dramatically to Kyūshū in July to aid the striking coal miners at Miike; they quickly discovered that they were not welcome, however, and returned to the capital. This hard core continued to demonstrate around Tokyo, and with their sudden world fame, came to be sought after by visiting tourists and scholars. As they began to take themselves more seriously, however, their power to influence the political scene all but vanished: it was clear that the high tension and massive *demo*

[25] Much was written about Miss Kamba in the weeklies and monthlies at the time of her death; in October 1960, a small volume of her writings as a student, edited by Kamba Akiko, her mother, was published by San'ichi Shobō under the title *Hito Shirezu Hohoeman* (With a Smile in My Heart); see also Zen Kyoto Shuppan Iinkai, ed., *Ashioto wa Tayuru Toki Naku* (The Sound of the Footsteps Will Never Die Away), Kyoto: Shirakawa Shoin, 1960, a collection of memorial poems and essays by well-known leftists.

were the necessary conditions for further extremism. Meanwhile, the superior organizing capabilities of the Communist Party's youth arm, Minseidō, increased JCP influence on many campuses throughout Japan, and by late 1964 the JCP was leading a new movement to "rebuild Zengakuren" under its own influence.

A bewildering series of changes in leadership occurred in the year after the crisis, and by the end of 1961, Zengakuren had broken into at least five quarreling factions.[26] The Communist League (Kyōsandō) which had controlled the CEC during the crisis, was ousted in April 1961 by the Marxist Student League (Marugakudō, the action wing of the former Kakkyōdō Zenkoku Iinkai-ha) which then defended itself in a wild brawl at the 17th National Convention in July 1961. The Komaba Campus of Tokyo University—a mainstream stronghold during the crisis —swung to the anti-mainstream (Zenjiren) in the spring of 1961, and after Zenjiren followed Kasuga from the JCP, swung again to the Socialist Youth League (Shaseidō), a newly formed youth organization under the JSP. In 1963, for the first time in postwar history, a non-Marxist, moderate student was elected Chairman of the Self-government Association at Komaba, but by 1964 leadership was again in the hands of the Socialist Youth League, and the Communists. The same sort of changes occurred on all the campuses, and in 1964 there were five major factions (subdivided into fifteen minor groups) competing for leadership of the student movement.[27] The average student could not be blamed for losing interest in these switches, which were accompanied by heavy doses of theorizing and, occasionally, fist-fighting. There were signs that the post-1960 student generation was less interested in extremism, more critical of

[26] The mainstream's evaluation of events may be found in "Wareware no Tatakai no Sōkatsu" (Our Evaluation of the Fight), in *Zengakuren Dai-Jūrokkai Teiki Zenkoku Taikai Gian* (Resolutions of Zengakuren's 16th National Convention), July 4–7, 1960, pp. 2–12.

[27] For a useful summary of developments in the student movement after 1960, see Fujita Kyohei, "Ryōkyoku Bunkai ni Mukau? Gakusei Undō" (The Student Movement: Facing Polarization?), *Ekonomisuto*, December 15, 1964.

317

Marxism, and more realistic in its view of itself and of its place in society.

A final attempt to keep the campaign alive was the much publicized "Back-Home Movement" (Kikyō Undō) during the summer following the crisis. Organized by a small group of students and instructors in Tokyo University's Law Faculty, and supported by members of Mingakken, its purpose was to send students into the countryside to their home towns to spread the word on the government's undemocratic procedures and brutality of the police, hoping that these tales would win votes in the fall elections. About 700 student organizers left Tokyo in mid-July carrying small packets of pamphlets, recordings, and photographs of the crisis; regional centers were set up in prefectural colleges and young faculty members traveled to rural areas to give lectures. The movement was not a success, according to its organizers. It appeared that the farmers, like the Miike coal miners, were not interested in the violence at the Diet.

Left wing bunkajin have helped to perpetuate the "ampo spirit" in the arts. Abe Kōbō, well-known leftist playwright, wrote a play called "Ishi no Kataru Hi" (The Day Stones Speak), which was produced by Senda Koreya and performed in Japan and Communist China during the fall of 1960 by a professional modern drama group. It featured an heroic cleaning-shop proprietor in Maebashi who joined with labor leaders in the strike of June 4. Another play, Nihon no Yoru to Kiri (The Night and Mist over Japan), by playwright Ōshima Nagisa, dealt with personal problems of the students during the crisis, dramatizing their heroic acts in the face of oppression. This play first appeared as a movie around the time of Asanuma's assassination, but closed down after four days. Leftists claimed it had been suppressed by the government while others said it was a financial failure. Professional and student groups continued to produce the play during the following year, however, and the movie later reappeared in second-run theaters. The magazine Shin Nihon Bungaku (New Literature of Japan) devoted its August 1960 issue to essays on the crisis by leftist writers; literally hundreds of articles in the leftist cultural journals continued to discuss the events over the following year.

318

Several years after the crisis, one could still hear the "ampo" songs being sung in the "singing bars" of Shinjuku. It is too early to know—but it will be interesting to observe—whether the "ampo spirit" finally takes root in the popular culture, or whether these efforts were a kind of leftist *gagaku* with symbols and appeal exclusively for the leftist cultural elite.

The Right Wing and the Resurgence of Violence

A disturbing postscript to the treaty crisis was the resurgence of rightist terrorism in Japan; there were signs that the leftist outbursts resulted in a revival of extremist activity on the right during 1960 and afterward. Of course the revival of the right had been under way long before the crisis [28] but it appeared that the leftist disturbances accelerated the process and created the climate for new outbreaks of terrorism of the prewar variety.

Rightist groups in the postwar period were characteristically small bands of petty racketeers, gamblers, and extortionists, fiercely loyal to individual bosses, parading under meaningless patriotic slogans. As the anti-treaty movement gathered momentum, such gangs appeared at *demo* and rallies in their helmets, khaki uniforms, and combat boots, harassing the demonstrators, drowning out the speakers, and distributing leaflets proclaiming the imminence of a Communist revolution. The most active of these groups were the Dai-Nippon Aikoku Tō (Great Japan Patriotic Party) under Akao Bin, the Gokokudan (State Guardians Corps), the newly formed Ishin Kōdō Tai (Renovation Action Corps) and the Matsuba Kai (Pine Needle Society). The Matsuba Kai had already achieved notoriety on April 2, 1960, by pouring sand in the presses of the *Mainichi Shimbun* for an alleged insult.

Sixteen of these organizations met in Hibiya Hall on July 25, 1959, to unify under the National Council of Patriots' Organizations (Zenkoku Aikokusha Dantai Kyōgi Kai), the largest assembly of rightists since the war. Inspired by Akao Bin, their purpose was to oppose the anti-treaty movement and support

[28] An excellent account of right wing activities up to 1958 may be found in I. I. Morris, *Nationalism and the Right Wing in Japan,* London: Oxford University Press, 1960.

319

the new treaty (which promised ultimate independence for Japan).[29] This attempt at unity was apparently not successful, and a second attempt in June 1960 was equally futile; the nature of these small, jealous, and unideological groups made unity difficult if not impossible. In any case, as the treaty crisis reached its climax in June, sporadic attacks from small bands of rightists increased, culminating in the attack of the Ishin Kōdō Tai on the Modern Drama Group on June 15, near the Diet (above, p. 295).[30] Though these small-time rightists (*gaitō uha*) inflicted injuries and were seriously annoying, they were not, it is fair to say, a major factor in sparking the *demo* against the treaty and Kishi.

About the time of the Hagerty affair, however, police noted the first stirrings since the war of the "real right wing" (*honkaku uha*)—rightists with significant past and present connections with influential conservatives.[31] A number of these individuals, of the old "*ichinin ittō*" (one-man, one-party) school gathered from all over the country around the time of the LDP convention in July to discuss ways to combat the recent emergence of Communist strength. These individuals, who were of a different order from the common hoodlums of the postwar era, saw themselves as latent repositories of true patriotism; dark rumors began to circulate that they were receiving financial support from business circles and government officials. It is not

[29] *Japan Times*, August 19, 1960, article by Murata Kiyoaki; and Iwakura Tomohide, "Uha Shisō no Taitō to Sayū Tairitsu" (Resurgence of Rightist Thought and Confrontation between Right and Left), *Seikai Ōrai*, January 1960, pp. 24–30.

[30] Other acts of rightist violence connected with the treaty crisis included: (1) The arrest on May 25, 1960, of an eighteen-year-old youth for the intended assassination of Kishi (*Asahi Evening News*, May 26, 1960); (2) efforts by a seventeen-year-old youth to wreck Zengakuren headquarters on June 28, 1960 (*Asahi Evening News*, June 29, 1960); (3) a bottle of ammonia thrown at Asanuma near the Diet on May 26, 1960; (4) the stabbing of Kawakami Jōtarō on June 17, 1960; (5) the stabbing of Kishi on July 15, 1960. Leftists also charged that the LDP used members of the Gijin Tō to pack the gallaries and threaten the Socialists on the night of May 19–20.

[31] *Asahi Shimbun*, July 15, 1960, and *Asahi Evening News*, June 18, 1960.

clear precisely what took place at this time, but the following months saw a succession of terrorist plots—some by the "new right" and some by the old—which gave clear proof that the prewar terrorism had not been entirely eradicated by defeat and the Occupation.

The nation was stunned by the assassination of Asanuma on October 12, 1960. In the middle of a nationally televised pre-election debate and before an audience of over 1,000, seventeen-year-old Yamaguchi Otoya leapt to the stage and stabbed the Socialist leader to death. Though it was never officially proved, there seemed little doubt that Yamaguchi had been inspired by Akao Bin, of whose party he had formerly been a member. Yamaguchi later committed suicide in jail and became a martyr for rightist fanatics. The left issued fresh charges of a conspiracy between the LDP, business circles, rightists, and even U.S. imperialists, and particular attention was drawn to the fact that the killer's father was an officer in the Self-defense Forces.[32]

A second act of terrorism occurred in the following February when another seventeen-year-old, Komori Kazutaka, appeared at the home of Shimanaka Hōji, President of the Chūō Kōron Publishing Company; finding Shimanaka absent, he attacked his wife with a knife, seriously wounding her and killing a maid who tried to intervene. Komori had also been a member of Akao's Dai-Nippon Aikoku Tō. Akao himself, infuriated by a story in Chūō Kōron describing the murder of the Imperial Family,[33] had stormed into Shimanaka's offices with other thugs just two days before this incident, demanding apologies and the dissolution of the firm. Akao was ultimately sentenced to eight months in jail in connection with this and other episodes.[34] Judge Iimori Shigeto of the Tokyo District Court aroused the anger of the left when he said on February 24, 1961, that the

[32] The father subsequently resigned. For discussions of the Asanuma assassination and its aftermath, see: Naoi Takeo, "Japan After the Assassination," New Leader, Vol. 43, November 7, 1960, pp. 8–9; and Japan Times, October 15, 1960, article by Kuroda Kazuo.

[33] Fukazawa Shichirō, "Fūryū Mutan" (Romantic Dream Story), Chūō Kōron, December 1960, pp. 228–240.

[34] Asahi Evening News, September 12–13, 1960.

rightist terrorist cases since late 1960 should be ultimately attributed to earlier leftist mass violence such as the Diet demonstrations.[35] There seemed no doubt, though (regardless of the impropriety of the Judge's remarks), that a connection existed. Shimanaka Hōji himself admitted the relationship and said that the conservatives, under pressure from the left, had turned to the rightists for aid during the treaty crisis; this had "politicized" the rightist gangsters for the first time since the war.[36]

A third instance of the right wing's revival was the discovery in December 1961 of a plot by thirteen ultranationalists to assassinate Ikeda and other prominent figures and take over the government.[37] Some of the conspirators in this weird plan were members of the Kokushi Kai (National History Association), an association of classmates from the fifty-ninth and sixtieth classes of the defunct Military Academy who had entered in 1943–1944. Five of the thirteen were former army officers, and one was a former navy man. Two ringleaders were Mikami Taku, who had taken part in the assassination of Prime Minister Inukai and Sakurai Tokutarō, a former Major General from Fukuoka. Others involved were a Chinese trader and a prominent industrialist. Police discovered hidden caches of weapons and uniforms and the subsequent investigations were far-reaching and bewildering. The conspirators admitted they wanted to kill Ikeda and others because the present government was not able to prevent a Communist revolution in Japan.[38] The National Council of Patriots' Organizations, composed of thirty-one member groups, publicly supported the "intent" and "spirit" of the arrested plotters, and the famous Kokuryū Kai (Black Dragon Society), which had reconstituted itself on October 23, 1961, similarly upheld the "spirit" if not the methods of the thirteen.[39] From evidence available, it did not appear that Self-

[35] *Japan Times*, September 28, 1961. The JSP made an unsuccessful attempt to impeach Iimori for this statement.

[36] Interview with Shimanaka Hōji, November 25, 1961.

[37] For details, see *Japan Times*, December 13, 15–16, and 28, 1961; and October 12, 1962; and *Asahi Evening News*, December 12, 14, and 31, 1961, and January 11, 1962. This was also called the "Sanmu Case."

[38] *Japan Times*, December 13, 1961.

[39] *Japan Times*, December 15, 1961. See also *Japan Times*, November 2, 1961, article by Murata Kiyoaki.

defense Force officers were involved in the conspiracy, though some had been approached. At least one critic, Murakami Hyōe, himself a graduate of the Military Academy, blamed Kishi's failure to deal properly with the left in May and June for creating the "mood" that led to the plot.[40]

In 1963, various rightist groups were again active, burning down the new home of Kōno Ichirō, threatening politicians and businessmen who favored trade with Communist China, and attempting to assault Prime Minister Ikeda and JCP Chairman Nosaka Sanzō during the election campaign.

It is hard to know at this stage how seriously these incidents and the resurgent right should be taken. The police in 1961 estimated that there were 400 ultranationalist organizations with a total membership of 100,000—a total which, if accurate, would have outnumbered the JCP in that year. In 1961 a postwar record of 217 ultrarightists were arrested—63 more than in 1960.[41] Small bands of demonstrating rightists became regular features at all "political" occasions in Tokyo, along with their Zengakuren counterparts of the left. There is no doubt that the turmoil of 1960 created conditions favorable to extremists of the right, and there was a growing tendency for both right and left to use the other as justification for unsavory conduct which the nation as a whole had genuinely come to abhor. As violence breeds on itself, hope for stability and moderation in Japan seemed to lie in the avoidance of excessive political excitement and exorbitant moods—such as those of May and June 1960.

General Elections, 1960 and 1963

This account of the turbulent politics of Japan in 1960 would not be complete without brief mention of the general elections of November 1960 and afterward; the results, both puzzling and revealing, lend perspective to the crisis.[42]

The conservatives, ignoring Opposition demands for elections immediately after the crisis, allowed the "mood" to settle and

---

[40] *Japan Times*, December 13, 1961.

[41] *Japan Times*, December 28, 1961.

[42] I am indebted for the summary that follows to, among others, the analysis of Douglas H. Mendel, Jr., "Behind the 1960 Japanese Diet Election," *Asian Survey*, Vol. 1, No. 1, March 1961, pp. 3–12.

Ikeda's popularity to grow before dissolving the Diet in October. Meanwhile, gubernatorial elections in Aomori, Saitama, and Gumma Prefectures were watched carefully to see if the protest movement had affected voters in the countryside. The LDP won all three elections, as expected, but the Gumma results were particularly disappointing to the Socialists.[43] In Gumma the JSP and JCP had worked closely together to build one of the strongest prefectural "joint struggle councils" under the People's Council. "Minyoren," the short name for this council, consisted of 70 member organizations with 130 chapters; it had conducted joint struggles against the U.S. base at Mt. Myōgi, the revised Police Bill and the treaty. During the treaty crisis, Gumma's capital, Maebashi, had been one of the most active smaller cities in Japan. There were no JSP factional complications, nor was there competition from the DSP in this election, and the JSP candidate was Tsunoda Giheiji, who had headed Minyoren in the crisis. Asanuma, Eda, and Suzuki, as well as Nosaka Sanzō of the JCP campaigned vigorously for Tsunoda, stressing the treaty issue and trade liberalization. The LDP candidate, Kanda Konroku, avoided the treaty issue almost entirely. In short, the ingredients for a substantial increase in votes for the left were there, and yet the LDP candidate won by 401,000 to 214,000 votes—roughly the same conservative-opposition margin as in previous elections. Coming so soon after the crisis (July 27), the results seemed to show that the joint struggles outside Tokyo had not added substantially to leftist strength across the nation.

In the three-week campaign before the general elections of November 1960, a number of factors favored the LDP: the new, calm mood; Ikeda's relative popularity; prosperity; the Socialist split; and the reaction against leftist extremism. On the other hand, reactions against Kishi and the treaty gave hope to the Opposition of gaining at least a few seats in the Diet. The assassination of Asanuma was generally considered to be a factor favorable to the left.

[43] "Chijisen Sanrenpai no Shakai Tō" (Three Consecutive Defeats for the Socialist Party in Gubernatorial Elections), *Asahi Jānaru*, August 7, 1960, pp. 74–75.

The treaty and the May-June crisis were the most important issues in the campaign, but the Japanese saying, "Even a rumor about a person lasts only seventy-five days" seemed to apply: the fact that the treaty was a *fait accompli* and that Kishi was out removed the heat from the issues. Ikeda, Eda Saburō, and Nishio clearly spelled out their views on the treaty in an unprecedented television debate; the Socialists campaigned on "positive neutralism" (friendly relations with both East and West), restored relations with Communist China, and abrogation of the treaty.

The voters returned the LDP to power with 296 seats—13 more than in 1958—representing 57.6 percent of the vote. The Socialists won 145 seats and 27.5 percent; their increase of 23 seats came largely at the expense of the DSP, which dropped to 17 seats and won only 8.8 percent of the vote.[44] The Communists gained about 125,000 votes and two new seats for a total of three in the Lower House. In Tokyo, the Socialists won 11 of the 27 seats. The combined total of the parties opposed to the security treaty (including the DSP) was 15.4 million votes, or just over 39 percent. The next general elections in November 1963 told essentially the same story: 294 conservatives, 144 Socialists, 23 for the DSP, 5 for the JCP, and 1 independent.

At this writing (1965), it appeared that, while the conservatives were continuing to lose some ground to the combined left, it was by no means certain that the left would gain a majority in the near future. The annual rate of growth in the combined popular vote for the left fell from 1.4 percent in 1958–1960 to 0.4 percent in the 1960–1963 period. In 1964, the public opinion polls showed for the first time since the War

---

[44] The story of the DSP's decline in 1960 was probably connected with its somewhat unclear position during the treaty crisis; in some ways the most moderate of all the parties, there was irony that it should become the major victim of the struggle. But there were other, unconnected reasons as well. For DSP views and statements on the treaty issue and the events of May and June, see Minshu *Shakai Tō, Saiken Zenkoku Taikai Tōmu Hōkokusho* (DSP, National Reconstruction Convention Party Report), January 23–25, 1961, pp. 250–276.

a trend toward the conservative party in the twenty to thirty age bracket. Other factors favored the conservatives, such as the waning influence of doctrinaire Marxism, rising prosperity, a new sense of responsibility and "image-consciousness" within the LDP, and the growth of nationalism. Though predictions are probably unwise, it may be that the doctrinaire left reached a high-water mark in 1960 in its ability to influence the political scene, and that future changes in party strength will be brought on by new forces, such as Sōka Gakkai. In any case, it is certain that the security treaty issue itself did not substantially affect the voting habits of the Japanese people.

The controversy goes on to this day whether these election results can be read as an endorsement of the security treaty itself, as Ikeda claimed, or whether other issues and factors accounted for the LDP victories. It has never been proved that *any* single issue plays an important part in determining the overall national election results in Japan. For this reason no one was sure how 1970—the first year in which the Japanese Government may call for an end to or changes in the treaty—will affect domestic politics. The left was already talking of another great struggle, and the conservatives were planning countermeasures, but no one could say how Communist China's nuclear weapons and Japan's own defensive efforts, as well as developments in Vietnam and elsewhere, might change the setting.

In any event, the strong, emotional, and elusive resistance to the government was not easily able to be channeled into the Japanese party system in 1960; even the DSP, with its relatively fresh image, failed to capture it. Illustrating the distance between the parties and popular trends was the fact that both the former Kishi and Satō factions—objects of much of the protest in May and June—increased their strength within the party in November 1960, Satō's increase being second only to Ikeda's among all the factions. And as we have seen, Satō was able to rise to the Prime Ministership in the fall of 1964.

With the elections of 1960, the "ampo period" came to an end; it remained only for the scholars and analysts to sift through the rubble and make sense of it all.

Japanese Views of the Crisis

If Japanese scholars were agreed on no other point, they all believed, at least, that the treaty crisis was the most important political event since the recovery of independence. It has received the most careful attention from the progressive intellectuals who were part of the struggle, and in this short space, we shall touch briefly on the major trends of thought among leftists who were deeply involved.[45]

The two "schools" into which the progressives split during the anti-treaty campaign produced differing evaluations of the results. The first group, led by Shimizu Ikutarō (sometimes called the Zengakuren-ha), began with the premise that the primary object of the struggle had been to block the treaty; since this goal had not been achieved, the movement had failed.[46] In this view, the leading elements on the People's Council—the JSP, Sōhyō, and the JCP—were to blame for the failure. Instead of stressing the class character of the struggle and building the movement around organized labor, these leaders had become infected with *petit bourgeois* ideology (the *shimin* concept) and had mistakenly lumped together diverse and unmanageable elements in an abortive united front. Throwing together all protesting groups, whether or not they opposed the treaty itself, had weakened the movement and diverted it from its proper goal. In stressing citizen participation, the leaders had closed their eyes to the fact that 70 percent of the demonstrators were organized workers. *Demo* under the People's Council were "manneristic" and served no useful purpose; instead of dissolving them, for example, the council should have kept the Diet surrounded until Kishi surrendered and the Lower House was dissolved. The JCP emphasis on U.S. imperialism diverted the

[45] This summary does not cover, of course, the great variety of interpretations outside the camp of the *kakushin interi*, where interest in the treaty issues has also been high, if less emotional.

[46] The best exposition of this view is found in Shinobu Seizaburō, *Ampo Tōsō Shi* (A History of the Security Treaty Struggle), Tokyo: Sekai Shoin, 1961, pp. 495–602. Shinobu differed from Shimizu only in that he was slightly more critical of the mainstream students' extremism.

movement from the main enemy: Japanese monopoly capital. The mainstream of Zengakuren carried much of the burden— it alone was responsible for the cancellation of Eisenhower's visit and Kishi's resignation. The energy shown by workers in the November 27 Incident and afterward had been suppressed by union leaders who were more interested in preserving their positions than in creating a revolutionary situation.

In short, this group concluded that very little had been achieved in the struggle. Ikeda succeeded Kishi with no change in the system. The council's claim that the treaty had been made a "dead-letter" was nothing but self-praise (*jiga jisan*); both in name and in fact the treaty remained in force. The hegemony of labor had not been established and important unions in the basic steel and chemical industries were under misguided leadership. The rural areas remained unmoved throughout. The only bright note was the energy and duration of the movement, which were considered "epochal"; the struggle marked an end to the "MacArthur era" and opened up new horizons toward the day when the Japanese people might control their own destiny.[47]

The views of the Shimin-ha are not easily characterized because of their diversity around the single theme of citizen participation. Two points on which most of them agreed were that Professor Maruyama was the leading theoretician of the Shimin-ha during and after the crisis, and that the struggle had been,

[47] With Shimizu Ikutarō as its mainspring, this group consisted of a variety of Trotskyite students, Marxian economists, nihilists, and others who had little in common besides antipathy for the JCP and for the Shimin-ha intellectuals whom they considered close to the JCP. Under Shimizu's editorship, they launched a small journal, *Gendai Shisō* (Modern Thought) in May 1961 which, however, failed after five issues. For samples of their writing, see Miura Tsutomu, "Chishikijin: Hidaka Rokurō no 'Shimin-ron'" (Intellectuals: Hidaka Rokurō's *Shimin* Theory), *Gendai Shisō*, May 1961, pp. 7–35; and Hayata Kunio (pseud.), "Ampo Soshi Kokumin Kaigi Ron" (Discussion of the People's Council), *Gendai Shisō*, June 1961, pp. 29–39. Shimizu himself has subsequently attacked aspects of Marxist doctrine. See, for example, "Atarashii Rekishikan e no Shuppatsu" (A Start toward a New View of History), *Chūō Kōron*, December 1963, pp. 34–49.

all things considered, a success.[48] They emphasized the struggle after May 19 to defend fundamental human rights more than the struggle to block the treaty. In Professor Maruyama's words: ". . . never before in Japan's history have the masses, in the face of the abuse of power by the government, organized almost spontaneously, without reference to their own personal direct interests, to protest on such a large scale and for a period of so many consecutive days. In that sense, this was a revolutionary event in Japan's history. Furthermore, it did not occur during a period of economic depression." [49]

The unseating of Kishi was a legitimate objective, in this view, and the movement therefore achieved a "great victory." Since there had never been much hope of blocking the treaty— the government would have called out the Self-defense Forces in a real emergency—the ratification could not be considered a defeat. The important by-product was the increased popular awareness of the power of protest to protect the democratic process against apathy and "mechanized politics." Maruyama was critical of the *"innaishugi"* (literally: inside the Diet-ism) of both the LDP and the Zengakuren; both stressed the formal aspects of democracy but overlooked its substance. The gap between the elected majority and the popular will must be closed "from below" by *ingai tōsō* (outside-the-Diet struggles) in a country where democracy has been imposed from above but has yet to take root. There was a positive value in the very act

[48] The best exposition of Professor Maruyama's position can be found in "Gikaisei Minshushugi no Yukue" (The Future of Parliamentary Democracy), *Ekonomisuto Bessatsu*, "Ampo ni Yureta Nihon no Kiroku" (Record of the Treaty Struggle that Shook Japan), September 10, 1960; the book that most fully embodies the *Shimin* concept is Hidaka Rokurō, ed., *Gogatsu Jūkunichi* (May 19), Tokyo: Iwanami Shinsho, 1960—so named because of the *shimin* emphasis on events *beginning* with Kishi's acts on May 19. For other examples, see "Ampo Kaitei Hantai Tōsō no Seika to Tenbō" (Accomplishments and Views of the Struggle Against the Revised Treaty), symposium, *Shisō*, August 1960, pp. 61–79; Fukuda Kanichi, "Minshushugi, Kokkai, Kokumin" (Democracy, the Diet, the People), *Sekai*, July 1961, pp. 32–38. In English, see "Japanese Intellectuals Discuss American-Japanese Relations," *Far Eastern Survey*, Vol. 29, No. 10, October 1960.

[49] *Ekonomisuto Bessatsu*, September 10, 1961, p. 93.

329

of demonstrating—a better expression of the people's will than the "ritual of the ballot." The greater the citizen participation, the less chance the Communists have of taking over such a protest movement. The rôle of organized labor was played down by exponents of the Shimin-ha; they tended to portray workers protesting as private citizens rather than as part of a class struggle. Much praise was given to the voluntary and spontaneous character of citizen participation and to the order and self-control of the demonstrators. A final by-product was that the struggle had cast doubt upon the moral validity and effectiveness of the treaty itself.[50] Professor Ishida Takeshi saw in the movement the seeds of a new organizational principle: voluntary association for a shared purpose rather than the old (*marugakae seizoroi*) principle of lumping together incompatible elements and slogans in meaningless coalitions to fight for the whole range of leftist causes under fossilized and bureaucratic leadership.[51] One trend in the Shimin-ha that may have some significance was a renewed interest in (and recognition of) left wing nationalism; it was not coincidental that *Shisō*, a year after the crisis, devoted a whole issue to the subject.[52]

A bitter dialogue between the two main schools has gone on since the end of the crisis.[53] Deep and complex personal relationships were involved, and, in reading the literature, one senses that they were speaking to each other as much as to Japan and the world, in interpreting the crisis. Their views are, of course, preliminary judgments. No scholarly book has yet been pub-

[50] Students of Japanese may wish to ponder this statement by Maruyama: "Sore o hikkuri-kaeshite ieba, kondo wa shin ampo jōyaku ga hijun sarete mo, sore ga dono teido jikkō o motsu ka dō ka to iu koto wa jitsu wa jikkō o *motaseru* ka dō ka to iu mondai da to omou no desu." *Ekonomisuto Bessatsu*, p. 96.

[51] Ishida Takeshi, *Gendai Soshiki Ron* (Modern Theory of Organization), Tokyo: Iwanami Shoten, 1961, pp. 227–235.

[52] *Shisō*, June 1961.

[53] See *Chūō Kōron* of July 1961, which contains articles by Shimizu Ikutarō, "Ampo Tōsō Ichinengo no Shisō," pp. 45–57; and Shinohara Hajime, "Demokurashii no Saihakken," pp. 148–160; and then the criticism of both by Inoki Masamichi in "Rondan Jihyō," *Asahi Shimbun*, June 25–27, 1961.

lished in Japan which claims to be objective, i.e., neutral as to the outcome of the "struggle." One suspects that, since the emotions are still warm and the sense of involvement deep, it will be some years before such a treatment does appear. Meanwhile, it will be interesting to see whether the differences among the progressives lead to new approaches and stimulate new thought, or whether they are part of a family quarrel that will be quickly dismissed when the next vital problem arises.

 CHAPTER 10

Conclusion

THE CRISIS in Japanese politics of 1960 was produced by a combination of elements, no single one of which could have accounted for it alone. To summarize briefly those elements, there was, first of all, a vigorous and prolonged campaign by the "regular" left wing against the new treaty—a campaign built upon unprecedented cooperation among the JSP, JCP, and Sōhyō—supplemented by the revived and radical student movement. Despite disunity arising from differences in ideology, political objectives, and generations, this leftist movement exploited deep-seated antipathy toward foreign troops and bases to cast fresh doubts among the uncommitted as to the wisdom of the alliance. International events—the relative increase in Communist Bloc strength vis-à-vis the West, U.S. intervention in the Straits of Taiwan and Southeast Asia, advances in nuclear strategy, and Communist propaganda—convinced many Japanese that any revision of the treaty should give them a large voice in its implementation. The anti-treaty forces successfully spread the idea that the new treaty would increase the danger of war. Disunity among the conservatives during revision negotiations reinforced leftist attacks; opponents of the alliance itself joined with those who opposed the government's revision policies as the campaign progressed.

The movement until the spring of 1960 was mainly an expression of Sōhyō's Marxist theories, executed by unionists who were experienced and confident after successfully blocking the Police Bill in 1958. Though there had been widespread support for the idea of negotiating a new treaty with the United States in 1957, public opinion in 1959 offered no clear mandate for either side on how to go about it. The Socialists, strongly influenced by Sōhyō and discouraged by the "one-third barrier," leaned towards extraparliamentary methods in the struggle, losing the right wing Nishio faction in the process. The JCP threw its superior organizational apparatus behind the movement, seeking always to increase its influence through a united front. Zengakuren extremists who had broken with the JCP embarrassed the older left with pointless violence which, however, was stimulated and made possible by the larger protest movement. The People's Council, which claimed to be against *revising* the treaty, was in fact made up of elements who wished to abolish it altogether.

The Socialists mounted an effective attack on the new treaty in the Diet; concurrently, the U-2 incident weakened the conservative case for trust in the United States. The summit breakup heightened ever present fears of war in Japan. At this moment, Prime Minister Kishi, whose political future was tied to the new treaty, chose unilateral tactics to win Diet approval, stirring widespread anger. Kishi, who had been more closely associated with war and defeat than any postwar Prime Minister, and whose "image" aroused deep hostility among Japanese of varied viewpoints, lost the support of many in his own party during the ensuing crisis. The press, already critical of the new treaty, led demands for his resignation, and the progressive intellectuals threw themselves as never before into the popular protest movement. With the Opposition boycotting the Diet, the People's Council (after fourteen months of preparation) channeled new protest groups into its demonstrations and rallies around the Diet.

The impending visit of President Eisenhower projected the United States more deeply into the crisis. The tense atmosphere created by the strikes and demonstrations helped the Communists to carry out anti-American objectives in the Hagerty affair and enabled Zengakuren to launch new attacks on the Diet. The bloody riot of June 15, involving the death of a student, was decisive in the government's conclusion that it could not protect the President and the Emperor during the visit; though Kishi hung on until ratification, the concellation forced his retirement.

With his resignation and Ikeda's accession to office, the excitement subsided; left wing unity dissolved, and parliamentary debate resumed. The elections of November 1960 and again in November 1963 showed that the protest movement had not significantly affected the basic alignment of the Japanese electorate. Despite outbreaks of rightist terrorism, trends toward moderation in the JSP, Sōhyō, and the LDP made a new crisis seem unlikely in the near future.

The Nationalist Theme

Having observed the multiplicity of causes for the crisis, we are prepared to suggest that one of the significant themes running through these events was the growth of Japanese nationalism.[1] We noted that the new nationalism, built partly on pride in economic achievement, partly on reaction to foreign influences (and bases), and partly on ambitions for power, gave birth to the treaty issue in 1957. In 1960, fifteen years after the atomic bomb and disaster, that movement burst into flames. The process of becoming self-conscious as a nation, begun in the Meiji period and accelerated by the "double-patriots" of the 1930's, was in motion again. The pendulum, which for fifteen years had swung toward absorption of foreign—especially American—culture, was swinging back toward self-reflection and assimilation. This trend was of course apparent before the anti-treaty movement began, and it continued afterward; it was a natural, predictable development in view of Japan's history and the 20th century contagion of nationalism. But it achieved its most dramatic expression on the streets of Tokyo in May and June 1960.

Every group involved in the crisis exhibited some form of the new nationalism. Conservatives promoted the revised treaty in terms of realistic self-interest: greater independence, a veto over undesirable actions by the United States, closer trade relations with the U.S.—all leading to greater strength and security for Japan. This was natural enough, but there was a notable lack of the accompanying view heard in NATO countries that the treaty contributed to the strength of the free world, to freedom, to democracy. There was good reason for this lack: such arguments did not interest the Japanese people, who have had no experience with "international solidarity." The concept of collective security in which a country fights far from its own shores

[1] This subject is discussed in my article, "Japan's New Nationalism," *Atlantic Monthly*, Vol. 211, No. 4, April 1963, pp. 64–69.

to preserve world peace and thus its own security was alien to all wisdom and common sense in Japan.

The conservatives, who claimed only that the treaty was the best expedient for the times, were as fearful of disruptive military actions by the U.S. as the left, and not merely because of political repercussions at home. Publicly, their pro-treaty statements revealed lack of confidence in U.S. motives. Pro-American statements were uttered ritualistically by Kishi and Fujiyama during the Diet debate, but a far more typical strain of conservative thought was that of Nakasone Yasuhirō (Kōno faction) who wrote in the midst of the crisis that it was absurd for Japan to be divided into pro-U.S. and pro-Soviet camps at a time when the people should be overwhelmingly pro-Japanese.[2] There was no question that the treaty had its strongest support from financial circles who had most to lose by a tremor in U.S.–Japan economic relations.

The left wing, in spite of a strong attachment to Marxist principles and proletarian internationalism, showed unmistakable signs of the new nationalism. The Socialists and Communists, painting an image of Japan as a subservient client state, with Kishi as a cowardly dog wagging his tail submissively before President Eisenhower, successfully pricked the skin of national pride. It was noteworthy that the Socialists argued less against the Self-defense Forces in 1960 than they had in 1951, and understandably, for these forces had come to enjoy a considerable degree of popular acceptance. One great appeal of the Socialists' neutralism was its promise of a middle, vital rôle in world affairs. As an expensive broker between East and West, the presumption was that Japan could (and should) avoid involvement in the problems of both. There was a strain of isolationism in this leftist nationalism—a desire to avoid harsh inter-

[2] Nakasone Yasuhirō, "Genka no Sōran ni Omou" (My View of the Current Disturbances), *Daiyamondo*, June 18, 1960, p. 33.

Kishi avoided a clear opportunity to deny that the U.S. was imperialistic in the following interesting section of the Diet debate: Dai-Sanjūyon-kai Kokkai, Shūgiin, Nichibei Anzen Hoshō Jōyaku Tokubetsu Iinkai, *Giroku* (Special Committee on the Japan–U.S. Security Treaty, *Proceedings*, No. 5), April 8, 1960, pp. 2–3.

national realities and withdraw into an uncommitted, insular refuge.

The massive participation of students had as much to do with their feelings of shame and inferiority left over from World War II as it did with their proclaimed desire to prevent World War III. It revealed the disgust of the younger generation for anything that smacked of defeatism and subservience: Kishi had been a Class A War Criminal; Eisenhower and MacArthur were names that symbolized American victories and supremacy in the war. The alienation of Zengakuren from the JCP epitomized the resentment of youth over all forms of foreign domination—whether from Moscow, Peking, or Washington. The acceptance by major Zengakuren leaders of aid from the right wing seemed a good indication that nationalism, not social revolution, was at the heart of their movement.

The progressive intellectuals were also purveyors of the new nationalism. The insistence by the Shimin-ha that Japan must achieve its own form of democracy was valid in itself, but it also reflected a continuing preoccupation with Japan's "uniqueness"—a presumption that *forms* of democracy applicable elsewhere could not be suited to Japan. Their pleas for solidarity, unity, harmony; their idealistic views of majority-minority relations; their mistrust of diversity and plurality of interests were reminiscent of themes in *Kokutai no Hongi*.[3] Anti-American overtones were present in their unanimous opposition to Eisenhower's visit. One sensed a desire to strike back at the source of the postwar intellectual environment—at concepts they could neither live with nor live without. There was evident satisfaction in bludgeoning Kishi (and, by association, the United States) with political theories imposed by the occupation. Other themes in their writings were the advocacy of closer ties with Asian people, and the self-glorifying, morally superior claim that they were the only true defenders of peace by virtue of being the only victims of the atomic bomb. This is not to deny that the intellectuals found valid and legitimate arguments against the treaty,

[3] See, for example, Hidaka Rokurō, ed., *Gogatsu Jūkunichi* (May 19), Tokyo: Iwanami Shinsho, 1960, p. 85.

but they also provided themes for which their massive audiences hungered, as part of the shedding of guilt and recovery of national self-respect. Whether by design or chance, they appealed successfully to the innate aspirations of the people.

1960 was the year in which the very subject of nationalism, long suppressed as an evil associated with the militarists, emerged again as a respectable topic of conversation. New ways for the individual to relate himself to the state, and new bases for pride in the nation became subjects of deep concern. Beginning in 1960, leftist scholars explored new foundations upon which to legitimize nationalism, such as the shared experience of the atomic bombing and postwar economic privations. University students for the first time since the war discussed ways to contribute to Japan's and Asia's future—such as giving technical aid to Southeast Asia—without fear of ridicule. New and more comforting interpretations of the road to Pearl Harbor filtered out, of which Hayashi Fusao's attracted much attention. Hayashi argued that World War II simply culminated the "100-year war" which began when the United States made its first attempt to "colonize" Japan in 1845. During these 100 years, according to Hayashi, Japan accomplished her historic mission of checking the Western colonization of Asia (where India and China had failed) and of proving to the world that the white and colored races were equal.[4] In other moves to soften the picture of the war, the Tokyo District Court ruled, in an *obiter dictum* of December 1963 that the atomic bombing of Hiroshima and Nagasaki was a violation of international law, and the government, in April 1964, began awarding posthumous decorations to those who died in World War II.

It was not surprising that the war and the defeat were vital issues in the process of reconstructing national pride. The ready acceptance by the Japanese of the occupation and their swift

[4] Hayashi has presented this argument in "Dai Tōa Sensō Kōtei Ron" (Affirmation of the Greater East Asia War), *Chūō Kōron*, September-December 1963, and in "Dai Tōa Sensō o Naze Minaosu no ka?" (Why Take a New Look at the Great East Asia War?"), round-table discussion, *Ushio*, Vol. 44, New Year's Edition, 1964, pp. 66–94. But this and similar ideas were already being discussed in the universities in 1960.

embrace of democracy have led many foreign observers to conclude that the memories of the war already belonged to the dim past. Nothing could be further from the truth. The war and defeat were still the central facts in the lives of most adult Japanese, breeding feelings of guilt, inferiority, and insecurity. The psychological wounds on this proud and sensitive people would probably not heal until the present generation of college students took over, and the scars were apparent in 1960 to those who would look beneath the surface.

The security treaty crisis did not in itself produce all these developments, but most Japanese—even those who were not involved—view it today as a kind of watershed in the postwar era. From this point on, they argue, the people became more conscious of their sovereignty, more secure in their self-respect, more confident of their future. To the extent that this new nationalism remained healthy and constructive, the treaty crisis ushered in a bright and promising new era for the Japanese people.

The Alliance

Much has been written on both sides of the Pacific about the meaning of the treaty crisis for the alliance and for U.S.-Japanese relations in general. Some experts on both sides went so far as to say that the treaty had been so morally discredited that it would be useless or ineffective in time of need. The contrary seems to be the case, and U.S. bases in Japan are, at this writing, functioning and prepared to strike back instantaneously with air and sea power against any aggressor. The danger of sabotage—a sudden disruption of electric power, of communications or transportation—or the possibility of invasion by mobs, has always been present and was not substantially affected by the crisis. Today, relations between the U.S. Forces and their Japanese hosts are no worse, and on the whole, are probably better than before the crisis. Still, the large naval base at Yokosuka—the only base west of Pearl Harbor that can drydock U.S. aircraft carriers—as well as the other large air bases in Japan, depend to a large extent on locally supplied labor. If this supply were cut off, or became unreliable, serious problems would arise for the United States. At present, there are no signs of such a development.

If the crisis did not render the alliance meaningless, there were continuing irritants in implementing the treaty. The troops and bases were still considered undesirable but necessary evils by most Japanese.[5] There were the usual number of unfortunate incidents: jet sounds disturbing classrooms, stray dud bombs landing near the Atomic Energy Research Institute, farmers' groups protesting exclusion from traditional grass-cutting areas, and jet crashes in residential areas. The left continued to exploit the situation, stirring fears of U.S. bad faith and rallying against the introduction of nuclear powered submarines into Japanese ports (a U.S. right under the treaty). Diplomatic problems continued to arise: the government was reported "jolted" by the U.S. "unilateral decision" to send troops to Thailand in May 1962, even though it acknowledged that this was not a matter for prior consultation under the treaty.[6] And landings by military transport planes used for supplying U.S. forces in Vietnam aroused adverse comment in 1965. None of these problems has shaken the alliance, but all have contributed to the complexity of maintaining close relations between nations with different international commitments and interests.

If the above difficulties could be resolved through skilled diplomacy (the U.S. after the crisis took important steps to improve relations), the events of 1960 foreshadowed a deeper problem for the future. Essentially, this was the lack of firm ideological or practical commitment by many ruling conservatives to the concepts of containment and deterrence which the new treaty represented, and serious doubt that the Soviet Union and Communist China were threats to Japan's security. This was of course an aspect of the new nationalism—the desire to play a larger rôle in world affairs by avoidance of "one-sided relationships." It also stemmed from doubts about the relative strength of the United States and from fears over U.S. motives in Asia.

---

[5] The number of troops had been reduced to about 50,000 by 1960; they occupied some 85,000 acres of land in 175 facilities as of August 15, 1961 (figures from the U.S. Embassy, Tokyo).

[6] *New York Times*, May 19, 1962.

From glimpses of conservative thought during the great national debate over the treaty, one could not escape the impression that their lack of conviction enabled the crisis to go as far as it did, and that in 1970, when the first opportunity to give notice to Japan's intention to terminate or revise the treaty would arise, some among present conservatives would join a movement to do so. On the other hand, there were signs of growing "defense-mindedness" on the part of some conservatives and the public in the years following the crisis, and it seemed likely that the Japanese people would be willing, by 1970, to devote more of their resources to their own defense budget. The criteria for determining most conservative attitudes on the treaty would be its effect on Japan's security, the economy, and domestic politics in that order. To the extent that Japan seemed secure from aggression, the other two factors would come into play. Missing from all thinking were abstract notions of collective security for the free world; so long as the United States shouldered this burden, it would not be a central factor in Japan's attitude toward the treaty.

A final word must be addressed to the question so often asked about the crisis: did it reflect widespread anti-Americanism? Many experienced observers, noting that Americans could mingle freely with the most violent demonstrators, and pointing to the "conversion" of radical student leaders once they joined a company after graduation, have concluded that anti-American feelings had little or nothing to do with the affair. These conclusions should not be accepted too quickly. We have already seen that the new nationalism resented *all* foreign encroachments, and to the extent that the U.S. was the dominant foreign influence, it inevitably became a prime target. One should also consider the lack of moral conviction in the alliance by its supporters in Japan.[7] The most careful examination should be given

[7] We Americans are often criticized for excessive "moral conviction"— for crusading in our relations with the world. But the serious question remains: how long can a democratic society espouse foreign policies *like Japan's* without some degree of emotional if not moral commitment on the part of a majority of the people?

to the ideas of Professor Ōhira Zengo—the foremost *supporter* of the new treaty among articulate Japanese intellectuals:

> The guide to our action must first of all be the "maintenance of the balance." But morally, we must be neutral, and with regard to the action of both East and West, we must take a realistic view of diplomacy. I think that we must not let our judgment be affected by ideologies, but rather that we should, freely and fairly, become the conscience of the world, and in the U.N. General Assembly form a healthy floating vote. It is wrong to say that either Russia or China—being red dictatorships— are morally evil by nature, or conversely, that the U.S. is an imperialist aggressor. We must look at both sides impartially, and rejecting totally pro-U.S. or totally pro-Soviet positions, make judgments objectively, based on the national interest. This is a theory of moral neutralism, and I think this form of neutralism is tenable even though we belong militarily to the joint defense structure of the free world. It is a mistake to brand those who favor treaty revision as pro-American, ideologically. Only when we are ideologically neutral can we make impartial judgments on our foreign affairs.[8]

If this view accurately represented the revised security treaty's most enthusiastic intellectual supporters, the reader can judge the range of opinion on this issue. In this sort of "moral neutralism" there was the desire to escape from the overwhelming political, cultural (and, in Japanese eyes, materialistic) influence exerted by the U.S. since the war; it was a desire to reassert Japan's initiative and her peculiar virtues, and to preserve the Japanese identity. This was a kind of "reactive nationalism"; it was also a form of anti-Americanism, and it thrived among broad sections of the people. In the writer's opinion, the demonstrations in 1960 did express to some extent pent-up feelings of hostility toward the United States. As Ambassador Reischauer

---

[8] *Nihon no Anzen Hoshō to Kokusai Hō* (Japan's Security and International Law), 5th ed., Tokyo: Yūshindō, 1960, p. 156.

has pointed out, "during the twentieth century as a whole, no country has more consistently regarded itself as in essential conflict with the United States than has Japan. . . ."[9] It would not be hard for the hostility to return under certain circumstances. Thus, while the treaty crisis did not create a lasting wave of anti-Americanism, and though the U.S. remained at the top of most popularity polls in Japan, it did reveal the potential for such a movement and it pointed up the fragile underpinnings of the alliance.

The United States has loomed so large, not only economically and politically, but psychologically in Japanese eyes since World War II that a kind of love-hate fixation has developed. Americans are excessively praised for their successes and excessively blamed for the world's ills. As the Japanese discover that new centers of power are growing throughout the world and that U.S. influence does not lie behind all international crises, this relationship may become more healthy and stable. For the foreseeable future, however, the United States would have to work hard to establish trust and good will in the mind of a wary, and sometimes overly sensitive ally.

Most of all, the United States needed to note the satisfaction in Japan over the new attention it received as a result of the crisis. There had been grumbling before 1960 that Washington policy-makers took Japan for granted as a kind of "back yard" in the Pacific, and the United States took important steps to set these anxieties at rest after the crisis. President Kennedy appointed Edwin O. Reischauer, a leading expert on East Asia and a scholar who could speak the Japanese language, as Ambassador to Japan, a move that was to prove highly popular in Japan, and then met Prime Minister Ikeda in Washington in June 1961 to launch a new era of "equal partnership." Annual meetings of cabinet members to discuss vital trade and economic questions were begun, and special committees were set up to discuss scientific and cultural matters of mutual concern. All these developments might eventually have come about anyway,

[9] *Japan and America Today*, Stanford: Stanford University Press, 1953, p. 2.

but the events of May and June provided the necessary impetus. They went far to persuade Japanese leaders that Japan was getting as good treatment from Washington as our European allies were, and they were warmly received.

One serious weakness remaining in the military alliance—though it was seldom brought into the open—was the conviction among many conservatives that the U.S. would aid Japan in a crisis whether or not the treaty existed; there was no sense, according to this view, in putting up with the troops and bases until that crisis occurred. Against this view was the recognition that Japan was buying security cheaply: her military budget took a smaller share of the gross national product (1.1 percent in 1964) than that of any other Asian country, Communist or non-Communist. This remained a factor in Japan's remarkable growth, and a potent argument among top Japanese business leaders.

Ultimately support for the security treaty rested on the extent to which the Japanese people believed in the existence of an external threat and in the superior strength of the United States. The alliance would quickly lose its meaning if a majority of Japanese became convinced that the treaty brought them insecurity—the threat of retaliation—in each international crisis involving the United States. The maintenance by the United States of real power, a real image of that power, and above all an understanding of Japan's deep sensitivity to war, would help to preserve the strength of the alliance.

Democracy

The political parties have not been able to channel and provide leadership for the strong tides of emotional protest that have engulfed Japan since the war. This was never so evident as in 1960 when the Prime Minister was forced from office and the President of the United States prevented from visiting Tokyo by crowds in the street—yet, only five months later, the LDP was returned to power. Kishi's faction was larger within that party, and the security treaty was still a cornerstone of Japan's foreign policy. Part of the explanation lies in the rapid economic and social change which has produced a militant labor

343

movement, urban unrest, and a nervous new middle class, even as conservative patterns of thought and behavior prevail among businessmen, smaller enterprisers, farmers, and fishermen. But we should also reexamine longstanding concepts of Japanese docility in the face of authority.[10] The obverse side of their "yield to the powerful" philosophy has resulted in the massive protest movements of the past century, in which prolonged apathy has turned suddenly into panic and violence—as in the Hibiya riots of 1905, the Constitution Protection Movement of 1912–1913, and the rice riots of 1918, which reflected elements of nationalism, manipulation by out-group elites, and emotional antipathy to the exercise of authority. The parties, with their in-group mentality and narrow paths of access, have in some cases used but have never completely captured this popular force in the postwar period. It may be that contemporary Japan, with its highly developed mass media, will be more susceptible than ever to such waves of emotion. As one intellectual observed, "This is an age where it is taught that resistance is democracy." [11] Even with universal suffrage, a high voting rate, free press, free speech, and protection for human rights, the political system has not removed the need for popular outbursts.

The major characteristics of the protest movement of 1960 were the calculated—even sophisticated—use of force, the pre-

[10] G. B. Sansom has observed: "There is evidence in past history that the Japanese people are, despite the rigid structure of their society, by no means incapable of revolt against what they deem oppression. The record of agrarian risings and religious martyrdoms in the feudal period shows that they have not always submitted tamely to authority. Indeed their story tells perhaps as much of turbulence as of docility, and their fatalism has found expression not only in patient acceptance of misfortune but also in reckless disregard for life itself. Therefore it cannot be predicted of them that they will in whatever circumstances conform to a prescribed pattern of behavior. The very fact that social pressure has in the past been so severe and unrelenting raises a presumption that, once the course of events removes that pressure, their reactions will be strong if not violent." *Japan: A Short Cultural History*, rev. ed., New York: Appleton-Century-Crofts, Inc., preface, p. vii.

[11] Nakamura Kikuo, *Gikai Seiji to Taishū Kōdō* (Parliamentary Politics and Mass Action), Tokyo: Yūshindō, 1960, p. 96.

dominance of the middle class (more white collars than blue in the demonstrations), the dearth of outstanding individual leaders, limited objectives, lack of positive alternatives, the strong stamp of the *bunkajin* Establishment (particularly the university intellectuals) and the erratic but powerful popular "mood"— reinforced by the press—that enabled the movement to grow and then helped to cut it off.

The intellectuals defined the movement's objectives and evaluated its results, revealing a characteristic penchant for theorizing even in the heat of the crisis. By intellectuals is meant not only the opinion leaders of Tokyo University, Iwanami and *Asahi*, but also the "field commanders" who went to the universities: Asanuma Inejirō (Waseda), Nosaka Sanzō (Keio), Miyamoto Kenji and Minaguchi Kōzō (Tokyo), Ōta Kaoru (Osaka), Kitakoji Satoshi (Kyoto) and Karoji Kentarō (Hokkaidō), to mention a few. Extraordinarily few of the prominent leftist leaders had "come up through the ranks." All spoke the language of the disaffected intellectual elite. One result was their concept of *keimō katsudō* (edification activity): the belief that the masses could be enlightened and educated through the act of demonstrating, based on the presumption that the masses, especially the inactive rural elements, were incapable of recognizing their own true interests.[12] Another result was the Shimin-ha intellectuals' concept of spontaneity, despite the fact that there was almost no spontaneous participation in the movement. There was an element of the fantastic in the fact that these intellectuals (1) organized the *shimin* demonstrations almost single-handedly and then (2) theorized afterward that the movement represented a spontaneous outburst of citizens' protest. A third result was their fundamental mistrust of the elective process. Their dedication to the task of safeguarding

[12] Tsurumi Shunsuke, who played, perhaps, a greater rôle than any other progressive intellectual in the movement, had this to say of Japanese scholars: "Now Japanese scholars, from Meiji down to the present, have the habit of talking about the necessity of 'enlightening,' 'modernizing,' and 'democratizing,' with the unconscious postulate that they are not part of the object criticized." Katō Hidetoshi, ed., *Japanese Popular Culture*, Tokyo: Charles E. Tuttle Co., 1959, p. 207.

the democratic process—though most of them refused to run for office or support political parties openly and actively—bore strong hints of the persistence of elitism.

Traditional Japanese mistrust of power in the hands of a single, overtly ambitious individual was also evident. Power must be exercised discreetly, from behind the scenes, and in the name of a higher Cause—if not in the name of the Emperor, then in the name of the people (*kokumin*). Power has been traditionally held by oligarchies with competing interests and multiple initiative. Kishi's bold attempt to win a third term was an affront to this tradition and aroused almost unbelievable hostility. His personality was not well suited to the rôle of strongman: a Yoshida or even an Asanuma with blunt, visceral reactions would have had a better chance of surviving in office than Kishi, with his suspiciously polished responses and "smooth" personality. A type like Yoshida could seem to be "divining the will of the people," but Kishi's image as a bureaucrat (implying legalism, arrogance, and distance from the ordinary people) could only be despised as selfish, egotistical, and dangerous.

If Kishi could not appeal to the nation at large in time of crisis, the fact that he survived in office as long as he did tells something of the qualities necessary for a political leader *within* the parties: toughness, durability, endless patience, willingness to compromise, ability to be ruthless, delicacy in playing off enemies, maneuverability on issues, and of course outside financial support. Paradoxically, some of the very qualities most resented by the public were most needed to stay at the top of the LDP. The Japanese bias against overt power-seeking has two sides: it checks the climb to power of a dictatorial fanatic, but it also fosters an undiscriminating mistrust of all politicians, which inhibits popular participation in party politics.

Japan's lack of a genuine two-party system has had unfortunate effects on all the parties. The LDP has become absorbed in factional struggles and less responsive to the popular will, while the Socialists, frustrated by the "one-third barrier," have lost touch with the realism that is bred by power (or proximity to power). The Socialists moved so far to the left in 1960 that a victory for them at the polls would have been a major revolution, a fact which in itself retarded their growth. Their acceptance of the "Sakisaka thesis" forced moderate leftists to the center, and it appeared, in the elections of 1960, at least, that there was no "center" for the Japanese voter. The far left Socialists have said that once the party takes over, there will be no possibility for the conservatives to take back the reins. If this position becomes the position of the party (and many conservatives suspect that it already is) and if present voting trends place the Socialists within range of victory, Japanese politics will undergo a serious crisis in the future. This confrontation may be avoided by trends toward the center among some conservatives and some Socialists.

Factionalism in all the parties seriously detracted from responsible intraparty debate on policy and strategy, but it should not be overlooked that it also served as a kind of check on the power of the mainstream in the LDP, preventing the Prime Minister from moving too swiftly with his absolute and seemingly permanent majority. If Kishi had enjoyed full support from all LDP factions in May-June 1960, he would not have had to resign over the crisis; it was this potential for an anti-mainstream coalition—or even for defection—and this alone that kept the Prime Minister within acceptable bounds of authority.

The confrontation on the night of May 19–20 showed clearly how little the concepts of majority rule and minority rights have been accepted in Japan. The traditional preference for unanimity or consensus, stemming from the "small village mentality," could be seen not only in the Diet, but in the party conventions as well. Much has been written on this subject, and we shall not dwell on it here, except to suggest that a prerequisite in the decision-making process—even when it appears to be by consensus—is the existence of overwhelming real or assumed power in the leadership—power which can reconcile conflicting opinions. Without that power, decisions are avoided, postponed, or obscured, so that the parties to the discussion themselves may not know what has been decided even when

347

a "decision" has been made.[18] Even on the most controversial legislation, the LDP can get its way when it is united (the education bills, rearmament, and others). When the party is faced with internal disunity, the left has been able to stir up popular anxiety and protest.

Certain basic conditions must be present in any democratic system if the delicate balance between majority rule and minority rights is to be maintained. These are: (1) the commitment by all parties to the preservation of the parliamentary system itself; (2) the possibility for the minority some day to become the majority; (3) legal checks to protect minimum minority rights; (4) a cultural tradition which respects the minority; (5) multiple interest groups enabling bipartisanship on some issues and shifting majorities on others. These conditions were either partly or wholly lacking in the Japanese scene in 1960, and this led to a temporary breakdown of the system.

The individual human being has not yet won full acceptance in the Japanese social or political scheme of things. Beyond any doubt, the group—the organization, the collectivity—is the recognized basic unit in all endeavor. It may be that circumstances of geography and population dictate this system, but it raises questions as to the viability of democratic institutions as we know them in the West. In the treaty crisis, those who joined in demonstrations did so by *groups* in almost all cases; the People's Council was a perfect example of an organization composed only of groups and subgroups. No individuals joined *as* individuals. The same was true of Zengakuren. This led to extraordinary situations: on one hand there were students, clerks, and laborers shouting "Down with the Treaty!" who had no interest or knowledge whatsoever in the issues involved. On the other hand, there were some young businessmen, writers, and students who were genuinely disturbed by Kishi but could not demonstrate because their "group" was officially for the treaty. Both situations were accepted, by and large, with resignation.

[18] The folk tale *"Sannin Ichi-ryō Son"* about Judge Ooka-sama illustrates this point.

348

The result of submerging individuals in groups was to obscure personal responsibility for everything; paradoxically, the question of *responsibility* was a constant preoccupation: Kishi's responsibility for the Socialist boycott of the Diet; rightist responsibility for left-wing extremism; the demonstrations' responsibility for rightist terrorism; Speaker Katō's responsibility for the November 27 Incident; President Kaya's view that students were *not* responsible for the violence, and so forth. The demonstrations, it should be added, were organized and directed by professional cadres who were elected by no one and responsible to no one. This massive escape from personal, individual responsibility led to a feeling that the whole movement was somehow inevitable. The traditional supremacy of the goals of the group kept most individuals from having to make a conscious, reasoned political judgment on the treaty—on Kishi—on the Socialist sit-down. Until the concept of membership in a group came to be seen as conferring responsibility rather than absolving the individual, the Japanese political system would be susceptible to control by the organizers who manipulate the groups.

Another aspect of this lack of individual responsibility noted by many writers was the massive—almost joyful—plunge into unity and solidarity during the anti-treaty drive by many new participants in the political process. The Japanese people are not happy, as a rule, with the persistence of conflict, and prefer to resolve competing ideas by seeking harmony around the broadest possible framework of agreement. The anti-Kishi, or anti-treaty drive, coming as it did after a long period of bitter, divisive debate, seemed for a time to offer this sort of framework. One need only sample the self-congratulatory literature of the anti-treaty forces to sense the relief and gratification over the newly discovered bonds of solidarity. Rapid social change since the war has perhaps stimulated this hunger for unity in Japan's new urbanized and rootless middle class, but it may be asked whether this sort of rush for togetherness will produce mature political behavior in the future.

Much has been written on the disillusionment and rebellion in Japan's younger generation. Another outstanding aspect of this was the tolerance—if not sympathy—extended by the older generation to the students. As the novelist, Mishima Yukio, has put it, the "old people in Japan today eagerly attempt to ingratiate themselves with the young." [14] Students were considered to be in a different category from the rest of the nation —partly because of the alleged "purity" of their motivation, partly because of the enormous gulf in understanding between generations. Without this tolerance, the Zengakuren extremists could not have functioned for long. There is reason to hope that the younger generation will reject the tendencies represented by Zengakuren—that the dismal emptiness of the Diet invasions will be replaced by some new sense of purpose, that feelings of inferiority and despair will give way to constructive and positive involvement in the life of the nation.

Some leftists in Japan liked to quote Nehru's statement that "essentially there is no difference between United States Forces in Japan and Soviet Forces in Hungary and Poland." [15] The absurdity of this statement was proved beyond all doubt in 1960: demonstrators who marched to the Diet showed with their feet that they knew the *locus* of state power. Protesting Hungarian students had marched against the State security forces and then against the Soviet troops, with results that were all too tragic. In Japan, the last serious attempt to overthrow the government was in the February 26, 1936 Incident, when Army officers took over government buildings, ignoring the Diet completely. In 1960, the Diet was at the heart of the crisis at all times; the simple fact that it survived offered hope for the future.

The crisis of 1960 gave many Japanese their first opportunity to show what they meant by democracy and freedom. For some, it was the first chance to involve themselves personally with an important foreign policy decision. Some saw the protest against the government as a kind of fulfillment of their new rights under the Constitution; some felt that marching against the Diet and demonstrating against the Prime Minister were vital to the preservation of Japanese democracy, regardless of the policy at stake. Those on the far left saw in the disorder a

[14] "Party of One," *Holiday*, Vol. 30, No. 4, October 1961, p. 12.
[15] *New York Times*, October 9, 1957.

glimmer of hope that their own style of democracy, under a "dictatorship of the proletariat," might prevail.

Given the diverse interpretations of democracy and freedom and the strongly emotional bent in the Japanese character, there would undoubtedly be new disturbances—perhaps again over the security treaty—in future years. If the individual citizen emerged from the turmoil as he did in 1960 with the power to choose his own form of government, and his own foreign policy, these crises would be overcome and democracy would grow stronger in Japan.

351

APPENDICES

APPENDICES

Security Treaty Between the United States of America and Japan[1]

Signed at San Francisco September 8, 1951
Ratification advised by U.S. Senate, March 20, 1952
Ratified by President, April 15, 1952
Ratified by Japan, November 19, 1951
Ratifications exchanged at Washington, April 28, 1952
Entered into force April 28, 1952

TREATY

Japan has this day signed a Treaty of Peace with the Allied Powers. On the coming into force of that Treaty, Japan will not have the effective means to exercise its inherent right of self-defense because it has been disarmed.

There is danger to Japan in this situation because irresponsible militarism has not yet been driven from the world. Therefore Japan desires a Security Treaty with the United States of America to come into force simultaneously with the Treaty of Peace between the United States of America and Japan.

The Treaty of Peace recognizes that Japan as a sovereign nation has the right to enter into collective security arrangements, and further, the Charter of the United Nations recognizes that all nations possess an inherent right of individual and collective self-defense.

In exercise of these rights, Japan desires, as a provisional arrangement for its defense, that the United States of America should maintain armed forces of its own in and about Japan so as to deter armed attack upon Japan.

The United States of America, in the interest of peace and security, is presently willing to maintain certain of its armed forces in and about Japan, in the expectation, however, that Japan will itself increasingly assume responsibility for its own defense against direct and indirect aggression, always avoiding any armament which

---

[1] U.S. Department of State, *Security Treaty Between the United States of America and Japan* (Vol. 3, *United States Treaties and Other International Agreements*, TIAS 2491), Washington: U.S. Government Printing Office, 1955, pp. 3329–3340.

could be an offensive threat or serve other than to promote peace and security in accordance with the purposes and principles of the United Nations Charter.

Accordingly, the two countries have agreed as follows:

ARTICLE I

Japan grants, and the United States of America accepts, the right, upon the coming into force of the Treaty of Peace and of this Treaty, to dispose United States land, air and sea forces in and about Japan. Such forces may be utilized to contribute to the maintenance of international peace and security in the Far East and to the security of Japan against armed attack from without, including assistance given at the express request of the Japanese Government to put down large-scale internal riots and disturbances in Japan, caused through instigation or intervention by an outside power or powers.

ARTICLE II

During the exercise of the right referred to in Article I, Japan will not grant, without the prior consent of the United States of America, any bases or any rights, powers or authority whatsoever, in or relating to bases or the right of garrison or of maneuver, or transit of ground, air or naval forces to any third power.

ARTICLE III

The conditions which shall govern the disposition of armed forces of the United States of America in and about Japan shall be determined by administrative agreements between the two Governments.

ARTICLE IV

This Treaty shall expire whenever in the opinion of the Governments of the United States of America and Japan there shall have come into force such United Nations arrangements or such alternative individual or collective security dispositions as will satisfactorily provide for the maintenance by the United Nations or otherwise of international peace and security in the Japan Area.

ARTICLE V

This Treaty shall be ratified by the United States of America and Japan and will come into force when instruments of ratification thereof have been exchanged by them at Washington.

In witness whereof the undersigned Plenipotentiaries have signed this Treaty

Done in duplicate at the city of San Francisco, in English and Japanese languages, this eighth day of September, 1951

FOR THE UNITED STATES OF AMERICA:

Dean Acheson
John Foster Dulles
Alexander Wiley
Styles Bridges

FOR JAPAN:

Shigeru Yoshida

Joint Communiqué, June 21, 1957

issued by President Eisenhower and Prime Minister Kishi [2]

The President of the United States and the Prime Minister of Japan concluded today valuable discussions on topics of interest to both countries. Their talks focussed mainly on United States–Japanese relations but they also discussed international subjects of mutual concern, especially the situation in Asia.

During his three-day visit the Prime Minister and members of his party met at length with the Secretary of State and also met with the Secretary of the Treasury, the Secretary of Commerce, the Chairman of the United States Joint Chiefs of Staff, the President of the Export-Import Bank and appropriate representatives of the President and of the Departments of Defense and Agriculture, and with leaders of the United States Congress. After leaving Washington, the Prime Minister will visit other parts of the United States and meet with leaders of business and other private organizations.

I

The President and the Prime Minister agreed that, although the dangers of general war had somewhat receded, international communism remains a major threat. Accordingly, they agreed that the free nations should continue to preserve their strength and their unity. It was mutually recognized that the deterrent power of the free world had, in recent years, been effective in preventing overt aggression in the Far East and the world.

The President and the Prime Minister are convinced that relations between Japan and the United States are entering a new era firmly based on common interests and trust. Their discussions covered the many mutual advantages and benefits of close relations between the United States and Japan. The President and the Prime Minister decided, therefore, that it would be appropriate to affirm the following principles of cooperation between the two countries:

(1) Relations between the United States and Japan rest on a solid foundation of sovereign equality, mutual interest and cooper-

[2] U.S. Department of State, "Joint Communiqué of June 21, 1957, issued by President Eisenhower and Prime Minister Kishi," *Department of State Bulletin*, Vol. 37, July 8, 1957, pp. 51–53.

ation beneficial to both nations. In the years ahead, this relationship will provide a vital element in strengthening the Free World.

(2) Both nations are dedicated to peace based on liberty and justice in accordance with the principles of the United Nations. They are resolved to work toward the establishment of conditions under which peace and freedom can prevail. To this end they will support the United Nations and contribute their best efforts to preserve and enhance the unity of the Free World. They will oppose the use of force by any nation except in individual or collective self-defense as provided in the United Nations Charter.

(3) In the interests of continued peace, the Free World must maintain its defensive capability until armaments are brought under effective control. Meanwhile, the free nations need to intensify their efforts to foster the conditions necessary for economic and social progress and for strengthening freedom in Asia and throughout the world. Free Asian nations, which desire assistance, should be aided in carrying forward measures for economic development and technical training.

(4) The United States and Japan reaffirm the desirability of a high level of world trade beneficial to free nations and of orderly trade between the two countries, without unnecessary and arbitrary restrictions.

(5) The two countries fully agree that an effective international agreement for the reduction of armaments, both nuclear and conventional, is of crucial importance for the future of the world. They will continue in close consultation on this important problem.

Within the context of these principles the President and the Prime Minister reviewed the great changes which have taken place in Japan in recent years, including Japan's extensive economic recovery and admission to the United Nations, both of which the President warmly welcomed.

II

Existing security arrangements between the United States and Japan were discussed. It was agreed to establish an inter-governmental committee to study problems arising in relation to the Security Treaty including consultation, whenever practicable, regarding the disposition and employment in Japan by the United States of its forces. The Committee will also consult to assure that any action taken under the Treaty conforms to the principles of the

United Nations Charter. The President and the Prime Minister affirmed their understanding that the Security Treaty of 1951 was designed to be transitional in character and not in that form to remain in perpetuity. The Committee will also consider future adjustments in the relationships between the United States and Japan in these fields adequate to meet the needs and aspirations of the peoples of both countries.

The United States welcomed Japan's plans for the buildup of her defense forces and accordingly, in consonance with the letter and spirit of the Security Treaty, will substantially reduce the numbers of United States forces in Japan within the next year, including a prompt withdrawal of all United States ground combat forces. The United States plans still further reductions as the Japanese defense forces grow.

The President, while recognizing that Japan must trade to live, stressed the continuing need for control on exports of strategic materials to those countries threatening the independence of free nations through the extension of international communism. The Prime Minister, while agreeing with the need for such control in cooperation with other Free World governments, pointed out the necessity for Japan to increase its trade.

The Prime Minister emphasized the strong desire of the Japanese people for the return of administrative control over the Ryukyu and Bonin Islands to Japan. The President reaffirmed the United States position that Japan possesses residual sovereignty over these islands. He pointed out, however, that so long as the conditions of threat and tension exist in the Far East the United States will find it necessary to continue the present status. He stated that the United States will continue its policy of improving the welfare and well-being of the inhabitants of the Islands and of promoting their economic and cultural advancement.

Economic and trade relations between the United States and Japan were discussed at length. The President and the Prime Minister mutually confirmed not only the desire for a high level of trade but also the need for close relations between the two countries in other economic fields. The Prime Minister, while expressing his deep concern over certain movements in the United States for import restrictions, explained that in consideration of the predominant importance of the United States market for Japanese trade Japan is taking measures for an orderly development of her exports to the United States. The President confirmed that the

United States Government will maintain its traditional policy of a high level of trade without unnecessary and arbitrary restrictions. He expressed his hopes for the removal of local restrictions on the sale of Japanese products.

The Prime Minister described his recent tour of certain Asian countries and said that he had been deeply impressed with the serious efforts these countries are making toward economic development. He expressed his conviction that further progress in the economic development of these countries would greatly contribute to stability and freedom in Asia. The President expressed his full agreement with the Prime Minister. The President and the Prime Minister discussed ways in which free Asian countries might be further assisted in developing their economies. The views of the Prime Minister will be studied by the United States.

The President and the Prime Minister discussed the early cessation of both the testing and the manufacture of nuclear weapons as part of a first step in a safeguarded disarmament program. The President told the Prime Minister that the latter's views are being taken into account in formulating the United States position at the current United Nations disarmament session in London.

The President and the Prime Minister are convinced that their exchange of views will contribute much to strengthening mutual understanding and to agreement on fundamental interests which will further solidify the friendly relations between the two countries in the years to come.

Joint Statement of September 11, 1958

issued to the Press after meeting of September 11, 1958
between Secretary of State Dulles and Foreign Minister Fujiyama [3]

The Secretary of State and Foreign Minister of Japan met together at the Department of State this afternoon and had a constructive exchange of views in an atmosphere of cordiality and mutual understanding. They reviewed the international situation, discussed Japanese-American security arrangements and took up other matters pending between their two countries. Others present at the meeting included Ambassador Asakai, Ambassador MacArthur, Assistant Secretary Robertson, Assistant Secretary (Defense) Sprague and General Lemnitzer.

Security problems facing the two countries were the principal subjects of the discussion today. It was agreed that the Japanese-American Committee on Security, whose establishment was agreed upon in the talks between President Eisenhower and Prime Minister Kishi last year, had been successful in strengthening mutual cooperation and understanding in the security field. Foreign Minister Fujiyama pointed out at the same time that seven years have passed since the United States–Japan Security Treaty was signed. He stated that with the re-established position of Japan in the intervening years the situation has now evolved to the point where it would be advantageous to re-examine the present security arrangements with a view to adjusting them on a basis entirely consistent with the new era in relations between the two countries affirmed by Prime Minister Kishi and President Eisenhower in the Joint Communiqué of June 21, 1957. It was agreed that the two governments will consult further on this matter through diplomatic channels following Mr. Fujiyama's return to Tokyo.

With respect to the Ryukyu Islands, Foreign Minister Fujiyama welcomed the current discussions taking place between the United States authorities and Ryukyuan representatives looking toward a satisfactory resolution of the land problem. Secretary Dulles ex-

---

[3] U.S. Department of State, "Joint Statement of September 11, 1958, issued to the Press after meeting of September 11, 1958, between Secretary of State Dulles and Foreign Minister Fujiyama," *Department of State Bulletin*, Vol. 39, October 6, 1958, pp. 532–33.

pressed his understanding of Japanese interest in the Ryukyus and it was agreed that on Ryūkyuan matters the two governments would continue to exchange views through diplomatic channels.

The Foreign Minister also touched upon specific issues among which was included the Japanese desire for compensation of former inhabitants of the Bonin Islands who are unable to return to their former homes. The Secretary assured Mr. Fujiyama that the United States is sympathetically aware of the problem and is studying it carefully in the hope of achieving a reasonable solution.

Discussions will be continued tomorrow.

APPENDIX D

Treaty of Mutual Cooperation and Security Between the United States of America and Japan [4]

Signed at Washington January 19, 1960
Ratification advised by the Senate June 22, 1960
Ratified by Japan June 21, 1960
Ratifications exchanged at Tokyo June 23, 1960
Proclaimed by the President of the U.S. June 27, 1960
Entered into force June 23, 1960
With Agreed Minute and Exchange of Notes

TREATY

The United States of America and Japan,

Desiring to strengthen the bonds of peace and friendship traditionally existing between them, and to uphold the principles of democracy, individual liberty, and the rule of law,

Desiring further to encourage closer economic cooperation between them and to promote conditions of economic stability and well-being in their countries,

Reaffirming their faith in the purposes and principles of the Charter of the United Nations, and their desire to live in peace with all peoples and all governments,

Recognizing that they have the inherent right of individual or collective self-defense as affirmed in the Charter of the United Nations,

Considering that they have a common concern in the maintenance of international peace and security in the Far East,

Having resolved to conclude a treaty of mutual cooperation and security,

Therefore agree as follows:

ARTICLE I

The Parties undertake, as set forth in the Charter of the United Nations, to settle any international disputes in which they may be

[4] U.S. Department of State, *Security Treaty Between the United States of America and Japan* [and related documents] (Vol. 11, *United States Treaties and Other International Agreements*, TIAS 4509), Washington, U.S. Government Printing Office, 1961, pp. 1633–1635.

involved by peaceful means in such a manner that international peace and security and justice are not endangered and to refrain in their international relations from the threat or use of force against the territorial integrity or political independence of any state, or in any other manner inconsistent with the purposes of the United Nations.

The Parties will endeavor in concert with other peace-loving countries to strengthen the United Nations so that its mission of maintaining international peace and security may be discharged more effectively.

ARTICLE II

The Parties will contribute toward the further development of peaceful and friendly international relations by strengthening their free institutions, by bringing about a better understanding of the principles upon which these institutions are founded, and by promoting conditions of stability and well-being. They will seek to eliminate conflict in their international economic policies and will encourage economic collaboration between them.

ARTICLE III

The Parties, individually and in cooperation with each other, by means of continuous and effective self-help and mutual aid will maintain and develop, subject to their constitutional provisions, their capacities to resist armed attack.

ARTICLE IV

The Parties will consult together from time to time regarding the implementation of this Treaty, and, at the request of either Party, whenever the security of Japan or international peace and security in the Far East is threatened.

ARTICLE V

Each Party recognizes that an armed attack against either Party in the territories under the administration of Japan would be dangerous to its own peace and safety and declares that it would act to meet the common danger in accordance with its constitutional provisions and processes.

Any such armed attack and all measures taken as a result thereof shall be immediately reported to the Security Council of the United Nations in accordance with the provisions of Article 51 of the Charter. Such measures shall be terminated when the Security Council has taken the measures necessary to restore and maintain international peace and security.

ARTICLE VI

For the purpose of contributing to the security of Japan and the maintenance of international peace and security in the Far East, the United States of America is granted the use by its land, air and naval forces of facilities and areas in Japan.

The use of these facilities and areas as well as the status of United States armed forces in Japan shall be governed by a separate agreement, replacing the Administrative Agreement under Article III of the Security Treaty between the United States of America and Japan, signed at Tokyo on February 28, 1952, as amended, and by such other arrangements as may be agreed upon.

ARTICLE VII

This Treaty does not affect and shall not be interpreted as affecting in any way the rights and obligations of the Parties under the Charter of the United Nations or the responsibility of the United Nations for the maintenance of international peace and security.

ARTICLE VIII

This Treaty shall be ratified by the United States of America and Japan in accordance with their respective constitutional processes and will enter into force on the date on which the instruments of ratification thereof have been exchanged by them in Tokyo.

ARTICLE IX

The Security Treaty between the United States of America and Japan signed at the city of San Francisco on September 8, 1951 shall expire upon the entering into force of this Treaty.

ARTICLE X

This Treaty shall remain in force until in the opinion of the Governments of the United States of America and Japan there shall have come into force such United Nations arrangements as will satisfactorily provide for the maintenance of international peace and security in the Japan area.

However, after the Treaty has been in force for ten years, either Party may give notice to the other Party of its intention to terminate the Treaty, in which case the Treaty shall terminate one year after such notice has been given.

In witness whereof the undersigned Plenipotentiaries have signed this Treaty.

Done in duplicate at Washington in the English and Japanese languages, both equally authentic, this 19th day of January, 1960.

FOR THE UNITED STATES OF AMERICA:

Christian A. Herter
Douglas MacArthur 2nd
J. Graham Parsons

FOR JAPAN:

Nobusuke Kishi
Aiichirō Fujiyama
Mitsujirō Ishii
Tadashi Adachi
Koichirō Asakai

AGREED MINUTE TO THE TREATY OF MUTUAL COOPERATION AND SECURITY

Japanese Plenipotentiary:

While the question of the status of the islands administered by the United States under Article 3 of the Treaty of Peace with Japan has not been made a subject of discussion in the course of treaty negotiations, I would like to emphasize the strong concern of the Government and people of Japan for the safety of the people of these islands since Japan possesses residual sovereignty over these islands. If an armed attack occurs or is threatened against these islands, the two countries will of course consult together closely under Article IV of the Treaty of Mutual Cooperation and Security. In the event of an armed attack, it is the intention of the Government of Japan to explore with the United States measures which it might be able to take for the welfare of the islanders.

United States Plenipotentiary:

In the event of an armed attack against these islands, the United States Government will consult at once with the Government of Japan and intends to take the necessary measures for the defense of these islands, and to do its utmost to secure the welfare of the islanders.

C.A.H.
N.K.

Washington, January 19, 1960

FIRST EXCHANGE OF NOTES

(p. 1646)

Washington, January 19, 1960

Excellency:

I have the honour to refer to the Treaty of Mutual Cooperation and Security between Japan and the United States of America signed today, and to inform Your Excellency that the following is the understanding of the Government of Japan concerning the implementation of Article VI thereof:

> Major changes in the deployment into Japan of United States armed forces, major changes in their equipment, and the use of facilities and areas in Japan as bases for military combat operations to be undertaken from Japan other than those conducted under Article V of the said Treaty, shall be the subjects of prior consultation with the Government of Japan.

I should be appreciative if Your Excellency would confirm on behalf of your Government that this is also the understanding of the Government of the United States of America.

I avail myself of this opportunity to renew to Your Excellency the assurance of my highest consideration.

Nobusuke Kishi

His Excellency
    Christian A. Herter
        Secretary of State
            of the United States of America

(p. 1647)

Department of State
Washington
January 19, 1960

Excellency:

I have the honor to acknowledge the receipt of Your Excellency's Note of today's date, which reads as follows:

"I have the honour to refer to the Treaty of Mutual Cooperation and Security between Japan and the United States of America signed today, and to inform Your Excellency that the following is the understanding of the Government of Japan concerning the implementation of Article VI thereof:

Major changes in the deployment into Japan of United States armed forces, major changes in their equipment, and the use of facilities and areas in Japan as bases for military combat operations to be undertaken from Japan other than those conducted under Article V of the said Treaty, shall be the subjects of prior consultation with the Government of Japan.

I should be appreciative if Your Excellency would confirm on behalf of your Government that this is also the understanding of the Government of the United States of America.

I avail myself of this opportunity to renew to Your Excellency the assurance of my highest consideration."

I have the honor to confirm on behalf of my Government that the foregoing is also the understanding of the Government of the United States of America.

Accept, Excellency, the renewed assurances of my highest consideration.

Christian A. Herter
Secretary of State of the
United States of America

His Excellency
Nobusuke Kishi
Prime Minister of Japan

SECOND EXCHANGE OF NOTES

Department of State
Washington
January 19, 1960

Excellency:

I have the honor to refer to the Security Treaty between the United States of America and Japan signed at the city of San Francisco on September 8, 1951, the exchange of notes effected on the same date between Mr. Shigeru Yoshida, Prime Minister of Japan, and Mr. Dean Acheson, Secretary of State of the United States of America, and the Agreement Regarding the Status of the United Nations Forces in Japan signed at Tokyo on February 19, 1954, as well as the Treaty of Mutual Cooperation and Security between the United States of America and Japan signed today. It is the understanding of my Government that:

1. The above-mentioned exchange of notes will continue to be in force so long as the Agreement Regarding the Status of the United Nations Forces in Japan remains in force.

2. The expression "those facilities and areas the use of which is provided to the United States of America under the Security Treaty between Japan and the United States of America" in Article V, paragraph 2 of the above-mentioned Agreement is understood to mean the facilities and areas the use of which is granted to the United States of America under the Treaty of Mutual Cooperation and Security.

3. The use of the facilities and areas by the United States armed forces under the Unified Command of the United Nations established pursuant to the Security Council Resolution of July 7, 1950, and their status in Japan are governed by arrangements made pursuant to the Treaty of Mutual Cooperation and Security.

I should be grateful if Your Excellency could confirm on behalf of your Government that the understanding of my Government stated in the foregoing numbered paragraphs is also the understanding of your Government and that this understanding shall enter into operation on the date of the entry into force of the Treaty of Mutual Cooperation and Security signed at Washington on January 19, 1960.

Accept, Excellency, the renewed assurances of my highest consideration.

Christian A. Herter
Secretary of State of the
United States of America

His Excellency
Nobusuke Kishi
Prime Minister of Japan

Washington, January 19, 1960

Excellency:

I have the honour to acknowledge the receipt of Your Excellency's Note of today's date, which reads as follows:

"I have the honor to refer to the Security Treaty between the United States of America and Japan signed at the city of San Francisco on September 8, 1951, the exchange of notes effected on the same date between Mr. Shigeru Yoshida, Prime Minister of Japan, and Mr. Dean Acheson, Secretary of State of the United States of America, and the Agreement Regarding the Status of the United Nations Forces in Japan signed at Tokyo on February 19, 1954, as well as the Treaty of Mutual Cooperation and Security between the United States of America and Japan signed today. It is the understanding of my Government that:

1. The above-mentioned exchange of notes will continue to be in force so long as the Agreement Regarding the Status of the United Nations Forces in Japan remains in force.

2. The expression "those facilities and areas the use of which is provided to the United States of America under the Security Treaty between Japan and the United States of America" in Article V, paragraph 2 of the above-mentioned Agreement is understood to mean the facilities and areas the use of which is granted to the United States of America under the Treaty of Mutual Cooperation and Security.

3. The use of the facilities and areas by the United States armed forces under the Unified Command of the United Nations established pursuant to the Security Council Resolution of July 7, 1950, and their status in Japan are governed by arrangements made pursuant to the Treaty of Mutual Cooperation and Security.

I should be grateful if Your Excellency could confirm on behalf of your Government that the understanding of my Government stated in the foregoing numbered paragraphs is also the understanding of your Government and that this understanding shall enter into operation on the date of the entry into force of the Treaty of Mutual Cooperation and Security signed at Washington on January 19, 1960."

I have the honour to confirm on behalf of my Government that the foregoing is also the understanding of the Government of Japan.

I avail myself of this opportunity to renew to Your Excellency the assurance of my highest consideration.

Nobusuke Kishi

His Excellency
   Christian A. Herter
      Secretary of State
         of the United States of America

THIRD EXCHANGE OF NOTES

Washington, January 19, 1960

Dear Secretary Herter:

I wish to refer to the Treaty of Mutual Cooperation and Security between Japan and the United States of America signed today. Under Article IV of the Treaty, the two Governments will consult together from time to time regarding the implementation of the Treaty, and, at the request of either Government, whenever the security of Japan or international peace and security in the Far East is threatened. The exchange of notes under Article VI of the Treaty specifies certain matters as the subjects of prior consultation with the Government of Japan.

Such consultations will be carried on between the two Governments through appropriate channels. At the same time, however, I feel that the establishment of a special committee which could as appropriate be used for these consultations between the Governments would prove very useful. This committee, which would meet whenever requested by either side, could also consider any matters underlying and related to security affairs which would serve to promote understanding between the two Governments and contribute to the strengthening of cooperative relations between the two countries in the field of security.

Under this proposal the present "Japanese-American Committee on Security" established by the Governments of the United States and Japan on August 6, 1957, would be replaced by this new committee which might be called "The Security Consultative Committee." I would also recommend that the membership of this new committee be the same as the membership of the "Japanese-American Committee on Security," namely on the Japanese side, the Minister for Foreign Affairs, who will preside on the Japanese side, and the Director General of the Defense Agency, and on the United States side, the United States Ambassador to Japan, who will serve as Chairman on the United States side, and the Commander-in-Chief, Pacific, who will be the Ambassador's principal advisor on military and defense matters. The Commander, United States Forces, Japan, will serve as alternate for the Commander-in-Chief, Pacific.

374

I would appreciate very much your views on this matter.

Most sincerely,

Nobusuke Kishi

His Excellency
  Christian A. Herter
    Secretary of State
      of the United States of America

Department of State
Washington
January 19, 1960

Dear Mr. Prime Minister:

The receipt is acknowledged of your Note of today's date suggesting the establishment of "The Security Consultative Committee." I fully agree to your proposal and share your view that such a committee can contribute to strengthening the cooperative relations between the two countries in the field of security. I also agree to your proposal regarding the membership of this committee.

Most sincerely,

Christian A. Herter

His Excellency
  Nobusuke Kishi
    Prime Minister of Japan

Joint Communiqué, January 19, 1960 [5]

Between President Eisenhower and Prime Minister Kishi

The President of the United States and the Prime Minister of Japan conferred at the White House today prior to the formal signing of the Treaty of Mutual Cooperation and Security between Japan and the United States. Their discussions were devoted chiefly to a broad and comprehensive review of current international developments, and to an examination of Japanese-American relations. Japanese Minister of Foreign Affairs Fujiyama and American Secretary of State Herter also took part in the White House talks. Later the Prime Minister and his party conferred with the Secretary of State on matters of mutual concern to the two countries.

I

The President and the Prime Minister first discussed the international situation. The President told the Prime Minister of the profound impression made upon him during his recent trip to South Asia, the Near East, Africa and Europe by the overwhelming desire throughout these areas for early realization of the goals of the United Nations, international peace, respect for human rights, and a better life. In discussing the international situation, the President stated his determination to exert every effort at the impending Summit meeting to achieve meaningful progress toward these goals. The Prime Minister expressed full agreement and support for the President's determination.

In this connection, the President and the Prime Minister agreed that disarmament, with the essential guarantees of inspection and verification, is a problem of urgent and central importance to all nations, whose resolution would contribute greatly to reducing the burden of armaments and the risk of war. They expressed the further hope that early agreement can be reached on an adequately safeguarded program for the discontinuance of nuclear weapons tests. They concluded that the world is entering a period affording important opportunities which they have every intention of explor-

[5] U.S. Department of State, "Joint Communique, January 19" (White House press release dated January 19, 1960), *Department of State Bulletin*, Vol. 42, No. 1076, February 8, 1960, pp. 179–181.

ing most seriously, but only on the basis of tested performance not merely promises. Both leaders recognized that all of man's intellect, wisdom and imagination must be brought into full play to achieve a world at peace under justice and freedom. They expressed the conviction that, during this period and particularly until all nations abide faithfully by the purposes and principles of the U.N. and forego the resort to force, it is essential for free nations to maintain by every means their resolution, their unity and their strength.

II

The President and the Prime Minister considered the security relationship between the United States and Japan in the light of their evaluation of the current international situation and declared that this close relationship is essential to the achievement of peace in justice and freedom. They are convinced that the partnership and cooperation between their two nations is strengthened by the new treaty which has been drawn up on the basis of the principles of equal sovereignty and mutual cooperation that characterize the present relationship between the two countries. Both leaders look forward to the ratification of the treaty and to the celebration this year of the contennial of Japan's first diplomatic mission to the United States as further demonstrations of the strength and continuity of Japanese-American friendship.

In reviewing relations between Japan and the United States since their last meeting in June of 1957, the President and the Prime Minister expressed particular gratification at the success of efforts since that time to develop the new era in relations between the two countries, based on common interest, mutual trust, and the principles of cooperation.

Both the President and the Prime Minister looked ahead to continued close cooperation between the two countries within the framework of the new Treaty of Mutual Cooperation and Security. They are convinced that the treaty will materially strengthen peace and security in the Far East and advance the cause of peace and freedom throughout the world. They are convinced also that the treaty will foster an atmosphere of mutual confidence. In this connection, the Prime Minister discussed with the President the question of prior consultation under the new treaty. The President assured him that the United States Government has no intention of acting in a manner contrary to the wishes of the Japanese Government with respect to the matters involving prior consultation under the treaty.

The President and the Prime Minister also discussed the situation in Asia. They reaffirmed their belief that they should maintain close contact and consultation with relation to future developments in this area. They agreed that Japan's increasing participation in international discussion of the problems of Asia will be in the interest of the free world.

III

The President and the Prime Minister agreed that the expansion of trade among free nations, the economic progress and elevation of living standards in less developed countries are of paramount importance, and will contribute to stability and progress so essential to the achievement of peace in the world.

The President and the Prime Minister exchanged views on the European economic and trade communities and on the role that can be played by the industrialized Free World countries in the economic development of the less developed areas. Both leaders called particular attention to the urgent desire of peoples in the less developed areas of the world for the economic advancement without which they cannot preserve their freedom. They stressed the role which increasingly must be played by the industrialized nations of the free world in assisting the progress of the less developed areas. The President particularly referred to the increasing role the Japanese people are playing in the economic development of free Asia.

In considering economic relations between the United States and Japan, the President and the Prime Minister recognized that trade between their two nations is of great benefit to both countries, noting that the United States is the largest purchaser of Japanese exports, and Japan is the second largest buyer of American goods. They expressed gratification at the growth of mutually profitable trade between the two countries. They reaffirmed their conviction that the continued and orderly expansion of world trade, through the avoidance of arbitrary and new unnecessary trade restrictions, and through active measures to remove existing obstacles, is essential to the well-being and progress of both countries.

The Prime Minister stressed the importance of the United States and Japan consulting on a continuing basis with regard to economic matters of mutual interest. The President expressed full agreement to this view.

IV

The President expressed his particular gratification that the Prime Minister could come to Washington on this occasion so important in United States–Japanese relations. The Prime Minister expressed his appreciation for the opportunity to meet again with the President.

The President and the Prime Minister agreed that their talks will contribute to the continued strengthening of the United States–Japanese partnership.

Joint Declaration of the Seven Major Newspapers, June 17, 1960 [6]

WIPE OUT VIOLENCE, PRESERVE PARLIAMENTARY DEMOCRACY

Quite apart from whatever may have been the causes, the bloody incidents on the night of June 15 inside and outside the Diet were utterly deplorable and threw parliamentary democracy into a crisis. Never before have we been so deeply disturbed as we are now about the future of Japan.

In a democracy, differences should be contested with words. Whatever the causes and whatever the political difficulties may be, the use of violence to settle matters cannot be permitted under any circumstances. If a social trend permitting violence should once become general, we believe that democracy will die and a grave situation will arise which will endanger Japan's national existence.

Consequently, the Government, which bears the grave responsibility for the present situation, must speedily exert every effort to resolve the current situation. In this connection the Government must make it clear that it will respond to the sound judgment of the people. At the same time, since the suspension of the Diet's functions is one of the reasons for the current confusion, the Socialist and Democratic Socialist Parties should, at this time, lay aside their disputes for the time being and return to the Diet. We sincerely believe that it is the wish of the people that they return to the Diet and cooperate in resolving the situation by restoring Diet procedures to normal.

We therefore sincerely appeal to the Government and Opposition parties to respond to the fervent wishes of the people by agreeing to protect parliamentary democracy and by dispelling the unusual anxiety now troubling the people.

> The Sankei Newspapers
> The Tokyo Shimbun
> The Tokyo Times Shimbun
> The Nihon Keizai Shimbun
> The Mainichi Newspapers
> The Yomiuri Newspapers
> The Asahi Newspapers

[6] Translation from the *Asahi Evening News,* June 17, 1960.

BIBLIOGRAPHY
INDEX

Bibliography

NOTE: It has been difficult to make the usual distinction between primary and secondary source material because the same document has sometimes been used for its factual or interpretive content and for evidence of attitudes by the author which influenced the political situation. Where doubt has existed, such documents have generally been listed as secondary sources. In selecting Japanese materials, the approach has been to include all pertinent material even though it may have had only marginal use in this study, on grounds that such a listing may be helpful to scholars who are beginning research on related aspects of the treaty crisis. Though this study has made much use of the Japanese press, it has not been practicable to list each article consulted and only the most significant articles have been included. The newspapers most consulted are listed in Japanese language material, Section II-4.

ENGLISH LANGUAGE MATERIAL

I. PRIMARY SOURCES

Cole, Allan B. and Nakanishi, Naomi, eds., *Japanese Public Opinion Polls with Socio-political Significance, 1947–1957* (3 vols., Ann Arbor: University Microfilms, Inc., 1959).

Japan, Office of the Prime Minister, Bureau of Statistics, *Japan Statistical Yearbook, 1961* (Tokyo: Japan Statistical Association, 1962).

U.S., Congress, Senate, Committee on Foreign Relations, *Treaty of Mutual Cooperation and Security with Japan, Hearing before the Committee on Foreign Relations*, United States Senate, 86th Cong., 2d sess., June 7, 1960 (Washington: U.S. Government Printing Office, 1960).

U.S., Department of State, *Administrative Agreement Under Article III of the Security Treaty Between the United States of America and Japan, United States Treaties and Other International Agreements*, Vol. 3, Part 3, TIAS 2492 (Washington: U.S. Government Printing Office, 1955), pp. 3341–3419.

————, *Agreement Under Article VI of the Treaty of Mutual Cooperation and Security: Facilities and Areas and the Status of United States Armed Forces in Japan, United States Treaties and Other International Agreements*, Vol. 11, Part 2, TIAS 4510

(Washington: U.S. Government Printing Office, 1961), pp. 1652–1674.

U.S., Department of State, *Annual and Progressive Reduction in Japanese Expenditures Under Article XXV 2 (b) of the Administrative Agreement of February 28, 1952, United States Treaties and Other International Agreements*, Vol. 8, Part 2, TIAS 3886 (Washington: U.S. Government Printing Office, 1958), pp. 1377–1385.

————, *Conference for Conclusion and Signature of Treaty of Peace with Japan, 1951*, Publication 4613 (Washington: U.S. Government Printing Office, 1952).

————, *Interpretation of Security Treaty and Administrative Agreement: Relation to the Charter of the United Nations, United States Treaties and Other International Agreements*, Vol. 8, Part 2, TIAS 3910 (Washington: U.S. Government Printing Office, 1958), pp. 1571–1577.

————, "Joint Communiqué, January 19," *Department of State Bulletin*, Vol. 42, February 8, 1960, pp. 179–181.

————, "Joint Communiqué of June 21, 1957 Issued by President Eisenhower and Prime Minister Kishi," *Department of State Bulletin*, Vol. 37, July 8, 1957, pp. 51–53.

————, "Joint Statement of September 11," *Department of State Bulletin*, Vol. 39, October 6, 1958, pp. 532–533.

————, *Mutual Defense Assistance Agreements Between the United States and Japan, United States Treaties and Other International Agreements*, Vol. 5, Part 1, TIAS 2957 (Washington: U.S. Government Printing Office, 1955), pp. 661–716.

————, *Mutual Defense Assistance: References in Agreement of March 8, 1954, to Security Treaty and Administrative Agreement, United States Treaties and Other International Agreements*, Vol. 11, Part 2, TIAS 4511 (Washington: U.S. Government Printing Office, 1961), pp. 1758–1759.

————, *Security Treaty Between the United States of America and Japan, United States Treaties and Other International Agreements*, Vol. 3, TIAS 2491 (Washington: U.S. Government Printing Office, 1955), pp. 3329–3340.

————, *Treaty of Mutual Cooperation and Security Between the United States of America and Japan with Agreed Minute and Exchange of Notes, United States Treaties and Other International Agreements*, Vol. 11, Part 2, TIAS 4509 (Washington: U.S. Government Printing Office, 1961), pp. 1632–1651.

II. Secondary Sources

1. books

Battistini, Lawrence H., *The Postwar Student Struggle in Japan* (Tokyo: Charles E. Tuttle Co., 1956).

Borton, Hugh and others, *Japan Between East and West* (New York: Harper for the Council on Foreign Relations, 1957).

Burks, Ardath W., *The Government of Japan* (New York: Thomas Y. Crowell Co., 1961).

Cary, James, *Japan Today: Reluctant Ally* (New York: Praeger, 1962).

Cohen, Bernard C., *The Political Process and Foreign Policy: The Making of the Japanese Peace Settlement* (Princeton: Princeton University Press, 1957).

Cole, Allan B., *Japanese Society and Politics: The Impact of Social Stratification and Mobility on Politics* (Boston: Graduate School of Boston University, 1956).

Dore, R. P., *City Life in Japan* (Berkeley and Los Angeles: University of California Press, 1958).

Dunn, Frederick S., *Peace-making and the Settlement with Japan* (Princeton: Princeton University Press, 1963).

Ike, Nobutaka, *Japanese Politics* (New York: Alfred A. Knopf, 1957).

Japan Newspaper Publishers and Editors Association, *The Japanese Press, 1961* (Tokyo: Dai-Nippon Printing Co., 1961).

Katō, Hidetoshi, ed., *Japanese Popular Culture* (Tokyo: Charles E. Tuttle Co., 1959).

Kawai, Kazuo, *Japan's American Interlude* (Chicago: University of Chicago Press, 1960).

Levine, Solomon B., *Industrial Relations in Postwar Japan* (Urbana: University of Illinois Press, 1958).

Maki, John M., *Government and Politics in Japan: The Road to Democracy* (New York: Praeger, 1962).

McNelly, Theodore, *Contemporary Government of Japan* (Boston: Houghton Mifflin Co., 1963).

Mendel, Douglas H. Jr., *The Japanese People and Foreign Policy: A Study of Public Opinion in Post-treaty Japan* (Berkeley and Los Angeles: University of California Press, 1961).

Morris, I. I., *Nationalism and the Right Wing in Japan* (London: Oxford University Press, 1960).

385

Nakamura, Kikuo and Matsumura, Yutaka, *Political Handbook of Japan, 1958* (Tokyo: Tokyo News Service, Ltd., 1958).

Reischauer, Edwin O., *The United States and Japan* (rev. ed., Cambridge: Harvard University Press, 1957).

Scalapino, Robert A. and Masumi, Junnosuke, *Parties and Politics in Contemporary Japan* (Berkeley and Los Angeles: University of California Press, 1962).

Schwantes, Robert S., *Japanese and Americans: A Century of Cultural Relations* (New York: Harper for the Council on Foreign Relations, 1955).

Swearingen, Rodger, and Langer, Paul, *Red Flag in Japan* (Cambridge: Harvard University Press, 1952).

Whittemore, Edward P., *The Press in Japan Today: A Case Study* (Columbia: University of South Carolina Press, 1961).

Yanaga, Chitoshi, *Japanese People and Politics* (New York: John Wiley and Sons, Inc., 1956).

2. ARTICLES AND PERIODICALS

Ayusawa, Iwao, "Japanese Labor in 1959," *Oriental Economist,* Vol. 28, No. 591, January 1960, pp. 29–32.

"Basic Trends, Political: Bureaucracy on the Move," *Japan Quarterly,* Vol. 6, No. 1, January-March 1959, pp. 1–5.

"Basic Trends, Political: The 'Back Home' Movement," *Japan Quarterly,* Vol. 7, No. 4, October-December 1960, pp. 398–401.

Cary, Otis, " 'University' a Romantic Word," *Washington Post,* May 20, 1962.

Chiba, Yūjirō, "Revision of Police Duties Law," *Contemporary Japan,* Vol. 25, No. 4, March 1959, pp. 621–634.

Colton, Kenneth E. and others, eds., "Japan Since Recovery of Independence," *Annals of the American Academy of Political and Social Science,* Vol. 308, November 1956.

Colton, Kenneth, "Japan's Leaders, 1958," *Current History,* Vol. 34, No. 200, April 1958, pp. 228–236.

Cowley, George, "Study of Contemporary Attitudes of Japanese Youth" (Unpublished manuscript dated May 25, 1961), made available by the author from the Embassy of Canada, Tokyo.

Dore, R. P., "Attitudes, Power and Ideas," *Pacific Affairs,* Vol. 30, No. 3, September 1957, pp. 260–265.

———, "The Japanese Socialist Party and 'Structural Reform,' " *Asian Survey,* Vol. 1, No. 8, October 1961, pp. 3–15.

———, "The Tokyo Institute of Science of Thought—A Survey

Report," *Far Eastern Quarterly*, Vol. 13, No. 1, November 1953, pp. 23–26.

Dubrovsky, D., "The Sharpening Political Crisis in Japan," *International Affairs* (Moscow), August 1960, pp. 16–21.

Feuer, Lewis S., "A Talk with the Zengakuren," *New Leader*, Vol. 44, No. 18, May 1, 1961, pp. 16–20.

Finn, Dallas, "What the Japanese Intellectuals Are Thinking," *American Scholar*, Vol. 24, No. 4, Autumn 1955, pp. 443–455.

"Firmly Oppose the Japan–U.S. Military Alliance," *Peking Review*, No. 3, January 19, 1960, pp. 6–7.

Fujiyama Aiichirō, "The United States of America and Japan," *Contemporary Japan*, Vol. 26, May 1960, 383–388.

Herter, Christian A., "The Department Recommends Senate Approval of Mutual Security Treaty with Japan," *Department of State Bulletin*, Vol. 42, June 27, 1960, pp. 1029–1032.

Hook, Sidney, " 'Common Sense' in Japan," *New Leader*, Vol. 42, October 5, 1959, pp. 10–12.

———, "Which Way Japan?" *New Leader*, Vol. 42, February 9, 1959, pp. 3–7.

Hosokawa, Ryūgen, "Portrait of a Premier," *Japan Times*, May 16–17, 1957.

Howells, William Dean, "The Japanese Socialist Party and National Security, 1955–1960" (Unpublished M.A. thesis, East Asian Institute, Columbia University, 1960).

Hudson, G. F., "Neutralism and 'Re-insularization,' " *New Leader*, Vol. 43, No. 34, September 5, 1960, pp. 6–7.

Info (Tokyo), August 1960 (A round-table discussion by Japanese business leaders on the effects of the security treaty crisis).

Jansen, Marius B., "Education, Values and Politics in Japan," *Foreign Affairs*, Vol. 35, No. 4, July 1957, pp. 666–678.

"Japan Today," *New Leader*, Section Two, November 28, 1960.

"Japanese Intellectuals Discuss American-Japanese Relations," *Far Eastern Survey*, Vol. 39, No. 10, October 1960.

"Japan's Treaty Trouble," *Eastern World*, Vol. 14, No. 6, June 1960, pp. 18–19.

Johnson, Chalmers A., " 'Low Posture' Politics in Japan," *Asian Survey*, Vol. 3, No. 1, January 1963, pp. 17–30.

Kano, Hisaakira, "Views on U.S.-Japanese Relations," *Japan Quarterly*, Vol. 4, No. 2, April-June 1957, pp. 152–158.

Kerlinger, Fred N., "Decision-making in Japan," *Social Forces*, Vol. 30, No. 1, October 1951, pp. 36–41.

Kimura, Kihachirō, "Effects of the Administrative Agreement," *Contemporary Japan*, Vol. 31, Nos. 1–3, 1952, pp. 113–117.

Koyama Kenichi, "The Zengakuren," *New Politics*, Vol. 1, No. 2, Winter 1962, pp. 124–134.

Kublin, Hyman, "Japanese Politics and the Socialist Minority," *Yale Review*, Vol. 46, No. 4, June 1957, pp. 571–585.

Kudashev, L., "Contrary to Japan's National Interests," *International Affairs* (Moscow), No. 1, 1960, pp. 63–68.

Kuo Mo-jo, "Resolutely Crush the Military Alliance between the U.S. and Japanese Reactionaries," *Peking Review*, No. 4, January 21, 1960, pp. 14–19.

Kuroda, Kazuo, "Whither the Student Movement?" *Japan Times*, July 12, 1958.

Lange, William, "Some Remarks on the Japanese Press," *Japan Quarterly*, Vol. 7, No. 3, July-September 1960, pp. 281–287.

Langer, Paul F., "Japan and the West," *Current History*, Vol. 34, No. 200, April 1958, pp. 208–213.

———, "Moscow, Peking and Japan: Views and Approaches," *RAND Corporation Paper* P-2098, September 12, 1960.

Lifton, Robert Jay, "Japanese Youth, The Search for the New and the Pure," *American Scholar*, Vol. 30, No. 3, Summer 1961, pp. 332–344.

Maruyama, Masao, "Nationalism in Postwar Japan" (Tokyo: Japan Institute of Pacific Relations, 1950).

Matsushita, Masatoshi, "The Japanese Intellectual: Who Is He? What Is He Like?" *Japan Times*, July 7, 1961.

McNelly, Theodore, "The Japanese Constitution: Child of the Cold War," *Political Science Quarterly*, Vol. 34, No. 2, June 1959, pp. 176–193.

Mendel, Douglas H. Jr., "Behind the 1960 Japanese Diet Elections," *Asian Survey*, Vol. 1, No. 1, March 1961, pp. 3–12.

Millian, Kenneth W., "The Labor Scene," *Japan Times*, January 28 and July 14, 1957.

Moos, Felix, "Religion and Politics in Japan: The Case of the Sōka Gakkai," *Asian Survey*, Vol. 3, No. 3, March 1963, pp. 136–142.

Morris, I. I., "Policeman and Student in Japanese Politics," *Pacific Affairs*, Vol. 32, No. 1, March 1959, pp. 5–17.

Murata Kiyoaki, "Fujiyama: Kishi's True Friend," *Japan Times*, July 23, 1957.

———, "Kishi: A Reformed Fascist?" *Japan Times*, March 2, 1957.

Naitō, Kunio, "Japanese Leader Views American Policy, New Treaty, Meaning of Neutralism," *Amherst Student*, January 30, 1961, pp. 4ff.

Naoi Takeo, "Behind the Japanese Socialist Split," *New Leader*, Vol. 42, November 16, 1959, pp. 19–20.

———, "Japan After the Assassination," *New Leader*, Vol. 43, November 7, 1960, pp. 8–9.

———, "Japanese Socialist Mission to Peking," *New Leader*, Vol. 42, April 13, 1959, pp. 9–10.

———, " 'New Course' in Japanese Trade Unionism," *New Leader*, Vol. 43, April 25, 1960, pp. 20–21.

———, "Socialist Setback in Japan," *New Leader*, Vol. 42, June 29, 1959, pp. 7–8.

Nishi, Haruhiko, "Some Comments Upon the Projected Revision of the Japan–U.S. Security Treaty" (mimeographed), February 11, 1959.

Ōi, Atsushi, "Rearmament and Japan: Thoughts on a Familiar Bogey," *Asian Survey*, Vol. 1, No. 7, September 1961, pp. 10–15.

Olson, Lawrence, "The Police Bill Controversy: An Episode in Parliamentary Growth," *American Universities Field Staff Letter* LO-12-'58, November 28, 1958.

———, "A Japanese Marxist—Itsurō Sakisaka: Theoretician and Activist," American Universities Field Staff, *East Asia Series*, Vol. 9, No. 4 (Japan), Tokyo, March 15, 1961.

Oppler, Alfred C., "The Sunakawa Case: Its Legal and Political Implications," *Political Science Quarterly*, Vol. 76, No. 2, June 1961, pp. 241–263.

Parsons, J. Graham, "The Mutual Security Program in the Far East," *Department of State Bulletin*, Vol. 42, May 16, 1960, pp. 782–789.

Passin, Herbert, "Japan and the H-Bomb," *Bulletin of the Atomic Scientists*, Vol. 11, No. 8, October 1955, pp. 289–292.

———, "The Sources of Protest in Japan," *American Political Science Review*, Vol. 16, No. 2, June 1962, pp. 391–403.

Quigley, Harold S., "Revising the Japanese Constitution," *Foreign Affairs*, Vol. 38, No. 1, October 1959, pp. 140–145.

Reischauer, Edwin O., "Some Thoughts on Japanese Democracy," *Japan Quarterly*, Vol. 8, No. 1, January-March 1961, pp. 98–103.

———, "The Broken Dialogue with Japan," *Foreign Affairs*, Vol. 39, No. 1, October 1960, pp. 11–26.

Rockefeller, John D. IV, "Student Gripes as Heard by Son of Famous Family," *Life*, Vol. 48, No. 24, June 20, 1960, pp. 28–29.

Rockefeller, John D. IV, "Students of Japan," *New York Times Magazine*, June 5, 1960.

Rovere, Richard H., "Letter from Washington, June 18," *New Yorker*, June 25, 1960, pp. 85–90.

Rōyama, Masamichi, "The U.S.–Japanese Security Treaty: A Japanese View," *Japan Quarterly*, Vol. 4, No. 3, July-September 1957, pp. 284–295.

Scalapino, Robert A., "Japanese Politics Since Independence," *Current History*, Vol. 34, No. 200, April 1958, pp. 198–204.

———, "Japanese Socialism in Crisis," *Foreign Affairs*, Vol. 38, No. 2, January 1960, pp. 318–328.

Seidensticker, Edward, "An Eastern Weimar Republic?" *New Leader*, Vol. 43, No. 34, September 5, 1960, pp. 7–9.

———, "True Rebel Is Rare in Highbrow Crowd," *Washington Post*, May 20, 1962.

Seki, Yoshihiko, "New Trends in Japanese Socialism," *Japan Quarterly*, Vol. 7, No. 2 (April-June 1960), pp. 142–151.

———, "Outdated Sakisaka Theory on Socialism," *Japan Times*, February 2, 1959 (translated and condensed from *Keizai Ōrai*, February 1959).

———, "The Democratic Socialist Party," *New Politics*, Vol. 1, No. 2, Winter 1962, pp. 144–150.

Shimbori, Michiya and others, "Comparison Between Pre- and Postwar Student Movements in Japan," *Sociology of Education*, Vol. 37, No. 1 (Fall 1963), pp. 59–70.

Shimizu, Ikutarō, "The Intellectuals," *New Politics*, Vol. 1, No. 2, Winter 1962, pp. 151–158.

Sissons, David C. S., "Recent Developments in Japan's Socialist Movement," *Far Eastern Survey*, Vol. 29, No. 1, March 1960, pp. 40–47, and No. 2, June 1960, pp. 89–92.

———, "The Dispute Over Japan's Police Law," *Pacific Affairs*, Vol. 32, No. 1, March 1959, pp. 34–45.

Smyth, Hugh H., "New Look in Japanese-American Affairs," *Eastern World*, Vol. 14, No. 6, June 1960, pp. 16–17.

Soukup, James R., "Labor and Politics in Japan: a Study of Interest-group Attitudes and Activities," *Journal of Politics*, Vol. 22, No. 2, May 1960, pp. 314–337.

Sugai, Shichi, "The Japanese Police System," in Robert E. Ward, ed., *Five Studies in Japanese Politics* (Ann Arbor: University of Michigan Press, 1957), pp. 1–14.

Tiltman, Hessell, "The Threat from the Left," *Asahi Evening News*, June 28, 1960.

Totten, George O., "Problems of Japanese Socialist Leadership," *Pacific Affairs*, Vol. 28, No. 2, June 1955, pp. 160–169.

Ukai Nobushige, "The Japanese House of Councillors Election of July 1962," *Asian Survey*, Vol. 2, No. 6, August 1962, pp. 1–8.

U.S. Embassy, Tokyo, *Summaries of Selected Japanese Magazines*, 1959–1960.

Uyehara, Cecil H., "The Social Democratic Movement," *Annals of the American Academy of Political and Social Science*, Vol. 308, November 1958, pp. 54–62.

Wakatake (Bulletin of the Wakatake Kai, London), No. 7, September 1960.

Wada Hirō, "The Socialist Party," *New Politics*, Vol. 1, No. 2, Winter 1962, pp. 135–143.

"What Happened in Japan? A Symposium," *Japan Quarterly*, Vol. 7, No. 4, October-December 1960, pp. 402–427.

Wint, Guy, "Japan's Incalculable New Role," *Asahi Evening News* (from the Observer Service, London), June 27, 1960.

Wurfel, David, "The Violent and the Voiceless in Japanese Politics," *Contemporary Japan*, Vol. 26, No. 4, November 1960, pp. 663–694.

Yanaga, Chitoshi, "Japanese Political Parties," *Parliamentary Affairs*, Vol. 10, No. 3, Summer 1957, pp. 265–276.

Yoshida, Kenichi, "Intellectuals Hoard the Truth," *Washington Post*, May 20, 1962.

3. NEWSPAPERS

Asahi Evening News (Tokyo), January-July 1960.

Japan Times (Tokyo), 1957–1960.

Mainichi Daily News, April-July 1960.

JAPANESE LANGUAGE MATERIAL

I. PRIMARY SOURCES

1. OFFICIAL DOCUMENTS

Gaimushō (Ministry of Foreign Affairs), *Waga Gaikō no Kinkyō* (Recent State of Our Diplomacy), No. 4, June 1960.

Keishichō (Police Agency), Sōmubu, Kōhōka (General Affairs Department, Public Information Section), *Ampo Tōsō o Megutte* (On the Security Treaty Struggle), pamphlet, June 1960.

Keishichō (Police Agency), Sōmubu, Kōhōka (General Affairs Department, Public Information Section), *Shōwa 35-nen Jōhanki no Keibi Jiken o Kaerimite* (Looking Back over the Police Incidents in the First Half of 1960), pamphlet, October 1960.

―――, *6:15 Totsunyū Jiken o Chūshin ni Shite* (Focusing on the Diet Invasion Incident of June 15, 1960), pamphlet, June 1960.

Kōan Chōsa Chō (Public Security Investigation Agency), *Ampo Tōsō no Gaiyō* (An Outline of the Security Treaty Struggle), December 1960.

Kokkai, Dai-Sanjūyon-kai Kokkai, Sangiin, Nichibei Anzen Hoshō Jōyaku Nado Tokubetsu Iinkai, *Giroku* (National Diet, 34th Diet, House of Councillors, Special Committee on the Japan–U.S. Security Treaty, etc., *Proceedings*), February-June 1960.

―――, Dai-Sanjūyon-kai Kokkai, Sangiin, Yosan Iinkai, *Giroku* (34th Diet, House of Councillors, Budget Committee, *Proceedings*), February-March 1960.

―――, Dai-Sanjūyon-kai Kokkai, Shūgiin, Honkai, *Giroku* (34th Diet, House of Representatives, Plenary Session, *Proceedings*), February-March 1960.

―――, Dai-Sanjūyon-kai Kokkai, Shūgiin, Nichibei Anzen Hoshō Jōyaku Nado Tokubetsu Iinkai, *Giroku* (34th Diet, House of Representatives, Special Committee on the Japan–U.S. Security Treaty, etc., *Proceedings*), February-May 1960.

―――, Dai-Sanjūyon-kai Kokkai, Shūgiin, Yosan Iinkai, *Giroku* (34th Diet, House of Representatives, Budget Committee, *Proceedings*), February-March 1960.

2. UNOFFICIAL DOCUMENTS

a. *Party Publications*

Jiyū Minshu Tō (Liberal Democratic Party), *Nichibei Ampo Jōyaku o Naze Kaitei Suru Ka?* (Why Is the Japan–U.S. Security Treaty Being Revised?), pamphlet, August 1959.

―――, *Shin Ampo Jōyaku Hantairon no Mujun* (Contradictions in the Arguments Against the Treaty), Tokyo, June 1960.

Minshu Shakai Tō (Democratic Socialist Party), *Shin Ampo Jōyaku no Shōtai* (The True Character of the New Security Treaty), pamphlet, March 30, 1960.

―――, *Saiken Zenkoku Taikai Tōmu Hōkokusho* (National Reconstruction Convention Party Affairs Report), January 23–25, 1961.

Nihon Kyōsan Tō (Japan Communist Party), "Aikoku to Seigi no

Tōsō o Hatten Saseyo!" (Develop the Patriotic and Just Struggle), handbill, June 10, 1960.

———, *Akahata* (organ newspaper), 1959–1960.

———, "Kishi Naikaku no Arata na Inbō to Danatsu o Funsai Shio!" (Crush the Kishi Cabinet's New Plot and Coercion), *Akahata*, Special Report, June 15, 1960.

———, *Zenei* (monthly organ), 1959–1960.

Nihon Shakai Tō (Japan Socialist Party), *Gekkan Shakai Tō* (monthly organ), 1959–1960.

———, *Kōzō Kaikaku no Riron* (Theory of Structural Reform), 3d ed., Tokyo, March 10, 1961.

———, *Reisenka no Jieiken* (Right of Self-defense in the Cold War), pamphlet, November 10, 1961.

———, *Sekkyoku Chūritsu to Heiwa Undō* (Positive Neutralism and the Peace Movement), pamphlet, October 15, 1961.

———, *Shakai Shimpō* (organ newspaper), 1959–1960.

b. *Newspapers*

Koe Naki Koe no Tayori, 1960.

Kyōtō Nyūsu, bulletin of the People's Council to Prevent Revision of the Security Treaty, 1959–1960.

Mingakken Nyūsu, bulletin of the National Society of Scholars and Researchers For the Protection of Democracy (*Mingakken*), June 10-August 15, 1960

Tokyo Daigaku Shimbun (Tokyo University Newspaper, May 25-June 22, 1960.

Waseda Daigaku Shimbun (Waseda University Newspaper), June 15, 22, 1960.

Zengakuren Tsūshin, June 25, 1960.

c. *Pamphlets and Leaflets*

Ampo Jōyaku Mondai Zenkoku Konwa Kai, *Konwa Kai Shiryō* (Conference Material), Nos. 1–8, December 20, 1958–February 15, 1960.

Ampo Kaitei Soshi Hōritsuka Kaigi, ed., *Yugamerareta Kempō Saiban* (Distorted Constitutional Decision), February 20, 1960.

Ampo Kaitei Soshi Kokumin Kaigi, "Ampo Jōyaku Kaitei Soshi Tōsō Nenpyō" (Chronology of Struggles to Prevent Revision of the Security Treaty), mimeographed, undated.

Doyōkai, *Ampo Kaitei ni Yoseru Waki-ryōshiki no Iken* (Youthful, Sensible Opinion on Treaty Revision), appendix to *Keizai Ōrai*, December 1959.

Katō Shūichi and others, eds., *Kokumin no Chikara de Ampo Kaitei Soshi, Nitchū Kokkō Kaifuku E* (Using the People's Strength, Block the Revised Security Treaty and Restore Japan-China Diplomatic Relations), Tokyo: Nihon Chūgoku Bunka Kōryū Kyōkai, July 1, 1959.

Kiyose Ichirō, *Kaiki Enchō to Ampo no Saiketsu* (Extension of the Session and Passage of the Treaty), May 31, 1960.

Konnichi no Mondai Sha, *Ampo Hantai no Haikei* (Behind the Opposition to the Security Treaty), Tokyo, October 10, 1959.

Koyama Ken'ichi, ed., *Nihon Kyōsan Tō no Kiki to Gakusei Undō: Zengakuren no Ikensho* (The Crisis in the Japan Communist Party and the Student Movement: a Zengakuren Position Paper), January 1, 1959.

Nihon Jānarisuto Kaigi, ed., *Kiken na Jōyaku* (Dangerous Treaty), Tokyo: Nihon Hyōron Shinsha, November 30, 1959.

Nihon Seinen Mondai Kenkyū Kai, ed., *Ampo Jōyaku Hantai no Mondaiten* (Problems in Opposing the Security Treaty), May 10, 1960.

Seinen Hōritsuka Kyōkai, Goken Bengoshi Dan, *Ampo Jōyaku Kaitei o Meguru Mondai* (Problems in Revising the Security Treaty), Tokyo: Rōdō Hōritsu Jumpō Sha, June 1, 1959.

Sekai Seikai Kenkyū Kai, ed., *Kikan-nai Kaitei to Jizen Kyōgi no Kyohiken* (Revision within a Certain Period and Veto in Prior Consultation), November 25, 1959.

Shinsanbetsu, *Ampo Soshi Undō to Kokumin Kaigi ni Tsuite* (Regarding the Anti-treaty Movement and the People's Council), June 20, 1960.

Tokyo Daigaku, Shakai Kagaku Kenkyūjo, *Ampo Tōsō no Bira* (Handbill Collection on the Anti-treaty Struggle).

Zengakuren Ampo Hikoku Dan, *Wareware no Genzai* (Our Present State), June 25, 1961.

Zengakuren, Chūō Shikkō Iinkai, *Zengakuren Dai-jūrokkai Teiki Zenkoku Taikai: Gian to Kōdō Hōshin* (Zengakuren 16th National Convention: Agenda and Action Program), July 4–7, 1960.

———, Chūō Shoki Kyoku Jōsenbu, ed., *Tatakau Zengakuren* (Fighting Zengakuren), April 1, 1960.

d. *Photograph Collections*

Hamatani Hiroshi, *Ikari to Kanashimi no Kiroku* (A Record of Anger and Tragedy), Tokyo: Kawade Shobo Shinsha, August 7, 1960.

Konnichi no Mondai Sha, *Ampo Hantai wa Ika ni Tatakawareta ka: Demo to Bōryoku no Kiroku* (How the Anti-treaty Battle Was Fought: A Record of *Demo* and Violence), August 1960.

Mugi Shobo, comp., *Yurusenai Hi Kara no Kiroku: Minshushugi o Mamoru Tatakai no Sanjūnichi* (A Record of the Unpardonable Day: 30 Days' Struggle to Protect Democracy), Tokyo: Mugi Shobo, July 1960.

Nihon Jānarisuto Kaigi, ed., *Shukensha no Ikari* (Wrath of the Sovereign), August 15, 1960.

Nihon Kyōsan Tō, Chūō Iinkai, ed., *Nihon Jinmin no Shōri e no Zenshin* (Marching Forward to the Victory of the Japanese People), September 1960.

Tokyo PEN Club, ed., *Nihon no Hansei: Ampo o Megutte* (Japan's Self-reflection: On the Security Treaty), Tokyo: Union Shoji, July 5, 1960.

II. Secondary Sources

1. BIBLIOGRAPHIES AND REFERENCE WORKS

Gendai Nihonjin Jinmei Jiten (Biographical Dictionary of Modern Japanese), rev. ed., Tokyo: Heibonsha, 1961.

Kokuritsu Kokkai Toshokan, Chōsa Rippō Kōsakyoku, Gaimuka, and Etsuranbu Seiji Hosei Sankōshitsu, comp., *Nichibei Anzen Hoshō Jōyaku Kankei Bunken: Showa 34-nen 11-gatsu-matsu Genzai* (Documents Relating to the Japan-America Security Treaty Up to the End of November 1959), January 1960.

———, Chōsa Rippō Kōsakyoku, comp., *Nichibei Anzen Hoshō Jōyaku Kaitei Mondai Shiryō Shu* (A Collection of Materials on the Problem of Revision of the Japan-America Security Treaty), *Shiryō* A-94, November 1959.

———, Etsuranbu, comp., *"Ampo Tōsō" Kankei Bunken, Shiryō Mokuroku, 1960-nen Go-roku-gatsu* (The Security Treaty Struggle: A List of Related Documents and Materials, May and June 1960), September 1960.

Nihon Seikei Shimbun Shuppanbu, *Kokkai Benran, 1961* (Diet Handbook, 1961), Tokyo, April 1, 1961.

Shakai Undō Chōsa Kai, ed., *Sayoku Dantai Jiten, 1961 Nenpan* (Annual Directory of Left Wing Organizations, 1961), 4th ed., Tokyo: Musashi Shobo, 1961.

2. BOOKS

Anzen Hoshō Kenkyū Kai, ed., *Anzen Hoshō Taisei no Kenkyū* (Research on the Security System), Tokyo: Jiji Press, 1960.

395

Etō Jun, *Hizuke no Aru Bunsho* (Certain Dated Essays), Tokyo: Chikuma Shobo, 1960.

Fukuda Tsuneari, *Jōshiki ni Kaere* (Return to Common Sense), Tokyo: Shinchōsha, 1960.

Gakusei Undō Kenkyū Kai, *Gendai no Gakusei Undō: Sono Shisō to Kōdō* (Modern Student Movements: Their Ideology and Action), Tokyo: Shinkō Shuppan Sha, 1961.

Gendai Shisō Sha, ed., *Sōkōsha to Seishun: Zengakuren Gakusei no Shuki* (Armored Cars and Youth: The Notes of Zengakuren Students), Tokyo: Gendai Shichō Sha, 1960.

Hidaka Rokurō, ed., *Gogatsu Jūkunichi* (May 19), Tokyo: Iwanami Shinsho, 1960.

Hirata Yoshisuke [Tada Minoru], Shin Ampo Jōyaku no Zenbō (The Full Story of the New Security Treaty), Tokyo: Gekkan Jiji Sha, 1960.

Ide Busaburō, ed., *Ampo Tōsō* (The Security Treaty Struggle), Tokyo: San'ichi Shobo, 1960.

Inaoka Susumu and Itoya Hisao, *Nihon no Gakusei Undō: Sono Rekishiteki Yakuwari Ga Oshieru Mono* (Japan's Student Movements: An Explanation of Their Historical Rôle), Tokyo: Aoki Shoten, 1961.

Ishida Takeshi, *Gendai Soshiki Ron* (Theory of Modern Organization), Tokyo: Iwanami Shoten, 1961.

Ishimoto Yasuo, *Jōyaku to Kokumin* (The Treaty and the People), Tokyo: Iwanami Shinsho, 1960.

Kamba Akiko, ed., *Hito Shirezu Hohoeman* (Smile in My Heart), Tokyo: San'ichi Shobo, 1960.

Kamiyama Shigeo, *Ampo Tōsō to Tōitsu Sensen* (The Security Treaty Struggle and the United Front), Tokyo: Shindokusho Sha, 1960.

Kempō Mondai Kenkyū Kai, ed., *Kempō o Ikasu Mono* (Keeping the Constitution Alive), Tokyo: Iwanami Shinsho, 1961.

Kenkyūsha Kondan Kai, ed., *Shin Ampo Jōyaku* (The New Security Treaty), Tokyo: San'ichi Shobo, 1960.

Koe Naki Koe no Kai, *Mata Demo de Aō* (Let's Meet Again at the Demo), Tokyo: Tokyo Shoten, 1962.

Koyama Hirotake, *Saisei to Hatten* (Rebirth and Development), Vol. 3 of *Gendai Hantaisei Undō* (A History of Modern Opposition Movements), Tokyo: Aoki Shoten, 1960.

Koyama Ken'ichi, "Ampo Tōsō Shōshi" (A Short History of the Treaty Struggle), Unpublished manuscript, 1960.

Kuroda Kan'ichi and others, eds., *Minshushugi no Shinwa: Ampo Tōsō no Shisōteki Sōkatsu* (The Myth of Democracy: General Ideological Background to the Treaty Struggle), Tokyo: Gendai Shichō Sha, 1960.

Nakamura Kikuo, *Gikai Seiji to Taishū Kōdō* (Parliamentary Politics and Mass Action), Tokyo: Yūshindō, 1960.

Nihon Daigaku Kokusai Kenkyūjo, ed., *Senryaku to Anzen Hoshō* (Strategy and Security), Tokyo: Shobun Sha, 1960.

Nihon Kokusai Mondai Kenkyūjo, *Shin Ampo Jōyaku no Kokkai Shingi* (Diet Deliberations on the New Security Treaty), Tokyo: Nihon Kokusai Mondai Kenkyūjo, International Problems Series, No. 2, June 10, 1960.

Nihon Kokusai Seiji Gakkai, ed., *Nihon Gaikō to Shinjōyaku* (Japan's Diplomacy and the New Security Treaty), 2d ed., Tokyo: Yūshindō, 1959.

Nikkan Rōdō Tsūshin Sha, ed., *Zengakuren no Jittai: Sono Habatsu o Chūshin to Shite* (The Actual State of Zengakuren: Focusing on Its Factions), Tokyo: Nikkan Rōdō Tsūshin Sha, 1959.

Nishimura Kumao, *Anzen Hoshō Jōyaku Ron* (A Discussion of the Security Treaty), rev. ed., Tokyo: Jiji Press, 1960.

Ōhira Zengo, *Nihon no Anzen Hoshō to Kokusai Hō* (Japan's Security and International Law), 5th ed., Tokyo: Yūshindō, 1960.

———, *Shudan Anzen Hoshō to Nihon Gaikō* (Collective Security and Japanese Diplomacy), Tokyo: Hitotsubashi Shobo, 1959.

Rekishigaku Kenkyū Kai, ed., *Sengo Nihon Shi* (History of Postwar Japan), Vol. IV, Tokyo: Aoki Shoten, 1962.

Rōyama Masamichi, *Gikaishugi to Seitō Seiji* (Parliamentarianism and Party Politics), Tokyo: Chūō Kōron Sha, 1960.

———, *Kokusai Seiji to Nihon Gaikō* (International Politics and Japanese Diplomacy), Tokyo: Chūō Kōron Sha, 1959.

Saitō Ichirō, *Ampo Tōsō Shi* (History of the Security Treaty Struggle), Tokyo: San'ichi Shobo, 1962.

Saitō Makoto, *Amerika Gaikō no Ronri to Genjitsu* (Logic and Reality in American Diplomacy), Tokyo: Tokyo Daigaku Shuppan Kai, 1962.

Sakisaka Itsurō, *Miike Nikki* (Miike Dairy), Tokyo: Shiseidō, 1961.

Sengo Shisō Sōsho, ed., *Zen Sekai o Kakutoku Suru Tame* (To Win the Whole World), Kyōsanshugisha Dōmei Bunken Series, No. 1, Osaka: Osaka Daigaku Shimbun Kai Shuppanbu, 1965.

Shin Hōgaku Series, *Ampo Taisei to Hō* (Tokyo: San'ichi Shobo, 1962.

BIBLIOGRAPHY

Shinobu Seizaburō, *Ampo Tōsō Shi* (A History of the Security Treaty Struggle), Tokyo: Sekai Shoin, 1961.

Tabata Shigejirō, *Ampo Taisei to Jieiken* (The Security System and the Right of Self-defense), Tokyo: Yūshindō, 1960.

Takano Yūichi, *Kempō to Jōyaku* (The Constitution and the Treaty), Tokyo: Tokyo Daigaku Shuppan Kai, 1960.

Takei Takehito (also Kenjin), ed., *Ampo Tōsō: Sono Seiji Sōkatsu* (The Security Treaty Struggle: A Political Summary), Tokyo: Gendai Shichō Sha, 1960.

Takeuchi Yoshimi, *Fufukujū no Isan* (A Legacy of Disobedience), Tokyo: Chikuma Shobo, 1960.

Terasawa Hajime, *Ampo Jōyaku no Mondaisei* (The Nature of the Security Treaty Problem), Tokyo: Yūshindō, 1960.

Tokyo Daigaku Shokuin Kumiai, ed., *6:15 Jiken Zengo: Ichō Namiki Kara Kokkai E* (Before and After the June 15 Incident: From the Row of Gingko Trees to the Diet), Tokyo: Tokyo Daigaku Shokuin Kumiai, 1960.

Tsutsumi Yasujirō, *Taiheiyō no Kakehashi* (Bridge Across the Pacific), Tokyo: Sanko Bunka Kenkyūjo, 1963.

Usui Yoshimi, ed., *1960-nen Nihon Seiji no Shoten* (The Focus of Japanese Politics, 1960), Supplement to *Gendai Kyōyō Zenshū* (Modern Culture Series), Tokyo: Chikuma Shobo, 1960.

Yamanaka Akira, *Sengo Gakusei Undō Shi* (A History of Postwar Student Movements), Tokyo: Aoki Shoten, 1961.

Yoshimoto Ryūmei, *Gisei no Shūen* (Death of a Fiction), Tokyo: Gendai Shichō Sha, 1962.

Zen Kyoto Shuppan Iinkai, *Ashioto wa Tayuru Toki Naku* (The Sound of the Footsteps Will Never Die Away), Tokyo: Shirakawa Shoin, 1960.

3. ARTICLES, PERIODICALS, AND PAMPHLETS

"Ampo Hijun Kokkai o Mae ni Shite" (The Diet Before Treaty Ratification), interview with Narita Tomomi (JSP) and Sone Eki (DSP), *Sekai*, March 1960, pp. 36–51.

"Ampo Jōyaku Chōin" (Signing of the Security Treaty), *Mainichi Shimbun*, September 10, 1951.

"Ampo Jōyaku de Futatabi Seimei" (Another Statement on the Security Treaty), *Akahata*, April 27, 1957.

"Ampo Jōyaku no Kaitei wa Kirikae ka?" (A Change in Treaty Revision?), *Tokyo Shimbun*, April 22, 1957.

"Ampo Jōyaku wa Kaitei Subeki ka?" (Must the Treaty Be Revised?), debate between Kaino Michitaka and Ōhira Zengo, *Sankei Jiji Shimbun*, March 7, 1959.

" 'Ampo' ni Yureta Nihon no Kiroku" (Record of the Treaty Struggle that Shook Japan), *Ekonomisuto Bessatsu*, September 10, 1960.

"Ampo o Meguru Shimbun Ronchō" (Tone of the Press on the Security Treaty), series of three articles, *Tokyo Daigaku Shimbun*, June 15, 22, and 29, 1960.

Arase Yutaka, "Hatashite Genron wa Jiyū de Aru ka?" (Is the Press Really Free?), *Sekai*, August 1960, pp. 203–216.

————, "Shizuka Naru Seigan no Soko ni" (At the Bottom of the Quiet Petitioning), *Sekai*, June 1960, pp. 6–10.

Asanuma Inejirō, "Ima Koso Tatakai no Kajitsu o" (Now for the Fruits of the Struggle), *Gekkan Shakai Tō*, No. 39, August 1960, pp. 4–5.

"Chi ni Somatta Kokkai" (The Diet Soaked in Blood), Radio Kantō Broadcast, *Shūkan Asahi*, July 3, 1960, pp. 30–32.

"Chijisen San-renpai no Shakai Tō" (Three Consecutive Defeats for the Socialist Party in Gubernatorial Elections), *Asahi Jānaru*, August 7, 1960, pp. 74–75.

"Fubyōdō Jōyaku wa Nani ka?" (What Does Unequal Treaty Mean?), *Sankei Shimbun*, editorial, April 24, 1960.

"Fubyōdōsei no Genshō Hakaru" (Plan to Reduce Inequalities), *Nihon Keizai Shimbun*, commentary, March 18, 1957.

Fujiwara Hirotatsu, "Shijō Kūzen no Kutsujoku Jōyaku" (The Most Humiliating Treaty in History), *Bungei Shunjū*, April 1960, pp. 62–68.

Fukushima Shingo, "Jijo oyobi Sōgō Enjo no Na no Moto ni" (In the Name of Self-defense and Mutual Assistance), *Chūō Kōron*, February 1960, pp. 30–45.

"Gakusei to Keikan: Kizutsukeru Nihon no Musukotachi" (Students and Police: Sons of Japan Injure Each Other), *Tokyo Daigaku Shimbun*, panel discussion, June 15, 1960.

Gendai Seiji Kenkyū Shūdan, "Nihon o Bunretsu Saseta Ninenkan" (Two Years That Split Japan), *Jiyū*, July 1960, pp. 2–38.

Hashimoto Kiminobu, "Hōteki Nimo Mukō de Aru" (It Was Legally Invalid Too), *Chūō Kōron*, July 1960, pp. 42–46.

Hashimoto Tetsuma, "Tai-GHQ Tōsō Jidai" (Era of Struggle Against GHQ), *Bungei Shunjū*, February 1957, pp. 76–78.

Hoshino Yasusaburō, "Kokkai Ronsō kara: Kyokutō no Han'i, Jizen

Kyōgi, Kempō" (From the Diet Controversy: Scope of the Far East, Prior Consultation, the Constitution), *Sekai,* April 1960, pp. 52–64.

Inaba Michio, "Aru Shiminshugisha no Tsubuyaki" (The Muttering of a *Shiminshugisha), Shūkan Dokushojin,* June 12, 1961.

Inoki Masamichi, "Rondan Jihyō" (Current Criticism) series of three articles, *Asahi Shimbun,* June 25–27, 1960.

―――, "Seijiteki Kiki no Soko ni Aru Mono" (At the Bottom of the Political Crisis), *Chūō Kōron,* August 1960, pp. 73–79.

Irie Keishirō, "Kyokutō no Han'i to Soren Oboegaki" (The Scope of the Far East and the Soviet Memorandum), *Sekai,* April 1960, pp. 29–35.

―――, "Nihon wa Kokuren ni Nani o Kiyo Shi-uru ka?" (What Can Japan Contribute to the U.N.?), *Sekai,* February 1957, pp. 227–233.

Ishida Takeshi, "Sho-Soshiki Kan no Minshushugi-teki Shidōsei" (Democratic Leadership Among the Organizations), *Shisō,* February 1960, pp. 114–128.

Itō Masami, "Gikaishugi no Hametsu o Fusegu Tame ni" (For the Prevention of the Collapse of Parliamentarianism), *Jiyū,* July 1960, pp. 44–51.

Iwabayashi Toranosuke, "Torotsukisuto to no Arasoi to Tō Kensetsu" (Fight Against Trotskyites and Party Construction), *Zenei,* February 1960, pp. 53–60.

Iwakura Tomohide, "Uha Shisō no Taitō to Sayu no Tairitsu" (Resurgence of Rightist Thought and the Confrontation Between Right and Left), *Seikai Ōrai,* January 1960, pp. 24–30.

"Jiki Seiken wa Dō Naru" (What Will the Next Administration Be?), *Asahi Jānaru,* June 26, 1960, pp. 96–97.

Kaikō Ken, Maruyama Masao, and Takeuchi Yoshimi, "Giji Puroguramu kara no Dakkyaku" (Emancipation from Bogus Program), debate, *Chūō Kōron,* July 1960, pp. 30–41.

Kamiyama Shigeo, "Ampo Tōsō to Puroretaria Kokusaishugi" (Antitreaty Struggle and Proletarian Internationalism), *Zenei,* November 1960, pp. 19–29.

Kano Tsuneo, "Ampo Hantai Tōsō Kiji no Naiyō Bunseki" (An Analysis of the Contents of Anti-treaty Struggle Articles), *Shimbun Kenkyū,* June 1961, pp. 16–20.

Katō Hidetoshi, "Nichijō Seikatsu to Kokumin Undō" (Daily Life and the National Movement), *Shisō no Kagaku,* July 1960, pp. 28–35.

Kawakami Jōtarō, "Giketsu e no Gigi" (Doubts About the Approval), *Jiyū*, July 1960, pp. 64–68.

"Kedamono no Yō na Kenryoku no Bōgyaku" (Atrocities of the Beastlike Authorities), *Jānarisuto*, June 20, 1960, p. 3.

"Kishi Kaizō Naikaku o Shindan Suru" (Examining the New Kishi Cabinet), panel discussion, *Sekai*, September 1957, pp. 190–201.

Kishi Nobusuke, "Ima ni Shite Omou" (Thinking Back on It Now), *Sandei Mainichi*, August 28, 1960, pp. 12–16.

"Kishi Shushō no San Dai-misu" (Kishi's Three Great Misses), *Sekai Ōrai*, July 1960, p. 1.

Kiyose Ichirō, "Gichō no Tachiba kara" (From the Standpoint of the Speaker), *Jiyū*, July 1960, pp. 59–63.

" 'Koe Naki Koe' Yo Te o Musube" (Let the Voiceless Voices Join Hands), *Shūkan Asahi*, July 3, 1960, pp. 11–17.

Koizumi Shinzō, *Shin Ampo Jōyaku wa Kyū Jōyaku ni Masaru* (The New Security Treaty Is Better than the Old One), pamphlet, Tokyo: Nihon Gakujutsu Sōsho Bessatsu, October 20, 1960.

"Kokkai Demo Jiken o Mokugeki Shite" (Witnessing the November 27 Incident), panel discussion, *Sekai*, February 1960, pp. 120–127.

Kokuritsu Kokkai Toshokan, *Shin Nichibei Anzen Hoshō Jōyaku* (The New Japan–U.S. Security Treaty) and related subjects; a collection of newspaper clippings on all aspects of the Security Treaty (1951–1961), deposited in the Newspaper Research Section of the National Diet Library.

Konno Jun'ichi, "Nihon no Shakai Tō no Genjō" (The Current State of Japan's Socialist Party), *Zenei*, June 1958, pp. 52–58.

Kumagai Junko, "Yomigaeru Matsuri" (Revived Festival), *Koe Naki Koe no Tayori*, No. 2, August 1, 1960, pp. 8–9.

Kuwabara Takeo, "Shin Ampo ni Interi wa Hantai Da" (Intellectuals are Against Security Treaty Revision), *Sekai*, April 1960, pp. 26–28.

Maruyama Masao, "Kono Jitai no Seijiteki Mondaiten" (Political Problems in the Current Situation), *Asahi Jānaru*, June 12, 1960, pp. 11–17.

———, "Sentaku no Toki" (Time for Choice), *Tokyo Daigaku Shimbun*, special supplement, July 11, 1960, p. 2.

Matsumoto Shigeharu, "Reisen no Naka no Daisanji Demokurashii" (Third Democracy in the Cold War), *Fujin Kōron*, August 1960, pp. 50–55.

Matsuoka Yōko, "Gijidō o Kakonda Hito no Nami" (The Wave of People Surrounding the Diet), *Sekai*, July 1960, pp. 44–45.

Matsuoka Yōko, "Yureru Shakai to Yuruganu Shihyō" (Wavering Society and an Unwavering Barometer), *Gendai no Me*, September 1961, pp. 24–28.

Matsuyama Zenzō, "Kono Bōkyō Yurusumaji" (This Outrage Is Not to Be Tolerated), *Shūkan Asahi*, July 3, 1960, pp. 18–21.

Mikami Masayoshi, "Gyōsei Kyōtei Hakusho" (A White Paper on the Administrative Agreement), *Chūō Kōron*, June 1960, pp. 71–83.

"Minshushugi no Genri wa Kō Shite Yaburareta" (How Democratic Principles Were Violated), *Gekkan Shakai Tō*, July 1960, pp. 11–21.

Miyamoto Kenji, "Waga Tō no Tatakatta Michi" (The Course of Our Party's Struggle), *Zenei*, September 1960, pp. 15–27.

"Moshi Ampo Kaitei Ga Nakattara" (If the Treaty Had not Been Revised), Discussion with Kishi Nobusuke, *Seikai Ōrai*, February 1964, pp. 34–42.

Nakaya Takeyo, *Ampo Seihen Shi no Hitokuma* (A Scene from the History of Political Change over the Security Treaty), pamphlet, December 15, 1960.

Nosaka Sanzō, "Atarashii Shōri ni Mukatte Zenshin Shio" (Let Us Move Forward to New Victories), *Zenei*, September 1960, pp. 4–14.

Ōe Kenzaburō (and others), "Rokugatsu Jūgonichi" (June 15), *Nihon Dokusho Shimbun*, June 12, 1960.

"Otona Nayamasu 'Daijin-kyū'" ("Cabinet Level" Headache for Adults), December 20, 1959, pp. 3–10.

Nakamura Kikuo, "Gakusei no Seijika Kan" (Student Views of Politicians), *Nihon Bunka Fuōramu Niyūzu*, No. 35, August 1960, p. 8.

———, "Kokkai Konran no Teisei-saku" (A Corrective Policy for Diet Confusion), *Tokyo Shimbun*, June 8, 1961.

Nakano Yoshio, "Gogatsu Hatsuka o Miushinau na" (Don't Forget May 20), *Shūkan Asahi*, June 26, 1960, pp. 9–12.

———, "Kimyō na Gaikō Kōshō wa Tsuzuku" (The Strange Diplomatic Negotiations Continue), *Sekai*, September 1959, pp. 27–35.

Nakasone Yasuhirō, "Genka no Sōran ni Omou" (My View of the Current Political Situation), *Daiyamondo*, June 18, 1960, p. 33.

Nakaya Takeyo, *Ampo Seihen Shi no Hitokuma* (Scene from the History of Political Change Over the Security Treaty), pamphlet.

Nambara Shigeru, "Beikoku Daitōryō no Rainichi to Nihon no

Genjō" (U.S. President's Visit Here and Present Conditions in Japan), *Sekai*, July 1960, pp. 10–15.

"Nichibei Ampo Jōyaku Kaihai o Meguru Shomondai" (Problems Concerning Revising or Abolishing the Japan–U.S. Security Treaty), series of 40 articles, *Yomiuri Shimbun*, March 13–May 1, 1957.

"Nichibei Kankei Saikentō no Toshi" (Year of Reexamination of Japan–U.S. Relations), *Yomiuri Shimbun*, editorial, April 28, 1957.

"Nihon no Shio" (Trends in Japan), *Sekai*, February 1957, pp. 234–237.

Nihon Shimbun Kyōkai, ed., "Nihon no Seiji Kiki to Shimbun Ronchō" (Japan's Political Crisis and the Tone of the Press), *Shimbun Kenkyū*, September 1960.

Nishi Haruhiko, "Nihon no Gaikō o Ureeru" (Worrying About Japan's Diplomacy), *Chūō Kōron*, February 1960, pp. 92–104.

———, "Nihon Gaikō o Ureete Futatabi" (Worrying Again About Japan's Diplomacy), *Chūō Kōron*, April 1960, pp. 30–45.

Noda Ryōsuke, "Nihon no Ichi-Kirisuto-sha to Shite" (As One Japanese Christian), *Sekai*, July 1960, pp. 66–68.

"Roku-ten-jūgo Ryūketsu Jiken no Kiroku" (Record of the Bloody Affair on June 15), *Asahi Jānaru*, July 3, 1960, pp. 4–21.

"Roku-yon Suto to Kongo no Seijō" (The June 4 Strike and the Subsequent Political Situation), *Shūkan Asahi*, June 19, 1960, pp. 86–87.

"Rokkiido, Baishō, Kuroi Jietto-ki" (Lockheeds, Reparations, and Black Jets), *Chūō Kōron*, February 1960, pp. 116–128.

"Rokuon Kōsei: 'Yuganda Seishun' no Hamon" (Repercussions from the Taped Broadcast, "Warped Youth"), *Shūkan Asahi*, March 22, 1963, pp. 12–20.

Rōyama Masamichi, "Ampo Jōyaku no Kaihai o Megutte: Ampo Jōyaku no Paradokkusu" (Concerning the Revision or Abolition of the Security Treaty: Paradoxes in the Treaty), *Chūō Kōron*, May 1957, pp. 56–64.

Ryū Shintarō, "Ampo Kaitei o Dō Shitara Yoi ka?" (What to Do About Treaty Revision?), *Bungei Shunjū*, June 1960, pp. 64–72.

Saionji Kinkazu, "Ampo Kaitei to Chūritsu Kankei" (Security Treaty Revision and Neutral Relations), *Sekai*, April 1960, pp. 36–41.

"Saishō Gendo no Hitsuyō" (Minimum Needs), *Asahi Shimbun*, editorial, January 14, 1960.

Saitō Chū, *Nichibei Anzen Hoshō Jōyaku no Shimei to Nihon no*

Chii (Japan–U.S. Security Treaty's Mission and Japan's Position), pamphlet, Tokyo: Kokumin Gaikō Chōsa Kai, July 15, 1960.

Sakamoto Yoshikazu, "Heiwa Kyōzon ni Gyakkō Mono," (Contrary to Peaceful Coexistence), *Sekai*, July 1960, pp. 16–30.

Sakisaka Itsurō, "Shakai Tō no Susumu Beki Michi" (The Way the Japan Socialist Party Should Proceed), *Ekonomisuto*, November 3, 1959, pp. 6–16.

———, "Tadashii Kōryō, Tadashii Kikō" (Correct Platform, Correct Structure), *Shakaishugi*, No. 88, December 1958, pp. 46–52.

———, "Waga Shōgai no Tōsō" (My Life's Struggles), *Bungei Shunjū*, July 1960, pp. 78–88.

"Shimbun wa Shinjitsu o Hōdō Shita ka?" (Did the Newspapers Report the Truth?), panel discussion, *Jiyū*, August 1960, pp. 77–92.

"Shimin to Shite no Teikō" (Protesting as Citizens), *Shisō no Kagaku*, No. 19, special edition, July 1960.

Shimizu Ikutarō, "Ampo Tōsō Ichinen-go no Shisō" (Thoughts on the Security Treaty Struggle One Year Later), *Chūō Kōron*, July 1961, pp. 45–57.

———, "Ima Koso Kokkai E!" (Now to the Diet!), *Sekai*, May 1960, pp. 18–28.

Shinohara Hajime, " 'Gikaishugi' no Kokufuku" (Conquest of So-called Parliamentarianism), *Jiyū*, July 1960, pp. 52–58.

"Shukensha wa Kokumin de Aru" (The People Are Sovereign), *Sekai*, special edition, August 1960.

"Sōhyō to Nihon-teki Kumiaishugi" (Sōhyō and Japanese-style Unionism), *Asahi Jānaru*, February 14, 1960, pp. 8–13.

Suzuki Ichizō, "Ampo Tōsō no Seika no Ue ni Rōdō Undō no Zenshin o Kachitorō" (Let the Labor Movement Move Forward on the Success of the Treaty Struggle), *Zenei*, September 1960, pp. 28–42.

Takeda Taijun, "Kishi San wa Kangei no Shikaku wa Nai" (Mr. Kishi Is Unqualified to Greet Eisenhower), *Shūkan Asahi*, June 26, 1960, pp. 6–9.

Taketani Mitsuo, "Saidai no Kyōkun" (The Greatest Lesson), *Sekai*, December 1957, pp. 84–97.

Takeuchi Yoshimi, "Arasoi no Tame no Yotsu no Jōken" (Four Conditions of the Struggle), *Shisō no Kagaku*, July 1960, pp. 17–19.

———, "Nitchū Kankei no Yukue" (Future of Japan-China Relations), *Chūō Kōron*, March 1960, pp. 77–87.

Tamura Kōsaku, *Ampo Jōyaku Mondai to Chūritsushugi no Hihan* (Problems of the Security Treaty and Criticism of Neutralism), pamphlet, Tokyo: Hōkoku Shimbun Sha, September 5, 1959.

————, *Jiyū Sekai no Bōei to Nichibei Shin Ampo Jōyaku* (Defense of the Free World and the New Japan–U.S. Security Treaty), pamphlet, Tokyo: Hōkoku Shimbun Sha, April 5, 1960.

Tanaka Seigen, "Busō Tero to Haha" (Armed Terror and Mothers), *Bungei Shunjū*, February 1960, pp. 117–121.

Tanaka Seigen, "Ima Koso Iu: Ampo Tōsō to Watakushi" (Now I Speak Up! The Security Treaty Struggle and Me), *Bungei Shunjū*, May 1963, pp. 220–231.

Tanaka Toshio, "Ampo Tōsō no Seika to Atarashii Mokuhyō" (Achievements of the Security Treaty Struggle and New Objectives), *Gekkan Shakai Tō*, July 1960, pp. 4–5.

————, "Shizuka na Seigan kara Hageshii Kōgi" (From Calm Petitioning to Fierce Protests), *Sekai*, July 1960, pp. 58–62.

————, and others, "Watakushi no Mita 'Hanedo Demo Jiken' " (The Haneda *Demo* as I Saw It), *Shūkan Asahi*, June 26, 1960, pp. 12–13.

Tanikawa Tetsuzō, "Mattaku Mucha Da" (It Was Really Outrageous), *Sekai*, July 1960, pp. 35–36.

"Tō no Konran o Nerau Torotsukisuto no Sakudō ni Tsuite" (Concerning the Plot of the Trotskyites Who Aim to Cause Trouble in the Party), *Zenei*, August 1958, pp. 15–30.

Tōgawa Isamu, "Shin Ampo Jōyaku to Kokkai" (The New Security Treaty and the Diet), *Gaikō Jihō*, July 1960, pp. 87–91.

"Tōnai Chōsei Kusuburu" (Smoldering Intraparty Adjustment), *Asahi Shimbun*, April 12, 1959.

"Torotsukisuto to Iwarete mo" (Even if We Are Called Trotskyites), *Chūō Kōron*, April 1960, pp. 126–145.

Tsuda Tatsuo, "Shin Jōyaku e no Arata na Giwaku" (New Doubts About the Security Treaty), *Sekai*, June 1960, pp. 80–88.

Tsuji Kiyoaki, "Mushiro Kokkai Tōhyō-hō no Seitei o" (Instead the Diet Election Law Should Be Changed), *Sekai*, April 1960, pp. 12–15.

————, " 'Yasui na Ryō-Seizai-ron' ni Tsuite" (The Easy "Both Sides Were Wrong" Theory), *Sekai*, July 1960, pp. 36–38.

Tsukamoto Jūichi, "Ampo Seikyoku ni Hatashita Masu Komi no Yakuwari" (The Rôle of the Mass Media in the Current Political Situation), *Seikai Ōrai*, July 1960, pp. 72–75.

Tsurumi Shunsuke, "Nemoto kara no Minshushugi" (Democracy from the Roots Up), *Shisō no Kagaku*, July 1960, pp. 20–27.

————, "Nihon no Naka no Amerika to Amerika no Naka no Nihon" (America in the Midst of Japan and Japan in the Midst of America), *Fujin Kōron*, August 1960, pp. 44–49.

Ukai Nobushige, "Gikai Seidō to Shōsū-sha no Kenri" (Parliamentary System and Rights of the Minority), *Sekai*, July 1960, pp. 52–53.

————, "Kyōkō Saiketsu no Mondaiten" (Problems in the Forceful Passage), *Shisō*, July 1960, pp. 124–128.

Usui Yoshimi, "Gogatsu Nijūrokunichi no Nampeidai 41-banchi" (Number 41 Nampeidai and the May 26 Demonstration), *Shūkan Asahi*, June 12, 1960, pp. 14–15.

Utsunomiya Tokuma, "Ichi Jimin Tō Daigishi to Shite Chokugen Suru" (My Frank Opinion as an LDP Diet Member), *Chūō Kōron*, June 1960, pp. 42–57.

Uzaki Kōhei, "Tenki ni Tatte Sōhyō no Giin-dan" (Sōhyō-affiliated Diet Members Stand at Crossroads), *Jitsugyō no Nippon*, June 1, 1960, pp. 38–40.

Yanaihara Tadao, "Minshushugi o Mamoru Yūki o" (Have Courage to Safeguard Democracy), *Shūkan Asahi*, July 3, 1960, pp. 22–23.

Yokota Kisaburō, "Chūhei to Shuken" (Stationing Troops and Sovereignty), *Yomiuri Shimbun*, October 21, 1951.

Watakushitachi wa Kō Kangaeru (This Is What We Believe), pamphlet (undated) published in June 1960 by the "Minna de Minshushugi o Mamoru Kai" (Let's All Protect Democracy Association) at Tokyo University.

"Zengakuren Mafutatsu" (Zengakuren Split Down the Middle), *Mainichi Shimbun*, July 11, 1961.

"Zengakuren: Uchiwa-mome no Donsoko ni" (Zengakuren: The Roots of the Internal Dissension), *Asahi Shimbun*, July 11, 1961.

4. NEWSPAPERS

Asahi Shimbun (Tokyo)
Mainichi Shimbun (Tokyo)
Nihon Keizai Shimbun (Tokyo)
Sankei Shimbun (Tokyo)
Tokyo Shimbun (Tokyo)
Yomiuri Shimbun (Tokyo)

INDEX

417

421